Ripples of Hope in the Mississippi Delta

Studies in Social Medicine

Allan M. Brandt, Larry R. Churchill, and Jonathan Oberlander, *editors*

This series publishes books at the intersection of medicine, health, and society that further our understanding of how medicine and society shape one another historically, politically, and ethically. The series is grounded in the convictions that medicine is a social science, that medicine is humanistic and cultural as well as biological, and that it should be studied as a social, political, ethical, and economic force.

A complete list of books published in Studies in Social Medicine is available at https://uncpress.org/series/studies-social-medicine.

Ripples of Hope in the Mississippi Delta

Charting the Health Equity Policy Agenda

....

DAVID K. JONES

EDITED BY DEBRA BINGHAM,
NICOLE HUBERFELD, AND SARAH H. GORDON

The University of North Carolina Press Chapel Hill

This book was published with the assistance of the Lilian R. Furst Fund of the University of North Carolina Press and the David K. Jones Health Equity Fund of Fidelity Charitable.

© 2024 Sarah Sacuto Jones
All rights reserved
Set in Charis by Westchester Publishing Services
Manufactured in the United States of America

Complete Cataloging-in-Publication Data for this title is available from the Library of Congress at https://lccn.loc.gov/2024035233.
ISBN 978-1-4696-8108-5 (cloth: alk. paper)
ISBN 978-1-4696-8109-2 (pbk.: alk. paper)
ISBN 978-1-4696-8110-8 (epub)
ISBN 978-1-4696-8111-5 (pdf)

Cover art: Crumpled sheet graph paper by angelmaximaxim/stock.adobe.com; Mississippi River Delta by Marco Attano/stock.adobe.com.

"Now More Than Ever" by Morgan Parker is © 2017 Morgan Parker. Reprinted by permission of ICM Partners.

David's book is dedicated to Sarah Sacuto Jones, the love of his life, and their three amazing children, Oliver Kerrie Jones, Anne Debra Jones, and Thomas Jeffery Jones, whom David cherished and adored more than words can ever express.

David and his family, from left to right: Thomas, Sarah, Ollie, Anne, and David. September 2020. Photographer Sonia Targontsidis.

Contents

List of Illustrations, ix

Editors' Foreword, xi

Preface, xv

Prologue, 1
The Health Equity Policy Agenda

1 Food, 27

2 Neighborhoods, 59

3 Jobs, 90

4 Education, 131

5 Health Care, 189

Conclusion, 227
Advancing the Health Equity Agenda

Notes, 233

Index, 297

Illustrations

Figures

P.1 Factors that affect population health, 3

P.2 Public health framework for reducing health inequities, 6

P.3 Percentage of population enslaved by county, 1860, 20

2.1 Highway 61 at the Piggly Wiggly in Tunica, Mississippi, 77

2.2 Martin Luther King Jr. Drive near Smith Elementary School in Cleveland, Mississippi, 78

Maps

P.1 Percentage of babies born low birthweight by state, 2021, 11

P.2 Low birthweight in Mississippi by county, 2022, 12

P.3 Delta Regional Authority, 15

P.4 Mississippi Delta core, peripheral, and Delta Regional Authority counties, 17

1.1 Prevalence of obesity among adults by state, 30

1.2 Prevalence of obesity among Mississippi adults by county, 31

1.3 SNAP enrollment as a percentage of county population, 40

5.1 Percentage of rural hospitals classified as "vulnerable" by state, 2015, 195

Graphs

P.1 Life expectancy at birth in years, Mississippi, 1939–1991, 9

2.1 Mortgage denial rates, 66

Editors' Foreword

On September 11, 2021, our lives were changed forever when David Kline Jones died from a preventable accident. While training for an ultramarathon, David fell to his death when he accessed a rusted staircase at the Massachusetts Bay Transportation Authority JFK/UMass station. The staircase was not properly labeled as unsafe, nor had the rusted staircase with its missing stairs been properly secured or removed. Many months before his death, these stairs were identified as a safety hazard. Immediately after his death, the stairs were finally made inaccessible to the public, and about a week later, they were completely removed.

David's death underscores the main thesis of his book: individuals should not be blamed for the conditions that lead to poor health or preventable deaths. Even if individuals make optimal choices for health, tragic consequences can occur when social structures and institutions do not provide safe, healthy environments.

Our desire is that this tragic loss for his family, his colleagues, and indeed the world will foster a renewed commitment to create safe and healthy environments for all people. David cared wholly and deeply about people, about communities (those of which he was a part and the broader communities in which all people live), and about humanity. He believed how much we care for each other will be reflected in how safe and nurturing every community is.

David knew that local policies and politics matter. He did more than give these ideas lip service. He advocated tirelessly for social and racial justice in his public health work as well as in his community. Despite his busy career, family life, and his wife's illness, David made time to be active in local and national politics. For example, he served as a town meeting representative in his neighborhood of Milton, Massachusetts, and supported the formation and work of the Milton Anti-Racist Coalition.

This book was undergoing peer review at the time of David's death. Our goal as co-editors has been to honor David's original research, voice, and vision. Given these unusual circumstances, we worked to preserve David's writing by changing as little of the book as possible while responding to peer review and editorial suggestions. We reorganized some text to clarify points David was making, and we corrected any drafting errors. We did not perform additional research. Instead, we kept the book true to the approach David described in the prologue, which was to let the people he interviewed in the Mississippi Delta guide the national, state, and local policy goals, recommendations, and examples he outlined. His guiding principle was that the policies that will support health in the Mississippi Delta are relevant to supporting health in other states and communities.

Working on David's book without him has been emotionally and intellectually challenging. We hear his voice in his writing, which makes us miss him more than ever. We wish that he were here to talk to us and to readers about what he learned and why he wrote this book.

Because of the support of our family, friends, and colleagues, in particular David's colleagues at Boston University, we have been able to do the work necessary to get his book published. We appreciate the insights and feedback from the reviewers and the support of the University of North Carolina Press's series editor Jonathan Oberlander, executive director Lucas Church, and the board of governors, who supported the publication of David's book before and after his death. We are also grateful to all of David's colleagues at Boston University School of Public Health. In particular, we appreciate the wholehearted support of Dean Sandro Galea and department chair Michael Stein. We are grateful to everyone who has made it possible to publish this work.

David was a hopeful person. He was also practical. He knew if his vision was to be achieved, the narrative would need to shift to foster a deeper understanding of the barriers to health equity. He knew that policies needed to be revised, but structural change would require that people's hearts and minds be opened in new ways. David's life was shaped by his deep kindness, big heart, and genuine compassion for others, and his life has had a lasting and positive impact on everyone who knew him. We are grateful that David is a part of our life journeys, and we are honored to be a part of the process of sharing what he was writing and thinking about before he died. We are also committed to doing everything we can to support his vision of securing health equity. To honor his life and desires, David's family has committed to donate the entirety of the proceeds from this book to support Mississippi Delta–based initiatives like those described in the Ripples of Hope sections throughout this book.

We agree with the first sentence he wrote in the prologue of this book: "Health equity is possible." We hope you will join us in deepening understanding of the barriers to health equity and then work to enact the policies that will advance health in your community, state, and beyond.

Debra Bingham, DrPH, RH, FAAN
David's mother
info@perinatalQI.org; @Debra_Bingham
Founder and CEO, Institute for Perinatal Quality Improvement
 (www.perinatalQI.org)
Retired Associate Professor, University of Maryland School of Nursing

Nicole Huberfeld, JD
Edward R. Utley Professor of Health Law and Professor of Law
Boston University School of Public Health and School of Law

Sarah H. Gordon, PhD, MS
Assistant Professor
Department of Health Law, Policy, and Management
Boston University School of Public Health

Preface

I stood outside the US Supreme Court on June 25, 2015, speaking with reporters about the impact of the *King v. Burwell* decision released that morning. This was the second time the Court had saved a major portion of the Affordable Care Act (ACA). I had a lot to say, as I had recently completed a dissertation and book manuscript about the law's implementation. Millions of people would have lost insurance and millions more would have seen their premiums and deductibles dramatically increase if the Court's decision had gone the other way.

But a nagging question in the back of my mind would not let go: What next? The ACA was the most comprehensive health reform law enacted in decades, and it had enormous potential to improve lives. If every state fully cooperated with the law, the number of people without insurance would be dramatically reduced. Health care facilities and doctors would be compensated for care they were already providing rather than swallowing these costs. The federal government would pay a large share of these costs, and the money coming to states would ripple through other sectors of the economy.

However, there was much reformers could not do because of political constraints. I also understood concerns that giving someone insurance would not mean they had access to good health care. There might not be enough providers near them, nearby providers might not accept Medicaid, their deductibles might be prohibitively high, or the care received might not be high quality. But these criticisms seemed shortsighted, as if we could not also work on these problems. Focusing on these criticisms also ignored the even bigger picture of why the places with the greatest access issues also have particularly unhealthy populations. What should policymakers and scholars do next to broaden the conversation beyond health insurance in order to advance population health?

Every time I looked at a map of health outcomes or policy decisions, my eyes were immediately drawn to the Deep South. Nearly every statistic is worse across this region, particularly in a belt of counties with the highest concentration of Black residents. These counties are located within states with the deepest opposition to ACA programs such as Medicaid expansion. I wondered what it would take for leaders in these states to expand Medicaid so that more people have access to health insurance, whether the health care system in these states could handle increased demand, and what could be done so that people were healthier more generally and fewer people needed health care in the first place.

The 2016 primary elections played out as I was reflecting on these issues. The role of racism in America was one of the most intensely polarizing topics during these debates. Some said we should examine the structural factors shaping health and economic outcomes, while others argued that people could be healthier and more financially secure if they just tried harder. In the latter paradigm, people are blamed for their problems, and it is deemed unpatriotic to consider the role of structures, systems, and history. My public health training and intuition convinced me it isn't right to blame people for circumstances often out of their control. I wanted to create something for my relatives and friends who thought this way that would help them understand why structural changes are needed.

Around this time, I happened to be reading Arthur Schlesinger's biography of Robert F. Kennedy and realized that it would soon be the fiftieth anniversary of his iconic trip to the Mississippi Delta in 1967. The idea emerged for a book in which I retrace Kennedy's steps in the Delta and highlight conditions in the places he visited. I took my first trip to the region in February 2016 and visited Clarksdale, Cleveland, and Greenville, the main stops on his trip. I went back every chance I could over the next four years to conduct interviews and focus groups with leaders and residents of the Delta. I loved every second of these trips, including the many opportunities to enjoy good food and live music at places like Doe's Eat Place, Abe's BBQ, Red's Lounge, Ground Zero, and Hey Joe's, not to mention the fun I had flying in and out of Memphis, Jackson, and New Orleans.

Using Kennedy's visit as my entry point to the region is still reflected in the brief story about his trip I tell at the beginning of each chapter. However, it quickly became clear that rather than focus on what Kennedy and I experienced while visiting the area, I needed to focus on the individuals and neighborhoods themselves, as well as the food, neighborhoods, and economic, educational, and health systems that surrounded them. Others have written about the effects of these social structures on health, but I do not know of any work that brings together statistics and stories to comprehensively examine how these factors intersect and interact in a single place.

Looking at these interrelated systemic issues in a specific place clarifies the role of racism in creating a constellation of barriers that prevents people from improving their situations, no matter how hard they try.

The more time I spent in Mississippi, the more I came to appreciate that the Delta is not an outlier in the American landscape but that the dynamics of race and class here epitomize what is happening in the rest of the country. I came to better understand that racism is more than people maliciously and intentionally harming someone else they view as inferior. It can take that form, but it is also people—sometimes including me—who believe they are not racist but who are unable to acknowledge or unwilling to change the systems that structurally benefit them while disadvantaging others. The more time I spent in Mississippi, the more I was able to see the same inequities and racism in my own community.

My Place

Four key formative experiences shaped how I asked and addressed questions about the role of race, class, history, and policy in Mississippi and helped me see how these lessons are relevant to the rest of the country. The first was in March 2016, just one month after my first trip to the Delta and long before I started writing. Jonathan Metzl invited me to a conference at Vanderbilt University on the politics of health in the US South to talk about why and how I planned to write a book about health equity in the Delta. This was one of the most stimulating academic meetings in which I have ever participated, largely because Metzl made a point of bringing together people from many disciplines and fields, including poets and authors such as Jesmyn Ward.

But the moment that stood out to me the most was the question I received from a Black undergraduate student who approached me after my talk. She asked how I, as a white northerner with all my privilege, would do justice to this topic and show respect to the people and places of the Delta, Mississippi, and the South. I had already thought a lot about these questions and have continued to reflect on them throughout every step of this research. Part of my answer is to acknowledge that I am an outsider. No matter how much time I spend in the Delta or with people in focus groups or over meals, I cannot presume to understand them or know what their lives feel like.

It is inappropriate to do place-based research without amplifying the voices of local residents, but it is also unfair to place demands on these individuals to tell their stories. This concept is beautifully explained in the following poem, "Now More Than Ever," by Morgan Parker.[1]

> Phrase used by Whites to express their surprise and disapproval of social or political conditions which, to the Negro, are devastatingly usual. Often accompanied by an unsolicited touch on the forearm or shoulder, this expression is a favorite among the most politically liberal but socially comfortable of Whites. Its origins and implications are necessarily vague and undefined. In other words, the source moment of separation between "now" and "ever" must never be specified. In some cases, it is also accompanied by a solicitation for unpaid labor from the Negro, often in the form of time, art, or an intimate and lengthy explanation of the Negro's life experiences, likely not dissimilar to a narrative the Negro has relayed before to dead ears. Otherwise, in response to the circumstances occurring "now," as ever, but suddenly and inexplicably "more" than ever, this is an utterance to be met with a solemn nod of the head and, eventually and most importantly, absolution, which all Good Whites are convinced they deserve. When a time or era achieves "more than ever" status, many Negroes will assume duties kindred to those of priesthood, e.g., receiving confessions, distributing mercy, et cetera. Though, as noted above, the precise connotation of this phrase is quite obscured in its usage, it seems to be uttered in moments of "Aha!" or, more bluntly, "I straight up did not believe you before," wherein "before" = "ever." (See also: Negro Lexicon entries #42 & #43: "same shit, different day" and "samo samo.") Subtexts, then, underscoring this phrase are quite sinister in nature, varying from "Your usefulness, Negro, is married to your misfortune" and "Time is linear," the implications of which are that (1) value is time sensitive, (2) conditions of despair are temporary, and (3) anything at all can be new, belonging exclusively to "now" and untethered to "ever" (i.e., past, future). These understandings of time versus import are likely due to the fact that spurs to action and empathy for the Whites are often directly correlated to any present dangers facing their individual freedoms, or even simply when one "feels like it." (See also: Case Study #5: "Empathy.") This reveals in Whites a compulsion to reformation based upon desire, excitement, guilt, or otherwise self-indulgent emotions, whereas it would appear that the Negro must live the life of the Negro ever, now, and ever

and ever [. . .] and ever and ever and ever and ever and ever and ever and ever and ever and ever and ever and ever and ever and ever (cont.)

I have tried to strike a delicate balance by seeking input from local leaders and using research methodologies that give participants a say in the process. But it is important to acknowledge that a power dynamic is inherent in our interactions and stems from who I am, where I am from, why I am there, and how this work benefits me.

I committed to giving 100 percent of my share of the proceeds of this book to nonprofit organizations based in the Mississippi Delta, and I naturally hope that publishing this book will contribute to policy conversations. While we cannot presume to understand another culture and should not try to speak on behalf of others, this should not mean that topics and research questions are off limits to anyone but insiders. This is unrealistic and too limiting. Reaching across boundaries is valuable if done with humility and respect. The ACA and other policies developed in Washington, DC, and around the country would be better if more people had a fuller picture of the range of lived experiences in our country.

The second formative experience that shaped my approach to this book was in early 2017 as I was beginning to launch a series of focus groups in Clarksdale, Cleveland, and Greenville. I made time in my schedule to drive out to Sumner in Tallahatchie County to visit the courthouse where Emmett Till's murderers were acquitted. This beautiful building is still the county courthouse and had recently been renovated to its appearance in 1955 as a memorial to Till and this pivotal moment in the civil rights movement.

As I stood outside waiting for the tour guide to arrive—next to a statue honoring Confederate soldiers and across the street from the offices of the law firms still open for business sixty years after representing Till's murderers—my research assistants and I said hello to a ninety-year-old white man getting out of his car to go into a nearby shop. He struck up a conversation that led to him talking about serving in World War II. I did the math in my head and realized that at the time of the Till murder trial, he would have been my age now, and his children would have been around the same age as Till. When asked what he remembered about that period, he replied without much hesitation that "there was plenty of killing in the other direction too, you know." Even with sixty years of hindsight, he did not seem to see the structural power dynamics at play in what happened to Till and the men who murdered him.

This conversation haunted me as I stood in the jury room a few minutes later contemplating the short "deliberation" that led to acquittal. The man on the sidewalk helped me better appreciate that everything in the jurors' cultural education reinforced a racist worldview. I realized that it was easy to judge and be angry about such obvious injustices when they were done by other people in a faraway place. I left Sumner that day asking myself what aspects of my cultural upbringing make me blind to the structures and power dynamics around me, and what my role is in perpetuating and changing them.

The third formative experience was the context in which I wrote this book. Much of it was written in the spring and summer of 2020 as the nation grappled with the racial inequities of the health and financial effects of COVID-19, as well as the killings of Ahmaud Arbery, Breonna Taylor, George Floyd, and many others. In this context, I was stunned in early June 2020 when my child's sixth-grade English teacher was put on administrative leave for talking about these killings. I was pleased that Ms. Zakia Jarrett—a young Black woman whose father had worked in the Student Nonviolent Coordinating Committee during the civil rights movement of the 1960s—was using "I, Too" by Langston Hughes to open a discussion with my child's class about racism in America and the role of the students in working for progress.

Apparently not all parents were happy with Ms. Jarrett for talking about racism. We were still in the throes of COVID-19, and so the lesson took place online. Someone recorded the discussion—a fourteen-second clip of her saying that the people responsible for these killings are racist and that "many cops are racist"—and circulated it to other parents, including a state trooper. The superintendent and principal—both white—immediately suspended her and froze her access to email and online materials. School leaders quickly reversed Ms. Jarrett's suspension as they caught wind of the community uproar and since made commitments to examine and change the structures driving inequitable experiences and outcomes. But any efforts to advance equity have faced an intense backlash as some parents feel that school curriculum and administrative decisions should not focus on racism.

The root of the issue is that Milton, Massachusetts, is a town of about twenty-five thousand just south of Boston where the median income and health outcomes are dramatically better than in the neighboring communities of Mattapan and Hyde Park. Milton has a split identity. One side of town is among the most diverse neighborhoods in New England,[2] while the rest of the town is almost entirely white and wealthy. Three of the four elementary schools are incredibly homogeneous, while the other is diverse along racial, ethnic, and class lines. All four schools are excellent academically, though parents often have strong feelings about which school their children attend. Some push for the diverse school, while others insist that their kids be sent to any of the other three. This tension comes to a head when all four schools feed to a single middle school.

The week my daughter's teacher was suspended, I happened to be writing the section in chapter 4 on tension in Cleveland, Mississippi, over the 2017 court ruling that forced racial integration of its schools. As I learned more about the history of "white flight" throughout the Delta, in which parents with means sent children to private schools or moved just outside of town rather than allow them to be with Black children in public schools, I came to better understand that even though my community did not have the same history of explicit segregation through Jim Crow laws, policy and power dynamics created de facto segregation that would be defended vigorously. This experience reinforced that what I was learning in Mississippi was not unique to red states or the South, as many northern liberals have seemed to think as I tell them about this book project, but rather has a lot to teach all of us.

Finally, my fourth formative experience came as my wife was diagnosed with stage 3 colon cancer in July 2020 just as I was wrapping up the first full draft of the manuscript. I supported her through multiple surgeries, eight months of chemotherapy, and six weeks of daily radiation, all while helping our children navigate seventh, fourth, and second grades remotely during the pandemic. To put it mildly, this was a traumatic experience for our family.

We were optimistic that treatment would lead to a cure, but the four years I had spent reading, talking, and writing about inequities in Mississippi made me particularly aware of the many layers of privilege that increased the likelihood of success in our case. My wife is otherwise in excellent health. She does not smoke or drink and has benefited from a lifetime of access to healthy foods she can afford to buy and has time to cook. She enjoys living in a neighborhood with sidewalks and jogging trails. The property values in our community mean that our neighbors have also benefited from privilege and have the resources to generously provide meals and gift cards so that we did not have to cook meals on the busy days we met with doctors.

Our privilege extends to my wife's medical care, as she was treated at one of the best hospitals in the world. We can afford this care because a lifetime of educational opportunities has led to employment with good income and good insurance. Our insurance not only covered my wife's treatment but also covers therapy and counseling to address our family's emotional and mental health. Our deductible is lower, and the annual limit on out-of-pocket expenses such as copays and coinsurance is far lower, than what is available in many plans across the country. And this does not come close to comparing to the challenges that people without insurance face.

Our experience epitomizes one of the main takeaways of this book: that all the factors that influence health are interrelated and mutually reinforcing. The opportunity for good health increases when people have good options, when the best choices are available and intuitive, and when the people around them benefit from the same privileges. This is not to say that everyone who makes good choices will be healthy. My otherwise healthy wife could die of cancer while someone with no insurance who smoked their entire life might survive. But striving for health equity at the population level means that everyone has the best chance possible to live a long, healthy, and happy life.

A Note on Methods

My research questions grew bigger and broader the deeper I dug, such that my goal became to examine how the multitude of factors that influence population health come together in a single place. In writing this book, I disregarded the main piece of advice I give to doctoral students when serving on their dissertation committees. I encourage them to continually narrow their research questions, so they are as focused as possible.

I did follow the other major advice I give to students, which is to choose the methods that answer the questions, not the other way around. This approach was exciting and daunting given the scope of my overarching question. No single research methodology is sufficient to examine a complex set of interrelated dynamics. With valuable input from mentors, colleagues, friends, and leaders in Mississippi, I landed on a process that integrated four main approaches.

First, I looked to the existing literature. So much great research has already been published on the issues that affect health at the individual and population levels. More needs to be done to synthesize these findings, place them in a fuller context, and translate them for non-researchers. Therefore, much of the work of researching and writing this book was focused on reviewing the literature on the root causes of these issues, the relevant policies, and what approaches work, then connecting this information with learning from my other methodologies. I relied heavily on scholars in diverse fields for guidance on theoretical and conceptual frameworks.

Second, I used quantitative data to get a broader picture of what was happening in the Delta and beyond. Most of this was descriptive analysis relying on a wide variety of sources. The Robert Wood Johnson Foundation's County Health Rankings was particularly helpful for analyzing measures that capture the demographic, health, and social infrastructure context at a local level and over time.

Third, I used qualitative methods to deepen my understanding about what it was like to live in the Delta and beyond. I conducted interviews with dozens of local leaders in public and private sectors in large and small communities throughout the Delta, such as mayors, city council members, state legislators, county officials, and the leaders of nonprofits and organizations focused on health care, education, tourism, business, and other issues. My goal in these meetings was to learn about their work and to listen. I did not try to convince them of anything. I did not lobby or do anything that might resemble lobbying. I promised to respect the confidentiality of our conversations and so do not name these interviewees in the book.

Fourth, I also talked to residents of the Delta to learn about their lives and how they view the issues that affect health.[3] Their perspectives and voices are critical to this work and are an essential complement to the literature reviews and quantitative analysis. One of the challenges of qualitative research is balancing breadth and depth. I chose something in between: surveys of a large number of people and an ethnographic approach of becoming deeply enmeshed in the lives of a small number of people.

All told, about fifty people participated in eight focus groups. Five of these groups, each with about seven people, met on a weekly basis for four weeks during the late summer and fall of 2017. These participants engaged in a visual ethnographic method called Photovoice in which they were given cameras (or encouraged to use the cameras on their phones) to take photographs each week in response to a series of prompts. The first meeting of each focus group was devoted to getting to know each other, talking about experiences with health care, and discussing how factors beyond medical care influence health. In subsequent weeks, each participant chose three to five photos they had taken to answer a question such as where people buy food or what they do and do not like about their neighborhoods. Their photos served as a launch pad to conversations about these issues and in many cases facilitated a richness of insight and description that might not have happened otherwise. The technology sometimes got in the way because the cameras I initially provided were too low quality or this was the first time some had used digital cameras.

Recruitment for the focus groups was a challenge given the intense time commitment required. I went through local organizations whose leaders were supportive of the project and worked within their networks to find willing participants. At each meeting I fed participants a meal, and when the interviews were over, they kept the cameras. I aimed to have participants whose demographic characteristics were as reflective of their communities as possible. Three of these groups were focused on working with youth, so the participants were teenagers who participated with their parents' consent.

Leaders of local organizations did not participate in the focus groups but served as members of an informal advisory committee to provide feedback on the research plan and answer specific questions. This approach of recruiting through organizations had the major advantage of establishing a higher level of trust at the outset than might otherwise have been possible. A disadvantage was that these groups were not random or representative cross sections of a particular community. Some people already knew each other, which may have made them more comfortable sharing feelings, though some may have chosen to be less open.

I filled gaps in stories and insights by circling back to some participants for one-on-one conversations and used a snowball approach in which participants in my study recommended other people whom they thought I should interview. I conducted three additional focus groups that were onetime conversations that did not involve photos. These groups included individuals from groups that were underrepresented in terms of the geography and demographics of the other focus groups. One meeting involved college students at the University of Mississippi who were from the Delta, one involved members of a church in Clarksdale, and the third involved users of the James Kennedy Wellness Center in Charleston.

It is important to emphasize that the focus groups did not include a huge number of participants. It would not have been feasible to go into much depth with many more people, and I do not claim these perspectives are definitive or representative of everyone in the Delta. Even so, the stories and insights I include in this book are consistent with the academic literature, quantitative data, and perspectives shared by others.

It is also important to appreciate that I did not do this work alone. Each of the five multiweek focus group sessions was led by Linda Nicole Stringfellow. At the time, Linda was the director of the AmeriCorps Vista program at Delta State University. She is deeply connected and widely trusted throughout the Delta, and her leadership was invaluable. Two doctoral students, Kathleen Banks of Boston University and Laura Jean Kerr of Mississippi State University, played a critical role in organizing and carrying out focus groups. Amy McInerney was instrumental in the final stages of the writing, editing, and formatting of the manuscript.

At each step, I tried to be respectful, reflective, and self-aware.[4] I tried to follow best practices in community-based research, including listening to and following the advice of community leaders.[5] I am sure I had blind spots and made mistakes while researching and writing. For these I am sorry and take sole responsibility. I hope they can be learning opportunities.

Ripples of Hope in the Mississippi Delta

Prologue
The Health Equity Policy Agenda

....

Few will have the greatness to bend history itself, but each of us can work to change a small portion of events. . . . It is from numberless diverse acts of courage and belief that human history is shaped. Each time a man stands up for an ideal, or acts to improve the lot of others, or strikes out against injustice, he sends forth a tiny ripple of hope, and crossing each other from a million different centers of energy and daring, those ripples build a current which can sweep down the mightiest walls of oppression and resistance.
—Robert F. Kennedy, June 6, 1966, Cape Town, South Africa

Let's start on an optimistic note: I believe health equity is possible. We can become a country in which we cannot predict how likely someone is to be healthy based on their race, their ethnicity, where they live, or other demographic characteristics—a society in which everyone has equal opportunity to be healthy in the fullest sense of the word, not just the absence of disease but "a state of complete physical, emotional, and social well-being."[1] This may sound naively hopeful given the challenges so many people face. But hope is a good thing, as long as it is rooted in a deep understanding of these barriers.

The COVID-19 pandemic clarified two things about who is healthy and why: individual choices are important, but a person's health is also deeply affected by the interconnected sets of relationships, structures, systems, and policies that shape the communities in which they live, and these dynamics inherently disadvantage some populations while they benefit others. Black, Indigenous, and other people of color are more likely than white people to work at jobs and live in communities in which social distancing is difficult, so they were more likely to be exposed to the virus. They were also less likely to survive COVID-19 once they contracted the disease, given that they are more likely to already have underlying health conditions such as obesity, cancer, or asthma and face greater barriers to accessing high-quality health care.[2] The long-term effects of the pandemic have reverberated more intensely through communities of color in which people are more likely to have lost loved ones and are more vulnerable to financial instability.[3]

The importance of relationships, structures, systems, and policies has been old news to scholars, students, and practitioners in the field of public health since the discovery in 1854 by John Snow that cholera is waterborne and that this disease could be prevented by removing the handle to the Broad Street pump in London.[4] Thousands of articles have since been published in academic journals on what have been called "the social determinants of health," or the underlying conditions that shape a population's opportunity to be healthy. A deep body of research has shown that issues that on the surface may seem unrelated to health, such as housing, education, and income, are deeply connected to life expectancy, obesity, mental health, quality of life, and other health outcomes.

However, there also seem to be two uncomfortable realities in the wake of the pandemic: (1) the disproportionate effect of COVID-19 on particular populations has strengthened the prevailing paradigm that health is a product of individual choices rather than convincing the broader public of the importance of structures and systems,[5] and (2) the field of public health has largely failed to explain social determinants of health or the changes to social structures needed to improve population health.[6]

In this book I acknowledge that individual choices affect a person's health, but I also challenge skeptics who believe that people are to blame for the choices that make them more likely to have chronic diseases. Seeing these decisions in context makes it clear that being healthy is more than making good or bad choices about what to eat and whether to exercise. At the same time, public health leaders need to explain the interconnected factors that shape health and be focused more on corresponding policy change. The terms of the national health reform debate need to be broadened so that we are not narrowly focused on health insurance. Presidential and congressional debates about health reform over the last century have primarily revolved around how to increase access to health insurance and thus medical care so that more people benefit from the drugs, devices, and expertise doctors use to help patients who are sick. Yes, good health care is critical, but health care does not address why people in some communities are so much more likely to be sick in the first place. The key to having the largest effect on health is not only to make changes that help clinicians more effectively treat individual patients or even to educate people on the benefits of eating vegetables and exercising but also to understand the underlying structural factors that shape the

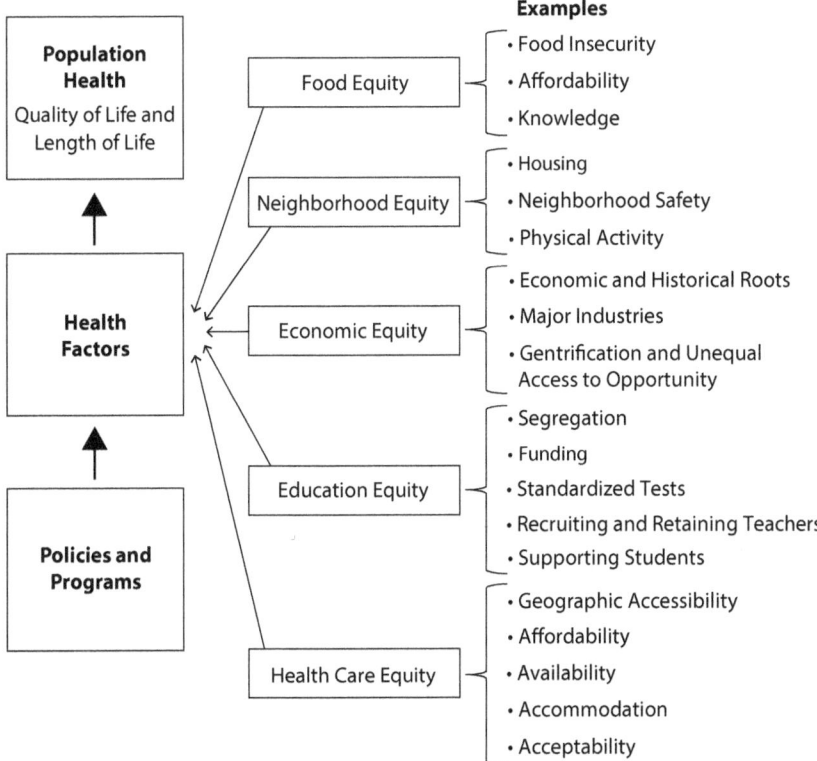

FIGURE P.1 Factors that affect population health. Population health outcomes are affected by policies and programs that are cumulative and mutually reinforcing among five areas of a person's life experience. Enacting policies and programs that ensure equity within each of these five domains improves population health. Copyright 2023 Institute for Perinatal Quality Improvement. All rights reserved. For requests to use or reprint, email info@perinatalQI.org.

distribution of health and disease, to identify the policies that drive these differences, and to change them. The goal of health reform should be health, not just health care.

The bridge between these paradigms is that it is a false dichotomy to view health as a function of individual choices or of contextual factors (see figure P.1). People are indeed more likely to be healthy if they eat well, maintain an active lifestyle, and have access to high-quality medical care. But it's much harder to make good choices when you don't have good options. Our goal should be ensuring that everyone has an equal opportunity, based on equitable policies and programs, to make healthy choices and is empowered to do so.

Poverty, Racism, and Power

Everyone having an equal opportunity to lead their healthiest lives is not the same as everyone having equal outcomes. This is simply not possible at an individual level because there will always be people who die young of cancer and people who live to be ninety years old while smoking two packs of cigarettes a day. But it is possible at the population level such that the distribution of people who get sick despite a lifetime of good choices is similar between groups and places. We will have achieved the goal of health equity once we are unable to predict a person's health or life expectancy based on their demographic characteristics or place of residence.

Though not the prevailing view, awareness is growing of the connection between health and place. For example, authors in *Time* magazine and *Forbes* make the case that "your ZIP code might determine how long you live—and the difference could be decades"[7] and "where you live impacts your health."[8] But such articles rarely go the next step to identify what drives these differences.[9] Particular populations or a particular geographic area do not inherently predetermine health outcomes. Generations of inequities persist not because of genetics or the fact that certain people are unlucky enough to inhabit a particular piece of land but because of policy decisions, cultural dynamics, and systemic forces that create, exacerbate, and perpetuate differences within these populations. As Paula Braveman and Laura Gottlieb write, we must dig into "the causes of the causes" of health inequities.[10]

The intense connection between health and place is largely a reflection of the multitude of policies that reinforce the geographic concentration of poverty. Therefore, a health reform conversation more fully oriented toward improving health should emphasize using policy to mitigate the effects of—and ultimately eradicate—poverty. We need a health equity policy agenda, a set of policies designed to create an environment in which the healthiest choices are accessible and natural.[11] Such a health equity policy agenda will be broad and encompass a variety of issues and fields that do not have the word *health* in their names, such as housing, education, and economic development. These conversations are already happening, but the people who participate in them often do not know they are doing public health and do not have enough engagement from public health scholars and leaders.

Poverty cannot be eradicated, and health equity cannot be achieved without addressing the important connections between race and the social, cultural, and political systems that shape health in the United States. Race is tightly correlated with who is poor, their opportunities to move out of poverty, and their ability to pass on physical, emotional, and financial health to subsequent generations. The geographic concentrations of poverty and race across this country are intensely related.

But in this book, I outline how the importance of race transcends its connection to class. Study after study shows that nonwhite populations with the same educational attainment and income as their white counterparts do not experience the same degree of long-term benefits in terms of life expectancy and generational wealth. Decisions that would help white populations emerge from poverty and become financially stable have diminishing returns for other populations because of a lifetime of being treated differently by teachers, law enforcement, mortgage lenders, employers, neighbors, and health care providers.[12]

To be clear, the problem is *racism*, not race.[13] Race is not a risk factor for disease. Race is a social construct, the definitions of which have shifted over time.[14] The Human Genome Project shows that all humans are 99.9 percent the same regardless of the color of our skin. "Genetic diseases" are related to geography and other factors, not skin color. No particular race or ethnicity is inherently predisposed to being less healthy or financially secure. The issue is whether people have the same access to opportunity, and how they are treated when they try to take advantage of it (see figure P.2).

Few topics are as sensitive and likely to shut down conversations as racism. Attempts to discuss the role of race and racism in our nation's founding and subsequent history are criticized as un-American and unpatriotic. Some states and cities have banned critical race theory from being taught in their schools. Leaders become defensive and cautious when race enters the conversation and decide it is safer to develop policies that are seemingly colorblind. At times this approach is a thinly veiled way to enact policies harking back to an era when racist goals were explicitly stated. But even when not motivated by racist intent, a colorblind approach to policymaking willfully ignores the ways the same policies affect populations differently. These approaches also tend to be guided by a mistaken philosophy that outcomes are entirely a function of individual choices and that fault should be assigned for not taking advantage of opportunities that are assumed by many to be the same for all.

A more productive conversation is possible if we frame policymaking in terms of structural racism, meaning the recognition that policies and structures can have racial implications whether they are motivated by racist intentions or not.[15] The inequitable distribution of opportunity in the United States means that it is not enough to avoid actively discriminating against certain groups in particular communities. We need equitable or fair policies.

← UPSTREAM ─────────────────────────────── DOWNSTREAM →

Socially Constructed Inequities on the Basis of:
- Class & Income
- Race/Ethnicity
- Gender & Gender Expression
- Sexual Orientation
- Immigration Status
- Abilities

Structural Barriers to Health

Institutional Inequities
- Grocery Stores
- Corporations & Businesses
- Voting Access
- Laws, Regulations, & Enforcement
- Schools
- Number & Location of Health Care Facilities
- Public Health Efforts
- Banks & Loans
- Budget Decisions

Living Condition Inequities
- Food, e.g., Insecurity, Affordability, Knowledge
- Neighborhood, e.g., Housing, Neighborhood Safety, Support for Physical Activity
- Economic, e.g., Historic Roots, Gentrification, Unequal Access to Opportunity
- Education, e.g., Segregation, Funding, Standardized Tests, Recruiting & Retaining Teachers, Supporting Teachers
- Health Care Services, e.g., Access, Affordability, Availability, Acceptability, Accommodations

Examples of Behaviors That May Contribute to Risk
- Food Choices
- Low Physical Activity
- Low Educational Attainment
- Not Accessing Healthcare or Following Treatment Recommendations

Examples of Disease Processes & Injuries Affected by Options & Behaviors
- Diabetes
- Heart Disease
- Hypertension
- Accidents
- Despair
- Weathering

Health & Well-Being
- Morbidity & Mortality
- Life Expectancy
- Quality of Life

Strategic Partnerships & Advocacy

Community Capacity Civic Engagement Community Organizations

Health Literacy

Quality & Accessibility of Health Care

POLICY AND LAW

Equity or fairness means striving to ensure everyone has what they need to be healthy based on where they started. Looking through an equity lens is recognizing that white people enjoy unearned privileges, and applying policies equally for everyone does not lead to equal outcomes. Equity means reforming structures, systems, and policies so that it is not possible to predict health outcomes based on ethnicity, gender, sex, sexual orientation, immigration status, or any other aspect of identity. My focus here and throughout this book is primarily on racism, though I believe we should simultaneously work to eliminate differences based on all other "isms."

Ibram X. Kendi goes one step further by arguing that *racist policies* is an even clearer term than *structural racism*.[16] The key insight is that we should focus on the thoughts, ideas, and policies as racist rather than the people behind them. This is not to say that we should absolve leaders or resist calling out people who are espousing racist ideas, but we should sharpen our focus on power and policy. In some cases, it will not be possible to change policies without changing who has power.

Policymakers who are not deliberately righting past and present wrongs perpetuate structures that limit opportunities along racial lines.[17] As Kendi explains, the opposite of racism is not to ignore race or be "not racist"; the opposite is *antiracism*. Kendi defines antiracism as "expressing the idea that racial groups are equals and none needs developing, and is supporting policy that reduces racial inequity."[18] This is in contrast to assimilationists or segregationists who express the racist ideas that one or more racial groups are inferior to others and therefore must be segregated or assimilated through policies designed to develop that group: "[Antiracism] can become real if we focus on power instead of people, if we focus on changing policy instead of groups of people. It's possible if we overcome our cynicism about the permanence of racism."[19]

Major political leaders have argued in recent years that structural racism does not exist in the United States.[20] Many people bristle at the idea of explicitly bringing racial considerations and equity into policymaking. They may be willing to agree that poverty is the underlying factor that drives

FIGURE P.2 (OPPOSITE) A public health framework for reducing health inequities. Underlying determinants, factors, and structures of health: policies dictate structures that affect options, behaviors, and outcomes. Based on the research conducted by David K. Jones in the Mississippi Delta. Copyright 2023 Institute for Perinatal Quality Improvement. All rights reserved. For requests to use or reprint, email info@perinatalQI.org.

differences in outcomes, but they are more likely to blame people for making bad decisions than to acknowledge the role that racism plays in shaping the opportunity someone has to make healthy decisions. And even if they are willing to accept this, they argue that explicitly considering race when pursuing equity is unfair. Why should they have fewer opportunities or seemingly be made worse off in the name of racial justice?

Addressing racial inequities does not necessarily require widespread redistribution or taking anything away from middle-class, white Americans. In fact, addressing racial inequity would most likely benefit them. As Jonathan Metzl shows in *Dying of Whiteness,* Black populations feel the effects of racism first, deepest, and longest, but racism hurts the health of white populations too: "Politics that claimed on face value to bolster White America ended up making even white lives sicker, harder, and shorter."[21]

Root Cause Analysis

The first step to developing a health equity policy agenda is to be clear about which problems need solving. Root cause analysis is needed to achieve greater consensus on the barriers that make it harder for people to live their healthiest lives. Some in public health might find this question redundant given the deep body of work already published. They are right—we already know a lot about the problems and what must change. Scholars have shown that controlling for a variety of factors, people are more likely to be healthy if they have safe housing, greater educational attainment, and higher income. They have also identified the independent effects of many specific policy changes.

But this work has not reached far beyond public health and has certainly not fully penetrated mainstream thinking. It also does not fully account for the interconnected complexity of factors that shape health. People do not live their lives controlling for other factors. People who experience inadequate housing are often the same people who experience food insecurity, unsafe neighborhoods, fewer job opportunities, limited educational opportunity, and lack of access to health care. The important work that has already been done must be complemented by a different kind of research that connects the dots between individual choices and the mutually reinforcing dimensions of relationships, structures, systems, policies, and the cumulative weight of dealing with multiple challenges simultaneously.

Place-based research is a valuable complement to the work that has already been done. A better understanding of problems at the commu-

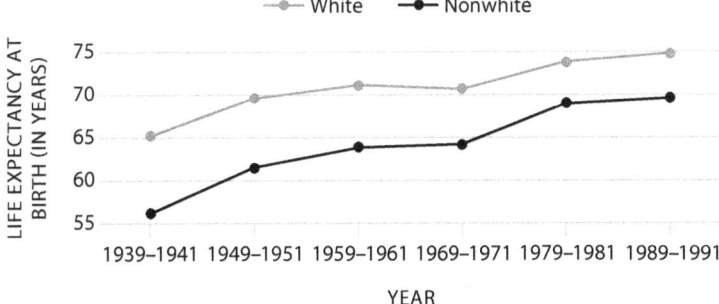

GRAPH P.1 Life expectancy at birth in years, Mississippi, 1939–1991. Data from Mississippi State Department of Health, *Abridged Life Tables for Mississippi, 1989–1991* (Jackson: Mississippi State Department of Health, n.d.), https://msdh.ms.gov/msdhsite/_static/resources/162.pdf.

nity level and their root causes makes it more likely that policy change will happen and work as intended. Place-based research is challenging, and digging into the complexities of context takes time, energy, resources, and humility. Thoughtful use of quantitative and qualitative methods and theoretical frameworks from a variety of disciplines is not natural to policymakers and scholars. But this approach is also infused with optimism and respect, and it pushes change makers not just to think about barriers but also to recognize and build on a community's unique assets.[22]

The Mississippi Delta

The Mississippi Delta is an ideal place to examine the interconnected dynamics of race, poverty, opportunity, and health because it is arguably the least healthy place in the United States. Mississippi is among the worst states, if not the very worst, in the country on most common health indicators such as obesity and life expectancy at birth. In 2019, life expectancy in Mississippi was the lowest in the nation at 74.4 years in comparison to the national average of 78.8 years.[23] Historical trends reveal that life expectancy at birth increased between 1939 and 1991 for white and nonwhite racial groups, but the gap between these groups narrowed only slightly (graph P.1). Between 1990 and 2008, life expectancy varied widely among counties within the Mississippi Delta, and there was a ten-year difference between Issaquena County (79.5 years) and Tunica County (69.0 years). Counties with lower life expectancies include neighborhoods of concentrated poverty and predominantly Black residents (see graph P.1).[24]

Some researchers may bristle at the idea of choosing one of the least healthy places as the focus for this book and worry that it might be an outlier or too different from the rest of the country. But the Delta is an ideal *example* because it reflects the problems faced by the entire country. The stark differences in experiences and outcomes between race and class groups and the issues that drive these inequities are on the surface to an intense degree. Of course, not every issue is exactly the same as in the rest of the country, but the Delta illuminates what is happening across the United States and the elements necessary for a health equity policy agenda. Readers of this book are missing the point if they come away shocked by conditions in the Delta but do not consider how the same inequities are perpetuated in their own communities everywhere in the United States.

On virtually every statistic in which Mississippi ranks worst in the nation, counties in the Delta are the worst in the state. In short, this is the least healthy region of the least healthy state. County-wide numbers may mask the scope of health problems across the Mississippi Delta since Black men, women, and children tend to have considerably worse outcomes than their white neighbors. Health in the Mississippi Delta—particularly among Black individuals—is a major crisis that deserves national attention.

One vivid example of this disparity is that 12.4 percent of newborns in Mississippi weigh less than 2,500 grams (5 lbs. 8 oz.) at birth,[25] a reliable indicator of significant health problems to come. This number is considerably greater than the national rate of 8.3 percent and more than a full percentage point greater than the state with the second worst rate, Louisiana, at 11.3 percent.[26] Based on 2020–2022 data, the March of Dimes gave the state of Mississippi an F grade for their high rates of preterm birth rate overall, and they calculated that the preterm birth rate among babies born to Black birthing people was 1.4 times higher than the rate among all other babies born in Mississippi (see map P.1).[27] With this national picture in mind, it is tragic that 17 percent of newborns in Coahoma County—one of the most highly populated parts of the Delta—are born underweight (see map P.2).[28] The racial differences within Coahoma County are even more drastic, since 20 percent of Black newborns are born underweight compared with 7 percent of white newborns. To put these numbers in a broader perspective, the rate of Black newborns in Coahoma County born underweight is worse than the known rate in most of the places classified by the United Nations as the least developed countries in the world.[29]

As dramatic as these numbers are, comparing the Delta to a third-world country is misleading, offensive, and counterproductive. This mindset may

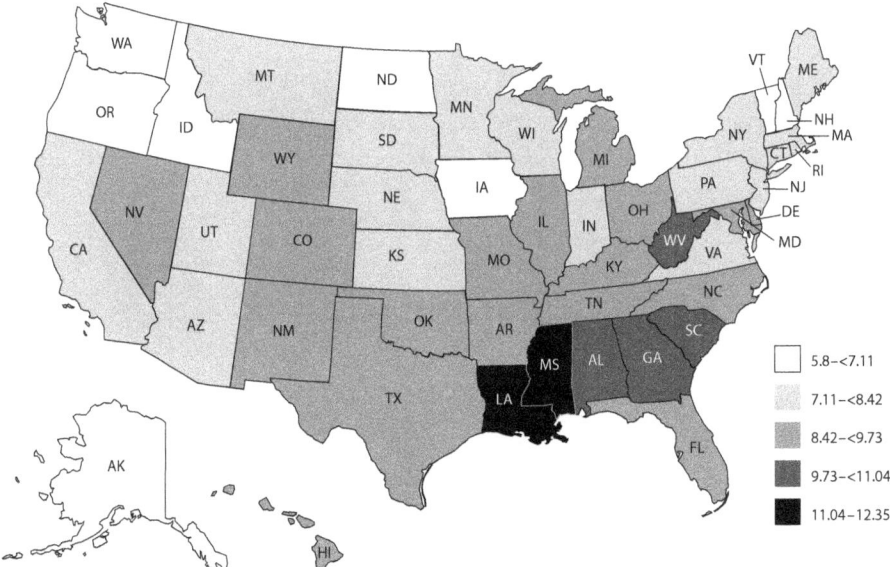

MAP P.1 Percentage of babies born low birthweight by state, 2021. From National Center for Health Statistics, last reviewed April 26, 2024, https://www.cdc.gov/nchs/pressroom/sosmap/lbw_births/lbw.htm.

unintentionally reinforce the idea that health outcomes in the Delta and the rest of the United States, and poorer countries for that matter, are inevitable and unsolvable. It makes the problems too distant, implicitly blames the residents of the Delta for these circumstances, and inappropriately absolves the rest of us from acknowledging inequities in our own communities and the role we each could play to improve national health disparities.

Health in Rural America

The Mississippi Delta is a particularly compelling place to study the connection between health and place, partly because rural America is so poorly understood by many national policymakers and researchers. As one scholar notes, "Rural people and issues generally receive little attention from the urban-centric media and policy elites."[30] More than forty-six million people live in rural parts of the United States, which is half the population of urban areas and about one-fourth the population of suburban areas,[31] but this is still a substantial number that deserves our close attention.

Health outcomes in rural communities also have implications for the rest of the country. Sociologist Kenneth Johnson argues that "few people

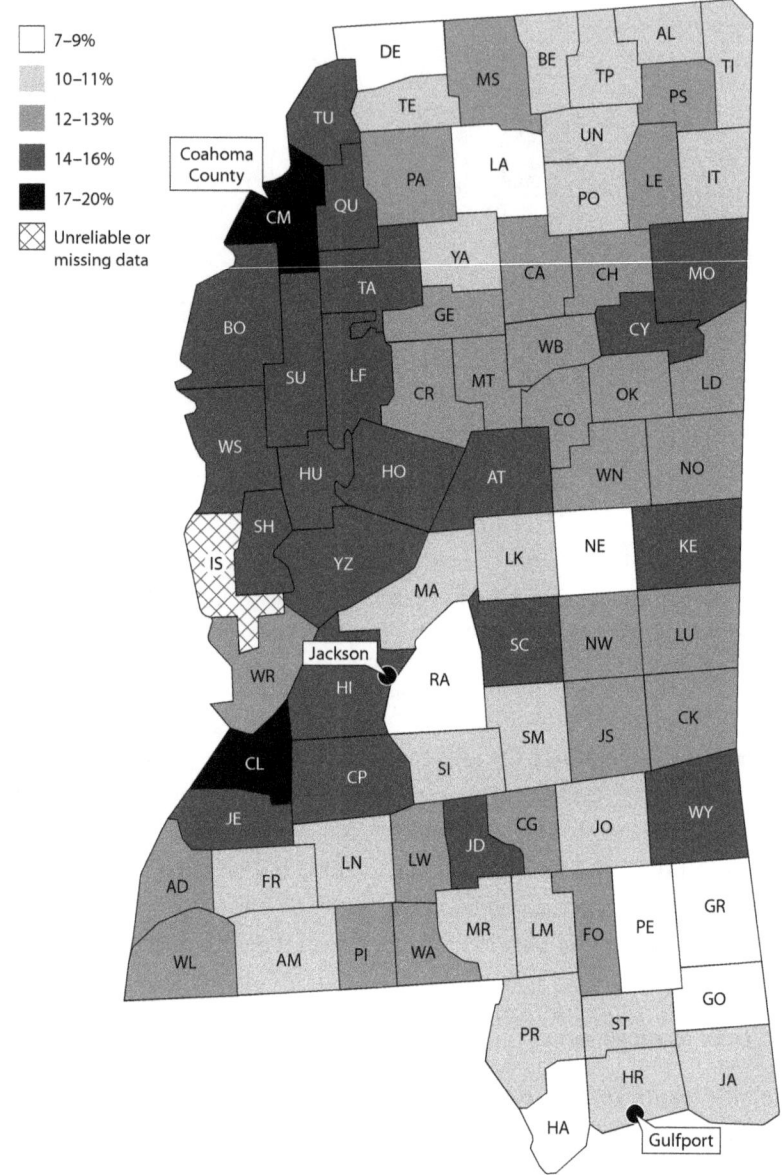

MAP P.2 Low birthweight in Mississippi by county, 2022. Percentage of live births with low birthweight (<2,500 grams). From "Mississippi: Low Birthweight," County Health Rankings, accessed June 10, 2024, https://www.countyhealthrankings.org/health-data/mississippi?year=2024&measure=Low+Birthweight. Used with permission from the University of Wisconsin Population Health Institute, County Health Rankings & Roadmaps.

appreciate that the fates of rural and urban America are inextricably linked. Improving the opportunities, accessibility, and viability of rural areas is critical—both to the 46 million people who live there and to the much larger urban population that depends on rural America's contributions to their material, environmental and social well-being. A vibrant rural America broadens the nation's economic, intellectual and cultural diversity."[32]

In a 2018 study, Arthur Cosby of Mississippi State University and colleagues examined 104 million deaths that occurred between 1970 and 2016. They found compelling evidence of a "mortality penalty" in high-poverty rural areas. The difference between rural and urban mortality rates in 2004 (913.13 vs. 836.16, respectively) resulted in 76.97 excess deaths per 100,000. The difference increased in 2016 (847.65 rural vs. 712.95 urban) to 134.70 excess deaths per 100,000. It's not that mortality increased dramatically in rural areas but that mortality in nonrural areas improved more dramatically.[33] In an earlier study, Cosby and colleagues estimated that the rural mortality penalty in 2000 to 2004 was 71.7 excess deaths per 100,000.[34] These studies show a close relationship between rurality and health even when controlling for poverty, other measures of socioeconomic status, and race.[35]

Comparatively little is known about what to do to improve health in rural America. Part of the problem is that rural communities are often talked about as if they were all the same. New research is making it increasingly clear that rural communities are not homogeneous and that more work needs to be done to understand their unique challenges and assets.[36] Rural communities in the United States fit into three broad categories. First, some are rich in amenities such as coastlines or mountains and have seen population increases of 19 percent between 1990 and 2015. Second, some are transitioning in that they have seen a 10.6 percent population increase during this same time period but a decrease in twenty-five-to-thirty-four-year-olds. Third, others are chronically poor in that they have lost 13.7 percent of their populations, have median incomes $15,000 to $21,000 less than the other two places, and nearly 40 percent of children live in poverty.[37]

Labeling communities in this third group—which is predominant in the South—"chronically poor" unfairly blames the residents. This label is inadequate because it fails to recognize that these communities face more hurdles to overcoming poverty because they do not have the resources and advantages of communities in the other two categories. In these communities, we need to do a better job of understanding the unique barriers to good health, identifying their unique assets, and developing policies tailored to address barriers and leverage assets.

Defining the Delta

The Mississippi Delta defies easy definition. Even the geographical boundaries of the Mississippi Delta are amorphous, and the term *Delta* means slightly different things depending on the context. In the broadest sense, *the Delta* refers to the alluvial plain that leads from Illinois to the mouth of the Mississippi River into the Gulf of Mexico near New Orleans. It encompasses parts of the states of Illinois, Missouri, Kentucky, Tennessee, Arkansas, Mississippi, Alabama, and Louisiana. This area is sometimes referred to as the "Lower Mississippi Delta" to distinguish it from the upper part of the river that extends from Lake Itasca in Minnesota. The Lower Mississippi Delta has a political identity through the Delta Regional Authority, a federal agency created in 2000 to distribute funds to and promote economic development in 252 counties straddling the river in these eight states (see map P.3).[38]

In a narrower sense, the Delta refers to the portion of the Lower Mississippi Delta in the northwestern part of the state of Mississippi bordered by the Mississippi River on the west and the Yazoo River on the east.[39] These rivers have played a major role in shaping the Mississippi Delta's cultural, economic, and political history. The soil is extremely fertile as a result of thousands of years of flooding, which made this a particularly attractive place for the native tribes that inhabited the land until the mid-nineteenth century, when they were displaced by primarily white farmers. The Mississippi River gave farmers and other business owners easy access to commercial centers from Chicago to New Orleans and beyond. Historian David Cohn had this political economy in mind when defining the boundaries of the Mississippi Delta as beginning in the lobby of the Peabody Hotel in Memphis, where much of the region's business with national and international leaders was conducted, and stretching south to Catfish Row in Vicksburg, where the Mississippi and Yazoo Rivers come together.[40]

These definitions are problematic because they do not match political boundaries such as county lines and legislative districts. A county that has any part between the Mississippi and Yazoo Rivers is often included in statistics about the region even though the demographics change dramatically moving east. For example, DeSoto County, along the Tennessee border, is sometimes considered part of the Delta because the Yazoo River cuts through its western edge. But it is very different from the rest of the region because DeSoto is one of the healthiest counties in the state, 63 percent white, and only 20 percent rural.[41] By contrast, neighboring Tunica County ranks

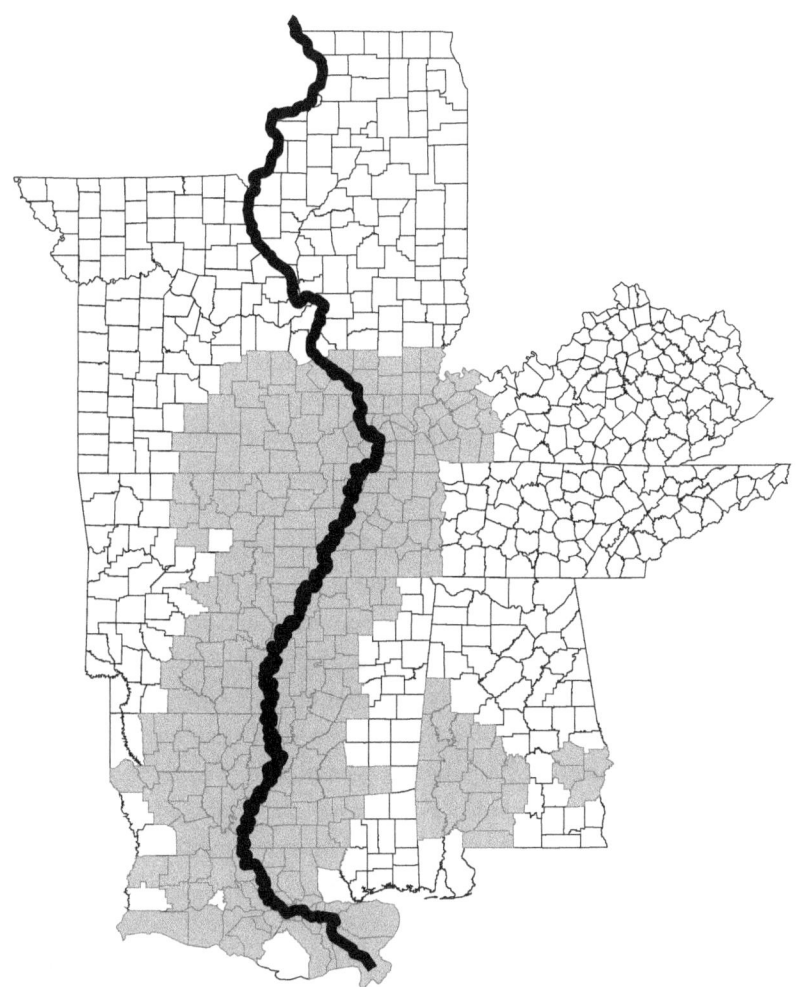

MAP P.3 Map of the Delta Regional Authority, with the Mississippi River represented here by a thick black line. Map produced by the Center for Population Studies, University of Mississippi. Used with permission from the University of Mississippi.

seventieth out of Mississippi's eighty-two counties in terms of overall poor health outcomes, is 77 percent Black, and is 66 percent rural.[42] The rest of the Mississippi Delta is much more like Tunica than DeSoto County.

Researchers deal with this boundary problem by conceptualizing the Mississippi Delta as three concentric circles: (1) core counties such as Tunica that are unquestionably within the heart of the region, (2) peripheral counties that are similar in many ways but on the edge, and (3) counties that are not culturally or demographically what people think of when they talk

The Health Equity Policy Agenda   15

about the Delta but that are part of the Delta Regional Authority's catchment area. This book is mostly about the core counties of the Mississippi Delta, though I try to be clear when I take a broader look (see map P.4).

The Political Determinants of Health in Mississippi

If the first step in developing a health equity policy agenda is identifying the systemic, structural, and policy root causes of the barriers to making healthy decisions, the next step is identifying the systemic, structural, and policy approaches to removing those barriers. But calls to action and calls for political reform run the risk of going unheard if driven by a weak understanding of local and state politics.[43] Public health leaders are likely to be frustrated by a lack of policy change without a fuller understanding of critical political forces.

We need to appreciate the historical and contemporary dynamics of power that gave rise to inequities.[44] We must ask who has the power to make changes, whether the people with power are convinced problems exist, and how they think potential solutions will affect them. The answers to these questions often lead to the conclusion that change will not happen until power dynamics are altered such that the people who make decisions more fully reflect and represent the affected populations. Health equity will not happen without a focus on politics and power dynamics, which makes voting rights one of the most fundamentally important public health issues.

The field of public health has a paradoxically uncomfortable relationship with politics because public health requires governmental action and so is inherently political.[45] In mainstream public health, the importance of politics is acknowledged, as evidenced by the World Health Organization's conceptual framework for action, which places all decisions about health within a broader context of public policy, political processes, and culture.[46] An informal scan of the leading public health journals suggests a growing appreciation for the importance of politics to our understanding of the conditions that shape health. Even so, some of the few researchers at the intersection of political science and public health argue that public health is "still commonly caught in a naïve, idealistic, and narrow view of public policy."[47]

A place-based approach to studying health inequities in the Mississippi Delta reinforces the importance of political power in shaping why circumstances are the way they are and what should and can be done to change these circumstances. The full history of voting, political participation, and

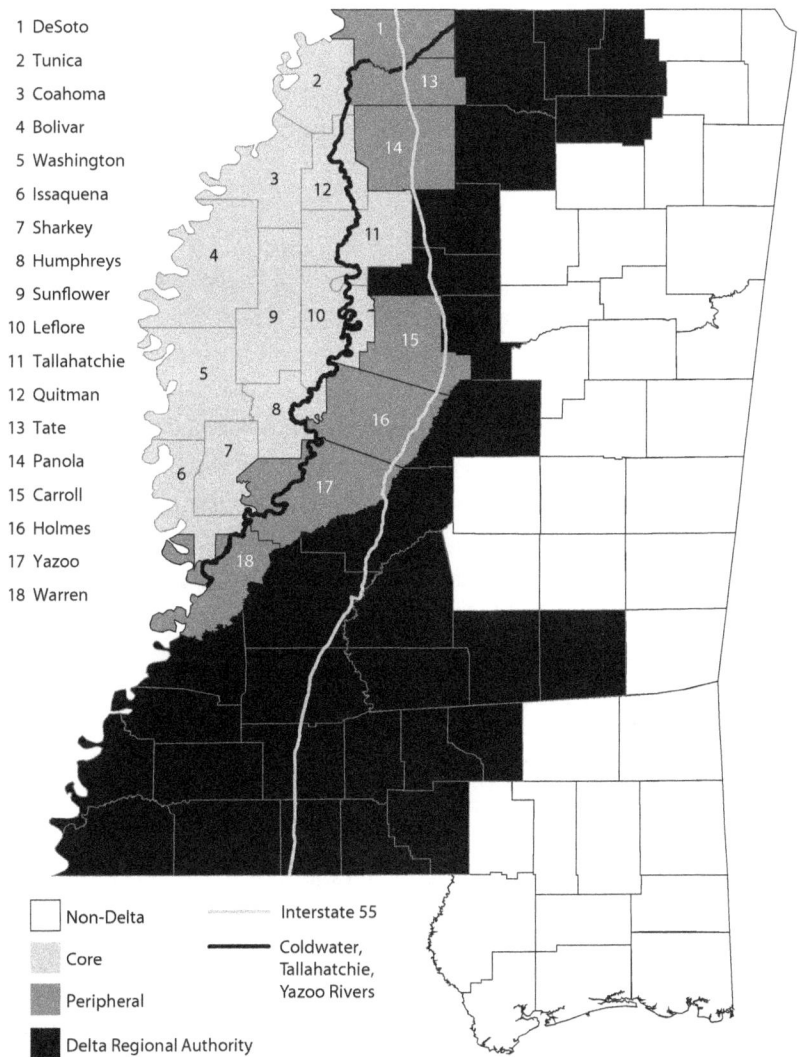

MAP P.4 Map of the Mississippi Delta core, peripheral, and Delta Regional Authority counties. Map produced by the Center for Population Studies, University of Mississippi. Used with permission from the University of Mississippi.

representation in Mississippi is far too complex to cover in depth. Entire books have been written on this subject.[48] However, it is crucial to appreciate how the evolution of power during four distinct periods affects the likelihood of a health equity policy agenda being adopted today.

Original Occupants

First, the Delta's demographics are deeply rooted in population changes that occurred in the nineteenth century. Slavery was not the region's first mass population displacement. Thousands of people in the Choctaw, Chickasaw, and other tribes occupied this land for centuries. The Delta was inhabitable by the primarily white farmers in the nineteenth century only because the native populations were forced to move west. One of the culminating events in this history of forced migrations was the Treaty of Dancing Rabbit Creek in September 1830. This was the first treaty negotiated by President Andrew Jackson's administration as part of the Indian Removal Act. The last of the Choctaw's twenty-three million acres, much of which covered what is today northern and central Mississippi, was ceded to the US government. More than two-thirds of the nearly twenty thousand Choctaws were displaced within three years to what is present-day Oklahoma.[49]

Similar stories played out for the other tribes in the area, such as the Chickasaw and the Quapaw. The Mississippi Band of Choctaw Indians still has a small presence in Mississippi, including reservations in the central part of the state, but they do not extend into the Delta. No county in the core or peripheral Delta has a native population greater than 0.5 percent.[50] One of the only traces that remain of the Delta's original inhabitants are the sporadic large mounds of dirt and grass that were built as burial sites or as a foundation for temples and other prominent structures. A group of twelve mounds near Greenville that were built in the twelfth century received protected status as a state park in the 1960s and as a National Historic Landmark in 1993.[51]

With the native population gone and primarily white farmers claiming the land, it is estimated that more than a million enslaved people were moved from the Upper South states of Virginia, Maryland, and Kentucky to work the tobacco and cotton fields in the Deep South states of Alabama, Louisiana, and Mississippi. This movement was twenty times larger than Jackson's Indian removals, larger than the number of people who migrated west by wagon, and double the number of Jewish immigrants who arrived in the United States from Russia and eastern Europe in the nineteenth century.[52]

A map of the prevalence of slavery in the 1860 census as measured by the proportion of a county's population that was enslaved shows that prevalence was greatest along the Mississippi River in what are now the core Delta counties. No other county in the United States had a higher prevalence of slavery in 1860 than Issaquena County, at the southern edge of the Delta, at 93 percent of 7,831 people.[53] However, this was not an outlier in the region. For example, 87 percent of people in nearby Bolivar County—named for South American liberator Simón Bolívar—were enslaved.

More than one-third of the population in Mississippi today is Black, which is the highest proportion in the country and dramatically higher than the national level of 12.3 percent.[54] The counties in the Mississippi Delta have some of the highest percentages of Black populations in the United States, and the highest is Holmes County at 81.6 percent. Ten other Delta counties are more than 60 percent Black, including the two with the largest total populations, Washington and Bolivar.[55]

One way plantation owners responded to the end of slavery was to recruit people from China to work their fields. These immigrants were desperate to make money to send home and worked for very little. The Chinese Exclusion Act, passed by Congress in 1882, severely restricted immigration from China, but a substantial number of Chinese people were already in the Mississippi Delta. This exclusionary anti-immigrant law was not repealed until 1943. Chinese immigrants occupied a unique place in society in that they were not on equal footing with white residents but were not subject to Jim Crow restrictions to the same degree as Black residents. Throughout the twentieth century, many Chinese Americans left the fields to operate independently owned grocery stores in small towns across the Delta. Many have since left, and based on July 1, 2021, census estimates, 0.3 percent to 1 percent of the population in Delta counties identifies as Asian alone, compared with 1.1 percent statewide and 6.1 percent in the United States. This is even lower than the relatively small Hispanic/Latinx population in the Delta, which is 2.4 percent to 3.1 percent in the same Delta counties.[56]

The effects of demographic shifts on today's conditions cannot be overstated. Avidit Acharya, Matthew Blackwell, and Maya Sen show compelling data that suggests "that counties with high shares of enslaved people just before the Civil War are places where whites today are more conservative,

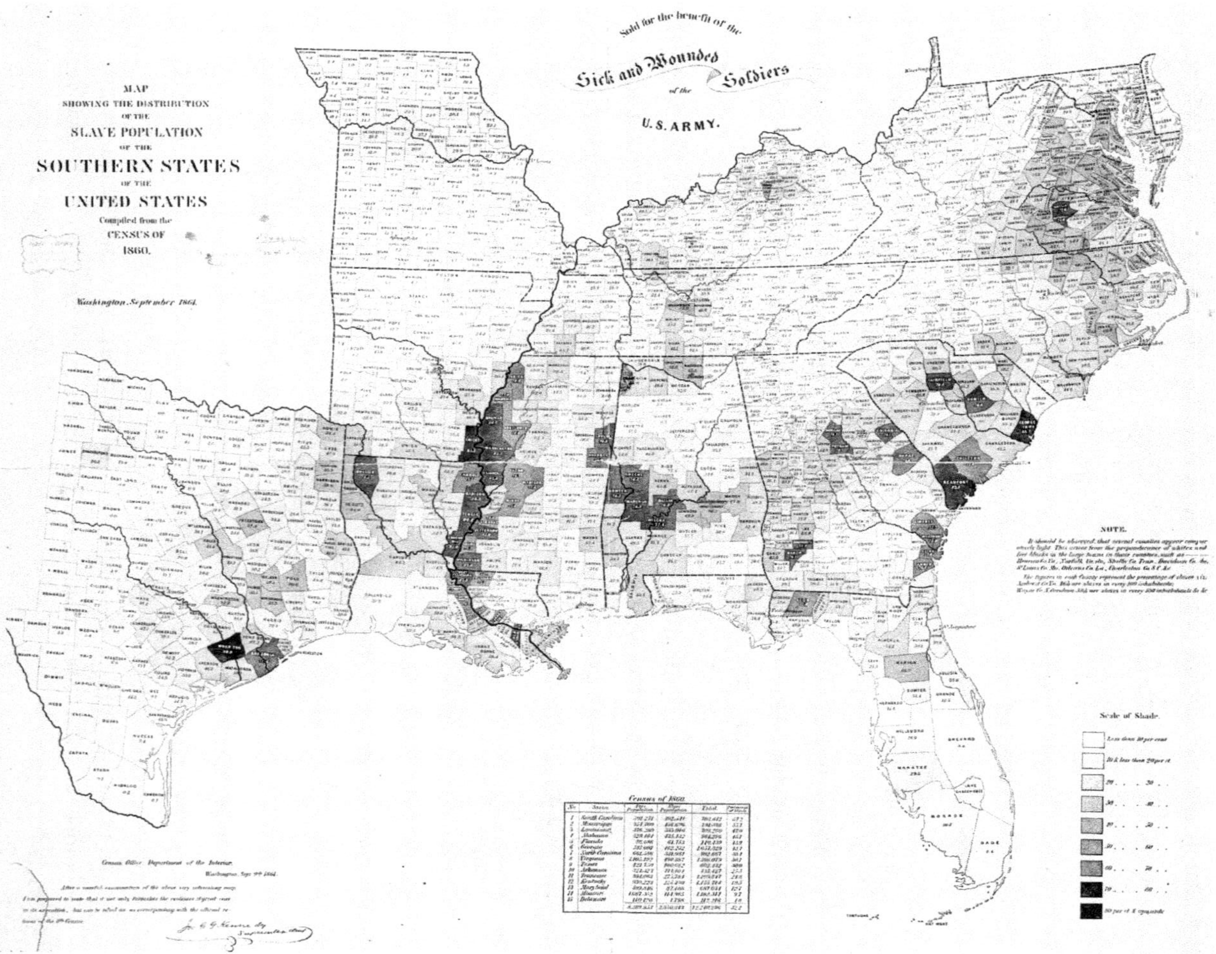

FIGURE P.3 Percentage of population enslaved by county, 1860. From Norman B. Leventhal Map and Education Center, Boston Public Library, Digital Collections, https://collections.leventhalmap.org/search/commonwealth:w950r836.

more opposed to affirmative action, more likely to agree with statements that indicate racial resentment, and more likely to express cooler feelings about Blacks."[57]

Constitution of 1890

The descendants of former slaves have struggled against poverty and white power structures that do not let them succeed, and changes to key institutions during the last 130 years have protected a purposeful power imbalance. The first post–Civil War elections in 1867 and 1869 allowed newly enfranchised Black voters to send 115 Black legislators to Jackson, with 13 in the Senate and 102 in the House.[58] US senators were selected at the time by state legislatures, meaning that this newly enfranchised group was able to send two Black men—Hiram Revels and Blanche Bruce—to Washington, DC, to represent Mississippi in the US Senate in the 1870s.

The white leadership of the state's Democratic Party felt threatened by these radical changes and responded by pushing for adoption of a new state constitution that would change the rules to their benefit. The new constitution did not need to be ratified by popular vote and could be written by a small group of delegates. Turnout for elections to select delegates was extremely low, which gave Democrats a dominant hand in the process. All but one of the 134 delegates were white. This group of white Democrats reestablished their dominance by using a poll tax, a literacy test, and a property requirement to determine who could vote.[59]

The new state constitution dramatically weakened the powers of Mississippi's governor just in case enough Black people voted to elect one of their own. Many of the functions given to governors in other states are held in Mississippi by freestanding boards and commissions appointed by legislative leaders or held by agencies led by independently elected heads. The legacy of these decisions lingers today, as the governor does not have direct control over the state's Department of Health or Department of Insurance, and the Mississippi Legislature has greater power than most state legislatures to oversee regulations adopted by the executive branch. Lest there be any doubt about the motivation behind these changes, Solomon Calhoon, president of the Constitutional Convention, explained, "Let's tell the truth if it bursts the bottom of the universe—We came here to exclude the Negro. Nothing short will answer."[60]

The new constitution had the intended effect. Voter registration among Black Mississippians fell from 70 percent in 1867 to 6 percent in 1892.[61] Black representation in the legislature ended immediately, and no Black person served in the state legislature between 1896 and the passage of the Voting Rights Act in 1965.[62] The Delta—or at least the Delta's wealthy white class—maintained a powerful presence in state politics during this period. Only three times between 1916 and 1940 was the Speaker of the House not from the Delta. These Speakers gave leadership positions for key committees to legislators from majority-Black districts to further consolidate power in favor of white Delta farmers.[63] Robert Mickey explained the [Democratic] party's primary method of operation in the Delta was possible because unequal distribution of populations among electoral districts supported white political cohesiveness. Other factors included legislator seniority systems, how planters were able to control legislative nominations, the influence of donors in statewide campaigns, and legislators' competence in keeping their office.[64]

Ending Jim Crow

Landmark judicial decisions and acts of Congress during the mid-twentieth century began to erode the grip on power enjoyed by white Democrats. For example, in 1944, the US Supreme Court held in *Smith v. Allwright* that states violate the US Constitution if they delegate responsibility for primary elections to white-only political parties that explicitly exclude voters based on their race. Dramatic and persistent political mobilization by activists such as Fannie Lou Hamer, Amzie Moore, Aaron Henry, and college-age northerners during the Freedom Summer contributed to important gains such as the Civil Rights Act of 1964 and the Voting Rights Act of 1965. On paper, these changes ended Jim Crow across the South and eliminated suffrage restrictions such as the poll tax and literacy test. Epidemiologists quantified the health effects of racial segregation at this time and found that Black people who lived under Jim Crow laws across the South were 20 percent more likely to die prematurely compared with those who lived in areas without Jim Crow laws.[65]

New federal laws such as the Voting Rights Act gave the US Department of Justice significant oversight over state elections to attempt to right these wrongs. Mississippi resisted the change required by federal law, which meant that federal officials had a stronger presence in Mississippi than other states. Between 1965 and 1980, 51 percent of Mississippi's counties were overseen by federal election examiners.[66] These changes had a dramatic effect on voting patterns. Less than 1 percent of voting-age Black Mississippians were registered to vote in 1940, so just 21 percent of white voters across the state could elect a majority of the legislature.[67] By 1960, the percentage of voting-age Black Mississippians registered increased to only 5 percent. Ten years later, this increased to 68 percent, the highest percentage in the Deep South.[68]

Gerrymandering

Mickey describes 1972 as the transition year in which democratization was fully consolidated in the South. However, despite having made major progress, recent changes did not necessarily ensure democratic responsiveness for Black Mississippians. The absolute number of new white registered voters was dramatically higher than the number of Black registered voters. This dramatic increase may have been in response to fears about what increases in Black voting would mean but was also likely a product of the removal of suffrage restrictions. Although not to the same extent as in the Black population, some poor white people were also limited in their ability to vote because of the poll tax, property requirement, and literacy test.[69]

Many states responded to national changes by switching their state legislative elections to multimember districts. Rather than elect a single candidate, voters would select who would fill the entire number of seats. The implication was that as a majority across the state, white people could select who served in the legislature, which denied Black-majority communities the opportunity to select their representative. For example, a district was created in Hinds County—which was 40 percent Black—such that all ten of the county's house seats would be elected at large. As a result, 60 percent of all voters, who were the white population, selected the ten elected officials.[70] The state legislature's decision in 1979 to respond to a Supreme Court ruling by eliminating multimember districts led to an increase in the number of Black legislators from four to seventeen. But this was still only 12 percent of the House membership and 4 percent of the Senate, far less than the statewide population of 36 percent.[71]

Redistricting following the 1990 census had the most profound effect on the racial composition of the legislature in a century. By 1992, thirty-one Black legislators were elected to the House and ten to the Senate. Of similar importance, a handful of these Black legislators were selected to serve in leadership positions, including Robert Clark as the Speaker Pro Tempore.[72] The increased numbers of Black people who were legislators and who held leadership positions did not necessarily translate to greater influence over policymaking. Districts were drawn so that large numbers of Black people were consolidated, which weakened Black representation. As a progressive white Democrat said after the 1992 elections, "You end up with radicalized White districts and radicalized Black districts in which the White representatives don't have to take into consideration the needs and wants of Black people in the state and Black people don't have to take into consideration the needs and wants of Whites because they represent such a small number that they don't have to cater to their interests to get elected."[73] The head of the Mississippi Legislature's Black Caucus had a similar response to the redistricting: "There is an effort to send a message to us, and to Black Mississippians, that no matter what your numbers are in the Legislature, we're going to still control things."[74]

A political scientist evaluated this claim by comparing the percentage of bills introduced by Black legislators with the percentage introduced by the control group of white legislators. Black legislators succeeded at passing 12 percent of the 166 bills they introduced in 1987 and 5 percent of the 285 bills they introduced in 1988. A comparison group of white legislators was able to pass 28.5 percent of the 281 bills they introduced and 21.1 percent of the 238 bills they introduced in these years. A follow-up analysis of the 2017 legislative session showed very similar results.[75]

The state did not technically ratify the Thirteenth Amendment to the US Constitution abolishing slavery until 2013. The legislature acted in 1995, but apparently there was a clerical error that meant the vote was never recorded. The error was discovered by a Mississippi citizen who researched the question after watching the movie *Lincoln* and contacted the Mississippi secretary of state.[76] This oversight may seem harmless to some, as the abolition of slavery occurred nationwide regardless of Mississippi's late ratification, but it epitomizes current tensions over the role of race in Mississippi. Key leaders argue that it is dangerous to focus too much on the past,[77] whereas others say it is impossible to move on without more fully grappling with how racism has shaped conditions today. The changing of the state flag in 2020 is a tangible symbol that progress, which at times seems impossible, can be made.

This brief history makes it clear that most of the policy ideas discussed throughout this book are not likely to be enacted unless leaders are more democratically accountable and responsive to all residents in the Delta. Simply calling for policy change or increased political will does not remove the obstacles to achieving health equity.

Charting the Health Equity Policy Agenda

As described earlier, this book is a response to skeptics who do not believe that seemingly colorblind policies have racial implications and those who believe that being healthy comes down to making good or bad choices. This is a false dichotomy, as people cannot make good choices if they do not have good options, but even good choices can only go so far if structural barriers remain in place. For example, people need to eat well and exercise to optimize health, but systemic issues make it hard for some people to access healthy foods (chapter 1) and live a physically active lifestyle (chapter 2). The availability of nutritious food, safe neighborhoods, job opportunities, high-quality education, and health care is not a luxury; these are well-established determinants of health that are essential to human functioning and often are cost effective to address. Structures and policies that shape these determinants directly affect the health of individuals. A skeptic might respond that the challenges highlighted in these chapters could be alleviated if people got better jobs, and if that is not possible, they should get more education. This is true, but chapters 3 and 4 highlight the many barriers that stand in people's way as they try to do this. Chapter 5 shows that all the factors that increase the likelihood of getting sick also make it hard to access high-quality health care.

Using a place-based approach to examining health equity requires a delicate balance. It is important to avoid a scarcity mindset or a framing that is overly focused on what is lacking. But it is also important to be honest and thorough about the wide range of problems that affect health. Optimism is empty unless we name injustices that need fixing and are specific about their root causes, as well as providing goals and recommendations for overcoming these barriers.

In each chapter of this book, I try to strike this balance with an in-depth look at the gaps and root causes of a specific issue that affects health, followed by highlights of people and organizations that are doing impressive work to address these gaps. This section of each chapter is titled "Ripples of Hope," which invokes Robert F. Kennedy's vision of the "centers of energy and daring" that together create a current powerful enough "to sweep down the mightiest walls of oppression and resistance."[78]

Just as poor population health outcomes are the result of a cumulative and mutually reinforcing set of factors, a multitude of complementary and mutually reinforcing solutions are needed to improve them. At the beginning of each chapter, I provide questions that highlight types of health barriers after offering context from Robert F. Kennedy's trip to the Delta. I then provide examples of individuals and groups who are creating ripples of hope in the Delta. Each chapter ends with a summary overview of policy changes that together constitute a health equity policy agenda.

There are multiple ways to solve some of these problems, so the health equity policy agenda is a list of *goals* that address specific problems through policy rather than a list of the specific policies that should be adopted. Associated with each goal are examples of national, state, or local policies that, if enacted, would improve health. Examples of policy recommendations are also outlined at the end of each chapter. However, which approach or policy will work best in a given context, and the legal mechanisms that will be best suited for achieving the goal, depends on the nature of the problem in a particular place and its political and cultural dynamics. The Robert Wood Johnson Foundation's Action Center is a starting point for identifying more specific policies that can be adopted to achieve these policy goals.[79]

Structural dynamics lead to de facto racial segregation, and as a result, people do not have the same access to food, neighborhoods conducive to an active lifestyle, jobs, education, and health care. In the following chapters, I examine each of these issues with an eye to the full context in which people live and the appreciation that we cannot solve any of these issues unless we improve all of them.

1 Food

Hunger affects every aspect of a person's life. Poor nutrition is associated with reduced productivity at work for adults and decreased performance at school for children.[1] Having adequate access to healthy foods is the strongest predictor of a host of outcomes essential to a full and healthy life, including overall well-being.[2] People who eat well are happier, more engaged, more creative, and therefore more likely to do well in school and at work.[3] Food policy is health policy.

On March 15, 1967, at the US Senate Subcommittee Hearing on Employment, Manpower, and Poverty, civil rights activist Marian Wright Edelman stated that "the single largest problem facing all of us in Mississippi right now is how can people eat during the winter. . . . This is an urgent situation which must be looked into and met."[4] Wright Edelman later said she had planned to talk about Head Start, the new preschool program she had been instrumental in implementing: "I don't know what moved me to talk about hunger. I guess I stayed out on the field a lot and was often visiting poor parents. . . . Hunger, and even starvation, was increasing, and that's what came out of my mouth that day."[5]

It would have been understandable if Robert F. Kennedy (D–NY) had been distracted during the hearing. Earlier that morning he stood in the rain at his brother's grave in Arlington National Cemetery with immediate family and President Lyndon B. Johnson for a private ceremony in honor of the former president, whose body was moved the night before to its permanent location. Yet Senator Kennedy seemed highly engaged during the hearing and asked typically pointed questions.

Wright Edelman invited the committee to go to Mississippi to see conditions for themselves. Chairman Joseph Clark (D-PA) accepted the invitation and held a hearing on poverty one month later at a hotel in Jackson. Senators Clark and Kennedy were the only members of the committee who agreed to stay an extra day in Mississippi to visit the Delta, the northwest region of the state, where Wright Edelman said poverty levels were particularly stark. A whirlwind tour on April 11 took Clark, Kennedy, their staffs, Wright Edelman, and a caravan of journalists through the Delta to visit the cities of Greenville, Cleveland, and Clarksdale and a few rural communities in between. Some of the trip was curated, and people were notified in advance that the group was coming. But Senator Kennedy did not want an entirely scripted experience and so regularly made a point of going off schedule to talk with people who had not been prepared.

Kennedy absorbed and retained Wright's Edelman focus on hunger as he traveled through the Delta one month later in April 1967 and asked almost everyone he met what was in their cupboards and what they had eaten that day. Young children answered that there was nothing but molasses.[6] A grandmother told Kennedy she could barely feed the fifteen people in her household twice a day and that they had eaten "bread and syrup" for lunch.[7] A father said that his family had their usual meals of sausage for breakfast and bread for lunch.[8] The entourage traveling with Kennedy noted that he was visibly stunned by what he saw and heard. Wright Edelman later said that the experience of watching him meet these hungry children convinced her that "somehow he would be a major part in trying to deal with hunger in Mississippi for children."[9]

The morning after their return from the Delta, Kennedy and his aide, Peter Edelman, made an unannounced visit to Agriculture Secretary Orville Freeman. They told him about the extreme hunger they witnessed and reported that the new food stamp program was not helping America's poorest families. People were required to buy the stamps before they could use them to purchase subsidized groceries, meaning that the program was inaccessible to families without any income. Freeman was skeptical about the picture Kennedy and Edelman painted and said, "Bob, there aren't people with no income in this country. That couldn't be. How would they exist?" Kennedy replied that one day earlier he had spoken with people in this situation: "I just don't know, Orville. I don't know why you can't just get some food down there."[10]

Freeman was hesitant, not because he opposed the food stamp program but because he was concerned that drawing attention to its shortcomings or calling for expansion would jeopardize its long-term existence. To appease Kennedy, he agreed to send members of his staff to Mississippi with Edelman to retrace the senators' trip through the Delta and to see conditions for themselves. They went a few weeks later and were similarly amazed by what they saw. Freeman then sent a team of nutritionists to provide an official account of hunger in the Delta. In their report, they explained that the diet of poor families there "was worse than had been that of the average Southern family with less than $2,000 annual income in 1955, twelve years earlier."[11]

Senator Kennedy kept pushing. On April 25, he testified at the Senate Agriculture and Forestry Subcommittee hearing on food stamp reauthorization and urged his colleagues to keep and expand the program. He told them, "I saw conditions of extreme hunger and saw people who eat only one meal a day. . . . We did see children with distended stomachs and with sores on their lips because of malnutrition, and who are really kept alive because of the food stamp program and the assistance they receive."[12] Later that day he wrote to Dr. Martin Luther King Jr. and said that while in Mississippi he had seen "enough evidence of widespread malnutrition and extreme hunger to convince me that a way must be found to provide more and better food to people with low income—or people with no income—in this country."[13]

Robert F. Kennedy was not alive to see these conversations culminate with the passage of the Food Stamp Act Amendment of 1970. This reform capped the amount people would have to spend to purchase stamps and ensured that people with no income would not have to pay. The Agriculture and Consumer Protection Act of 1973 subsequently made food stamps a national program available in all fifty states. Approximately forty-one million people benefit from what is now known as the Supplemental Nutrition Assistance Program (SNAP).[14]

Mississippi still has a malnutrition crisis, although the symptoms are no longer distended stomachs or sores on the lips of children because of hunger. The major problem today is an extreme level of obesity. Mississippi is the state with the most obese residents in the nation: 37.3 percent of adults had body mass indexes greater than 30 in 2016.[15] The rate was 15 percent in 1990, which at the time was one of the highest rates in the country.[16] More than 40 percent of school-age children in Mississippi are obese, and the prevalence of obesity among adults is projected to reach 40 percent by 2030 (see map 1.1).[17]

The rates of obesity are higher in the Delta. For example, 42 percent of adults in Coahoma County, where Kennedy made his final stop more than fifty years ago, are obese. Ten other counties in the Delta have adult obesity rates of at least 30 percent, including Sunflower and Sharkey Counties at 50 percent (see map 1.2).[18]

Gaps and Root Causes

Food epitomizes the debate about whether health is an individual responsibility or a systemic issue. While traveling throughout the Delta, I was often asked by hotel clerks and food servers what brought me to the area.

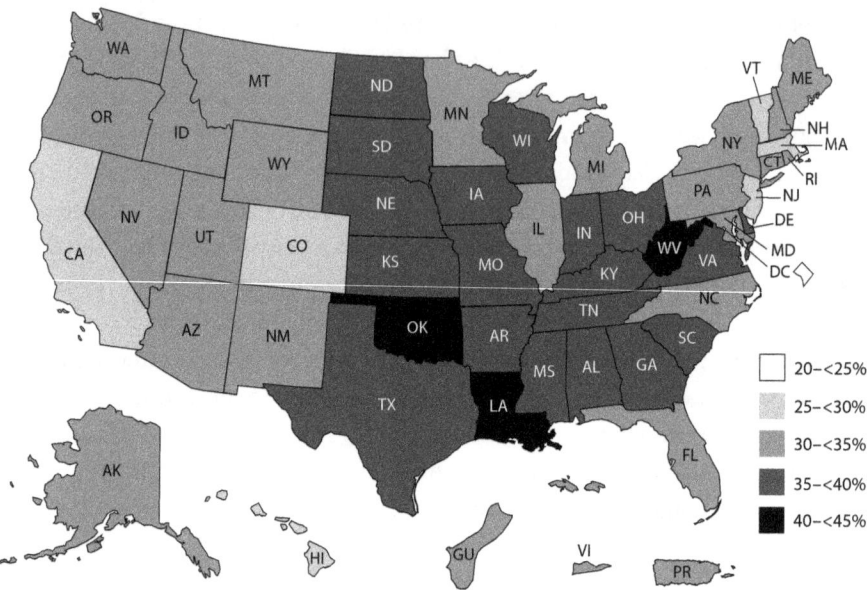

MAP 1.1 Prevalence of obesity among adults by state. Prevalence of self-reported obesity among US adults by state and territory, Behavioral Risk Factor Surveillance System (BRFSS), 2022. From "Adult Obesity Prevalence Maps," Centers for Disease Control and Prevention, last reviewed September 21, 2023, https://www.cdc.gov/obesity/data/prevalence-maps.html#overall.

When I explained that I was working on a book about health in Mississippi, they regularly said something like, "I can save you the trouble of doing all this research; people here are so unhealthy because they eat too much fried chicken. There wouldn't be so many health problems in the Delta if people ate better." The racially coded response I regularly heard from servers and clerks is deeply problematic. Focusing on the eating decisions of individuals dramatically oversimplifies the issue and fails to acknowledge the complicated factors that affect what people eat. In addition, how we understand and measure obesity has a complicated and arguably racist history.[19]

However, they are right in two ways. First, many of the people I interviewed did describe unhealthy eating habits. For example, a teenager in Clarksdale said, "[I have] a whole vending machine under my bed because I used to wake up in the middle of the night and get real hungry. So I just reach under my bed and get a honey bun or get some chips or something like that." A middle-aged woman in Cleveland explained that she regularly ate cornstarch straight out of the can while growing up. Studies confirm that residents of the Delta are more likely to eat empty calories or calorie-laden

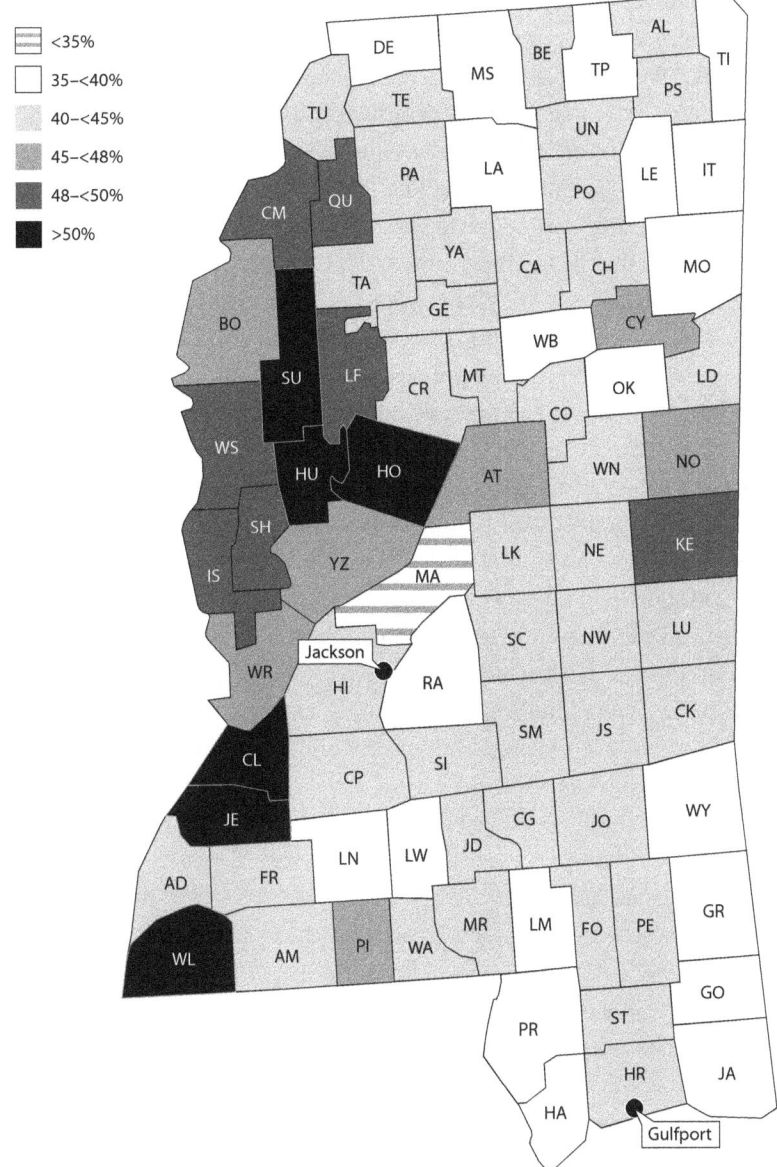

MAP 1.2 Prevalence of obesity among Mississippi adults by county. From "Mississippi: Adult Obesity," County Health Rankings, accessed March 29, 2024, https://www.countyhealthrankings.org/explore-health-rankings/mississippi?year=2022&measure=Adult+Obesity&tab=. Used with permission from the University of Wisconsin Population Health Institute, County Health Rankings and Roadmaps, 2022.

ultra-processed foods and are less likely to eat whole fruits, dairy, and healthy sources of protein than the national average.[20] But rather than blaming people, we should ask why a teenager woke up in the middle of the night hungry, or why a woman's family relied on cornstarch as a meal.

Second, the long-term health consequences of obesity are dramatic, and obesity significantly increases the likelihood of developing chronic diseases such as type 2 diabetes, hypertension, and many types of cancer.[21] More than half of all deaths in Mississippi each year are attributed to chronic disease.[22] In addition, health-related costs for an obese person are 40 percent higher than for a person who is not obese.[23] The estimated 2018 costs for obesity-related care in Mississippi were projected to be $3.9 billion. According to one estimate, if the average body mass index in the state were reduced by 5 percent, eighty-six thousand people would be spared from developing type 2 diabetes, sixty-seven thousand people could be spared from coronary heart disease and stroke, and fifty-six thousand could be spared from hypertension. This reduction would lower health care costs across the state by 6.9 percent per year and equal more than $6 trillion by 2030.[24] The Delta has a higher burden of obesity and the associated health risks than the rest of the state.

Obesity is a symptom of malnutrition as extreme as what Kennedy witnessed fifty years ago. People in poverty are more likely to miss meals or cycle between periods of undereating and overeating. When they do eat, their meals are less likely to be balanced and more likely to contain cheaper, calorie-dense, ultra-processed foods.[25] As a result, people become obese even though they are chronically hungry.

The Delta has a perfect storm of poor nutrition. Studies show that Americans who are Black, have access to lower levels of education or poor-quality education, are low income, or live in rural communities are less likely to be able to eat a balanced diet.[26] However, there is nothing inherent about belonging to any of these groups or living in this place that causes people to make worse decisions about food. The real issue is that these populations are more likely to face barriers that impede healthy choices. Nearly everyone I met in the Delta described how they and their families struggle to eat a balanced diet. One person referenced the movie *The Nutty Professor*, saying, "I come from a family of big people, and buffets, and big Sunday dinners, like the Klumps sitting down to eat. That's the type of family I come from." "My family's a fryaholic," another person explained, because they mostly eat food that is deep fried. A young man in Clarksdale described, "In our community, we have a get together. . . . But they always avoid the healthy food. Always. Sometimes, some people do actually bring fruits, vegetables. But those are the things that don't get eaten."

These eating habits are not unique to the Delta; many Americans do not have balanced diets. Researchers estimate that ultra-processed foods comprise about 60 percent of the calories and 90 percent of the added sugars consumed in all US households.[27] These numbers are even greater in the households of people with low socioeconomic status.[28] This pattern is problematic because ultra-processed foods are "industrially formulated products that are convenient, highly palatable, and contain few whole ingredients,"[29] and studies indicate that ultra-processed foods are harmful for health in a number of ways.[30] Ultra-processed foods are high sugar, low fiber, high fat, and calorie dense, with low or no nutritional value, and they contain chemical compounds not found in whole foods. These features increase risk for cardiovascular and metabolic diseases.

A food equity policy agenda should focus on removing three barriers:

(1) **Food insecurity.** Is there sufficient healthy food in the region, and is it accessible?
(2) **Affordability.** Are whole foods and other healthful food options affordable?
(3) **Knowledge.** Do people learn what constitutes a healthy diet, how to prepare healthy foods, and other essential information for eating well?[31]

The culminating insight from a close look at these questions is that people need to make good decisions about the food they eat, but most of our energy should be devoted to changing the structural risk factors that make it hard for people to make good decisions.

Food Insecurity

Mississippi is the most food-insecure state in the nation, and nearly one-fourth (23 percent) of the population has limited or uncertain access to healthy meals.[32] This is dramatically worse than the national average, in which approximately forty million people, or one in eight, are food insecure.[33] Food insecurity is a major driver of chronic disease and a wide range of other issues, including developmental delays, struggles in school, and depression.[34] For all of the eight years that Feeding America has systematically compared states, Mississippi has been the most food-insecure state in the nation.[35] Seven of the ten counties with the highest rates of food insecurity in the nation are in Mississippi, and five are in the Delta.[36] At least 30 percent of the population in nine Delta counties lacks food security. The food crisis in Issaquena County is the most severe at 35 percent.[37] All of these statistics predate the COVID-19 pandemic, which made food insecurity more common and more severe.[38]

Food Deserts

There are not enough places to buy healthy food in the Delta. Only two full-size supermarkets exist in the entire region: a Kroger in Cleveland and another in Greenville.[39] Walmart stores in Clarksdale, Cleveland, and Greenville have grocery sections, and Kroger and Walmart sit on the Delta's periphery in Batesville, Granada, and Vicksburg. Clarksdale lost its only full-size supermarket when Kroger permanently closed in 2018. The store had been open for seventy-five years, but executives in the corporate office said the store had not been profitable for a long time.[40] The effect of Kroger's closure was enormous for this town of about fifteen thousand. Some people switched to shopping at Walmart, but many said prices were higher, and the food was not as fresh. Few alternatives exist, so many people drive thirty-three miles south to Cleveland, forty-four miles east to Batesville, or seventy miles southeast to Granada. Some say they go to the Memphis area for doctors' appointments and other reasons often enough that they regularly grocery shop there, more than eighty miles away.

Let this sink in. This region, which spreads over more than seven thousand square miles, has between two and eight fully stocked supermarkets, depending on the stores being counted. This is far from adequate food access and makes the Delta one of the most extreme food deserts in the United States.[41] The average distance a resident of the Delta travels to a grocery store is thirty miles, which means that a large portion of the population must travel much farther.[42] However, many households do not have enough vehicles or any at all, and people often must pay family or friends to drive them.[43] As a result, distances much shorter than the average thirty miles effectively put grocery stores out of reach. A distance of even one mile can be too far, especially during the extremely hot summer months when it is difficult to travel on foot.

Food Swamps

Some communities are described as "food swamps" because they have an overabundance of unhealthy foods.[44] Living in a food swamp is a stronger predictor of obesity and other negative health consequences than living in a food desert.[45] The two problems typically go hand in hand because limited access to grocery stores makes rural communities such as the Mississippi Delta particularly attractive markets for fast-food restaurants. A business magazine article targeting entrepreneurs to open franchises explains, "If you open a fast-food restaurant in a food desert, you are more likely to attract customers who do not want to make a long trek to a grocery store or buy groceries from a gas station's convenience store."[46] Other advantages include cheap real estate, low advertising costs, and limited competition from sit-down restaurants.[47]

The same dynamics lead to abundant corner stores and gas stations stocked with junk food. For example, someone living in the predominantly low-income Black neighborhood west of Main Street in Greenville could walk to six different corner stores within a half mile but would have to walk three miles to Kroger or Walmart. Corner stores play a particularly large role in food purchases in small towns where no supermarkets exist. A woman in Shaw, a town of about two thousand people, said she counted nine places to buy food nearby: "None of them are a grocery store. None of them offer fresh fruits, fresh vegetables. Only one place sells meat. There are no good options." She went on to describe the daily temptation she faces to get sugary drinks from the convenience store across the street from her work: "I have very little willpower when it comes to food, and that's kind of hard for me." Another person in Shaw added, "If you look at the sign of what's offered, it's tobacco, beer, chicken, sandwiches, and salads. And then the meats and the pizza. So the only thing out there that's even remotely healthy is the salad, which depending on what oil you put on it, it's probably still not healthy."

Researchers confirm that the availability of food at these types of stores does not offset the gaps caused by a lack of larger grocery stores.[48] More than 80 percent of large grocery stores across the broader Delta region, including Arkansas and Louisiana, sell fresh produce compared with 20 percent of small or medium grocery stores and only 4 percent of convenience stores. Whole wheat bread is available in 85 percent of larger grocery stores compared with 23 percent of small or medium stores and 6 percent of convenience stores. All three types of stores tend to sell milk and cereal, but larger grocery stores are more likely to have skim milk and cereals high in fiber and low in sugar.[49]

Non-grocery chain stores such as Fred's, Dollar General, Family Dollar, and Dollar Tree are underappreciated parts of the food landscape in poor rural communities, as they may exist where grocery stores do not. Nearly every town in the Delta has at least one of these stores. As one person described, "When you get on Highway 61, there's one in Merigold, Shelby, all the way down till you reach Clarksdale, you're going to find a Dollar General in each of the towns that you hit. And even when you go the other way, it's pretty much the same." These stores do not typically sell fresh food but do have nonperishable items. A woman who lives a few miles outside of Cleveland added, "It's not just the food. They have the toilet paper, and the school supplies, and the cleaning supplies, and the coffee. It's more of a 'if I need something and I don't want to run to Cleveland,' I go to Dollar General."

These stores might seem like attractive candidates for expanding access to healthy foods in the Delta. However, the economic principles of supply and demand up and down the supply chain would make it very difficult for them to sell enough fresh produce to cover the costs, and the amount they would have to charge would make it hard to compete with stores such as Kroger and Walmart.

This example illustrates the reciprocal nature of the gaps in accessing healthy foods in the Delta. Choosing to buy fresh produce at local stores would require education on nutrition and healthful food shopping and preparation, and for people to be convinced by that education that they should eat healthier foods. However, from a structural perspective, it would also require people to have sufficient transportation for even short distances to purchase higher-quality food. Finally, people would need to be convinced that higher prices at local stores are worth the convenience of avoiding the drive to other towns. As the next section illustrates, this scenario seems unlikely, as affordability is also a major barrier to healthy foods.

Affordability

Food insecurity is a deeper problem than whether someone lives in a food desert or a food swamp. Food activist Karen Washington says these are outsider terms not used by the residents of these communities and fail to consider the root causes of the problem. She suggests we discuss "food apartheid" instead to focus on the whole food system that creates and perpetuates inequities.[50] Little evidence indicates that changing a region's food landscape so more healthy options exist substantially changes what people eat.[51] Social and demographic factors are estimated to be nearly twice as powerful predictors of unhealthy food consumption as where a person shops.[52] As one researcher describes, "Over the past decade, study after study has shown that differences in access to healthy food can't fully explain why wealthier Americans consume a healthier diet than poor Americans."[53] Questions should be asked about potential biases in these studies, including what it means to have a healthy diet. Even so, something else about poverty and the experience of being poor makes it harder to eat well.

One explanation is that people who experience poverty cannot afford to buy healthy food. Price has been shown to be a significantly more important factor in food-purchasing decisions for people in poverty than people in groups with better socioeconomic status, and price was more important than travel distance.[54] In American households with lower incomes, people spend less money on food than those in wealthier households, but they spend a larger share of their income on food.[55] This disparity—relatively lower spending that represents a larger share of household income—is more extreme in the Mississippi Delta than in any other part of the country.[56]

People told me they would be willing to eat better if they could afford it, but "fresh fruits and vegetables are really expensive down here." Other researchers found that "the bottom line is price."[57] A woman in Cleveland explained, "With our income threshold in the Delta, people are going to choose the cheaper option. That's how I have to be to be able to survive." She said one of her favorite treats—barbeque-flavored chips—cost $1.88, and "that should be how much a pack of lettuce should cost. . . . The romaine lettuce is like $3. And those $3 add up. If I get six packs of romaine lettuce, that's expensive. That's a lot."

The cost of food is different in Mississippi, because it is one of seven states that fully applies its 7 percent sales tax to groceries, although localities cannot add to it. Most states have no sales tax (five states), exempt groceries entirely (thirty-two states), or apply lower tax rates for groceries (six states).[58] Mississippi was the first state to impose a sales tax on groceries, beginning in 1930 during the height of Jim Crow. Governor Mike Connor's argument did not specifically mention race but was a thinly veiled message about people who did not own property or generate income not paying their fair share into the system: "There are today in Mississippi thousands of people who pay no taxes, but who enjoy all the rights and privileges of citizenship. These people will be glad of an opportunity to share in the responsibility of maintaining the government of the state in which they live."[59] The Mississippi sales tax on groceries disproportionately affects low-income families because they have less income to spend on necessities, and they must be more cost conscious in food-purchasing decisions.

Research shows that people living in poverty try to factor value into food-purchasing decisions to a greater extent than those not in poverty, not only in terms of taste and nutrition but also in terms of foods that provide energy, are used for more meals, are palatable to children so food is not wasted, and can be stored for longer periods of time.[60] Paychecks must be stretched, and people may be able to travel the distance to a grocery store only twice per month: "I'm going to use the Chef Boyardee just because if it's getting to the end of the week, and we don't have a lot of food left, I know that's just a staple item that will be in there so that if we don't have any food left one night [the kids] can always have that."[61] A mother in Clarksdale explained, "You got this amount of money and it's going to last a whole month or two, [until] the next time you get paid." She buys neck bones and beans even though "those things gain weight" because "you can get that to feed the whole family. . . . It's going to stick to your ribs, you'll get full for the remainder of the day." Carol Connell and colleagues cataloged the food available in the Delta and found that the price per serving of meat was higher than fruits and vegetables despite its lower nutritional value. Meat is the economically rational purchase because it has significantly greater energy density per serving. In the same study, fats, oils, and sweets were highly consumed despite the fact that they had the lowest nutritional value; they had the lowest prices per serving and the greatest energy density.[62]

A food equity policy agenda should help people overcome financial barriers to buying healthy foods, and some programs are designed to do so, including food stamps, community gardens and farmers' markets, and school lunches. While these programs help, they have important limitations.

Supplemental Nutrition Assistance Program

Approximately one-fifth (537,000) of Mississippians are enrolled in SNAP, which is sometimes referred to as food stamps. To be eligible, an individual must have less than $2,000 in their bank account and earn less than 130 percent of the federal poverty level. This equates to an annual income of about $27,000 for a household of three people.[63] The average person in Mississippi enrolled in SNAP receives $115 per month, or $1.26 per person per meal, and the money is credited to an account used like a debit card called an electronic benefits transfer (EBT) card that can be used at 3,600 participating stores across the state.[64] The American Rescue Plan Act of 2021 appropriated $3.5 billion to SNAP and increased benefits by $28 per beneficiary, but this temporary increase responded specifically to the economic crisis brought on by the COVID-19 pandemic.[65]

The number of SNAP enrollees in Mississippi represents only 83 percent of those eligible, which means that tens of thousands more people could enroll.[66] The paperwork burden and fear of being disrespected by someone in a small-town benefits office are obstacles for many. A teenager in Clarksdale described friends who are unable to get benefits even though they are single mothers and poor enough to be eligible: "I feel bad for them because they can't get the food stamps when they actually need it. Like, they be trying to pay bills on their own, have a child, and that would be so devastating to me."

In the Delta, SNAP is a major part of the food economy, and it is estimated that 36 percent of the region's population participates in the program.[67] Six of the twenty counties in the United States with the highest proportion of SNAP enrollees are in the Delta. For example, nearly half (48.1 percent) of the population of Humphreys County receives food stamps (see map 1.3).[68] Policymakers and researchers debate the effects of the program, and some claim that participation exacerbates obesity. Food stamps cannot be used to purchase alcohol, cigarettes, hot foods, or foods that are meant to be eaten in the store, but they can be used to buy just about any other food item.

State-level data on how these benefits are used are not readily available, but national reports suggest that 40 percent of food stamp benefits are spent on basic items (meat, fruits, vegetables, milk, eggs, and bread), 40 percent are used for prepared foods, and 20 percent are used for junk food such as soda and other sugar-sweetened beverages, salty snacks, and candy.[69] These proportions are not very different from purchasing decisions made by people who are not SNAP beneficiaries, but SNAP participants tend to consume fewer fruits and vegetables, more meat, and more calorie-dense processed foods.[70]

Evidence of the relationship between SNAP and obesity is mixed. In some studies, enrollment had no effect; in some studies, SNAP participants had an increased likelihood of obesity; and in a smaller number of studies, SNAP participants had a decreased likelihood of obesity.[71] The most recent research suggests that many of the earlier studies suffered from methodological challenges, which makes it difficult to gauge accuracy. Many studies are based on self-reported data, which are not very accurate and do not account for a person's full environmental context.[72] For example, in a study published in 2019, consumption of fruit and sugar-sweetened beverages

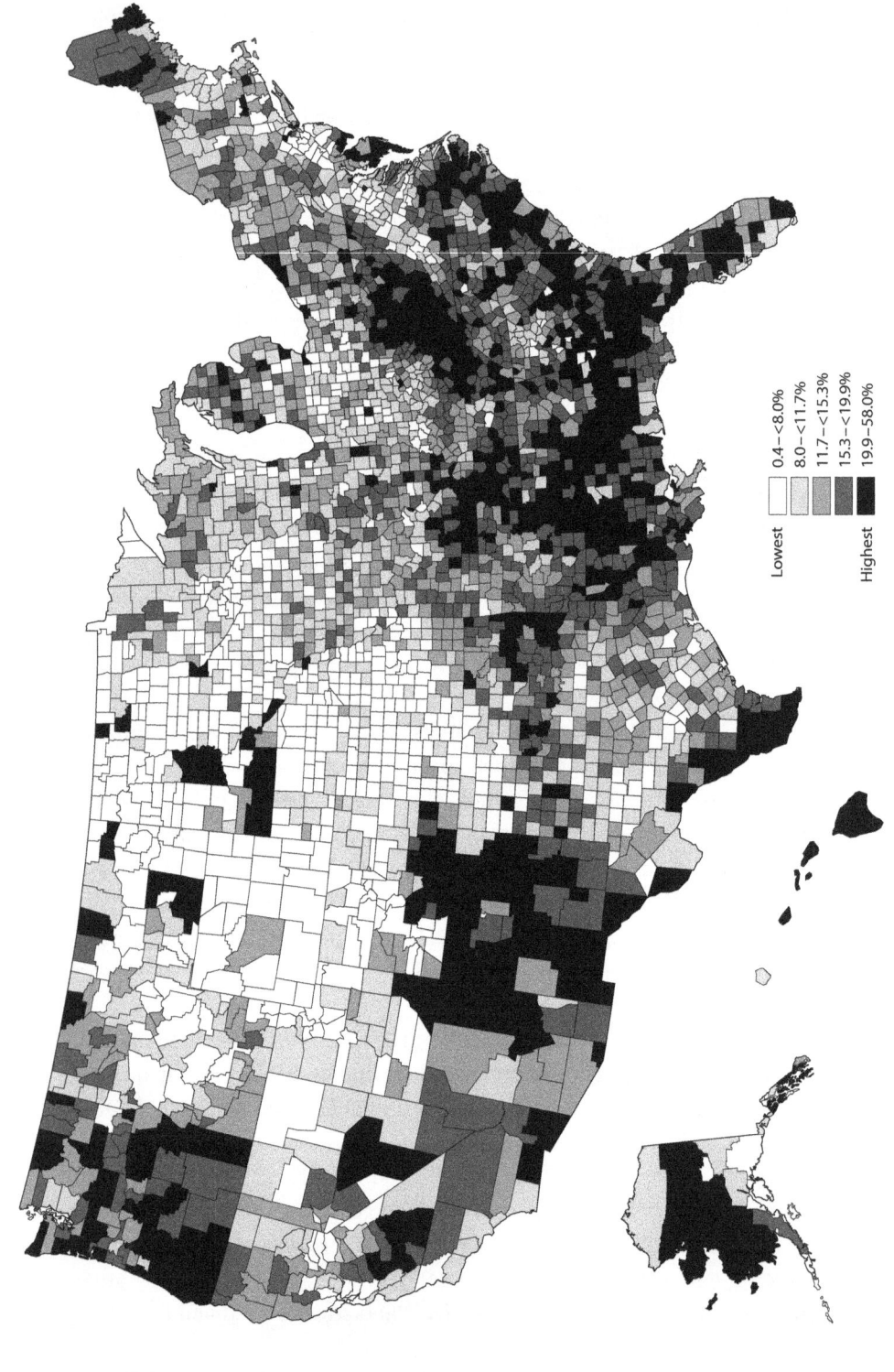

among SNAP participants varied according to whether they lived within a half mile of a store,[73] but this type of detail was often not included in earlier studies.

Most importantly, the debate over whether SNAP participation exacerbates obesity misses the key point that the appropriate comparison is not between SNAP recipients and nonrecipients. Instead, researchers should examine what recipients would do if they did not participate in the program. They would not be positioned to make healthier nutrition decisions if they lost SNAP benefits. They would lose the money that is directed toward education, housing, and transportation, and many would go hungry more often.[74] In testimony to the House Committee on Agriculture regarding the program, Diane Whitmore Schanzenbach of Brookings concluded that "SNAP is a highly efficient and effective program. It lifted nearly 5 million people out of poverty in 2014."[75] During the COVID-19 pandemic, SNAP helped many families, thanks in part to policies that increased eligibility and benefits, but Mississippi did not maximize extra federal funds.[76]

SNAP alone cannot address food environment issues such as food deserts or swamps, but a person living near a grocery store cannot benefit from its proximity if they cannot pay for food. The question is not whether SNAP is beneficial—studies like those just mentioned show that it is—but rather how to use the program to help more people. This includes expanding who is eligible. As with other social programs, a national debate lingers over whether adults without disabilities and without children should be allowed to enroll. The political argument often goes something like this: the people in this group—referred to in political terminology as "able-bodied adults without dependents"—could get jobs or more education but they do not, so they remain eligible for benefits when they do not deserve government assistance. This is not an evidence-based argument; as we will see in chapter 3, most people in this category work or want to work, but they face challenges that make it hard to fully provide for themselves.

Rather than maximize SNAP for a population known to be food insecure for structural reasons, Mississippi has taken more extensive measures than any state to limit the participation of adults without dependents in SNAP. Federal law allows SNAP payments for three months per year for people

MAP 1.3 (OPPOSITE) SNAP enrollment as a percentage of county population. From "The Geography of Food Stamps," *Daily Yonder*, December 31, 2018, https://www.dailyyonder.com/geography-food-stamps/2018/12/31/25422/. Data from the US Census. Used with permission.

who are not working unless they live in areas with high unemployment rates. Every state qualified for an exemption to this rule during the Great Recession, but the improved economy in the subsequent decade meant that the rule went back into effect in many states in January 2017. The unemployment rate in Mississippi meant the state could have received a federal waiver to exempt the entire state or specific counties from the work requirement. But Governor Phil Bryant directed the state's Department of Human Services to impose this restriction anyway.

The Mississippi Legislature subsequently passed the Act to Restore Hope, Opportunity and Prosperity for Everyone (the HOPE Act), which prevents a future governor from seeking a federal waiver of work requirements without legislative approval and further entrenches the work rule. The HOPE Act also gives the Department of Human Services authority to request proof of eligibility of any participant at any time and to disenroll them if they do not respond within ten days. Benefits can be restored once documentation is provided, but beneficiaries are permanently disenrolled if they cannot produce proof of eligibility three times.[77] Providing evidence of income and assets is a known hardship for members of low-income populations who struggle with limited transportation, literacy, and broadband access that leads to administrative disenrollment (meaning the person is program-eligible but cannot meet paperwork requirements). The HOPE Act also outsourced administration of SNAP to a private, nongovernmental organization.

Part of the legislature's motivation was to limit fraud. These laws and discussions among policymakers never use the word *Black*, but a racial undercurrent taints the debate based on who is perceived to benefit from a proposed change and whether they "deserve" help. Researchers suggest that abuse of SNAP by participants is effectively negligible,[78] but according to one estimate, 12 percent of stores authorized to accept SNAP in Mississippi have used the program illegally, yet these infractions account for less than 1 percent of the program's funds.[79]

Some people in the Delta described seeing occasional misuse of SNAP in their communities. Many said when misuse occurs, it is a symptom of the deeper structural issues related to food insecurity rather than a key problem: "Sometimes people do things for survival. I can't pay my light bill, so I'm going over here and I'm going to sell him my card, my EBT card." Similarly, access to food diminishes in a community when stores caught abusing the system are punished. Ironically, the person at the Mississippi Department of Human Services responsible for investigating fraud was sentenced in April 2019 to thirty-nine months in prison for extorting money from the stores he was investigating and pocketing the money he claimed was their fine.[80]

Rather than focusing on fraud, we should strengthen policies that help people who use SNAP to buy healthy foods, because $1.26 per person per meal does not go far. Purchases of ultra-processed foods using EBT cards spike at the beginning of the monthly benefit cycle in anticipation of scarcity at the end of it.[81] As a woman in Cleveland described, "It really frustrates me when I go to Walmart between the first and the fifteenth, between those times, you see these huge buggies and these moms, they're shopping, but the majority of the groceries that are inside of their shopping carts are carbs. You see pizzas, you see Tostino pizza rolls, and Hot Pockets. But they're getting what they can afford with their food stamps or whatever that they get."

Some policymakers have called for SNAP to incentivize healthier choices, including extending restrictions to ultra-processed food and sugar-sweetened beverages.[82] Grocery stores prey on enrollee purchasing power during peak SNAP disbursement periods by increasing in-store marketing of sugar-sweetened beverages.[83] In a 2014 study, researchers predicted that banning sugar-sweetened beverages could reduce the incidence of type 2 diabetes.[84] However, others argue that preventing people in poverty from enjoying their food of choice is difficult to administer and inappropriate paternalism. As Diane Whitmore Schanzenbach of Brookings testified to the House Committee on Agriculture, "Items should not be classified in a manner that suggests a particular food is always 'good' or 'bad.' The Academy of Nutrition and Dietetics, the largest organization of food and nutrition professionals, has adopted a position statement that the 'total diet' or overall pattern of food eaten should be the most important focus of healthy eating. All foods can fit into a healthy diet if consumed in moderation and with appropriate portion size, and as a result no particular food should be always banned."[85]

A more balanced approach would be to use carrots rather than sticks (pun intended) to facilitate healthier choices. For example, providing SNAP participants an additional thirty cents for every dollar they spend on fruits and vegetables would double the proportion who consume the recommended amount.[86] Some states offer an extra dollar for every dollar that is spent on fruits and vegetables.[87] States may also be able to influence the timing of when benefits are disbursed to influence food and beverage choices. However, neither states nor SNAP has much authority over the practices of grocery stores that market highly processed and other nutrient-deficient foods, which is partially why SNAP enrollees are targeted by proposals that try to encourage nutritious choices.

Gardening and Farmers' Markets

Many people I spoke to mentioned gardening as a way to access fresh vegetables but added that they know very few people who have skills to garden or can invest in learning. A woman in Cleveland told fellow focus group members, "There was a time when we grew the majority of our own food, if you can imagine, in our own backyards. I mean, I don't know if you all can remember back that far, but I still have uncles and aunts that raised chickens, goats. My granddad got a tomato garden in his backyard." A woman in Mound Bayou described her parents' struggles as sharecroppers in the 1950s and 1960s. They were perpetually in debt picking cotton on someone else's land for very little pay, but a byproduct of this lifestyle was that most of what they ate was fresh: "We had to grow our own foods and raise our own foods. When my father would kill the hog in November or October my mother would cut the meat up. She knew how to cure it for bacon. We had to do it for sausages. . . . Everything on the pig went for use, even the hooves. We got a cold, they would make hoof tea." She and others of her generation are concerned that gardening is not being continued by their children and grandchildren. But the history and legacy of sharecropping and its historical ties to enslavement make gardening a culturally complicated matter.

Some community leaders see farmers' markets as a promising way to increase access to locally produced fresh foods. This is a nationwide trend, and the number of farmers' markets across the United States grew from fewer than two thousand in 1994 to more than eight thousand today.[88] Evidence of the effects of farmers' markets on food insecurity is mixed, but some research has shown increased access to fruits and vegetables in low-income communities,[89] including in parts of the rural South.[90]

The Mississippi Department of Agriculture and Commerce lists ten farmers' markets in the Delta, including two in Clarksdale,[91] the city that lacked a grocery store when Kroger closed in early 2018. However, the same barriers of knowledge, geography, and affordability that make buying fresh food difficult in grocery stores also prevent the people most in need from using the farmers' markets.[92] In fact, access challenges are even greater with farmers' markets. Unlike grocery stores, which are open from early in the morning until late at night, farmers' markets are available during a limited window of time each week. People also perceive a lack of racial and ethnic diversity in sellers and a mismatch between their preferences and what is available.[93]

Ensuring that SNAP participants can benefit from farmers' markets is one way to increase access to healthy foods. However, according to a 2010 report, no farmers' markets in the Delta had the capacity to take EBT cards.[94] Some had authorization to accept EBT cards as payment but lacked the technology to process transactions. Giving a card reader to these merchants did not help because the locations of the markets in parking lots and fields made it difficult to plug them into electrical outlets. This partly explains why Mississippi is the only state in the nation that saw a decrease between 2012 and 2017 in the number of farmers' markets authorized to accept EBT cards.[95] Organizations have stepped in to help these merchants and to eliminate this barrier, and as of August 2018, the state's directory lists six markets in the Delta with the ability to accept EBT cards.[96]

The inadequate supply of affordable healthy foods in the Delta is vexing given that agriculture is such a prominent part of the region's economy. As a woman in Cleveland described, "I think it's very ironic that we have the most fertile soil in the world. We could grow lots of different things we can eat, and yet we don't. So my whole community is surrounded by fields that look like this. And it's just, it's kind of sad that our kids don't have enough food to eat, and yet they're growing stuff that is not edible." Despite the fertile soil, most of the region's crops are sold as commodities. Corn is abundant, but most is used for fuel or feed rather than food. Crop planting choices are largely driven by federal policy, and 40 percent of the industry's profits in 2020 came from government subsidies.[97] Promoting gardening and farmers' markets is unlikely to improve supply of or access to healthy foods compared with adjusting incentives so that small farmers who grow food are better supported.[98]

School Lunches

Public schools are the major source of food for many children in the Delta. The National School Lunch Act specifies that children in households with incomes below 185 percent of the federal poverty level are eligible for free and reduced-price lunch in school. Only two counties in the Mississippi Delta have fewer than 100 percent of children in public schools eligible for lunch: Bolivar and Tallahatchie, each at 92 percent.[99] National nutritional standards were updated in 2011 so that children would receive more fruits, vegetables, and whole grains, and the only milk served would be fat-free and low fat.[100] In studies from before and after this reform, children who regularly ate breakfast and lunch in school reported statistically significant but modestly higher levels of fruits, vegetables, whole grains, dairy, and calcium consumption.[101]

People in the Delta painted a less successful picture of the school lunch program. A high school student said, "I feel like the school lunch is overrated. They say that they're feeding us healthy foods, but I really don't feel like it's healthy. So I bring my own lunch and I fix my own lunch." She does not have the time and money to do much, so most days this consists of just cucumbers and water. A high school freshman in Clarksdale added, "I bring my own lunch to school, too, because I don't like the food that they serve. I can't actually watch what they're putting into the food. I don't know where they're getting their resources from. I don't know none of that. And half the time, they leave the food unattended and leave the door open. Flies just, oh, I cannot eat this. And then half the time they don't fully cook the meal." A parent in Greenville said, "They don't have a choice. When the food that you're giving them is not worth eating, they're throwing it in the garbage, so when they get out of school from 7:30 to 3:15 they run home to the freezer and fridge and eat up everything in there. That's how they get obesity because the variety of food that they have for them."

Others said an important part of the problem is that children reject healthy foods because they are unfamiliar: "I work at the school, and I do our ordering and stuff. And we got a grant through USDA and they do like fresh fruit and vegetables. Like Monday, Wednesday, and Friday, the kids, they get pineapples, they get apple slices, they get orange slices. It's already cut, it's pre-packaged, and they don't eat it. They're not used to it." Others in the same focus group added that when the workers go around to clean up after lunch, "the garbage can be full of food" and the kids "throw it all away. . . . They didn't know what a celery stick was."

Even so, schools are a major provider of food for children who might not have access to regular meals otherwise. During the 2019–20 school year, approximately 357,000 children (about 74 percent of the students in participating schools) were eligible for reduced-price lunch in Mississippi.[102] Hunger increases dramatically in the summer when school is not in session. The Summer Food Service Program addresses this gap, but the food sometimes is not available after July, which leaves a gap of a few weeks before school begins at the end of August.[103] Mississippi school buses do not run during the summer, so the program is only available to children who can reach one of the food service locations, which are not always in schools. For example, the Delta Hands for Hope summer camp is located in a community center in Shaw. This camp in a rural community far from a grocery store served approximately four hundred meals when it first began in the summer of 2014. This number grew to more than ten thousand meals during the next two summers.[104]

Knowledge

One explanation for poor eating habits could be that people do not believe they need to pay attention to nutrition, but this might change if they were convinced otherwise. Some people said they realized they needed to eat more healthfully after having health scares. For example, one participant said that warnings from his doctor were a reality check to learn more about nutrition: "About four months ago I told my mom, 'If I don't change the way we eat and live and exercise and stuff, I'm shortening my life.' I started eating different, and it motivates you to keep on going. And you sit there going, 'If I keep doing this consistently, if I've done it this long and this is happening, and I keep doing it consistently, I'll totally transform my situation.' And that is some self-discipline that I had to work on."

However, simply educating people that balanced meals are important is inadequate. Only 48 percent of people in the Delta are estimated to have a basic understanding of healthy eating.[105] People more often said they should be eating healthier but did not know where to begin. A woman in Charleston described struggles trying to help people in her family and community to eat better: "I don't even know where we would start here. I mean, a bunch of us that try and try and try—it's kind of like beating your head up against a wall. We're set in our ways. I mean we really tend to be set in our ways." A young woman in Clarksdale provided a particularly dramatic illustration of the difference between motivation and education. She decided to try a fruit cleanse because she heard that is what celebrities do to be healthy. For an entire week, she consumed only Hi-C fruit punch, a drink with virtually no nutritional benefit but eighty calories and twenty grams of sugar per twelve ounces.[106]

Many people said their families consume a lot of vegetables but prepare them in ways that they believe to be unhealthy. Greens are typically prepared in oil with large amounts of sugar. As one person in Cleveland described, "We eat greens, we eat string beans, we eat broccoli in some households, and things like that. But the way we're cooking is how we hurt ourselves. We put the ham hocks in, and we cook them down so all the nutrients that's in those greens, beans, and stuff like that is null and void. You really aren't supposed to cook it down that much. And some of us don't know that because we're more so traditional cooks than we are health-conscious cooks. And it's hard to teach an old dog new tricks, as my grandma would say." A teenager in Clarksdale explained, "[I] hate green foods. Yeah, I hate them so much, but it's so healthy for me. I don't know. I have to get where I would eat broccoli without something on it."

If the problem is lack of knowledge about eating well and how to do it, then the solution should be education. The Mississippi Department of Health developed an action plan in 2018 to address obesity, which includes a number of steps to increase awareness and understanding, including public service announcements targeting television, radio, and print media.

Relying on education as the primary strategy to improve nutrition is inherently limited. Educational messages are drowned out by advertising for food, drinks, and restaurants. In some cases, public campaigns about healthy eating have had negative effects by increasing stigma.[107] Public education campaigns about nutrition also run the risk of being grounded in an understanding of food choices that does not reflect or respect cultural differences. For example, studies show that people in the Delta who are poor and Black do not respond to the word *organic* and see it as an indication that something is meant for wealthy white people. Instead, *no-spray* is a more inclusive term.[108]

Even if educational interventions are successful at convincing people of the need to eat well and how to make healthy meals, and even if this education is done with respect and an appreciation of cultural differences, people cannot make good decisions if sufficient healthy food options are not nearby or if healthy options are inaccessible because of transportation or cost limitations. Until underlying structural barriers to food access are addressed, it will be hard for residents of the Delta to make healthy food choices.

Contrasts in the Meaning of Food

In this chapter, I explore obstacles to eating balanced diets for people in the Delta. The problem is much deeper than people making bad decisions. The problem is poverty. The issue of food insecurity in the Delta epitomizes Princeton scholar Eldar Shafir's research on behavior change: "All the data shows it isn't about poor people, it's about people who happen to be in poverty. All the data suggests it is not the person, it's the context they're inhabiting."[109] Time is an incredibly scarce resource for people living on the edge of financial viability. A woman in Clarksdale explained, "No one really has time to stay at home and cook, so everyone either goes to McDonald's or Burger King for their kids with themselves so they won't be hungry. So they go out, get the food, and then they're on their way. And that'll be pretty much an everyday thing because they don't have time to be home. Everyone is just on the move and trying to work." Another person added, "The fried foods is so quick and easy to cook. When you're a working mother, frying foods is the quickest meal you can do, and so that's how we got into that." Buying junk food is a way for parents to appease children and quickly get through shopping. One parent described the constant demands from her children: "Can I have this? Oh can I get these? Can we get that? And finally, I'm like, Shut up. Take it. Put it in the cart. Leave me alone."[110]

The effects of poverty are so intense that eating well is difficult even if the barriers of food insecurity, affordability, and knowledge are overcome. Research shows that living with chronic stress has the effect of diminishing cognitive capacity. In other words, the accumulation of stress with no end in sight changes how people make decisions.[111] Sometimes their calculations or priorities change, but stress also makes it fundamentally more difficult to follow through with priorities to bring about the outcomes desired.[112] This is a tricky argument, as it risks blaming people for their choices rather than the context, and a lack of good options.

Another way of looking at food insecurity suggests that poverty can change the very meaning of food. Priya Fielding-Singh found that low-income parents are just as likely to say they want their kids to eat healthy, balanced diets as affluent parents. Geography and cost affect who can buy healthy foods, but the dynamic is a little different with unhealthy foods. Both groups of parents are bombarded by requests from their kids for chips and other unhealthy foods. The key difference is that 96 percent of wealthier parents said they regularly declined these requests compared with 13 percent of low-income parents.[113]

The reason for this difference is not that affluent people are inherently better parents or even that for some parents the trade-offs for scarce resources such as time and money are less intense, but that these requests mean something different to each group. Low-income parents said they were disappointed by how often they had to say no to their children for things like a new pair of sneakers or a trip to an amusement park and that they "could almost always scrounge up a dollar to buy their kids a can of soda or a bag of chips."[114] As a low-income single mother told Fielding-Smith, "They want it, they'll get it. One day they'll know. They'll know I love them, and that's all that matters."[115] On the other hand, more affluent parents said the assurance that they consistently meet their children's basic needs and even provide many luxury items like iPhones made it emotionally easy to say no to food requests. Saying no is a way to teach children self-control and willpower.

Ripples of Hope

A number of people and organizations are working to change food systems in the Mississippi Delta and to help overcome the effects of poverty. The following three inspiring examples serve as models for what is possible elsewhere in the region and around the country. These programs do not solve all aspects of the food insecurity problem—no single program can. But they help a lot of people.

Baby Cafés

Mississippi has low breastfeeding rates—only Alabama and Louisiana have lower rates. One goal of Healthy People 2020 is to increase the percentage of infants in the United States who are ever breastfed to 81.9 percent and the percentage of those who are exclusively breastfed for six months to 25.5 percent.[116] The national rates are close to these targets, but Mississippi is far below, at 63.4 percent and 16 percent respectively.[117] Infants who do not get breastmilk are at a health disadvantage for the rest of their lives.

A group of local leaders is working to change this dynamic, and an important part of their efforts is the opening of Baby Cafés.[118] The first was in Greenville in April 2016, and locations in Clarksdale and Indianola soon followed.[119] Each is a place where women can come to meet other parents and talk with lactation specialists. Participation is limited to certain hours each week but is free of charge. The Clarksdale Baby Café is open Wednesdays from 11:00 A.M. to 2:00 P.M. in an inviting room at the hospital. Large comfortable chairs, a couch, two bathrooms, and sinks are available. Certified lactation consultants, including registered nurses and a regional breastfeeding coordinator, are present to provide support. Chelesa Presley helped launch the café in 2016 and said the number of attendees quickly jumped from four to five to an average of twenty women each week.[120]

Staff try to help women appreciate the nutritional benefits of breastfeeding and the money they will save by not using formula. This is part of a comprehensive approach that takes into consideration the broader context in which women live. Presley explained that "one of the most important ways to improve breastfeeding rates is to focus on mental health. You can't breastfeed if you're in poor mental health, or if it's too hot outside and you don't have air-conditioning, or if the lights are off. It's hard to think about anything, and you probably don't like the idea of putting another person against your body." Presley adds that mothers, grandmothers, and increasingly fathers come to the Baby Café to eat. She feels a responsibility to model good nutritional choices because "this is some of the healthiest food they'll ever eat." She adds that although breastfeeding is very important, it is a very small part of a child's life. She hopes the cafés will have a long-term effect by helping parents have the confidence to make good decisions about nutrition. The Baby Cafés address food insecurity, affordability, and knowledge by teaching people about infant nutritional needs and how to save some money on their basic necessities budgets.

The Good Food Revolution

A coalition of community leaders in Bolivar County believes that reforming the region's food system is critical for the "health and wealth for all in the Delta."[121] They came together with a focus on healthy foods and nutrition but are guided by the principles of equity and social justice. Deborah Moore explained, "People don't understand us, so outsiders are constantly trying to fix us. Needless to say, we have been researched to death and many organizations have received millions of dollars in grant funds to 'fix us.' This puts people in the Delta in a passive position and does not allow us to build our own capacity. While we have seen some positive results, what we normally see is once the funding dries up, the programs are gone and we are right back where we started."[122] Moore chairs the board of directors for the Delta Fresh Foods Initiative (DFFI), an organization she believes has lasted longer than previous initiatives because it prioritizes community engagement, even if that means slower progress. As Executive Director Judy Belue puts it, "We work hard to ensure equity—inclusion that will produce economic benefits to local communities and sustainable growth in local food production. . . . It takes more time and patience to make a deliberate effort to make space at the table for stakeholders with little or no power and voice."

Delta Fresh began in February 2010 when more than one hundred farmers, community leaders, and educators came together for a two-day meeting at Delta State University in Cleveland. Rather than impose a solution on these communities, they asked residents what changes they wanted to see and branded the initiative the North Bolivar Good Food Revolution. The coalition developed a four-pronged approach to food justice in the region: increasing the supply of fresh food, fostering demand, expanding the network of partners, and emphasizing sustainable structural change. They decided to start with churches and schools. Soon, thirty-six churches had gardens that produced fresh vegetables for members of the congregation to tend and pick,[123] and more than twenty schools built gardens and integrated their care into the fifth-grade curriculum.[124] Ryan Betz, coordinator for DFFI, worked with school districts in Bolivar and Coahoma Counties to place orders with local growers for thousands of pounds of potatoes. Betz said, "Everyone wins. Students are fed wholesome, local produce and educated on where their food comes from. The farmer makes money. The school districts are able to meet mandated nutrition guidelines and the overall community benefits."[125] This effort represents just a few orders in a couple of school districts, but it is a meaningful start.

Leaders of DFFI then decided to focus on three communities five miles apart along Highway 61: Mound Bayou, Shelby, and Winstonville. They trained twenty-three local youth on food insecurity and survey methodology, and these "Good Food Youth Ambassadors" interviewed people in 210 community households.[126] The results of this survey were shared at a town hall meeting in December 2017. One of the most striking findings was that 43 percent of respondents self-identified as food insecure, a number considerably higher than the reported county-wide level of about 30 percent. Nearly everyone surveyed (88 percent) said they would support a mobile market in their community.[127] The Good Food Revolution responded by securing funds for a mobile market, which launched in June 2018 and operated on Saturdays until late November. Youth Ambassadors remained engaged with all aspects of the initiative, including farming, transport, and marketing. The team tried to maximize the mobile market's effect by accepting SNAP and providing cooking classes and demonstrations to improve knowledge and accessibility. They were enthusiastic about the early successes and potential for growth and resolved to increase the number of days and locations and to more aggressively market to SNAP participants.[128]

Weather sometimes gets in the way. Chris Johnson described, "The mobile market was a success for two summers but then the third year was really wet. This past summer the weather was the worst these growers have ever seen, literally. Most of them, if not the worst, among the top two. . . . So, we had a tough year this year. We had less sales than we did the first." Even so, people were optimistic about the future and proud of their successes, particularly the Youth Ambassadors: "The kids have taken to it in a way we never expected. They love it. Of course, there are not jobs. And we were actually paid $10 an hour for every hour they participate, which is huge. . . . They're helping the growers on their farms doing whatever they ask them to do, which mainly the first year was harvesting. They're operating the mobile market. They're coming to leadership development classes. We even tried our 'Real Food Is Good Medicine' classes with them, which was so foreign to them. I mean they're college kids and high school kids, about the toughest audience you could tackle to try to change their eating habits."

Other organizations are pursuing parallel initiatives in other parts of the region. For example, the Delta Health Alliance runs Delta Edible Agriculture Teaching Students (EATS), which helps schools in Hollandale, Leland, and Shaw to establish gardens that contribute to learning and knowledge. These gardens become the centerpiece of a multifaceted approach that includes a curriculum aligned with the Common Core, taste tests, family nights, and summer garden camps.[129]

The Delta EATS website celebrates the empowering effect that participating in a school garden has for children. But it also prominently features a disclaimer that "Delta EATS improves knowledge from pre to post test, but not yet habits. Children are missing access to the food needed for healthy habits."[130] In other words, it will be very difficult for these children and their families to develop healthy lifestyles unless deeper, structural changes occur, and changes are not likely to happen unless demand from consumers builds. These programs are helping to spark a revolution by giving communities an accessible taste of good food and facilitating the learning that builds knowledge of healthful eating.

James C. Kennedy Wellness Center

Charleston is an unlikely place for a twenty-thousand-square-foot wellness center. This town of about two thousand people is by some definitions just outside the Delta because it is a few miles east of the Tallahatchie River, but it has the same challenges of poverty and poor health outcomes. All the barriers to food security are present. The area is deeply rural with an average of eighteen people per square mile throughout the 367 square miles of the East Tallahatchie School District. The median household income of $31,000 is $10,000 less than the state median and $18,000 less than the national median.[131] Only one grocery store exists, which residents say does not have a large selection of fresh foods and is considerably more expensive than stores in larger communities. People can buy processed foods at Fred's, Dollar General, and Family Dollar, as well as a handful of corner stores. A Google search for restaurants in the area yields eight results, all of which are fast food, diners, or gas stations.

Yet Charleston is home to a thriving community of people who have dramatically changed their relationship with food. At the center of this change is the James C. Kennedy Wellness Center, a beautiful building that opened in 2016 behind Tallahatchie General Hospital. In addition to focusing on nutritional education and support, the center has an array of services and resources they offer to people of all ages in the community and the surrounding areas. These services include physical and occupational therapy, intensive outpatient psychotherapy, an annual health fair with free health screenings, group and personal fitness training, diabetes and nutrition coaching, and other community-based programs that cater to the needs of the community. The center has an exercise room with modern equipment, a large multipurpose room where the group fitness classes are held, and a mile-long walking trail.

One person described the Wellness Center as "the second-best thing since church to come to this town." Another echoed this thought: "I was born and raised here and it's one of the best things that has ever happened to Charleston. Besides Jesus and my family it's the best thing to ever happen to me. It has literally changed my life, and I mean literally changed my life." They were proud to have access to what they said was widely known as the nicest facility of its kind in the region. A woman said, "I have a really good friend that goes to a wellness center in Greenwood and she said her wellness center is nothing like my wellness center. Absolutely nothing." Another person added, "We would have to go as far as Memphis or somewhere to find a place like this."

Participants give credit to Executive Director Catherine Woodyard Moring for making the center happen. Her doctoral dissertation at the University of Mississippi included a community needs assessment of eastern Tallahatchie County, which she used as the basis for a $550,000 grant from the Rural Health Care Services Program of the Health Resources and Services Administration to cover the center's programming costs. Jim and Sarah Kennedy provided funds to build the $4.2 million facility. The Kennedys live in Atlanta but own a duck hunting lodge in Charleston. Jim Kennedy explained, "I love coming here and we wanted to give back to this community."[132] Participants also commend Kennedy's commitment to doing this project well: "He didn't just bring a shabby job when he did it." Attention to detail is focused on the user experience, including a kitchen large enough for cooking classes, a community garden with fresh produce, and dieticians and nutritionists on staff.

The center runs food education programs. Participants take classes, and receive individual support. For example, they receive recipes for each day of the week and a list of healthy items they can buy at Walmart. One woman said that as a result of the education, she observed many benefits: "I changed my lifestyle. I don't eat man-made food. I don't eat junk food. I really changed. I mean, it changed my life."

It is hard to stick to a healthy diet when eating out, and so an important implication is that people cook many more of their own meals. One participant noted, "We usually eat out on the weekends, but now on Sunday after church, instead of going to eat with my friends, I go home and cook and fix my food to get through Thursday. Never before did you open up my refrigerator and it be boiled eggs and salad. I mean we were just grab and go people, just mainly ate out."

Some of the participants said they were skeptical at first. One woman said she tried other diets or programs before but "fell off the wagon with every challenge. I would be like, I just don't think I'm going to eat any of this. Catherine is like, 'Come over one day and let's cook.' And I mean, you have never seen somebody so organized and cook 15 meals, you know?" The personal encouragement made a big difference and convinced her that "this really isn't bad." Her husband did not want to do the program with her, and so for a time she cooked two separate sets of meals: "So I started sneaking it in on him, like spaghetti squash." She says he was always surprised to find out that the food he liked was compliant with her program, and he no longer resists her meals.

It is hard to quantify the effect of the Kennedy Wellness Center, but its opening coincides with Tallahatchie County's improving by twenty places in the state's county health rankings between 2011 and 2018.[133] People describe an effect that goes beyond metrics such as obesity levels and prevalence of diabetes, however: "[The center] did such a change in my life. I lived in chronic pain 24/7 . . . and learning how foods you eat can cause pain. Inflammation can cause pain in your body. There is no gym in the world that I know of that cares enough about their people to do that. And I'm just so grateful to have this place."

The Food Equity Policy Agenda

Few issues are as important to long-term health as what people eat, yet food is one of the most polarizing issues in the debate over whether health is a function of individual choices or systemic factors. Television shows and movies regularly reinforce the narrative that obesity is rampant in the Mississippi Delta and other predominantly Black communities because the residents eat unhealthy food. People need to make good decisions about what to eat, but this understanding is too narrow and racist. It pathologizes and blames these communities for circumstances with long histories beyond their control that remain entrenched because of state political structures.

A close look at life in the Delta reveals that healthy eating is both a systemic issue and an individual issue. It is harder to buy healthy food when you live far from a grocery store, when the prices are beyond your budget, and when you are too worried about necessities such as rent and medical bills to focus on vegetables.[134] How can people in Clarksdale—a town of about fifteen thousand people with extreme levels of poverty—be expected to consistently eat well when no grocery store exists in town?

The food equity policy agenda must remove structural barriers that perpetuate food insecurity, increase the affordability of healthy food, and improve learning and knowledge about the importance of eating well.

Food Equity Policy Goal #1: Remove Structural Barriers That Perpetuate Food Insecurity.

Examples of national, state, and local policies:

- Policymakers should work with local leaders and companies to make opening grocery stores in underserved areas a financially viable and attractive choice.
- Explore alternative approaches to bringing healthy foods into communities, including mobile markets, farmers' markets, and farm-to-school programs.
- Increase the selection of foods available at medium-size stores.

- Use zoning and licensing laws to reduce the density of businesses that primarily sell unhealthy items, such as liquor stores.
- National and state agriculture subsidies should prioritize the production of edible crops and reward farmers who bring what they grow to local markets.

Food Equity Policy Goal #2: Make Healthy Foods More Affordable.

Examples of national, state, and local policies:

- Strengthen SNAP so that everyone who is hungry is eligible.
  - Ensure that the administrative policies and structures support people to apply and stay enrolled.
  - Provide sufficient benefits to make healthy foods accessible.
  - Structure benefits so people are incentivized to purchase healthy foods.
  - Prevent retailers from preying on EBT card users.
- Reform tax policies to remove the sales tax on grocery items while specifically keeping or increasing taxes on unhealthy products such as sugar-sweetened beverages.

Food Equity Policy Goal #3: Expand Educational Efforts to Increase Knowledge about the Importance of Eating Well and How to Eat Well.

Examples of national, state, and local policies:

- Develop and provide education, including public awareness campaigns and other efforts, to increase knowledge regarding what constitutes a healthy, balanced diet, the importance of eating a balanced diet, and how to prepare healthful meals. Education should be culturally sensitive, developed in collaboration with the communities meant to be reached, and based on the concept that food represents more than nourishment.
- Develop regulations modeled after tobacco advertising restrictions that may be a path to addressing misleading advertising by the food industry.

As important as these issues are, food insecurity involves much more than food. Broader economic factors shape who lives in an area, who has stable and well-paying jobs, and how much income people can devote to healthy foods. These same economic forces affect which stores are nearby, what they sell, and how much they charge. Choices about eating are part of a broader structural context that includes the basic necessities of paying for health care, housing, and other essentials. As one person put it, "How do you think about something other than Cheetos for your child to eat when you can't pay the rent? You can't." The key to solving food insecurity is ensuring that everyone has an opportunity to achieve financial security in addition to living in environments where food is accessible both geographically and economically. We will see in the next chapter that this is also true for physical activity.

2 Neighborhoods

Health is most commonly talked about as the outcome of choices made about nutrition and exercise. We saw in chapter 1 that the first part of this equation is much more complicated than people needing to make better decisions about what they eat because their options are limited by what food is accessible and affordable. A close look at a person's neighborhood makes it clear that where you live affects your health in many ways. This includes the likelihood that your neighborhood has high levels of violence and whether your housing is safe and comfortable. A close look also requires recognizing how policies and structures systematically affect who lives in the neighborhoods with the fewest resources and the barriers people face to improving their neighborhoods or moving out. Policies that affect the built environment are health policies. The same is true with exercise because some neighborhoods are more conducive to physical activity than others. A health equity policy agenda needs to focus on removing the barriers to living an active lifestyle.

Robert F. Kennedy saw these dynamics at play during his visit to the Mississippi Delta in 1967. Photos of Kennedy's trip show him talking with families in one-room wooden shacks resting on blocks rather than foundations. Some people had boards missing from their walls, which exposed them to the Delta's heat, rain, and insects. Many of these photos were taken on Chrisman Avenue on the east side of Cleveland. As Kennedy made his way down the street talking with surprised families, he was confronted by Clifford Langford, editor of a local newspaper. Langford was furious at Kennedy for visiting Mississippi and accused the trip's organizers of deliberately showing him the worst areas. He denied that people were starving and living in unsafe housing. Langford told Kennedy that if they crossed the tracks, they would see that Cleveland was a nice town and that people lived well. He may have been right, but this would have undermined, not supported, his argument. Kennedy replied that it was unacceptable for anyone to have to live in the unsafe and unsanitary conditions he was witnessing. The fact that this level of poverty had geographic and racial borders did not make it better.

The locations chosen for Kennedy to visit were not isolated pockets of extreme poverty and inadequate living conditions. When the nearby Delta Health Center opened a year earlier, its leaders found that "about 65 to 70% of the housing in that entire area for Black folk would simply be unfit for human habitation."[1] An estimated 90 percent of Black people living in north Bolivar County at the time did not have toilets that flushed.[2] People regularly showed up at the clinic with broken bones from falling through planks in their floors or off their porches because of missing stairs. Doctors were surprised by the number of children who needed treatment for burns. It was not until they did home visits that they understood that the only source of heat in most homes was a large metal stove in the middle of the shack's one room. Children would trip and land on the stove or sit so close that their clothes caught on fire.[3] These experiences reinforced the insight the center's leaders were developing that medical care alone was not enough to help people in the Delta who lived in unsafe conditions. We need to think about health in the context of where people live.

Gaps and Root Causes

The stark disparities that Kennedy witnessed between the Delta and his homes in Virginia and Cape Cod, as well as within Mississippi, exemplify the intense connection between health and place. These inequities are not explained by geography per se or something inherent about the people living there but by how particular policies and decisions affect life for people in these communities. Just as with nutrition, population-level policy solutions are needed to make it easier for people to live active lifestyles in neighborhoods that are safe and comfortable.

A neighborhood equity policy agenda should focus on removing three barriers:

(1) **Housing.** Do all people have safe, high-quality, affordable places to live with a path toward nondiscriminatory, nonpredatory lending and home ownership practices?
(2) **Neighborhood safety.** Are neighborhoods safe and free from violence, with trusted and supportive police officers who ensure antiracist law enforcement?
(3) **Physical activity.** Does the environment support active lifestyles by being walkable with desirable places to go to exercise that are easily accessible and safe?

Housing

The ability to be healthy is shaped by physical infrastructure in which people dwell. At first glance, the quality of housing in the Mississippi Delta is much better than what Robert F. Kennedy observed in 1967. Few sharecropper shacks remain in the region. A law enacted by the state legislature in the 1980s requires landlords to provide indoor plumbing. However, a serious housing crisis exists in the region, and approximately one in five households in the Mississippi Delta is reported to have a severe housing problem. This rate increases to one in four in Tunica and Washington Counties.[4] One type of severe problem stems from the safety of the actual building. The second is rooted in financial instability resulting from inadequate housing.

Safe Places to Live

A woman in Clarksdale described how many houses in her predominantly Black neighborhood "look kind of nice on the outside, but on the inside the walls are leaking. There's mold growing everywhere in the inside of the houses and all this different type of stuff." Some people stay despite these hazards, but the homes eventually become unlivable. In many cases, the owners do not have the ability or motivation to destroy these abandoned homes and so they sit empty. As a result, the three most populated counties in the Delta have a vacancy rate that is three to six times greater than the rest of the nation (United States: 2.5 percent, Bolivar: 6.2 percent, Coahoma: 8.1 percent, Washington: 12.9 percent). Vacancies are even more common in other parts of the Delta, such as Issaquena County, where more than a quarter of all houses are abandoned.[5] These numbers likely represent an undercounting of the severity of the issue because many of the vacancies are localized to the poorest communities, and people said that houses that look vacant are in fact still occupied.

Living in a community with such visible housing problems has a profound effect on people's mental health. A Clarksdale teenager lamented that more of her neighbors did not take pride in caring for their homes: "It's bad enough that the Clarksdale majority is in poverty. . . . Just because you are [poor], that doesn't mean you have to look the part. So that's how I feel about Riverton. Like, some people think okay, I'm poor. I don't have enough money to do this and this and this and this and this, but they still don't understand like the little things count. Like picking up the trash that's on the ground in front of your door, or like cutting the weeds from your grass, or stuff like that. The little stuff count." Another Clarksdale teen added that when she drives around town, her reaction is, "Wow, this is poverty for real. Because there's so many burnt down buildings, vacant houses, and people on the street and everything. And you're just like, wow."

Having a run-down house on your block is not just an aesthetic issue, it's a major health hazard. Studies show that people who live in substandard housing conditions, such as places with water leaks, poor ventilation, dirty carpets, and pests, are more likely to have a variety of negative health outcomes such as asthma, lead poisoning, injuries, and increased risk of cardiovascular disease.[6] When these houses are left vacant, the rest of the neighborhood suffers. A woman in Greenville said they attract homeless people and criminals: "When they kill people, they put them in these abandoned houses or behind the houses." Others said that these houses attract snakes, rodents, and other pests that spread to the rest of the houses in the neighborhood.

Many people said they would rather see an empty lot and hoped their city governments would push people to tear down the abandoned houses. A woman in Cleveland felt that the city council should "start contacting those owners and you give them three to six months. They can clean it up, rent it out, or tear it down and send them the bill. Add it to their taxes. Tear it down, send them the bill and clean it up because it looks better to have a green space instead of a lot with a raggedy piece of whatever in it." However, even if these houses were torn down, many of the lots are too small or too wet to build something given modern safety codes. Flooding is a perpetual problem in the Delta's poorest neighborhoods because water drains poorly and sits for long periods. A resident of Greenville explained that their street floods every time it rains: "I walked around to try to figure out why it floods. The drain to the sewage is kind of uphill, so right in front of my house sometimes there is two feet of water, and so that is one of the things that I don't like about where I live." Similarly, a young woman in Clarksdale described, "Every time I go out to my mama's car in the morning, I am always stepping in water because it doesn't go down." She calls the landlord, but he does nothing. She says he doesn't understand the severity of the problem or the effect it has on her quality of life because he does not live in the area: "He doesn't like, wake up and see everything."

Financial Instability

Another type of severe housing problem is the financial instability that comes from not being able to afford where you live. An estimated thirty-nine million American families spend more than 30 percent of their income on housing. Nearly half of these households are considered severely cost burdened because they spend more than 50 percent of their income on housing.[7] The challenge of affordable housing can also be measured by the number of hours someone would have to work to pay for affordable housing in an area. The national median is slightly more than full time at 40.9 hours per week. Some parts of the Delta are comparable, although someone who lives in the most populated county (Washington, where Greenville is located) needs to work 44 hours per week. The burden is even higher in Sunflower County at 49.2 hours and Issaquena County at 66.1 hours.[8] These numbers, combined with the challenge of finding good jobs, which will be described in the next chapter, are part of the reason that Mississippi ranks eighth in the nation for evictions.[9]

Housing instability is very bad for your health and leads to increased risk of early drug use, teenage pregnancy, depression, anxiety, and suicide.[10] The health effects are greatest for people who experience homelessness, but even seemingly less extreme experiences of instability, such as struggling to keep up with utility bills, payments, and home repairs, are associated with lower levels of well-being.[11] One reason for the close connection between housing instability and health is that people need to make difficult trade-offs about what they are going to pay for. People with housing issues are less likely to have a usual source of health care, more likely to skip medications, and by one estimate twenty-three times more likely to struggle to purchase food.[12]

A Black man in a middle-class Cleveland neighborhood poignantly described how the dead pine tree that sits in his yard hovering over his house symbolizes the difficult trade-offs that come with trying to live in a nice place: "It's not a high priority on my list to pay someone to cut this dead tree down," even though it would cost much less to remove the threat than it would to fix the roof if it fell. This dead pine tree serves as a constant reminder of the looming threat of financial and housing insecurity.

Others worried about the trees that had already fallen around their neighborhoods. A woman in Shaw told a story about an elderly woman whose house still has a tree resting on the roof many months after it was knocked over by a storm: "I think it just goes to show what happens when elderly people or people on a fixed income, if you don't have home insurance or if your home insurance doesn't cover certain things, there's literally nothing you can do when something happens to your home."

Home Ownership

Many people wished their neighborhoods were safer, were cleaner, and had more amenities, but they were skeptical this improvement would happen anytime soon, and so they wanted to move somewhere else. For example, a Black woman in Cleveland described her motivation and struggles to land in a different type of neighborhood from where she lived as a child:

> I see a lot of extra stuff in yards. The yards are not acutely manicured, things of that nature. And I grew up wrestling with that. And one of the things I promised myself when I got out, Lord, please don't put me back in that type of environment. I've had that. It's like okay, I know what my race is, but I don't have to live, it reminds me of poverty, that's what I'll say. It constantly reminds me of poverty. So when I came here, I said, "No, I refuse to," and my rent was not easy, especially with a note, a car note. But at the same time, I was like, no, I refuse to go stay over here on this side of 61. I deserve better. I need to be able to leave my purse on the front seat right in my place and come back out and not wonder is my purse there. I don't want to hear people's loud music at night. I don't want the cars riding through with the windows vibrating. I lived enough of that, and I refuse to come over here and do this.

Studies suggest that she is more likely to have better physical and mental health after having moved out of the neighborhoods with greater poverty.[13] But that is only true if she can financially sustain her place in the area with better amenities. Some people described seeing friends and neighbors try to buy nicer places in what they saw as better communities, but this decision put them in highly precarious positions if their incomes dropped even slightly.

Many people said they wished they could own their own homes rather than rent. Homeowners are no longer at the mercy of absent landlords to solve their problems, and communities in which people own their homes tend to be more likely to have well-maintained parks and good schools. The social connections that result from home ownership have even been connected to lower risk of dying from cancer.[14] Unfortunately, relatively few people in the Mississippi Delta own their homes. Slightly more than half (56 percent) of homes in the Delta are owner occupied compared with 63.4 percent nationally. Tallahatchie County is higher at

75.8 percent, though others are considerably lower, such as Tunica County at 39.5 percent.[15]

Home ownership in the United States is intensely racialized, and only 44 percent of Black families own their own homes.[16] The implications of this disparity are enormous because home ownership is one of the primary modes of accumulating and passing on wealth in the United States. This stark difference is a major reason that the median wealth of white families in the United States is twenty times greater than that of Black families.[17] But this disparity is particularly dramatic in the Delta given that by 1900, less than half a century after emancipation, more than three-fourths of Black families in the region owned land. These families effectively were forced to become sharecroppers as the wealthy white class used new rules to take their land.[18]

Economic dynamics today continue to put home ownership out of reach for many people. Consider the families living in the Chapel Hill Heights apartments in Clarksdale. This is government-subsidized housing in which their share of the rent is set at 30 percent of their adjusted gross income. Eligibility requirements for receiving this assistance means that their income needs to be even less than the already low median income in the area. As a result, they are likely paying a few hundred dollars per month. Houses are available in Clarksdale with an asking price of less than $60,000, which would result in comparable monthly payments depending on the interest rate, taxes, and terms of the loan. But many of these houses are in poor condition, which means that a move would expose someone to serious financial and health risk. As one person described, maintenance is another financial trade-off when living in a house that costs a large share of someone's income: "We all want that nice house, but we can't afford to keep our nice house up. So like when mold and stuff is on the wall, we can't just go get that problem fixed. Or when we get a leak and all, we can't just go and get that problem fixed." For families in this situation, home ownership ends up not being a step up but exposes them to greater health and financial risk.

Inequities in who owns their home is not just a question of people needing to get better jobs, make more money, or be better at budgeting. Even families with sufficient income and savings struggle to make the move to home ownership because of discriminatory practices that disadvantage Black families. Many people told stories of real estate agents discouraging Black clients from looking at houses in the wealthiest neighborhoods. Many described being turned down for loans even though they saw their white

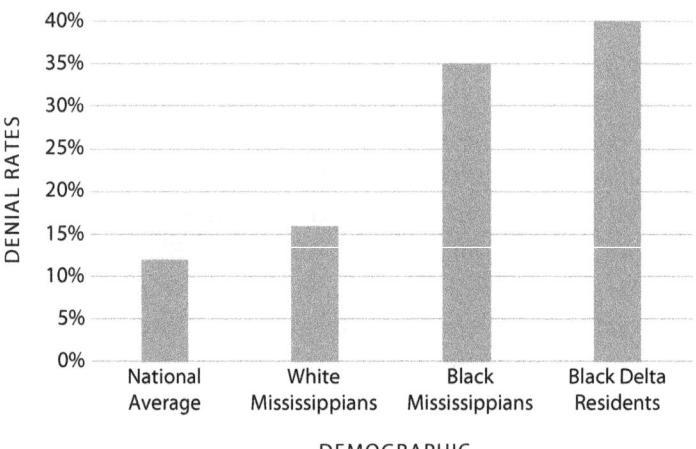

GRAPH 2.1 Mortgage denial rates. Based on data from "Download HMDA Data," Consumer Financial Protection Bureau, accessed March 29, 2024, https://www.consumerfinance.gov/data-research/hmda/historic-data/.

neighbors with similar incomes and credit histories receiving financing for boats and additional cars. A Black woman in Cleveland said that her father was denied many times before finally being approved for a mortgage. She still has the handwritten note from the white banker who offered to take a chance on her dad, and she called this decision a major turning point in her life that made it possible for her to own multiple investment rental properties of her own across northern Mississippi.

Not everyone is as fortunate as this woman's father. In fact, Black applicants for home loans are more likely to be denied in Mississippi than in any other state (graph 2.1). The national denial rate for mortgages is 12 percent. The rate for white applicants in Mississippi is higher at 16 percent, but this is still less than half of the statewide denial rate for Black applicants at 35 percent. The denial rate for Black applicants across the Delta is 40 percent.[19] Studies show that racial disparities in lending persist even when controlling for income, loan size, and other factors.[20] Some federal laws offer protection, but Mississippi is the only state in the country that does not explicitly prohibit discrimination in housing-related transactions.[21] It is not known how the credit scores of these applicants compare because this information is not publicly available, but it is known that the current methodology for determining credit scores systematically disadvantages nonwhite families.[22] Advocates have tried to convince lenders to develop a scoring model that includes factors such as a person's bank account history, work history, or utility payments. It is estimated that these alternate approaches would mean that potential borrowers whose credit scores are borderline under the status quo would be twice as likely to be approved.[23]

Not only do these systemic forces mean that nonwhite applicants are less likely to be approved for loans, but they also mean that the loans they are approved for are significantly more likely to be risky and higher cost.[24] Programs put in place to help minority families have actually exacerbated this problem. A series of federal laws passed in the 1980s and 1990s shifted the incentives for lenders and loan originators such that there was money to be made in origination charges and other fees, regardless of whether the borrower ultimately defaulted.[25] Many banks responded by targeting predominantly Black and Latino communities, obtained lists of people who had already taken out high-cost loans, and used coethnic intermediaries to solicit them for high-cost refinancing and other loans.[26] These predatory practices likely accelerated the foreclosure crisis of 2007–9.[27] According to one estimate, 25 percent of residential mortgage loans between 2003 and 2005 contained one or more indication of fraud, and this was significantly higher in counties with high levels of racial segregation.[28]

As a result of all these factors, the homes that Black families own are less likely to appreciate in value or to do so as quickly as the homes with white owners.[29] Minority households, therefore, have a particularly difficult time weathering recessions and other financial downturns. The median value of home equity fell about $20,000 for all families between 2005 and 2009, but the initial disparity meant that the equity for Black homeowners fell from $77,000 to $59,000 compared with the decrease from $115,000 to $95,000 for white families.[30] The confluence of all these factors is deeply troubling and epitomizes the argument that health is about more than people making better choices and that nonwhite populations are disadvantaged by structural racism. People who are seemingly playing by the same rules and making the same choices ultimately have very different options and very different outcomes.

Neighborhood Safety

Violence

The level of violence in the Delta is not just a barrier to physical activity, it is a major public health crisis. It is hard to live a healthy life if you are recovering from violence or afraid it is around the corner. Virtually everyone I spoke with personally experienced a crime that scared them or knew someone in their immediate circle who had. Many described incidents that happened within the last week or two. A woman in Cleveland said a burglar recently climbed in her bedroom window and took her TV. A man in Clarksdale heard ten to twenty shots the night before we spoke. A group of teenagers in Clarksdale was still shaken after one of their best friends was killed a few weeks earlier in the crossfire of gang violence. A group in Clarksdale described a recent shooting in which shots were fired into a neighbor's living room. They laughed at the absurdity of someone stealing the ambulance while the paramedics were inside tending to the victim.

The most extreme episodes make the news and reinforce the broader perception that the Delta is a dangerous place. Examples include a Clarksdale police officer being shot by two teenagers caught in the act of robbing a corner store,[31] a nun in Jonestown being stabbed and beaten after she was confronted by a robber at her front door,[32] a lawyer who was shot to death in Clarksdale by a building contractor during a deposition at which the mayor was present,[33] and a murder-suicide in a Greenville convenience store as a man shot his wife and then killed himself.[34]

Clarksdale has a reputation of being particularly dangerous. People from other parts of the Delta said they have been warned by parents and friends to avoid the city entirely because of crime: "Don't drive up 41," "It's just super dangerous, don't drive up there," "Just don't go to Clarksdale," and "I'm telling you, don't go back down there because that's a good way to get killed." Young adults from other cities said that when they were in high school and had sporting events in Clarksdale, the adults would line the sides of the school bus and tell the kids, "Quick, get in the building so we don't get shot." Many of the people making these comments were white, but not all. A young Black woman from Clarksdale said her mom's instructions are, "If I'm not here, you're not going out of the house. When I'm here, you're not going out of the house. The only time you go out of the house is when you go to school."

Local leaders struggle to know how to react. On the one hand, they do not want tourists and businesses to be scared to come to Clarksdale, and so they sometimes say that most of the crime is confined to the Riverton and Brickyard neighborhoods, which are predominantly Black, low income, and rarely visited by tourists. But residents become angry if they feel that local leaders are not taking crime seriously or blaming people in those communities. A local business owner described the challenge faced by former Clarksdale mayor Bill Luckett, who is now deceased, particularly given that he was a white man who owned a downtown blues club geared for tourists: "The mayor got in trouble when he first took office for saying Clarksdale had a 'perception of a crime problem' rather than a real crime problem.... The powers that be are so concerned about putting a good face on things that they can't really assess how bad things are and why." He added, "There is a real crime problem here."

The statistics bear this out. The homicide rate in Coahoma County, where Clarksdale is located, was thirty-four per one hundred thousand in 2018.[35] This is the second-highest rate in the nation: less than Orleans Parish in Louisiana and greater than St. Louis, Baltimore, Chicago, and Washington, DC.[36] These rates do not adequately capture the level of crime given that Clarksdale is so much smaller than these large cities, with a population of about fifteen thousand people. Another way to look at it is that in 2018, 1 in every 29 people in Clarksdale was involved in a burglary and 1 in every 120 people was involved in a violent crime.[37] These numbers are not unique to Clarksdale. Washington County, where Greenville is located, is also on the nation's top ten list for most homicides per capita.[38] In 2018, 1 in every 14 people here was involved in a property crime, such as burglary, larceny, motor vehicle theft, or arson. This is an improvement from the late 1990s when the rate was 1 in 9. Cleveland, the other largest city in the region, has similar rates, with 1 in every 16 people involved in a property crime, 1 in every 94 people involved in a burglary, and 1 in every 196 people involved in a violent crime each year.[39]

STRESS

It is worth pausing to acknowledge these crime statistics. Even for those not involved in a violent crime in Clarksdale, a good chance exists that everyone knows someone who was involved or affected. People are hyperaware that it could soon be their turn. These aggregate numbers may underestimate the intensity of violence for many people in the Delta in that many of these incidents happen in neighborhoods that are predominantly occupied by people who are low income and Black. Living in a community with this much violence is intensely stressful and affects every aspect of life. Eating well and exercising more become secondary concerns. As one person put it, "You can't worry about broccoli when you're worried about where you're going to lay your head down at night or where your kids are. You just can't. It doesn't fit in your head."

A woman in Clarksdale made a similar point while describing an episode that happened the night before we spoke in which two young men shot a cop while robbing a corner store a few blocks from her home. She said that these events have a profound effect on the community and add a layer of stress and intensity that is always there. As a result, she said that "people just want to go about their business, hurry home, and shut their doors." A young woman in Shaw said that she is so afraid of gun violence that she stays home: "Sometimes I hide under my bed." Another young woman said, "If I'm walking or something like this, especially by myself, I am worried that somebody is going to try to kidnap me or something."

Similarly, a woman in Cleveland said that people are afraid to leave their houses, even to put out the garbage: "I mean, all day and all night, all we're hearing is shooting. Pow, pow, pow, pow, all night." Another woman in Cleveland explained that the violence in her community makes it hard to sleep at night: "It is stressful, it's very stressful. I got to make sure that they don't shoot into my home. Make sure my son's okay. . . . You know, my alarm clock is going, it'll be 6:00 in the morning, it's time to get up. Then I got to function all day off of the, you know, the minimum amount of, the small amount of sleep that I've gotten that night because somewhere over the night, I've just fallen asleep and then somebody's texting me saying they're shooting in our area." She added that this "goes on all the time" and affects the whole community: "It's not just me because I hear my neighbors. I'll be talking to them the next day and they be like, 'Well, I was up all last night because all I could hear was shooting.' Then I go on Facebook and it's like everybody's up late at night and they're saying, 'They're done shooting tonight. Shooting going on.'"

A young man described the trauma of losing his uncle to gang violence: "I was a happy-go-lucky boy but then after all this stuff went down, all this stuff impacted me, I changed and that's kind of how I am today." But he did not realize how much living with this stress was affecting him until he visited his grandmother. "When I go down to her house, she live in Madison in the country, so it's like, for me that's like nostalgia. And when I go back home, I think about things and if I see something that reminds me of something, I end up reflecting on it. . . . Thinking about things from the past, it's like constantly going just like a storm in your mind. And then you got to tell yourself that you got to deal with all this now and you just got to accept it, but it's hard at the same time." A young woman in Clarksdale described how she tries to cope: "All of that was normalized to me. I grew up like hearing people shooting outside, and it was like, just go in the back room and sit on the floor, and like you'll turn on the TV, and you don't even hear that anymore. Like you hear it in like rap music. Like that's all they talk about, like I can relate to that because I hear the gunshots in our windows, too." She added, "It was just life. It was how you live life."

GANGS

Many people attribute the crime and violence in the Delta to gangs. Some of this is said to be rooted in the Great Migration and reverse migration, in which large numbers of people moved to northern cities such as St. Louis and Chicago and in which some have since returned (see chapter 3 for more on this). In 2004, the agent in charge of Mississippi for the federal Drug Enforcement Administration said, "In Greenville, people still have strong family ties in Chicago. Then you have people in the Delta who have been to Chicago, gotten into drugs and travel back and forth." Because these are rural areas, residents feel there is very limited enforcement or sophisticated police departments compared with Chicago: "They feel there is less chance they will get caught. And in a lot of ways, it's true."[40] A 2017 report documents that northern gangs have a presence in all eighty-two counties in Mississippi.[41]

But in a 2004 *Chicago Tribune* examination of gang violence in the Delta, Greenville police chief Lon Pepper noted that larger organized gangs are not the only or even biggest driver of crime here: "What we have now is a lot of wannabees."[42] Many people described this as the case today and theorized that the level of violence is more a reflection of the lack of jobs and educational opportunity. A young woman said teenagers have nothing to do in Greenville, "so you're just with your friends, chilling, outside doing whatever you're going to do, and you can get into trouble if you're not busy. So a group of friends started calling themselves 'N***** from [she named the street].' And like the reality is like that was just a group of kids who grew up together, who like sit around all day chilling at somebody's house because they live on the same street. But a few years ago, like those people started breaking into those same houses on the street. Like they got, they're in jail for shooting up houses on that street." She added, "It's the reality, like gangs are so normalized. It's just like a friend group, you know?"

When asked if any of the friends he grew up with have joined gangs and what that looks like, a young man in Clarksdale responded, "Plenty of them. . . . It's terrifying seeing my friends growing up to be this and being influenced by people that they don't even know. Or having to see them getting told what to do and being forced to do something like carry out a mission or something, like selling drugs and all that." Easy access to guns escalates the intensity of the violence. A young woman in Cleveland described buying shells to go duck hunting even though she was sixteen, which is under the legally required age of eighteen. She said, "[The clerk] asked for my birthdate. I told him. And he said it wasn't working. And then I said, 'Is it because of the age?' And he said, 'Maybe.' Then he typed something else in and he ended up just handing [me the shells]—I paid for them and left. Nobody stopped me or checked out when I walked out. I mean I just left with them." She was glad to go hunting but said the incident scared her because "everyone has a gun."

Police and Law Enforcement

The legacy of slavery and Jim Crow casts a large shadow over the region and colors what it means to feel safe in Delta communities, who is to blame for problems, and who is responsible for fixing them. Law enforcement in the region has a deep history of not only standing by as Black residents became the victims of racially motivated attacks but also actively facilitating and participating in the violence. Many struggle to trust the police and legal systems to impartially carry out justice. Police killed 108 people in Mississippi between 2013 and 2018, which is the tenth-highest rate in the country during this period.[43] The proportion of these people who are Black and the rate of Black people killed by police per capita is relatively low. But the stories of many of the people who have been killed sound eerily like what police said happened to George Floyd, Breonna Taylor, Ahmaud Arbery, and others before video evidence of these killings surfaced and the full truth emerged.

For example, Patrick Bryant was a forty-one-year-old Black man in Clarksdale who was walking home from the store with his ten-year-old son one evening around 9:00 P.M. Police officers showed up after receiving a call that there was a prowler in the area. The confrontation ended up with Bryant shot by police in someone's backyard and his son running away looking for help.[44] News reports say that Bryant pointed a gun at police but never fired. His wife and mother told reporters that he was licensed to carry a gun because of his job as a security officer, and they are frustrated by the lack of answers they have received to their questions.[45] It is unclear whether the police officers involved were charged. In another case, police officers were indicted for an incident that resulted in the killing of Willie Lee Bingham Jr., a twenty-year-old Black man who was allegedly breaking into cars in Cleveland when he was spotted by a police officer.[46] After a six-mile vehicle chase, Bingham and his friends ran on foot and were followed by an unmarked vehicle. One was caught, but when Bingham did not stop, officers shot him multiple times in the back. No weapon was found on Bingham, so an officer allegedly placed a police baton near the body. The officer was tried twice on charges of manslaughter, but both trials resulted in mistrials because jurors could not agree on a verdict. He was subsequently charged with evidence tampering and faced up to twenty years in prison, but a federal judge dismissed the case because prosecutors argued that the officer has since become too ill to stand trial. He remains free on bail.[47]

Many such stories exist in which little is publicly known other than that a Black person was shot by police officers during a traffic stop or response to an alleged crime when they found "a man matching the description given to them by callers and gave chase."[48] Also, many stories are told of officers shot in the line of duty and shooting only after shots were fired at them.[49] But the deep history of law enforcement being responsible for violence or allowing violence to go unpunished—from Emmett Till to the many names not widely known—has many residents skeptical about justice and safety in Mississippi. In June 2020, one of the organizers of a Black Lives Matter protest said that what happened to George Floyd and Breonna Taylor "could be anybody, plain and simple. Our thing is to get people aware and get people to understand that lynchings aren't just something that happened during the civil rights era, it's still happening."[50]

Many people were also concerned that those with power—that is, government leaders and residents who pay higher property taxes—did not prioritize fighting crime in low-income Black communities and that the police departments were therefore under-resourced to address the magnitude of the crisis. A woman in the small town of Shaw told a story of calling 911 while hearing gunshots near her home. The receptionist responded, "Our police officer is off duty." She was stunned. "Off duty! What police officer [is] off duty?! No one is at work but the receptionist. Off duty?!"

A white woman in Cleveland told a story that captures the lingering lack of trust between Black communities and government institutions, particularly those with white leadership. She described giving her daughter and some friends a ride home from an event: "I've got two white kids and two Black kids in the car, and a police officer goes by. The two Black kids go, 'Po, po!' and dive. That's when I'm concerned because I didn't teach that, but something in this seven-year-old and this nine-year-old, like driving in [my] Jeep, a safe place, a place they know is safe, they still feel the need to dive." She asked why they ducked down, to which the Black kids responded, "Because they could have seen me." When asked why this worried them, they replied again, "I don't want them to see me." She pushed further: "What have you done that you don't want them to see you? Did you steal from the store that we just got our snack from? Do you have a gun in your book bag that I'm not aware of?" They laughed at her question but insisted again they did not want the police officer to see them. She asked again, better understanding that as much as things have progressed from the Jim Crow era, their experience growing up in Mississippi was not the same as her white daughter's. She concluded, "That's like real talk. That's the shit that will keep me up at night."

Shortly after taking office as mayor of Clarksdale in 2017, Chuck Espy—a Black man—hired Sandra Williams as the first Black woman to serve as the chief of police. He was concerned that the police department was corrupt and telling lies about leadership.[51] Chief Williams conducted an internal assessment in which it was found that some officers were "insubordinate, have issues of adapting to change, a lack of discipline, a lack of training." Perhaps in response to this analysis, the department was soon short-staffed at thirty-three officers, down fifty from a year earlier. In November 2018, the board of commissioners that governs the force approved the hiring of five more officers.[52]

Mayor Espy received national attention in May 2019 for a unique plan to address gang violence in Clarksdale. He offered $10,000 of his own money as moving assistance to help "drug dealers, gang members, and want-to-be criminals" leave town. "I know there are some people who feel that they have some problems in the city like being drug dealers, or being gang members, or they just can't control themselves," said Espy.[53] He is quoted in *Newsweek* as saying, "It's not to say you just want one criminal to move from one city to the next. . . . They might just not have the good opportunities they need in this city. But make no mistake about it, we are asking those three groups of people, if you are just simply a criminal, if you are a gang member, or a drug dealer, move out of this city now."[54] It is unclear whether this approach has been implemented or yielded any results.

Physical Activity

National guidelines recommend that adults engage in 150 minutes of movement per week, with at least two sessions of muscle strengthening. Physical activity can include exercise such as jogging and cycling but can be as simple as going for a walk or doing yardwork. School-age youth (ages six to seventeen) should do 60 minutes of activity every day. People with active lifestyles are less likely to develop chronic disease and are more likely to have a higher overall quality of life.[55] Even a single episode of activity lasting less than 10 minutes brings physical and emotional benefits.[56] Mississippi is the least active state in the United States, which is saying a lot given that almost one-fourth of adults (22.9 percent) and children (24 percent) across the country do not get enough physical activity.[57] Only 13.5 percent of adults in Mississippi do the recommended level of activity.[58] The number is even lower for adult women, at only 9.5 percent.[59] Even more alarming is that 34 percent of Mississippians report having no physical activity at all. This number rises to 40 percent in many parts of the Delta and is most severe among Black women.[60]

It is interesting and potentially helpful to identify the populations who are and are not active, but this examination does not identify the root causes of physical inactivity. These characteristics should not be thought of as determinants in the sense that they cause inactivity. Being Black or a woman is not a risk factor that predisposes someone to a sedentary life. We need to better understand the underlying dynamics that lead to these differences.

Unfortunately, most of the evidence about how to design neighborhoods to facilitate physical activity comes from studies of urban and suburban areas.[61] Building dedicated bike lanes is a growing trend across the country that is unlikely to have the same effect on lifestyles in small Mississippi towns as it does in New York City. Much of the research on rural environments fails to take into consideration that not all rural communities are the same. They vary dramatically in terms of population density, distance from population centers, and the sizes of these population centers.[62] There really is not much evidence about the barriers to and opportunities for increasing physical activity in rural communities.

Even so, the key insight from this research is a valuable starting point to better understand the challenges and opportunities for active living in the Mississippi Delta. Leaders cannot make someone go for a walk, take a bike ride, or incorporate some other form of physical activity into their routine, but they can create conditions in which it is easy and natural to do so. What does that look like? The answer is that people are more likely to be active if they live in communities that are walkable, have desirable places to go, and feel safe.

Walkability

Residents of the Delta sometimes laughed when asked if their communities were walkable. When questioned why she was laughing, a woman in

Cleveland said simply, "You rarely see sidewalks." Large parts of the region are connected only by roads designed exclusively for cars. This makes sense on the back-country roads—sidewalks are not needed along fields of cotton and corn where houses are far apart. But sidewalks are missing from many of the neighborhoods in small and medium-sized cities. In a study of twelve communities in the Delta, it was estimated that three-fourths of the examined segments lacked sidewalks, defined shoulders, or pedestrian crosswalks.[63] City planners and budgets have not made these features a widespread priority. Few people can step outside their doors and go for a walk, jog, or bike ride without needing to be in the road for much of the trip. As a man in Clarksdale explained, "I don't see any biking trails where folks can ride bicycles, like on smooth streets and everything. I don't see any of that in Clarksdale." "Nah, ain't no smooth street," a fellow Clarksdale resident echoed.

Some people regularly travel on foot despite the lack of sidewalks and other features that would make a community walkable. This is the main way for some people to get around. Consider Tunica, a town on the northern edge of the Delta between Clarksdale and Memphis in which approximately 1,400 people live within two-thirds of a square mile.[64] The Piggly Wiggly, Dollar General, Family Dollar, and most of the gas stations are along Highway 61, a state highway with two lanes in either direction separated by a turning lane. Based on 2020 US census data, 5.8 percent of all households in Tunica have no vehicles, and 28.9 percent have only one car.[65] This means that for large numbers of people, the only way to buy groceries is to walk across five lanes of traffic. Some stretches have sidewalks that abruptly end. Roads have few crosswalks or traffic lights. As a result, it is common to see people walking in the narrow shoulder or standing in the turning lane waiting for a break in traffic. Figure 2.1 shows the road people need to cross to get from town to the Piggly Wiggly grocery store. A stoplight is not very far in the other direction, but it is entirely for vehicles, without any crosswalks or signage for pedestrians.

Children walking to school are particularly vulnerable. A woman in Cleveland described regularly seeing kids on Martin Luther King Jr. Drive, a road that runs through the predominantly Black side of town and near D. M. Smith Elementary School and Cleveland Central Middle School: "There's no sidewalk on that street. And there are people that are riding down that street 40 miles an hour maybe when school is getting out and you have kids that are walking. So what is it going to take, a child getting hit and possibly dying for the city to say, we need to do something?"

FIGURE 2.1 Highway 61 at the Piggly Wiggly in Tunica, Mississippi. Google Maps Street View.

Another woman in Cleveland described regularly having the same experience: "When I'm going to drop my sister off, there's kids walking in the road. And they're like in the middle of the road. And they don't go to the side, they just stay in the middle. You want to honk and roll down the window and just scream at them, tell them, 'Did your parents not teach you to walk in the road?' But, I mean, you can't really do anything about it." The point is not that kids are being careless but that they are so used to walking on streets without sidewalks that they are not concerned about sharing the road with cars. Their communities are not walkable, but they do not have a choice other than walking in the road if they want to get somewhere on foot (figure 2.2).

Desirable Places to Exercise That Are Accessible

When asked why she was laughing at the question of walkability, a woman explained, "The only sidewalks are downtown." In other words, some areas are connected by sidewalks, but these are not where most people spend their time. In Tunica, many of the most visited destinations—jobs, stores, churches, restaurants—are more likely to be in strip malls along a state highway than downtown. These important centers of activity are far from where people live, far from other common destinations, and only accessible by car.

Neighborhoods 77

FIGURE 2.2 Martin Luther King Jr. Drive near Smith Elementary School in Cleveland, Mississippi. Google Maps Street View.

The downtowns of the three largest cities in the Delta—Clarksdale, Cleveland, and Greenville—are exceptions in that each city has a handful of restaurants and shops, all of which are connected by sidewalks. But many residents feel that these businesses cater to the tastes and price points of a population other than the local Black residents, such as upper-middle-class white residents, faculty and students at Delta State University, and tourists from Europe and Australia visiting historical blues sites. People who visit downtown almost always drive and park directly in front of their destinations. If they do walk, it is rarely more than a block or two. As a community leader in Greenville put it, "What does walkability mean in Greenville or Cleveland. You know what I mean? And let alone like Leland, or Ruleville, or something like that?" Even the biggest downtown in the Delta is too small for traveling between stores to be a source of physical activity for many people.

What about out in the country? A persistent misconception is that rural areas have unlimited access to outdoor recreational activities.[66] It is true that people in some areas with natural amenities have many options and do lots of physical activity.[67] For example, residents of Colorado are among the healthiest and most active in the nation because they regularly hike, jog, bike, and ski in the mountains.[68] But many people in rural America, including those in the Mississippi Delta, do not live near such natural amenities. Popular websites for identifying trails for hiking and jogging, such as Alltrails.com, suggest very few options within an hour's drive of most parts of the Delta. The only ways to experience the region's most prominent natural feature—the Mississippi River—are through activities such as boating and fishing that are not particularly active or accessible to everyone. There are places to swim in Mississippi River State Park in Marianna, Arkansas, and a lake near Arkabutla, Mississippi, but nobody I spoke with said they made the hourlong trip to visit either location.

Neighborhood parks are a critical element of healthy and active communities but are a missed opportunity in most of the Delta. A handful of parks exist, but very few people live close enough to walk to one. In the United States, an estimated 38 percent of people live within a half mile of a park. The highest rate in the Delta is 34.5 percent in Washington County, where Greenville is located. In Coahoma County, where Clarksdale is located, only 20.5 percent of people live within a half mile of a park. The rates are even lower in more rural counties such as Sunflower (6.1 percent), Issaquena (4.7 percent), Holmes (0 percent), and Tallahatchie (0 percent).[69]

The parks that are near people offer little to entice them to visit and be active when there. Few have any amenities such as trails, playground equipment, or basketball hoops. Even fewer are well maintained. A young man in Clarksdale described, "We had, like a basketball court thing out there, but they tore it down. They said they was going to fix it, but they never committed to it." Another said that when her family first moved to Clarksdale a few years earlier, she was pleased that there was a park across the street where she could take her younger brother and sister. At first, she was surprised she rarely saw others, but she quickly discovered that "the playground was really nasty. . . . They would go months without cutting the grass, and so the grass would be tall out there at the park." She says that people treat the park like a personal trash can and leave candy wrappers and even entire garbage bags because they get the message from the city and other residents that this space is not important. The last straw for her mom was when they saw children urinating on the equipment: "After that my mom just stopped letting us go. She would take us to the park that's on Martin Luther King Drive. But, yeah, this park is still kind of nasty too, sometimes, because they leave little trash and stuff out there and it's still not safe."

This is a difficult cycle, as city officials are skeptical that their efforts to clean and maintain parks are worth the time and money because people will continue to litter. Some communities are working hard to break this cycle and are building new parks, particularly in lower-income neighborhoods that are predominantly Black. A community leader in Shaw said, "We have a location. We have a playground. We are going to be having a fence within the next month. The fence itself took four months to get. I did an online fundraiser. We needed $2,000. Within twenty-four hours we had $2,000."

This is an impressive accomplishment in a community of two thousand people where the median income is $20,000 per person. She explained that most of the money came from people who moved away after growing up in Shaw but still have family in the area: "I know there's a lot of pride specifically in the Delta about where you're from and where you went to high school. And that even if you've moved hundreds or thousands of miles away, that's still your hometown, those are still your people. And you still want to see your town succeed. It's not like people move away and forget about it. You still want to see opportunities and growth."

Safe Places to Exercise

Building sidewalks will not be enough to encourage physical activity if people do not have desirable places to go such as nice parks. But even making key destinations walkable and inviting will not be enough to change lifestyles if people do not feel safe. Residents of the Delta described many safety concerns that affect their willingness to spend time outside.

First, summers in the Mississippi Delta are brutally hot, with average temperatures in the nineties and daily highs regularly greater than one hundred degrees with high humidity.[70] Every summer, news media report farmers and athletes dying while working and playing in the heat.[71] Even so, weather does not adequately explain the region's low physical activity levels since the oppressive summer heat is offset by the relatively mild temperatures throughout the winter.

Second, many do not spend time outside because they are worried about stray dogs walking the streets. No statistics are available to show the number of dog attacks on pedestrians or the number of stray dogs in the Mississippi Delta, but leaders at the Mississippi Department of Health said they were stunned that "wild dogs" were one of the most commonly mentioned barriers to health they heard about while conducting the state health assessment. "That is where we are close to a third world country. Who knew that would be the answer to that question," one leader said. One explanation I was given is that people do not neuter or spay their dogs because they hope to make a little money with each new litter. Most of these puppies do not get sold, and some are neglected and may be abandoned.

It is not uncommon to see stray dogs on the streets of the larger cities of Clarksdale, Cleveland, and Greenville and in small towns such as Mound Bayou and Tutwiler. A woman in Drew—a town of about 2,500 people twenty minutes outside Cleveland and ten minutes from the entrance to the state penitentiary in Parchman—said that she was traumatized not only by the number of dogs but also by the cruelty she witnessed toward these animals: "They are really rough to stray dogs in Drew. They hang them off buildings, shoot them, stone them." A woman in Clarksdale described how stray dogs affected her ability to incorporate physical activity into her lifestyle: "I don't walk up and down my street because down at the other end, there's this dog and he runs after cars and everything, you know? And that will stop you from walking up and down the street and around if you're afraid that a dog might come out at you." Similarly, when asked where in Clarksdale he would recommend jogging, a pastor told me he did not think it was a good idea to exercise outside because of the likelihood of being confronted by a dog.

Third, people could drive to places to exercise, but traveling by car brings its own risk because Mississippi has the highest rate of motor vehicle deaths per capita in the country. The rate here is double the national average, and this is the single largest type of preventable death in the state.[72] The reasons for this are multifaceted but include that rural roads tend to have more accidents and that Mississippians are less likely to wear seatbelts (a law requiring backseat riders to buckle up was only enacted in 2017), less likely to properly harness young children, and more likely to drive while under the influence of alcohol.[73]

Finally, many people said they do not spend time being physically active outside because they are afraid of crime.[74] When asked how to increase physical activity levels in the Delta, one woman responded, "You say, well, people could walk. Okay, so let's think about that a second. If you live in a neighborhood that is not safe, it's hard to go for a walk, especially at night." A woman in Cleveland explained, "We've had a lot of murders in the area, the crime rate has grown very, very high. . . . I'm not comfortable sitting on my porch now." As a result, she said "the best thing to do is just stay in the house. And you know, most of the time you just stay in the house all day. Then you got to sit around and you're not going to be active. Because the majority of the time, you start watching TV or whatever, you're in your home on your laptop or whatever all day. Yeah, [safety] plays a big role. And I think that's for the whole community."

People in low-income neighborhoods said that the liquor stores and corner stores in their communities "create a different type of atmosphere for violence." For example, a woman in Cleveland described the area near the intersection of Chrisman Avenue and Highway 61, the same neighborhood Robert F. Kennedy visited fifty years earlier, as having multiple stores that are magnets for violent situations: "Anybody who lives in this area knows that this area, right across the street, has shootings, stabbings, fights, all those kind of things happen." As a result, she does not feel safe going for a walk or think that children in her community should spend time playing outside unsupervised. Parks were described not only as missed opportunities to facilitate activity but also as common gathering places for young adults in ways that felt threatening to parents of young children.[75] A woman in Cleveland mentioned this while describing that crime has gotten worse in recent years: "Nobody goes out. You don't see too many people out. Like we used to put our . . . on warm days, there would be so many kids walking around. Now, they have shootings in our park. Our kids can't even go to the park." She added, "Imagine the health disparities they're going to have sitting in the house all day. Because I can't let my son outdoors. He can't go outside. He has all his activities indoors, and we don't go to the park."

Some people said they would feel more comfortable being in their parks or walking outside if their communities had streetlights. A teenager in Clarksdale described an experience that keeps her from feeling comfortable walking around her community:

We went to McDonald's because back then, my momma had money to blow, so we just went out and we ate out like every other night. So we came back, we had our drinks and stuff in our hand and the streetlights were, the whole street was just black. And it was one streetlight over the garbage can, and that was the only streetlight on, and it was like flickering. And I looked back because I heard something like a thump or something, and I saw some guy standing beside the garbage can. And I was like, hurry up and get in the house, hurry up and get in the house, there's a dude standing beside the garbage can. So we went on in the house and later on, we heard gunshots, and the next day we had found out that our friend's daughter had been shot in her eye. And it was so bad. And I feel like that's another big part about it, too. Lights are important. I don't know how the lights ended up off because there was like, that wasn't normal because our lights were always on. Like all the lights on our street. That was the only time we had went home and all the lights was off like on that street.

But others said that having streetlights did not increase their confidence because "they'll shoot them out" so that the neighborhood is dark. These experiences reinforce the point that as important as it is to improve the built environment in ways that facilitate and encourage physical activity, deeper community-level issues must be solved.

Ripples of Hope

The three major issues examined in this chapter—housing, neighborhood safety, and physical activity—clearly demonstrate the powerful connection between neighborhoods and health. Residents of the Mississippi Delta face many barriers to living in neighborhoods that facilitate optimal health. A multifaceted approach to strengthening neighborhoods is needed to ensure that all people live where it is natural, easy, and safe to maintain an active lifestyle. This includes helping more people become homeowners and providing more amenities in underresourced communities. Many challenges exist on both fronts in the Delta, but some good things are happening, such as the work of HOPE Credit Union and the creation of more walking trails in Delta cities.

HOPE Credit Union

Bill Bynum has been working for more than twenty-five years to help low-income families in Mississippi achieve their dreams of buying a home. The HOPE Credit Union began as a volunteer effort run out of his church in Jackson but has evolved to include thirty-two branches in the mid-South.[76] This includes multiple cities in the Delta, such as Drew, Greenville, Moorhead, Robinsonville, and Shaw. The nonprofit is focused on communities that Bynum describes as "bank deserts" because traditional lending institutions are scared off by the Black and rural populations they deem too risky: "As a result, the money lenders that go into those areas charge excessive rates and fees for those who can least afford them. And so that is a market failure," Bynum said.[77]

HOPE's philosophy is to build communities: "Our difference is that we add a commitment to serving these markets. It's a matter of will. We are very committed to making sure people have access to capital regardless of who their parents were, or where they live, or what they look like. If we determine they have the ability to pay a loan at a responsible rate, then we make those loans."[78] Much of the initial focus was on helping small businesses get going, but home loans have emerged as a major part of HOPE's work. Bynum says that the program has been immensely successful in quantifiable terms. Since 2000, it has provided $300 million in financing for home ownership and the building of affordable housing. This has added up to more than six thousand homes and apartments.[79] More than 80 percent of loans have been to first-time homebuyers with average incomes of less than $40,000 per year. Despite funding this population that other banks avoid, HOPE has experienced a loss of less than half of a percent on home loans.[80]

HOPE's role in rebuilding the Eastmoor Estates epitomizes the intense need it is helping to fill. In 1969, sixty-eight single-family homes were built with the promise of subsidized rent for low-income families. The homes were placed just outside Moorhead, Mississippi, likely with the intention of preventing many Black families from being able to vote in municipal elections. Approximately five hundred people moved into Eastmoor Estates when it opened, excited by the future they thought was ahead of them with stable and safe housing. Unfortunately, moving into these homes quickly turned into a nightmare. Poor wiring meant that many of the houses suddenly caught fire and burned down. Foundations shifted, and homes sunk into the wet ground. Residents were forced to stuff rags into cracks in the ceilings and walls to protect themselves from the rain, wind, mosquitos, and mice. Sewage backed up onto people's lawns and onto broken sidewalks. About one-third of the original houses are no longer standing just fifty years later.[81] The federal Department of Housing and Urban Development ultimately withdrew its subsidies in 2001 because the houses no longer qualified as viable low-income housing.

Emma Bush suffered through this nightmare. Her husband of forty-five years died of a heart attack in 2006 after spending hours digging to fix the leak that caused sewage to overflow into their yard. Bush wanted to leave after his death but had nowhere to go.[82] HOPE Credit Union is stepping in to help Bush and others in her situation. It leveraged its own resources to raise $3 million from Goldman Sachs to completely refurbish the properties and build new homes where the others had burned to the ground. The sidewalks are being fixed, and a new playground designed by the community children is being built. In a recent annual report, Eva Bellmon, who has seen all the ups and downs at Eastmoor since moving in as one of the original occupants in 1969, was quoted saying, "HOPE brought life back to this area. Before, Eastmoor was an outcast area. Now it's revitalized, and the whole town is excited."[83]

A similar story is playing out in the Magnolia Crossing community in Yazoo City (at the southern edge of the Delta, about an hour northwest of Jackson). Houses built in 1976 are falling apart and need to be renovated, but no financial institution was willing to front the costs. HOPE put forward nearly $900,000, which helped open the door to raising additional funding from the Federal Home Loan Bank of Dallas, as well as tax credits and money from the federal, state, and local governments. The result of this $8.8 million effort will be homes for eighty-six families whose incomes fall below 60 percent of the area median income.[84] HOPE CEO Bill Bynum brings an equity framework to this work and sees it as an extension of the deep roots of the civil rights movement in Mississippi: "Martin Luther King, Medgar Evers, Emmett Till, they died so the work we're doing at HOPE could happen, so that economic justice could be available to all."[85]

Downtown Walking Trails

Cleveland's downtown is thriving, with few of the vacant shops or abandoned theater marquees seen in most other communities across the Delta. I explore why this is the case in the next chapter, on economic development, but a key feature of this downtown serves as a powerful example of the ways community leaders can shape the built environment to encourage physical activity.[86] Running through the middle of the main stretch of businesses is a beautiful walking trail.

Studies show that the likelihood of someone using a trail decreases substantially for every quarter-mile increase in the distance from the trail to their home.[87] This trail is strategically placed adjacent to the predominantly white, middle-class neighborhood near Delta State University and the predominantly Black, poor neighborhood that Robert F. Kennedy visited more than fifty years ago. The location of the trail is deeply symbolic, as it sits on the site of the old Illinois Central line that racially divided the city for generations. The last train went through in 1995, and the tracks were removed in 2000.[88] That this is still the de facto racial line in town underscores its importance as the location for the walking trail.

Research also shows that people are more likely to use walking trails that are well maintained, well lit, and near amenities.[89] The Cleveland trail is well lit and lined by well-manicured grass, tall trees, and public art. Ample free parking is spaced along the trail for the many downtown restaurants and shops, which means that people can drive to the trail and then get a meal or a frozen yogurt at Delta Dairy. The trail also happens to be in front of the city's police station. Many people mentioned that this helps to minimize the degree to which concerns over safety are a barrier to using the trail. One woman said there are a handful of other places to walk, "but people have been complaining because they have not been able to be out there and be safe. And the police does not really know about it." By contrast, "I haven't heard anybody complain about the walking trail . . . because it's near a police department because it is right there where the police department's located."

The effect of the trail on physical activity rates has not yet been evaluated, but many aspects indicate it has been positive. One is that the trail is almost always in use, and importantly, no obvious racial pattern has emerged as to who uses it based on the times I was there and what people told me. It is just as common to see a middle-aged Black couple walking as it is to see a young white woman jogging behind a baby stroller. The trail is about 1.5 miles long, which makes it a natural spot for the 5K races that occur throughout the year.

Other trails have been built in or near downtown Cleveland. These include a loop just west of the Delta State University campus that is well lit and near apartments and houses, as well as a short walking trail in front of the Renova City Hall just north of Cleveland. Other communities are looking to replicate the success of Cleveland's trails. Greenville, in particular, has built a 1.7-mile trail along the levee to take advantage of the city's location immediately adjacent to the Mississippi River. This was an expensive project for the city, but local leaders view it as critical to improving Greenville's physical, emotional, and financial health. The city was able to leverage resources from the state's Department of Transportation so that it is only paying one-fifth of the $1 million needed for construction. Other groups, such as the Community Foundation of Washington County, have contributed toward the city's share of the costs. Mayor Errick Simmons explained that the trail is worth the money, along with what will be required for maintenance, "Our overall aim in this administration is to create a healthier city population. So that walking trail provides that avenue for individuals to walk, to run and to jog, to be healthier individuals in the city of Greenville."[90]

The Greenville trail is not as central as the one in Cleveland, but its location is deeply symbolic given the levee's importance in the development of a civil rights consciousness across the South. The Great Flood of 1927 was one of the biggest natural disasters in the Delta's history, as more than twenty-three thousand square miles were submerged by the overflowing Mississippi River. Hundreds of thousands of people were displaced and at least 250 people died. The impact of the flood was intensely racialized in ways that were echoed by the response to Hurricane Katrina nearly one hundred years later. Black families were among the last to be rescued. Black plantation workers were forced to work on repairing and cleaning up the damage. Many were stranded for days without food and water as the waters continued to rise. At least one Black man was shot after refusing to work.[91]

These events laid the early foundation for the response that would emerge in the wake of Emmett Till's murder and the other major turning points in the fight for civil rights in the Delta. It was a major driver of the Great Migration, when thousands of Black families left Mississippi for northern cities such as St. Louis and Chicago. Choosing to place Greenville's new trail along the levee is a way for the community to literally build on this tragedy to promote physical activity and equity.

The Neighborhood Equity Policy Agenda

Robert F. Kennedy was stunned by the neighborhoods he saw during his visit to the Mississippi Delta in 1967. People lived in small wood shacks that had missing boards and no foundations. A car in his caravan hit a stray dog. He was confronted in Cleveland by a local leader who accused his staff of cherry-picking the worst areas to show him. However, the presence of major differences in the opportunities available to people in different neighborhoods was one of the major points that Marian Wright Edelman and others were trying to communicate to Senator Kennedy, Senator Joseph Clark, and the rest of the nation.

Where someone lives profoundly shapes the opportunities available for them to make healthy choices. Physical activity rates in the Delta are among the lowest in the nation partly because so few places to be active exist. But building sidewalks and bike lanes is not enough. We need to improve the full context in which people live, such as whether they live near well-maintained parks, they are likely to see stray dogs, they are afraid of crime, or their housing is not safe.

The neighborhood equity policy agenda needs to increase the availability of safe, affordable housing, ensure that neighborhoods are safe, and remove structural barriers to physical activity.

Neighborhood Equity Policy Goal #1: Ensure That Housing Is Safe, Affordable, and Available to All.

Examples of national, state, and local policies:

- Strengthen local infrastructure so that homes are protected from pests, lead, mold, or drainage problems and that residents receive help with removing dangerous branches and trees.
- Community leaders should prioritize removing abandoned homes and find new uses for land when abandoned homes are removed.
- Support renters so that they can afford monthly payments—for example, ensure affordable housing is available and regulate rent increases.
- Provide counseling for renters when they struggle to afford monthly payments.
- Enable protections for renters throughout the eviction process.
- Increase access to home ownership for members of historically marginalized populations.
    - Revise the approach to calculating credit scores.
    - Enforce tougher policies to prevent discrimination by realtors.
    - Prevent predatory lending practices.

Neighborhood Equity Policy Goal #2: Increase Neighborhood Safety.

Examples of national, state, and local policies:

- Strengthen seatbelt and drunk driving public health campaigns and laws.
- Equitably enforce seatbelt and drunk driving laws.
- Increase animal control efforts so that people are unlikely to encounter wild dogs on the streets.
- Restrict access to firearms so fewer people—particularly those at greatest risk of suicide and perpetrating intimate partner violence or who are members of gangs—have guns.
- Eliminate public access to assault weapons.

- Ensure that members of law enforcement are antiracist and work with leaders in communities with high crime rates to establish cultures of trust.
- Increase resources to ensure accountability for police officers and police departments, especially when trust is violated.

Neighborhood Equity Policy Goal #3: Remove Structural Barriers to Physical Activity.

Examples of national, state, and local policies:

- Ensure greater sidewalk connectivity to facilitate physical activity in higher-density neighborhoods, prioritizing areas near schools.
- Prioritize developing amenities that promote movement and accessibility, such as well-maintained and well-lit parks, sidewalks, and walking trails near homes and stores.

I have had many conversations with people who see health as primarily about individual choices or who do not believe structural racism exists but are willing to agree with the idea that where someone lives affects access to food, safe housing in safe neighborhoods, and physical activity. Their response tends to be that people should take responsibility for their situations by being proactive and moving to better neighborhoods. If they cannot afford to do that, the argument goes, they should get better jobs. If they cannot do that, they should get more education.

Not only does this "pull yourself up by your bootstraps" mindset inappropriately absolve the skeptic of any role in improving the conditions in which other people live, it is also offensive and wrong. The answer should not be that we give up on certain neighborhoods and expect people to move out if they want better lives. It is also not the case that everyone can make the decisions that will give them access to greater resources. We have already seen that Black applicants are treated differently by lenders and real estate agents, even when they have the same income and educational attainment as white applicants. We will also see in the next two chapters that Black people face intense systemic barriers to getting better jobs and accessing high-quality education.

3 Jobs

Most of the barriers to eating healthy and physical activity for people in the Mississippi Delta are rooted in economic conditions. Places with thriving economies are more likely to have grocery stores and communities with amenities conducive to physical activity. People with financial security are more likely to be able to afford healthy foods and to have the resources of money, time, and space that make it easier to have an active lifestyle. Economic policy is health policy.

Robert F. Kennedy made this point frequently after his trip to the Mississippi Delta and told leaders around the country that creating jobs and building a strong economy are the keys to addressing the problems of food and housing insecurity he witnessed.[1] Marian Wright Edelman talked about this with Kennedy at his home in Virginia in August 1967 a few months after showing him around the Delta. They discussed the racial tension that was bubbling to the surface in Detroit and other cities and brainstormed about what should be done next to draw attention to economic inequality in America. When Wright Edelman mentioned that she was on her way to see Dr. Martin Luther King Jr. in Atlanta, Kennedy suggested she tell Dr. King to mobilize people to make their presence felt in Washington. She did. Wright Edelman describes this conversation with Dr. King: "I told him that Bobby Kennedy said he ought to bring the poor people to Washington. And as simply as Bobby Kennedy said it, Dr. King instinctively felt that was right and treated me as if I was an emissary of grace here, or something that brought him some light. Out of that, the Poor People's Campaign was born."[2]

One reason Dr. King was so receptive to Kennedy's idea was that he also had recently visited the Mississippi Delta with Wright Edelman and was overwhelmed by the level of poverty he observed. Wright Edelman says that Dr. King was moved to tears while visiting a new Head Start center in Marks, Mississippi, watching a teacher serve each child nothing more than a handful of crackers and a single apple slice for lunch.[3] As Dr. King lay in bed at the motel that night, he told Reverend Ralph Abernathy, "I can't get those children out of my mind."[4]

Dr. King announced the Poor People's Campaign a few months later in November 1967 at a leadership meeting of the Southern Christian Leadership Conference. The idea was for people from across the country to descend on Washington, DC, the following summer to bring attention to systemic poverty in America. Some on Dr. King's team thought the idea was too ambitious and that the aims were too vague. But King insisted that the message of economic security was actually pretty simple: "It's as pure as a man needing an income to support his family."[5] He also called for specific policy goals such as better unemployment insurance, a higher minimum wage, and better education.[6] People would be coming from all over the country, but the Mississippi Delta was central to how King talked about the Poor People's Campaign. On March 31, 1968, he told an audience at the National Cathedral in Washington, DC, "I was in Marks, Mississippi the other day, which is in Quitman County, the poorest county in the United States. And I tell you I saw hundreds of black boys and black girls walking the streets with no shoes to wear."[7]

Dr. King was shot and killed in Memphis, Tennessee, just four days after that speech and just one month before the campaign was supposed to begin. The Southern Christian Leadership Conference went forward with the campaign anyway, and the first wave of people was led by Coretta Scott King. They marched in Washington on Mother's Day, May 12, 1968.[8] A group with about fifteen mule-driven wagons left Marks the next day and began moving east. The wagons were hand painted with messages of economic equity such as "Injustice is a sin in the eyes of God" and "Which is better? Send man to the moon or feed him on earth?"[9] They faced threats of violence across Alabama and Georgia, at which point they boarded trains for Arlington, Virginia. There, they once again hooked up the mules and marched, arriving in DC about one month after the beginning of their journey. They stayed at Resurrection City, a temporary collection of tents and shacks that had been set up on the Mall.

Robert F. Kennedy was assassinated on June 6, shortly before the mule train from Marks arrived and about two weeks before the permits for Resurrection City were set to expire. One participant describes the scene, "The single most poignant moment for me was when the hearse carrying Robert F. Kennedy's body to rest near his brother John Kennedy at Arlington National Cemetery crossed Memorial Bridge and paused for a brief time at the Lincoln Memorial allowing the poor people still in Resurrection City from the Poor People's Campaign to bid farewell while singing the Battle Hymn of the Republic. It was Robert F. Kennedy's last campaign."[10]

Are economic conditions in the Mississippi Delta better today than they were more than fifty years ago when Dr. King acted on Kennedy's idea to bring people from Marks to Washington? The answer is complicated since some of the most obvious symbols of the crushing poverty Kennedy and Dr. King observed are mostly gone. There has been progress, but the gains have not been enough and have not reached everyone.

Gaps and Root Causes

In 1968 there was very little epidemiologic evidence of the connection between economic security and health outcomes. As recently as 2006, literature reviews on the subject showed that the connection was controversial.[11] However, the evidence is now clear that populations with greater income inequality have worse population health outcomes. In a comprehensive literature review published in 2015, the authors concluded that in the minority of studies in which there was no association between income inequality and health outcomes, the method used to measure income inequality was inadequate. In addition, there were flaws in how the researchers treated constructs that mediated the relationship between income inequality and health in statistical models and how they measured health, including relying on less objective health assessments collected over time intervals that were too short for holistic health assessment.[12]

In a highly publicized 2016 study, economist Raj Chetty and colleagues estimated a nearly fifteen-year difference in life expectancy between the wealthiest 1 percent and poorest 1 percent in the United States.[13] A fifteen-year difference is astounding, especially after controlling for a wide variety of potentially confounding factors. Other researchers validated these gaps and used different data sources to suggest that the disparities might be even greater.[14] Inequitable outcomes do not just occur at the extremes, because people with moderate incomes are healthier than people with the lowest incomes but are less healthy than the wealthiest people.[15] People in high-poverty rural areas also face what Arthur Cosby and colleagues call a "rural penalty" for the negative health outcomes they face above and beyond the effect of being poor.[16]

The relationship between economic security and health goes in both directions. A better financial situation not only increases the likelihood of good health but also is more likely for those who are healthy, in part because they are less likely to miss work because of illness.[17] Health and economic development are reciprocal and mutually reinforcing. Economic factors also epitomize the connection between individual choices and population-level dynamics. A skeptic might say that people who want more financial security should get better jobs and that failure to do so reflects an inability or unwillingness to try harder. Yes, people need to make good decisions, but many people in the Delta face barriers to making the decisions that will improve their financial security, and the same decisions do not have the same positive effect for them as they do for others. We need to start by examining the state of the economy to understand the broader factors that shape economic opportunities and then dig deeper into the factors driving these disparities.

An economic equity policy agenda should focus on eliminating three barriers:

(1) **Economic and historical roots.** Do antiracist efforts focus on eliminating barriers to economic stability and prosperity for people who have been historically and are currently marginalized?
(2) **Major industries.** Are enough good jobs being created, and are they equitably accessible to all?
(3) **Gentrification and unequal access to opportunity.** Do people, especially historically marginalized populations, have equal access to services and supports (credit, job training), and are they protected from predatory practices so that they can become financially secure?

The Economy of Mississippi

The vitality of a state's economy is measured in many ways, none of which are favorable for Mississippi. According to *U.S. News and World Report*, the state has the forty-eighth best overall economy. Drilling down on the categories that drive this aggregate measure, Mississippi ranks last in economic growth, patent creation, and poverty rate; forty-ninth in household income, business environment, and growth of the young population; forty-eighth in venture capital and labor force participation; forty-seventh in unemployment; forty-fifth in top company headquarters; and forty-fourth in gross domestic product (GDP) growth and net migration.[18]

The state's economy has grown in recent years, but rankings indicate that this growth has been at a slower pace compared with the rest of the country.[19] In 2018, eleven thousand new jobs were added in Mississippi for an increase of 1 percent. Meanwhile, all four neighboring states experienced greater increases, and Alabama and Tennessee saw growth of at least 2 percent.[20] Similarly, the state's unemployment rate improved to 4.7 percent by 2019, but this was still higher than the national level of 3.9 percent.[21] As with many other issues, conditions in the Delta are even starker than these statewide numbers suggest. Before the COVID-19 pandemic, an average of more than 8.0 percent of people in the labor force across the Delta were unemployed. This number was driven largely by conditions in the three most populated counties (Bolivar at 7.7 percent, Coahoma at 7.8 percent, and Washington at 8.3 percent). However, unemployment was even greater in some other parts of the Delta, such as Sunflower County at 10.7 percent and Humphreys County at 11.1 percent.[22]

Recent data suggest that unemployment in some Delta counties has been improving over time. For example, the reported rate in Issaquena County, one of the smallest counties in the state by land area and population, dropped from 17.3 percent in 2014 to 8.9 percent in 2019. However, this drop may be driven more by changes in the denominator than an increase in employment because people are no longer included in the rate's calculation if they move out of the county or leave the labor force altogether. If everyone who was in Issaquena's labor force five years ago were still counted in the denominator, the current number of jobs would suggest an unemployment rate of more than 23 percent.[23]

One explanation for these statistics is that the effects of economic downturns are strongest, deepest, and longest in the areas that were already struggling.[24] The recession of 2007–9 had a dramatic effect on Mississippi's economy, which lingered for many years even after other parts of the country had mostly recovered. Mississippi's chief economist reported to the legislature in 2017 that the state's economy had grown by only 1.7 percent since 2009 despite the fact that the national GDP had grown by 14.1 percent and the GDP in the rest of the Southeast had grown by 16.9 percent.[25]

Early evidence suggests that we will see similar effects in Mississippi as a result of the health and economic crises caused by the COVID-19 pandemic.[26] For example, the number of unemployment claims increased from 2,026 claims to 36,465 claims (1,700 percent) over a two-week period in March 2020 as the governor ordered a shutdown of nonessential businesses.[27] The statewide unemployment rate increased from 5.1 percent to 16.3 percent between March and April 2020 before improving somewhat to a still very alarming 10.6 percent in May 2020.[28] The state's economy rebounded somewhat in 2021, but not as much as in other places, and indicators suggest that long-term stagnation is on the horizon.[29]

Historical Roots

Study after study shows that race is a factor that shapes who has access to opportunity and who can work within economic conditions to achieve security. We see racial differences in who gets better jobs with good incomes, which in turn affects who can afford nutritious, fresh foods; who lives in comfortable housing in safe neighborhoods; who is able to provide more educational opportunities for their children; and who can access high-quality health care. All these factors reinforce a generational cycle of improving or worsening outcomes. Recent findings make it clear that race predicts these outcomes even when controlling for socioeconomic status.[30] This is an important insight that makes it clear that the issue is not race but structural racism. It is not only that nonwhite populations are less likely to have equitable access to the things that lead to better incomes, but also that they are less likely to see the same improvements in health outcomes even when they do everything that is expected to improve their situations.

For example, research shows that Black people in the United States benefit when their incomes increase but with diminishing returns, such that the same increase in income does not lead to the same improvement in outcomes as for white families.[31] Shervin Assari explains, "Due to structural barriers that Blacks face in their daily lives, the very same resources and assets generate smaller health gain for Blacks compared to Whites. Even in the presence of equal access to resources and assets, such unequal health gain constantly generates a racial health gap between Blacks and Whites in the United States."[32] We saw an important example of this in the previous chapter, as Black families struggle to get mortgages to buy good homes, which in turn makes it difficult to develop assets and pass on wealth to subsequent generations.

These are provocative insights that make it clear that providing equal access to jobs or similar incomes is not enough to eliminate inequities. Charting an economic equity policy agenda in the Mississippi Delta requires going even deeper, including grappling with the historical roots of structural racism.

Displacement and King Cotton

The Mississippi Delta's economy is deeply intertwined with the growing and selling of cotton. It is beyond the scope of this book to provide a full history of the cotton industry in the Delta,[33] but it is important to appreciate five key dynamics. First, as the state's website for promoting business opportunities points out—with no hint of irony or historical awareness—"For hundreds of years, people have come to Mississippi to grow crops, timber, and other commodities."[34] Slavery was not the region's first displacement connected to agriculture. The Choctaw and Chickasaw tribes were forced from the area in the 1830s so that European American settlers could work the land.

Second, the number of settlers who came to the Delta was not initially large, but they recognized the land's profitability and brought huge numbers of slaves to the area. For example, John Clark arrived in 1848 and founded Clarksdale. By 1860 there were nearly 7,000 people in surrounding Coahoma County, 75 percent of whom were slaves.[35] The area grew dramatically after the Civil War, and the population in Coahoma County tripled from 6,606 in 1860 to 18,342 in 1890 and then doubled again over the next few decades. A similar trend happened a bit earlier in Washington County as Greenville became an important trading hub because of its location directly on the Mississippi River. The population went from 8,389 in 1850 to 25,367 in 1880 to 49,216 in 1900.[36] A large share of these new settlers were former slaves who were looking for financial independence and security.

Third, some Black families were able to own land in the early days of Reconstruction, but Jim Crow laws of the late nineteenth and early twentieth centuries pushed most into sharecropping arrangements.[37] Sharecroppers lived on a landlord's farm with the promise that they would earn more for higher yields. But they typically had very little control over key decisions and were usually so far in debt to the landlord and local store that it was very hard to ever catch up. No viable alternatives were available, in part because the wealthy white class deliberately limited educational opportunities for Black youth. Many families effectively had little choice but to accept living in a state of legal servitude.[38]

Fourth, changes in agricultural technology reduced the need for manual labor and thus dramatically altered the Delta's economy. Eli Whitney invented the cotton gin in 1794, but this innovation did not arrive in the Delta until the 1940s. The Hopson Plantation near Clarksdale was the first in the region to get a cotton machine. Records from 1944 indicate that each machine did the work of fifty people, and the cost of producing a bale of cotton dropped from $39.44 by hand to $5.26 by machine.[39] Many people suddenly found themselves without much hope of a livelihood. At the same time, demand for cotton decreased as synthetic fibers became increasingly common. European manufacturers were able to operate with even cheaper labor costs.

Fifth, Black residents began agitating for improved conditions, particularly after World War II gave young Black men the experience of living in freer places. The white power structure responded by organizing as well. The Delta Council was created in 1938 to support farmers, oppose labor unions, and undermine civil rights advocacy. The council's membership was explicitly all white. They deliberately created conditions in which economic independence was virtually impossible for Black residents of the Delta.

The Great Migration

Black people in the Delta in the mid-twentieth century wrestled with a difficult choice: stay in Mississippi despite racist laws, low pay, and the persistent threat of losing work to mechanization or move north in the hope of finding a better job and better living conditions. There were reasons to believe life would be better in northern cities, as the typical wage in Chicago for working in a laundry, factory, or restaurant was $7.50 per hour, three times what someone could earn picking cotton or working as a servant in the Delta.[40]

Some white leaders, concerned about losing their workforce, tried to intimidate Black people into staying. Reverend H. H. Humes, editor of the Delta Council's newspaper at the time, wrote, "Many people who have sold their possessions and have gone into northern industries will be flocking back this way after the war, empty-handed, depressed, and embarrassed." By contrast, those who "conformed" by staying "will be happy, comfortable, and secure against the dark days that follow all wars."[41] Delta Council leaders tried to convince Black families that it was in their best interest to stay because they did not have the experience or judgment to be independent: "Negroes ought to be happy and thankful for the privilege of enjoying the civilization that the White man is giving to them in America. . . . If the negro wants to know the outcome [of resisting], he need only look at the Indians."[42]

Between 1950 and 1960, more than two hundred thousand people in the Mississippi Delta took the risk of moving north.[43] This was part of a broader movement across the South in which more than six million people left in two large waves.[44] The first was between 1910 and 1940 when federal laws that limited immigration from other countries meant that there were not enough workers for all the manufacturing jobs in the North. The second was between 1940 and 1970 in response to Jim Crow and the mechanization of cotton.[45]

These shifts fundamentally changed the country. In 1910, 90 percent of all Black people in the United States lived in the South. This was reduced by half by 1970.⁴⁶ Migrants from the Deep South dramatically changed the racial composition of many northern cities. For example, the proportion of the population in St. Louis that was Black increased from 9 percent in 1930, to 17.9 percent in 1950, to 28.6 percent in 1960, and to 40.9 percent in 1970. Chicago saw a similar explosion, and the Black share of the population increased from 8.2 percent in 1940 to 32.7 percent in 1970. Detroit, Cleveland, Newark, New York, and Washington, DC, experienced similar changes.⁴⁷ Marian Wright Edelman connected racial tension in these cities during the mid-1960s to the legacy of Jim Crow in the Deep South: "I cannot think of a northern ghetto that has enough room for 20,000 people or 15,000 or even 10,000 people. And these people are attached to Mississippi."⁴⁸

This large-scale migration continues to have important implications for the Delta and the rest of the Deep South. The people who remained tended to be less educated and less financially stable than those who left.⁴⁹ The departures—combined with a lack of investment in education and economic opportunity for those who remained—had a spiraling effect. Communities with few skilled workers made it hard to attract and retain companies, which made it hard to have the jobs and amenities that would attract more people to the area, and so on.⁵⁰

Some companies have tried to make it work in the Delta in recent decades, but many have closed and gone elsewhere. Each company's departure has an intense economic and emotional effect on the community it leaves behind. A woman in Cleveland talked about a particular company that had "major factories in this area that employed a lot of people for several years . . . and now, it was a building, but they tore it down, and now it's just nothing. They put porta johns out there. Let people park there. Trucks out there. It's just nothing. It's just rubble and just a hopeless space." A man in Cleveland said that the number of deserted factory buildings gives the area a "hollowed-outness." He went on to say, "If you go to smaller towns you'll see just like whole streets of hollowed-out buildings where people used to have jobs in there and they used to provide services for people."

Reverse Migration

A growing number of Black families have returned south in recent years. Most of the movement is toward Atlanta, Dallas, and Houston,⁵¹ but even southern cities without the comparative advantages of jobs and amenities have seen people coming back. Many say they are driven by a sense of duty to care for relatives and loved ones who did not go north and now need help.

The story of a woman from Bolivar County epitomizes the broad demographic trends of her lifetime, including why people left the Delta and why they are coming back. She was born in 1954 on a plantation where her "family were sharecroppers." As she described, this meant, "The owner of the plantation would rent out certain amounts of land, and my father would cultivate it and get it where he could harvest it in fall. Whatever he made, then the owner got a part of that. So that's the kind of living that we did. Because of that, we didn't have a lot of money and stuff. So my mother made our clothes, and we had big gardens. My father raised cattle and pigs. That's how we got our food." When asked if her parents had hoped to own their own land, she responded, "Financially it was impossible because the amount that we received at the end of the year wasn't enough to sustain the whole family for a full year."

Her father died when she was young, and by 1974 her mother had died of a stroke. At that point she moved to Chicago as a twenty-year-old orphan in pursuit of an education and a career: "I first went to school as a medical assistant and doing that, I was working with a cardiologist that was wanting to do research. So he asked me if I would join his team to do clinical research in hypertension. He sent me to school to get the certificate that I needed to do to be in clinical research, and that's what I've been doing a lot of years." She moved back to the Delta after living in Chicago for more than forty years: "My siblings started to get old because I'm the youngest of the bunch." One of the most pressing needs was that two of her nephew's grandchildren were being given up for adoption, "and so, I chose to take them and raise them. One was five and the other one was seven when I got them." She explains that this was not easy because she "wasn't a young person."

She had been able to make a good life after moving away. Even so, she said, "it wasn't that hard to move back. I mean, of course I missed a lot of the amenities that the city has moving back to a rural area, but it wasn't devastating." She is fortunate that she has been able to continue working remotely for the same hospital in Chicago doing the budgeting and administrative side of setting up clinical trials. Many other people who returned to the Delta described taking deep cuts in pay or being unable to find new jobs altogether.

Major Industries Today

Each of these historical legacies and demographic shifts has shaped who is in the Delta today and what opportunities are available to them. Agriculture is still the largest industry in Mississippi, and there are more than thirty-four thousand individual farm operations across more than ten million acres.[52] More than one-third of the state's land is devoted to farming.[53] Soybean is the most common crop, followed by cotton and corn.[54] Agriculture is particularly dominant in the Delta, where approximately 70 percent of the region's land is occupied by farming. In the Delta counties with the largest populations, an even higher share of the land is farmed than in the rest of the region, with Bolivar at 73 percent, Coahoma at 75 percent, and Washington at 80 percent.[55] Farming in the Delta is also notable for being concentrated in the hands of a relatively small number of operators, many of which are corporations with headquarters in other states.[56] The average farm in Mississippi is about three hundred acres. Farms in the Delta are three to four times larger at 1,108 acres. The average farm in Washington County, the most populated in the Delta, is 1,357 acres.[57]

Agriculture is estimated to form 29 percent of the state's labor force, which is considerably higher than the national level of 11 percent.[58] This includes people who work directly on farms, people who manufacture and sell equipment, lawyers who work on contracts, and researchers who develop more efficient techniques. A large share of agriculture jobs are highly technical and require advanced training. Few people in the Delta are taught these skills, which means that few opportunities exist for advancement beyond labor-intensive, manual work. A Black woman in Cleveland observed that it is hard for people in this position to see a way out. "A lot of young men that may not necessarily finish high school or even those that finish high school and really don't know what they want to do with their lives, they go and work on a farm. . . . A lot of them get comfortable in those positions and they work for the farmers," she said. "And it's a generational thing, too. Their dad worked for them, and their granddad worked for them."

State leaders have pointed to a study by Georgetown University economists to celebrate that Mississippi is the second-best state in the nation for creating high-paying jobs that do not require four-year college degrees. These "good jobs" are defined as paying at least $35,000 to people under the age of thirty-five and at least $45,000 to workers older than forty-five.[59] However, reporters at *Mississippi Today* investigated this claim and found that this statistic is actually a reflection of the fact that the state is second to last in the nation in the percentage of workers who have bachelor's degrees. The more telling statistic is that just 30 percent of workers in the state without four-year degrees have a "good job."[60] Mississippi is tied with Arkansas for last place in the United States. This figure parallels another striking trend that retail cashier is the single most common job in Mississippi. In fact, no state has a higher share of its workforce working as cashiers. Fewer than one-third of the state's cashiers are teenagers, and 86 percent are women.[61] Families are living off cashier incomes.

Mississippi is one of thirty-one states that has not enacted a minimum wage higher than the federal level of $7.25 per hour. This amount equates to less buying power every year that it is not adjusted to keep up with the increased cost of living. Today's minimum wage is only worth $6.07 in 2009 dollars, the last time it was changed.[62] The forty-two thousand cashiers working in Mississippi earn an average annual salary of $19,620, which is just $2 more than people paid minimum wage for working forty hours per week for all fifty-two weeks of the year.[63] It is unrealistic and cruel to expect people to work without any days off—people get sick, their kids and families get sick, and people need time off work.

When asked about their plans after finishing school, many teens in the Delta said that most of the jobs they knew about or saw others doing were at Dollar General or in fast food. Some expressed gratitude that their communities had Walmarts because they employ a relatively large number of people. But not everyone agreed that Walmart's influence on the local economy is positive. For example, a woman in Cleveland said, "Walmart is a very large corporation; they employ a ton of people. And the bigger chains, when they come down to smaller towns, they can sometimes get rid of some of the smaller businesses that would serve as competition." She adds that the implications go even further because "Walmart does not pay that well. . . . A lot of employees have to end up on government benefits just to be able to feed their families." One study suggests she may be right. The opening of a new Walmart was associated with a 2.7 percent reduction in an area's average retail employment. This translates to an average loss of 150 retail positions per county for each new Walmart.[64]

Education and health care are the next two largest sectors of the Delta's economy after retail and represent 11 percent and 10 percent of all jobs, respectively.[65] A woman in Cleveland highlighted the dominance of these industries: "To be honest, in this particular area, if you're not in the education field or in agriculture or health care, it's really kind of hard to find an actual career outside of that." Most of these jobs are concentrated in a small number of organizations such as the local school district or a local health care facility.[66]

Many teens described high ambitions for productive careers in the health care sector. They imagined themselves becoming registered nurses, nurse anesthetists, obstetricians, or orthodontists. They described obtaining these jobs as a path to secure and comfortable lives for themselves and their future families. Many also said that they were not just thinking in financial terms. As a young woman in Cleveland described, "Not all jobs are about the money. Some people like to help people. Some people may be in the feeling of wanting to save a life or make someone comfortable, to help them with whatever they're dealing with or their family members. So when you say a good job or a bad job, I think it just depends on the person or their personal experience." A man in Cleveland put a somewhat different spin on this point: "It seems like a lot of the economy is becoming poor people taking care of other poor people. And health care and education, those two things are probably going to be important because of that."

Gambling

In recent years, local leaders have worked to grow the gambling and tourism industries, hoping the jobs and money they bring will diversify and strengthen the Delta's economy. This has to some extent turned out to be true, with some mixed results and some downsides. Casino gambling was legalized in Mississippi in 1990, although there was already a deep history of gambling that went back to the earliest days of western settlement in the mid-nineteenth century. The 1990 law was modeled somewhat after the approach Iowa and Illinois adopted to restrict gambling to boats so that it would not spread to neighborhoods where people live. This made some sense in Mississippi given that most of the illegal gambling was happening on the Gulf Coast and along the Mississippi River. A key difference to Mississippi's approach was that gambling was not restricted to when the boat was moving. It could occur on a boat that was permanently docked as long as the boat was on navigable waters.[67]

The new gambling law gave voters the option of rejecting the construction of casinos in their communities. DeSoto County, on the very northern tip of the state, was the only place to do so. This made Tunica County, at the northern edge of the Delta, a particularly compelling option for casino developers given its proximity to the relatively large population of DeSoto County as well as Memphis, which was the largest city in the area in a state where gambling was not allowed.[68] Local leaders in Tunica County embraced the casino industry. The president of the board of supervisors at the time said, "It's not the best industry, but it's the only one we can get. . . . We welcome the casino boats and I want the world to know it."[69] Another county leader said, "The people in this community were willing to take the risks involved by inviting the industry into their midst because they were that desperate for the potential economic development."[70] Similarly, the mayor of the city of Tunica said, "We needed it. The county didn't have anything and we had a 30% unemployment rate."[71]

There were two initial problems with building casinos in Tunica County. First, there were only two paved roads off the main state highway from Memphis, and second, the largest city in the county was not directly on the water as required by the state law. The first casino was built approximately six miles from town in an area called Mhoon Landing, named after a nineteenth-century settler. The floating casino, Splash, was on a barge that was permanently moored in a slip that had been dug out to house the casino. It was an early success, and eighty thousand people paid the ten-dollar cover charge to board the "boat" in the first month.

Splash did not last very long, but it did set a precedent: state officials would use a very loose definition of the term *navigable waters* and allow gambling to happen in facilities that barely resembled boats. Pretty soon the casinos that would be built were large hotel and entertainment facilities that were entirely on land and connected to the river by only thin pipes.[72] Policymakers tried to support the growth of the state's casino industry by establishing some of the most relaxed regulations in the country. Casinos were only required to pay $5,000 every other year to renew their licenses, which is dramatically less than the $100,000 casinos in Louisiana pay annually. Mississippi is one of the few states besides Nevada that does not restrict the number of casino licenses to control their locations and concentration. Similarly, Mississippi casinos are allowed to devote as much floor space as they want to gaming and are not required to place a limit on the size of bets.[73]

The effect on Tunica County's local economy was immediate and dramatic. Just two years after gambling was legalized in Mississippi, there was more casino square footage than had been constructed in sixteen years in Atlantic City. By 1997 it was a $1.9 billion industry. After ten years, Tunica passed Reno and Tahoe to become the third-largest casino tourist destination in the United States behind Las Vegas and Atlantic City.[74] Casinos are required to return 12 percent of their revenue in taxes, with 8 percent to the state, 2 percent to the county, and 2 percent to the city. The region also benefited from all the industries that grew around the casinos such as restaurants and hotels. Whereas not a single dollar was made on lodging in 1990 in Tunica, by 1999 $820 million in revenue was made from hotels. The county experienced a 344 percent growth in construction employment during this time and a nearly 5,000 percent growth in service employment.[75] The county's unemployment rate dropped from 17.2 percent in 1991 to 5.6 percent in 1999.[76]

Greenville is the other major gambling hub in the Delta, but its experience was not quite as dramatic given its history as an important port city when the Mississippi River was the main source of economic activity. It also benefited from the increased tax revenue coming to the city and Washington County in the years after the first casinos were built. According to supporters, evidence shows that the casinos continue to have positive effects on the economies of these communities. The gaming industry promotes the fact that thirty-seven thousand people work as chefs, security guards, accountants, caterers, florists, and meeting planners as well as in other roles in the state's twenty-nine casinos.[77] Tunica County was able to use the influx of tax dollars to build a new school, arena, fitness center, library, fire station, police station, post office, community center, and jail.[78] Even so, many signs show that the benefits have not been evenly distributed, and they have diminished over time.[79] One of the groups that benefited the most was the farmers who sold their land to make way for the casinos. Soybean and cotton prices had dropped so low that the land was worth very little in 1990. But as the first casinos were being built in Tunica County, the property value of surrounding land skyrocketed. For example, in 1990 Shea Leatherman's 150 acres of Delta farmland was worth less than $1 million, and in 1993 he sold the land to Sam's Town Casino and Gambling Hall for $25 million.[80]

Yes, the casinos brought new jobs to the area, but the high-paying jobs went to white outsiders rather than to Black residents living nearby. More than half the jobs are low paying, and even for these jobs, a large share of the workers commute in from Memphis or somewhere else. The people who work in these jobs say they are just as anxious about their financial stability as they were before starting work in the casino.[81] Casinos are not a stable source of economic security for their workers because the industry has a countercyclical relationship with the broader economy. People cut back on gambling during a recession, which means that workers are let go at a time when it is hardest to find a new job.[82] The dramatic increase in legalized gambling elsewhere makes it that much harder for all the existing casinos to maintain market share. Gamblers can now go to West Memphis, Tennessee, or Hot Springs, Arkansas, instead of coming to Tunica.[83]

The good news from the gaming industry's perspective is that revenue at the Tunica casinos stabilized after the 2008 recession and plateaued at around $600 million.[84] The bad news is that three casinos closed in the years between this recession and the COVID-19 pandemic, including the largest casino in 2014, which brought a loss of 1,300 jobs. No state has lost more casino jobs since 2012 than Mississippi.[85] Casinos shut their doors throughout much of 2020 because of COVID-19, which led to the lowest gaming revenue for the casino industry since 2003.[86] The long-term effects are likely to reverberate for many years.

Residents of the Delta are also concerned about the side effects that come with gambling. Evidence suggests that gambling is safe for many people but that problem gambling is associated with a host of consequences.[87] More research is needed on the mechanisms at play, but problems include increased risk of obesity, chronic medical conditions, lower overall quality of life, costly medical care, and perpetuating and being a victim of intimate partner violence.[88] It is not clear what pushes someone over the edge to problem gambling, but many aspects of the gambling environment are not healthy for people to experience on a regular basis. Workers and players spend many hours per day in smoke-filled rooms because public smoking is allowed.[89] Most Mississippi casinos give out free alcoholic beverages to players and process tax refund checks so that people can immediately use this money to gamble. A pastor in Clarksdale said he is worried that people in his congregation are spending their days driving up to Tunica and playing away the little savings and income they have.

The move to legalize gambling and promote the casino industry in Mississippi thirty years ago has had some positive effects, but these benefits are not evenly distributed and are getting smaller over time. This is not a sustainable approach to strengthening the Delta's economy going forward.

The Mississippi Lottery

Given the history of gambling in Mississippi, it is surprising and alarming that the state decided to create a lottery in 2018. Until then, it was one of only six states without a lottery. Leaders on both sides of the political aisle opposed it for moral reasons and out of concern that it would disproportionately harm families with lower incomes. The politics surrounding a lottery changed because of an infrastructure crisis in the state. Mississippi closed more than five hundred bridges following a report that said they were unstable and dangerous. A lottery was seen as a way to help the state come up with the hundreds of millions of dollars that would be needed on short notice to repair these bridges. Unfortunately, three layers of this problem exemplify the geographic and structural racism of economic inequities in the Mississippi Delta.

First, ten of the fifteen counties with the most bridge closures per capita were in majority-Black counties.[90] The state closed thirty-one bridges in Washington County, more than the number closed in Hinds and Rankin Counties combined, even though its population is a fraction of the hundreds of thousands of people who live in the latter two counties, which encompass the Jackson metro area. Sunflower and Bolivar Counties were also among the top five counties with the most closures at twenty-two and twenty, respectively. These closures were the result of years of inadequate maintenance and represented major inconveniences in areas in which many people already struggled with transportation.

Second, the distribution of funding did not match the needs, at least in terms of the number of bridges closed in an area. The state appropriated $250 million in August 2018 to repair 163 of the closed roads. Neither of the two counties that received the most money was in the Delta or had populations of Black residents at least as great as the state average of about one-third. By contrast, Washington County received $4 million for its thirty-one bridges.[91] It is hard to truly compare these situations without knowing the severity of the problems in each individual case, but this works out to $129,000 per bridge in Washington County compared with more than $4 million per bridge in Forrest and Jackson Counties and a little more than half as much spent per capita.

Third, the solution of creating a lottery to pay for these repairs is likely to disproportionately hurt the Delta. National evidence is clear that revenue from state lotteries comes predominantly from lower-income Black communities and is then redistributed to everyone.[92] Lotteries are effectively a regressive tax on the poor because they spend more on them than people with higher incomes, both as a share of their income and in terms of total dollar amounts.[93] In one study, it was estimated that 54 percent of lottery sales in the United States comes from 5 percent of players and that the amount spent is more than on sports tickets, books, video games, movies, and music combined. It is also money that otherwise would have gone to routine expenses such as clothes, transportation, and food.[94] By contrast, raising additional money through an income tax or property tax would have more evenly distributed the burden to homeowners and people with higher incomes, who in Mississippi are more likely to be white.[95]

Lottery supporters point to the large amounts of money that have been raised and earmarked for public goods. Mississippi's law specifies that the first $80 million must be spent on roads and that anything beyond that amount should go toward education.[96] This sounds good, but studies show that what this has meant elsewhere is that money in the state budget that would have gone to roads and education is shifted to other purposes and that these issues receive no more money than they did before. Funding for roads and education is now even more vulnerable because it is tied to the success of the lottery.[97]

Tourism

Tourism is an intriguing growth industry for the Mississippi Delta because it injects outside money into the local economy. But this is only possible if a community has a niche it can use to brand and market itself so that tourists come to visit or at least stop on their way to larger tourist destinations such as New Orleans and Memphis. Some communities celebrate famous people who lived there. Leland—a city of about 4,500 just outside Greenville—has a small museum called the Birthplace of Kermit the Frog at the boyhood home of Jim Henson.[98] Others honor important places in the civil rights movement. The main draw in Sumner—a small town of 400—is the restored courthouse where the trial of Emmett Till's murderers took place.[99] The Emmitt Till Interpretive Center gives individual tours and provides maps so people can visit the key sites connected to Till's kidnapping and murder. Both are worth visiting but on their own are not enough to revive a town's economy. The communities that are best positioned to entice visitors are those that offer multiple experiences and places to eat, drink, and sleep. This is a chicken-and-egg problem because it is hard to attract tourists without having events, restaurants, and hotels, but it is hard to operate any of these businesses without enough tourists.

The niche that many communities around the Delta have decided to market is their connection to the history of blues music. Statewide efforts to attract visitors to explore blues history began in the mid-1990s with the installment of 310 markers that commemorate sites where important people lived or noteworthy events took place. More than two-thirds of these initial markers were in the Delta.[100] This includes the birthplace of B. B. King in Berclair, the birthplace of Muddy Waters in Rolling Fork, and the gravesite of Robert Johnson in Greenwood.[101] One of the most prominent recent developments in blues tourism was the 2011 opening of the GRAMMY Museum in Cleveland.

No community has invested as deeply in blues tourism as Clarksdale, which was named in 2018 by Fodor's Travel as one of the best music cities in the country other than Nashville.[102] Legend has it that Robert Johnson sold his soul to the devil in Clarksdale at the crossroads of Highway 49 and Highway 61 in exchange for guitar-playing skills. Celebrated musicians from Ike Turner to Sam Cooke were born there.[103] Hopson Plantation just south of town played a similar role as Dockery Farms in Cleveland, and the WROX radio station broadcast from Clarksdale helped spread the blues beyond the Delta.[104] The legacy has extended to contemporary music, as rapper and producer Rick Ross was born there and local guitarist Christone "Kingfish" Ingram was nominated for a Grammy Award in 2019 as a twenty-year-old.

Roger Stolle has played an important role in marketing Clarksdale blues history by opening a record store, co-founding multiple music festivals, and working with local business owners to guarantee live music is happening somewhere in the city 365 nights out of the year.

Local leaders are looking for ways to expand the tourism industry in Clarksdale, which already supports approximately 950 jobs across the county.[105] An additional $7 million per year would come to the city if all visitors stayed the night rather than passing through on their way to Memphis, for example. Similarly, it is estimated that people who are already staying would bring in $14 million more if they stayed one extra night.[106] Convincing just 5 percent more of the people gambling in Tunica to come to Clarksdale—about an hour away on Highway 61—would bring in an additional forty thousand visitors.[107] Bubba O'Keefe, executive director of the county's tourism commission and the owner of much of downtown, believes that visitors are drawn to Clarksdale by the music history but will stay longer and spend more money if a deeper experience is available: "We want tourists to be holistically invested, not financially. We're not looking for people to give to us. We're looking for people to become a part of us. . . . [Clarksdale] is more than an attraction. We are a Sesame Street. We have a cast of characters. We want visitors to get to know those characters who are unique to Clarksdale."[108]

Many of the local leaders and business owners in town agree with the philosophy and explicitly try to foster a sense of connection with tourists. Before his death in 2021, former Clarksdale mayor Bill Luckett would often make the rounds at live music venue Ground Zero, greeting visitors. Luckett was co-owner of the club along with actor Morgan Freeman, who is from the area. In 2011 Luckett was the state's Democratic nominee for governor of Mississippi. People who stay at the Riverside Hotel, a small house that has been added onto over the years, are likely to receive a hug from Zee Ratliff, whose family has been operating the hotel since 1944. For many years, Riverside was the only racially integrated hotel in the area, which means that many of the most important Black musicians, such as Duke Ellington, Muddy Waters, and Sam Cooke, stayed there when they were in town. Bessie Smith died in one of the rooms in 1937 after a car accident on Highway 61.[109]

Visitors can stay at the Clark House, a bed and breakfast on the north side of downtown, in the beautiful Victorian home that once belonged to John Clark, the city's founder.[110] The manager, who goes by the name "Chilly Billy" Howell, also owns Delta Bohemian Tours, for which he drives visitors around in a Jeep Wrangler to see the cultural and historical sites in Clarksdale and Coahoma County. His company's website explains this philosophy of immersing visitors in the city's culture and people: "Clarksdale native and Delta Bohemian Tours docent Chilly Billy Howell provides premium, private, personal, always serendipitous, area tours right here in the birthplace of the Blues. His tours are relational, authentic, organic and rife with opportunity to meet local 'characters,' while garnering a fuller awareness and understanding of the land, its people and the terroir informing the blues."[111]

Visitors can also stay at the new Travelers Hotel. Now a bare-bones boutique hotel, the property sat vacant for many years following its original use in the 1920s as a place for railroad workers to stay overnight. The hotel's mission is to bring creative people to Clarksdale by establishing a cooperative in which artists, musicians, writers, and others are given a free place to stay in exchange for working a certain number of hours each week.[112]

It is too early to know what the long-term effects of the COVID-19 pandemic on the Delta's tourism industry will be, but the early signs are devastating. A large share of the profits for many of Clarksdale's businesses are derived from people coming for a handful of festivals. Many of these were canceled in 2020, which made it hard for these businesses to stay open, which will in turn make it hard to attract visitors back. Stolle says life in Clarksdale during the pandemic reminded him of what it was like when he first arrived: "It's just crazy to see nobody walking around. It reminds me frankly of 18 years ago when I opened up; before we really kick started the blues fueled downtown revitalization of Clarksdale. On a random weekday, you could kind of go downtown and it would be sort of like a ghost town. And temporarily that's what it feels like right now."[113] He and other leaders worked to keep live music going 365 nights a year, broadcasting

Clarksdale's musicians from their homes and other locations around town, but it is unclear when the tourists will be back in large numbers.[114]

Even before the pandemic, some leaders were concerned that the economic benefits that have come to Clarksdale through tourism are not being evenly distributed across the Delta because people who visit Clarksdale are not going to many of the surrounding cities. Leaders in Clarksdale are not antagonistic toward other communities or overly competitive because they recognize that they all benefit from more visitors to the region: "If tourists are headed from Clarksdale toward New Orleans, [Bubba] O'Keefe wants them to know about the GRAMMY Museum® Mississippi in Cleveland or the B.B. King Museum in Indianola. 'If we can be a good neighbor in their travel north or south, we want to be there,' he says. 'And we want our brother and sister towns in the Delta to know that we're sending them their way.'"[115] The bigger issue is that smaller surrounding communities such as Mound Bayou, Rosedale, and Tutwiler do not have the infrastructures to generate a critical mass that would drive cultural tourism, and developing this infrastructure is difficult without this critical mass of visitors.[116]

Gentrification and Inequitable Access to Opportunity

Another concern is that the cultural opportunities that attract tourists are not accessible to everyone in Clarksdale. Most residents cannot afford to eat at places like the Yazoo Pass or hear music at Ground Zero. Similarly, the bulk of the economic benefits of tourism primarily go to a relatively small number of people, most of whom are white. This dynamic is not the classic definition of gentrification because people and businesses are not being displaced by this economic development. More than two-thirds of the buildings downtown are still vacant, and rent remains relatively low. As a result, property values are unlikely to be driven up dramatically in ways that push out current occupants.[117] However, this has a similar effect as gentrification because Clarksdale is being remade in ways that reflect the values and tastes of one population at the expense of another.[118]

The dynamic is complicated by the intense history of racial segregation in Clarksdale. There was once a thriving downtown on the Black side of the train tracks, and in 1947, there were more than 150 businesses in this part of town, which was commonly referred to as "the New World." Today, fewer than a dozen account for 3 percent of the total occupied retail and office space in Clarksdale. By contrast, the north side of the tracks has 80 businesses that account for 69 percent of occupied commercial space. The rest is along DeSoto Avenue, such as the Save-a-Lot and Fred's Pharmacy.[119]

Development on the white side of the tracks did not push out businesses from the Black side. The biggest driver of this shift was the opening of the Walmart south of both sides of downtown in 1971.[120] A local business owner explained that the goal now is not necessarily to make sure both sides of downtown are thriving, which is unrealistic as approximately 80 percent of floor space in the New World is currently vacant.[121] Instead, the goal is to make sure that everyone is benefiting from the economic development that is happening. "I think there are a lot of Blacks who feel like downtown is not theirs, yet we have downtown businesses, Grandma's House of Pancakes, the barbershop over here," the business owner said. "There are Black and white businesses downtown now that years ago you wouldn't have a Black business over here, you would have them over there, but now everything is here."

Concerns over gentrification tap into the deep legacy of exploitation in the Delta, including the appropriation of music, which was epitomized by Elvis Presley becoming an international superstar by playing a version of the music developed by Black musicians in the Delta. Stephen A. King, a former professor at Delta State University, explains, "The African-American legacy of Blues music has been captured mainly by the White community, and today's promotion of blues bears little reflection on the torment the Black community suffered—and in many ways still suffers—in regards to depravations inflicted upon them generations ago."[122]

Nothing epitomizes this tension quite like the Shack Up Inn, which a writer for *Huffington Post* said may be "the coolest hotel in America."[123] For eighty-five dollars a night you can stay in a shotgun shack that has been relocated to a plot of land next to the same Hopson Plantation that was the first place in the state to have a cotton gin. The shacks have been minimally updated to include air-conditioning, heat, indoor plumbing, Wi-Fi, and electricity for a microwave and coffee machine but nothing else. These are not replicas but rather the actual homes that sharecroppers once lived in. Visitors can also choose to stay in a former grain silo.[124]

Many locals find it insulting that white tourists celebrate the opportunity to spend a night experiencing the poverty and living conditions their parents and grandparents suffered through. A reporter compared it to setting up a hotel at Auschwitz. The owner, a white local in his sixties, was quoted in the *Pittsburgh Post-Gazette*: "We've been criticized [for] taking advantage of the plight of the black man, but we've also had blacks say thank you."[125] He and other supporters say that staying in these shacks is a way to make sure history is passed on and not forgotten.

The issues in Greenville are a little different because the tourism is centered on casinos instead of the blues, but a similar Black-white gentrification dynamic exists. Local leaders are working to revive downtown, which has struggled to compete with Walmart and the strip malls south of town. But Black residents worry that they will be left out of this economic development. "Nelson Street used to be a hub in the Black community. . . . [Revitalizing downtown] kind of disturbs me because hey, you didn't include Nelson Street, which used to be the downtown for us," one resident said. "Why can't we revitalize Nelson Street also? But we don't think like that and that's what we've got to do. If you revitalize Nelson Street you cut out all the crime because you would have business down there like it used to be."

Cleveland struggles with the same dynamics of gentrification almost to a more intense degree given its relative prosperity. Some feel the GRAMMY Museum has not yet lived up to its promise of community building. One leader said it has been good for Cleveland's economy, but they have not yet figured out how to spread this to the surrounding communities such as Shelby, Shaw, and Mound Bayou. Another resident of Cleveland said, "I think that the GRAMMY Museum is an opportunity if it is used to be an opportunity. It's an opportunity to bring the community together around music. And I've taken a tour of the museum. It's beautiful inside. It focuses on talent that has come from Mississippi, and it's interactive and kids can go in and take advantage. But I think that it's underutilized. I think that it's catered to a certain group, a demographic of people and it's totally isolating another group of people that can benefit from it as well."

Black-Owned Businesses

One way to reverse the negative effects of gentrification is for leaders to explicitly promote Black-owned businesses. Black entrepreneurs face many barriers to starting and operating successful businesses. They often are not able to tap into resources in family or professional networks, and they are likely to have faced disadvantages, which makes it harder to raise the capital needed to get started. In 2016, Stanford University researchers found that 1 percent of Black business owners received bank loans during the first years of their business compared with 7 percent of white business owners. Similarly, 30 percent of white business owners can use business credit cards during their first year, whereas only 15 percent of Black business owners have access to this credit.[126]

As a local leader in Greenville described,

> It's hard for a Black man to get a small business loan to open up a business. It's hard. You have to go through so much red tape. You've got to put your children up, dog, and everything else that you got in order to try to get a small business loan. But then you see old Joe, he got two boats and three trucks in his yard without working on a side job. Now how in the world can he afford all that, and you can't even afford but one vehicle and it's broke down? So that means one thing, that the banks, the financial institution is more lenient towards white than they are towards Black.

The struggle that many Black people have faced in trying to start their own businesses has led to complicated feelings toward people of other nonwhite populations who have businesses. Chinese immigrants have been in the Delta since the 1870s and have largely been associated with small family-run grocery stores in Black neighborhoods. These immigrants were in a tough position because, while not on equal footing with white residents, they did not receive the same degree of animosity as Black residents.[127] Some of the stores in these communities are today run by immigrants from India and Pakistan. A Black woman in Cleveland said she felt that "they had come here to America and have a great life and get monies to establish businesses like this, whereas a person that's American who wants the American way, we can't get that same kind of loan that they can come into the country for. And a lot of times that's why they come. That's why America has become this great melting pot with various ethnicities. Because there are opportunities here. But who are they here for? And at what cost?"

Community leaders such as the HOPE Credit Union are trying to help the Delta's Black residents overcome barriers to starting their own businesses. Similarly, Higher Purpose Co. is a nonprofit organization whose mission is to "build community wealth with Black residents who have faced generations of poverty." Tim Lampkin, CEO, says, "Our goal is to help people who have been overlooked and underserved and provide them with the same resources and treatment as anyone else. . . . It's about leveraging the spirit of ownership to create generational wealth." The theory of change at Higher Purpose Co. is based on asset building, narrative change, and advocacy primarily with the goal of helping Mississippi's Black population experience land ownership, home ownership, and business ownership. Technical assistance, education, and financial support have been provided to more than seven hundred residents, including more than fifty Black entrepreneurs, which has led to the creation or expansion of fifteen businesses.[128]

Abe and Adrienne Hudson, a legislator in the state house of representatives and a leader in education policy whose nonprofit policy organization RISE is discussed in the next chapter, rent an office in downtown Cleveland. The office provides space for people who are trying to get businesses started and to build clientele to secure more funding. They describe this as an incubator for small businesses and have helped entrepreneurs offering everything from karate classes to photography.

Some see farming as a promising business opportunity for young Black people in Mississippi. A woman in Cleveland who has made this her career explained, "We are not an area where a tech company is going to come and lay roots. We're just not. Agriculture in this area is very, very, very profitable." She went on to explain that "ag is not a business for the dumbfounded. What those young men get in that time that they work for those big farmers, what our young men don't do that I hope to show them and teach them is, get your training, learn the business, but then step out of someone else's business and create your own. Because it is a profitable business. It is a respectable business. It is a business of very educated people. . . . I think that's the way for our people in this area." She adds that it has been incredibly empowering to think back on the generations of her ancestors who worked fields for someone else and to know that she is now making it in farming as her own boss.

Job Training

Some business leaders disagree that industries such as tech would not come to Mississippi. They argue that the key to moving out of the bottom of state rankings is "attracting industries that pay higher wages, getting people who are in poverty into the workforce, and stopping the loss of people who are leaving the state." This requires attracting "businesses that make products with big profit margins that then sell those products to people outside Mississippi. . . . Today, most of those high margin businesses sell tech products or services. And the trick to having those businesses is to have a thick labor market of college-educated or skilled people clustered together."[129]

The best way to create such an environment is deep investment in the local education system, which as we will see in the next chapter faces many obstacles in the Delta. Even so, it is important to find ways to train people who want to change careers without earning another degree and people who never completed school but want to learn employable skills. A woman in Cleveland explained how having a degree is not enough or the right path for everyone: "Yes, people can get degrees, but you're not seeing the employment and the need pertaining to degreed positions. It's going . . . back to skills and training whether you're a barber, a beautician, welding, carpentry. It's going . . . back to skills and training. Forklift driving, that's for males and females. We've got to find a way to teach our youth skills and trade."

The main resources for job training and employment in Mississippi are the Workforce Investment Network (WIN) Job Centers located around the state. Nine WIN Job Centers are in or near the Delta, including in the largest cities of Clarksdale, Cleveland, Greenwood, Greenville, and Indianola.[130] These centers are designed as hubs for job application and recruitment and where people file for unemployment benefits and receive training for new jobs. According to the website, several WIN centers also provide on-the-job training, which helps offset training costs.

The state has also gone in an intriguing direction by trying to provide job training through the community college system. This includes the Workforce Development Center at Coahoma Community College in Clarksdale. Similarly, the mission of the Center for Community and Economic Development at Delta State University in Cleveland is "to empower families in the Mississippi Delta who have continually suffered generational oppression for lack of knowledge" by increasing "awareness of postsecondary educational opportunities available to low-income and economically-disadvantaged adults, 19 and older, who desire to pursue a postsecondary education and to assist with postsecondary institution enrollment."[131] The state increased support for these programs in 2016 with the creation of the Mississippi Works Training Fund. This provides $50 million over ten years to "enhance training opportunities at the state's 15 community colleges." Services have been provided through this program to more than one thousand people across the Delta.[132]

However, little evidence suggests these job training programs are likely to have a broad, long-term effect. In a 2019 report, the White House Council of Economic Advisors examined the dozens of government training programs created by the federal government and found that participants do not seem to have significant gains in employment and wages, in part because of fundamental factors such as whether enough jobs are available in their areas.¹³³ Similarly, in a report from Brookings, authors found that the promised benefits of technology-focused government job training programs often go unrealized because "both students and the government have radically underestimated how long it takes the average person to transition into a high-skill career."¹³⁴ People also need guidance on how to access information and navigate opportunities.

It has been estimated that only 10 percent of the $50 million that has been appropriated for job training in Mississippi has actually been used.¹³⁵ People who tried to access services complained about their experiences. As a woman in Cleveland explained, "This building has no windows. And when you walk in, it is so dark. It is so drab. And then on top of that, the people make you feel dark and drab." Another person agreed with this description: "When you walk into this building, it's like you're walking in a police station or something. . . . It's like when you walk in and you look around, it's like you don't walk out feeling hopeful." A third person said, "It sucks, I'm sorry. This is just such a waste of space and funding in my personal opinion."

A woman in Cleveland had a slightly more nuanced take and said she knew someone who worked at the WIN Jobs Center and that this contact helped her have a good experience: "I had a child who went through WIN Job Center who got her first nursing degree; they paid for it. And once again, they have various programs, but it's all in who you know, who can tell you what's there to benefit you." Others elaborated on this and said that what many people really need is more training on soft skills such as how to network and how to interact in a professional setting. Unfortunately, not everyone has these connections, and very few opportunities allow people to learn these skills.

Bank Deserts

Even landing a job with a good income is not enough to ensure financial security for residents of the Mississippi Delta, in part because it is harder for them to save their money. More than 12 percent of Mississippians do not have bank accounts, and one-fourth are reported to be "under-banked," meaning they have limited access to banking services.¹³⁶ This can be as simple as not living close—or close enough to walk if your household does not have enough vehicles—to an ATM other than those at gas stations, which charge fees of around five dollars per transaction.¹³⁷

This gap in banking is driven in part by national economic forces, as thousands of branches closed across the country after the 2007–9 recession.[138] Many parts of the Delta do not look like bank deserts because a lot of banks exist. As one woman described, "Here in Cleveland we have a bank on every corner." She talked about one near her: "This is one of the, probably the newest banks here in Cleveland, and within 500 feet of this bank there's another bank, there's Cleveland State. Then around the corner there is a smaller Regions, and then on the other side of the lot, the same lot as Save A Lot, there's another Regions bank."

Some questioned how this oasis of banks could sit in the midst of a bank desert: "I see all these disparities that we have in our community, but we have a bank popping up probably every two to three years. And that concerns me because, okay, that means money's coming from somewhere. So where's it coming from? And is it really helping the communities where these banks are?" Others answered their own questions and believe that these banks are for the white farmers who still have most of the money in their communities rather than for working-class Black families. As one person put it, "There is money in Greenville, but it's only being distributed to a certain group of people."

Organizations are trying to help people overcome these barriers. HOPE Credit Union, highlighted in the previous chapter, is focused on increasing access to banking services in the Delta. A woman in Cleveland mentioned the role that HOPE is playing in Bolivar County and surrounding areas: "HOPE Credit Union is going into these small Delta towns. So Shaw has one, Drew has one, and Moorehead. And they're really helping the community. I mean, they have an ATM that I walk to. When a lot of businesses are leaving these small Delta towns, it's kind of cool to see there's purposely a financial institution coming to serve this small town."

Two Mississippi natives are trying to increase financial literacy and access to banking services for people who cannot reach a bank or an ATM. Sheena Allen and Tim Lampkin co-founded CapWay, an online banking app available to people anywhere. CapWay is FDIC insured and offers checking accounts, debit cards, and financial education.[139] There is no overdraft fee, no fee for cashing a check, and no minimum balance penalty.[140] Lampkin and Allen created CapWay to financially support underserved Americans, help them maximize the resources they do have, and promote financial health. Lampkin states that "one of the biggest problems is distrust in financial institutions. There is resentment from years of intentional discrimination." He goes on to explain that "there is a lack of transparency regarding banking fees and how services work. Banks need to train their employees on how to explain things like APR and overdraft fees."[141]

PAYDAY LENDING

One of the challenges of living in a bank desert is that people who are struggling to make ends meet are particularly vulnerable to being targeted for predatory lending by businesses whose financial model depends on desperate people making unwise borrowing decisions. As a woman in Cleveland described, "Now, just like there are banks popping up, there are check-cashing places popping up, too. So these may be for the more affluent that can deposit their money, whereas the check-cashing places are popping up for those that that's their last resort. And then they're being pulled into that cycle of, you know where that goes." Payday lending allows people to leverage their forthcoming paychecks for quick cash that can be used to pay a bill, buy groceries, cover medical expenses, or fulfill any other need. National research shows that the average payday borrower is in debt for five months to borrow $375. During that time, they pay an additional $520 in fees, which is more than the amount borrowed. Approximately 75 percent of borrowers take out at least eleven loans per year, and 70 percent of all borrowers use payday loans to cover recurring expenses such as rent.[142] These are not onetime emergency loans but instead reflect a reality that sacrificing long-term stability is the price many living in poverty feel they need to pay to survive the short term. Lenders prey on people's desperation and exacerbate a cycle that is very difficult to escape.

Mississippi has more payday lenders per capita than any other state and more relaxed regulations than some of its neighbors.[143] The maximum amount that someone in Mississippi is allowed to borrow is $500. This amount includes the initial fee, which means that the actual amount borrowed is closer to $400.[144] The amount of the fee depends on a variety of factors, but as an example, payday lenders in Clarksdale advertise an annual percentage rate of 521.43 percent on loans up to $200.[145] By contrast, Louisiana caps the borrowed amount at $350, and the annual interest rate is 36 percent.[146]

Local leaders are frustrated by the effect these predatory companies have in their communities. As a person in Cleveland described, "These places are targeted towards people in poverty. . . . These places are only successful if people patronize them. So that's our job, too, as community practitioners, to educate our community on, yes, true enough, these may be your only options, but at the same time it's an opportunity for you to see that these people are not here for your betterment. Because they can only get rich and keep planning stores if we keep putting our money into them." Another community leader in Cleveland added that "it's important to remember that none of this money is coming back to these communities."

Auditing

One of the key takeaways of this chapter might sound obvious but is important to highlight: poverty is a risk factor for deeper poverty. Poverty makes it much harder to emerge from financial struggles. Many of the exacerbating effects are felt disproportionately by minority racial and ethnic groups, such as lack of access to banking services and vulnerability to payday lending. Humphreys County, on the southeastern edge of the Delta, is per capita the most audited county by the Internal Revenue Service (IRS) in the United States, despite being one of the poorest. The audit rate is estimated to be 51 percent higher than Loudon County, Virginia, despite a difference in median income of more than $100,000.[147] Humphreys County is not an outlier, as most of the places with the highest audit rates are rural counties with large nonwhite populations. Poor white counties in eastern Kentucky are also heavily audited, but a larger share consists predominantly of counties in the Deep South with large Black populations, parts of South Texas with large Hispanic populations, and reservations in South Dakota where Native Americans live.

The IRS states that in these places, more than half the county's taxpayers claim the Earned Income Tax Credit (EITC). The EITC helps low- and moderate-income families reduce the federal taxes they owe and can increase their federal tax refunds.[148] The IRS claims audits are not targeted to any particular region or race.[149] Nonetheless, people who claim the EITC are twice as likely to be audited as people with incomes of $400,000.[150] This epitomizes structural racism, as applying a federal rule equally affects people of color very differently from those in other populations.

Being audited imposes a particularly intense burden for the low-income families that depend on the EITC. The IRS holds the tax credit until an audit is complete, which often takes more than a year.[151] Low-income households have greater difficulty documenting income and expenses because they are more likely to work for employers who pay cash or do not keep complete records or they work multiple, hourly wage jobs. They also are more likely to rent from landlords who only accept cash and do not sign leases.[152] Further, tax preparation services take advantage of their vulnerability. For example, the head of a Memphis company called Mo' Money was sentenced to five years in prison for falsifying more than five hundred returns and an estimated $3.5 million in refunds. Though this problem is federal policy, not state, the IRS's audit practice compounds the financial problems that flow from other governmental actions that are rooted in structural racism.

Ripples of Hope

Each of these examples highlights the structural barriers people in the Delta face in trying to build financial security. It is harder to get good jobs, and even if they do, nonwhite residents experience diminishing returns. Having the same income is not enough to lead to long-term improvements in outcomes because they can't build and transfer wealth to subsequent generations. These gaps and root causes make clear that the depth of inequality in the Delta is not accidental, nor is it a matter of poor people refusing to work or not trying hard enough to better their situations. It is the result of decisions made by policy and business leaders over centuries that have systematically privileged some at the expense of others. However, these conditions are not inevitable and can be changed through leadership and policy.

"Keep Cleveland Boring"

The research on economic development shows that communities do best when they are able to attract and retain a group of creative people. This can include artists and musicians, but the importance of a "creative class" extends beyond the arts to people who are creative problem-solvers, who develop new solutions for the issues a community is facing and have the energy to see them through.[153] Roger Stolle and the many people who are reimagining Clarksdale's future exemplify the power of a creative class and create a ripple of hope that progress is not just on the horizon but is happening.

A group of young people is playing a similar role in Cleveland. The economy is already comparatively strong there, largely because Delta State University (DSU) attracts faculty, staff, and students from around the state and from across the country. DSU regularly hosts cultural and sporting events that draw people to the area. The GRAMMY Museum is on DSU's campus and is just a few blocks from a thriving downtown with a walking trail, a new luxury hotel, a high-end clothing store, and multiple restaurants. Unlike in most Delta towns, storefronts do not stay empty for long. This neighborhood also has the unique distinction of being the first place that Eric and Donald Trump Jr. announced their family business would build a hotel after their father won the White House.[154]

One of the challenges community leaders face—along with trying to ensure that the benefits of economic development are distributed to everyone—is to convince young people to stay. Some are willing to stick around to get a degree at DSU but have a hard time envisioning remaining throughout their twenties and beyond. They say the question is more than whether they would find a job, but also whether they would have fun living there. They want places to eat good food, drink craft beer, and listen to live music. DSU students came together in 2011 to create an organization they ironically named Keep Cleveland Boring. The name was meant to be tongue in cheek, play off the perception that Cleveland is boring, and riff on the "Keep Austin Weird" slogan in the Texas capital. As the group's website explains: "Keep Cleveland Boring is a non-profit organization who's [sic] mission is to erase the phrase, 'Cleveland is Boring.' The idea is to inspire people to come together in support of the many activities organized and created by the group in Cleveland, Mississippi. Our aim is to provide entertainment by creating original events unique to the Delta and by promoting various events already taking place in Cleveland. We do not want to keep the city boring. In fact, quite the contrary. We want to make Cleveland an entertainment hub for the Delta and beyond."[155]

Keep Cleveland Boring has its roots in a concert put on in 2005 by Justin Huerta and William "Weejy" Rogers. They say they just wanted to create a space to see their favorite bands but gained confidence from the experience of breaking even that night.[156] They have continued the tradition of putting on a concert each year branded as Otherfest. The concert now happens over two days every October in a field just north of town on Highway 61. For twenty-five dollars, patrons camp for free, listen to a dozen bands, and choose from plenty of beer and food options.[157]

Initially, business and civic leaders were not enthusiastic about the branding Keep Cleveland Boring. Huerta said, "People thought we were out to make the town look bad at first."[158] They worried it would perpetuate the idea that Cleveland is boring or distract from the cultural activities already happening. The name Otherfest was somewhat provocative because it is one weekend removed from Octoberfest, which for more than three decades has been the largest event for the Chamber of Commerce and the city. More than fifteen thousand people of all ages come for music, face painting, and a barbeque contest that is sanctioned by the Memphis Barbeque Network.[159]

In 2009 Keep Cleveland Boring's leaders founded Hey Joe's, a restaurant and bar in a prominent location downtown. A second restaurant, Mosquito Burrito, was also opened and ultimately moved next door. Together they serve as the unofficial headquarters for Keep Cleveland Boring and are where DSU students and others come for the burger of the month, trivia night, and live music. Most patrons at these restaurants are likely to be white on any given night, but people say that one of the most attractive aspects of this movement is how inclusive it is of many dimensions of diversity. Youth who are LGBTQ+ said that engaging with the Keep Cleveland Boring scene was the first time in their lives they felt a safe space to be themselves.

The success of these restaurants and Otherfest built the momentum for more events. The largest of these is Anotherfest, a second music festival that takes place in April and happens progressively throughout the day as people move together from venue to venue. Weejy Rogers explains, "There are so many [bands] around here that they make [booking] easy because they're so good, between Jackson, Cleveland and Oxford."[160] A journalist for the *Clarion-Ledger* says that Cleveland becomes the epicenter of indie music in the state during the weekend of Anotherfest.[161] These festivals have made bands and booking agents more aware of the market in Cleveland, giving them an additional tour stop at Hey Joe's between nearby cities with larger music scenes such as Memphis and Jackson.

Local leaders have recognized that something exciting is happening and they have come around to what Keep Cleveland Boring is trying to do.[162] Some are still not quite sure how to engage, but they no longer feel threatened. One local business owner said, "Keep Cleveland Boring's thing is like they're the cool kids, and so like when you start partnering with adults, they lose a little bit of their coolness. . . . It's not really our scene anyway. I mean, they want live music, they want to camp, and they want to drink all day. And that's great, like that's awesome, because Cleveland needs that."

The organization has attracted regional and national media attention.[163] *Smithsonian Magazine* named Cleveland the number two small town to visit in America in 2013.[164] Keep Cleveland Boring won a Mississippi Main Street award in 2016 for its partnership with the local chamber of commerce.[165] The city's tourism office is trying to build on this momentum, with taglines on the city's promotional materials such as "Small town. Big vibe" and "Hip little town in the Mississippi Delta."[166] Similarly, Keep Cleveland Boring and

Team Cleveland, an organization affiliated with the Cleveland-Bolivar Chamber of Commerce, partnered in 2014 to create Restaurant Week. Patrons have many restaurants to choose from, including the Delta Meat Market, led by Cole Ellis, who in 2017 was a semifinalist for the James Beard Award for Best Chef South.[167]

Ellis's presence as a nationally recognized chef who is originally from Cleveland and has chosen to come back home epitomizes the success of these events and everything else that is happening in Cleveland. As the city's tourism director explains, "We really started seeing different people, whether they are people who are from Cleveland originally and moved back into town or went to Delta State and ended up staying, like I did."[168] Many factors come together to make it possible and desirable for young creative people to stick around. Making sure that Cleveland is anything but boring has been an important step.

The COVID-19 pandemic at least temporarily halted this momentum. Hey Joe's and Mosquito Burrito lost nearly 90 percent of their business throughout much of 2020. The Delta Meat Market laid off all its staff as it lost 95 percent of its business. Federal help through the Coronavirus Aid, Relief, and Economic Security Act helped, but navigating the applications was a major challenge. Local leaders are hopeful that enough of a foundation has been laid so that Cleveland's economy will be well positioned to rebound.

Meraki Roasting Company

Cali Noland is a white Clarksdale native who recognized that not everyone in town had the same opportunities she did or is benefiting equally from the economic development of the last decade. "The big battle we are facing in Clarksdale is the effects of the generational poverty cycle. The resources and the support system that these students need have not been in place. . . . They just need a chance to get over the hurdles that have been built into the community for so long."[169] She returned to Clarksdale after graduating from the University of Mississippi and in 2014 created an after-school program named Griot Arts for local middle and high school students. Noland explains that in many West African cultures the word *griot* means "storyteller," the keeper of the culture who passed on a community's stories through poetry, music, and dance.[170] She says that she feels she is in between two distinct Clarksdale cultures, the wealthy white residents and everyone else who built the wealth.

Griot's leaders noticed that many of the youth participating in the after-school program struggled to secure and hold jobs, even if they had GEDs or high school diplomas. The problem was not necessarily that they did not have an education or even specific hard skills, but that they did not have the soft skills that employers were expecting, such as showing up on time, following complex steps, and interacting with customers from different cultures. As one leader put it, "We often hear from people that, you know, 'Soft skills are nice, but it doesn't earn money, and people need to earn money down here. It's hard skills that earn money.' My argument to that is soft skills are the foundation—is if you don't have those soft skills first, it's very difficult to even maintain a job, or develop the hard skills to earn money."

Noland's team received a small grant to develop a job training program in which local youth did all aspects of growing, marketing, and selling local foods. Griot's board of directors saw the job training aspect of this program as a success but was concerned that it was not sustainable, as it was funded entirely through grant dollars. One person explained that the bottom line is "you're not going to make much money selling produce locally in a small town." Ben Lewis came into the picture around this time. Ben is a native of the Pacific Northwest who came to Clarksdale on a short-term project to help a high school that had received a school improvement grant. When that ended, he and his wife did not feel ready to leave. He got a job doing IT for an agricultural investment firm, but he did not love the work and hoped to find something else. He became friends with Noland and was intrigued by the challenge she faced of developing a sustainable job training program for Clarksdale's youth.

Griot's leaders felt that the way forward was to create an independent business that could ultimately be financially self-sufficient. They felt that "whoever ends up developing this project needs to be passionate about running the business." Lewis explained that they developed the idea of running a coffee roasting company: "Education and coffee are my two—aside from family—my two loves in life. And how many times in my life can you get to blend the two of those together?" They landed on the name Meraki, which their website explains means "to do something with soul . . . to put a piece of yourself into your work."[171] Meraki's business model includes engaging tourists who fall in love with Clarksdale and signing them up for subscriptions to receive freshly roasted bags of coffee delivered to them from the Delta every one to two months.

Lewis explained that coffee is an ideal business for a job training program focused on soft skills because roasting is scientific in nature and so many variables are constantly changing. Someone cannot just be trained on what steps to follow in a formulaic, linear way; they have to understand the why behind each step and develop critical thinking skills to adapt as circumstances change. This environment also gives employees opportunities to work under the pressure of interacting with customers, navigate working on a team, develop self-awareness and conflict management skills, and learn the sales and accounting skills needed to run a business.[172]

Meraki's program uses a cohort model open to people ages sixteen to twenty-four. Applicants are not eligible if they are currently in school, with the idea being that they are encouraged to continue their educations. Lewis explained, "We're there for those that have fallen through the cracks. . . . We get some that have dropped out of high school. Most of ours currently have either completed their GED, or graduated, and just haven't figured out that next step." The program for the initial cohort lasted four months. In addition to working at the coffee shop, participants engage in "circle time" in which they brainstorm together how to deal with a variety of personal and professional issues and opportunities. Each cohort is also expected to organize and collaborate on a service project, such as collecting garbage along the nearby Sunflower River.[173]

The business side of Meraki is gradually coming together, with the initial grants phasing out and revenue covering a larger share of operating expenses each year. But the job training aspect excites leaders most. Lewis said they saw impact after the first cohort: "The students who were going through the program were starting to hold down jobs, maintain them, and their careers started moving up, creating sustainable lives in their own personal life." More than seventy fellows so far have gone through the program.[174] Some youth stayed on at Meraki and help to train subsequent cohorts. Lewis said, "Four months is not a lot to build your resume. Yes, you can say we went through this intensive job training program for four months, which helps on a resume with nothing on it. But to say, you know, I've worked in a coffee shop for a year, it helps a lot more."

The fellows tell their stories in a documentary called *Griot Grit: Cultivating Community through the Arts*. Filmmaker E. B. Blakney has Mississippi roots and says he got the idea for this movie while getting a cup of coffee at Meraki. He asked the young man serving him what the program has meant to him and was struck to hear him say it changed his life. The server lost both his parents while still a teenager and struggled for a while before becoming involved with Meraki. Blakney says, "That was really powerful. . . . I immediately knew something special and unique was happening in that place in Clarksdale and it was a story worth telling." Blakney explains that his team chose this story to counter the narratives about Mississippi. "I've seen so many other documentaries and news stories and it's just poverty porn. The photography books show hopelessness and desperation and that's just not the Mississippi I know. Desperation can be told in other parts of the country as well. . . . Mississippi has this horrible reputation and some of it is well earned. At the same time, there's just incredible work happening in the Delta and incredible people doing the work."[175]

Lewis says that as word has spread about Meraki, he has been getting requests from all over the country to provide guidance on how to do something similar. He believes no single formula is possible and that what works in a community is a function of its people and particular history. One of the key ingredients in the Delta is the particular kind of tourist who comes for the blues and wants to remain connected to Clarksdale after leaving. Meraki's experience is a hopeful example of the good that a small number of people can accomplish. Job training programs focused on soft skills do not solve every economic problem communities like Clarksdale face, but they fill an important gap in a way that ripples beyond the people being trained.

Delta Foundation

The Delta Foundation has an ambitious mission: "To provide community, social, human, and economic development activities to underserved, mostly minority families, businesses and communities. This mission is undertaken to eliminate poverty within the Delta region."[176] One of the primary ways the Delta Foundation seeks to fulfill this mission is by providing small business loans to minority entrepreneurs who have promising ideas but no access to credit. These loans benefit not only the recipients but also the people who are employed at these businesses, the stores where they shop, and the broader communities in which they live. As the foundation's website explains, "The principle [sic] vehicle for the attack on poverty is the creation of for-profit enterprises that increase control and ownership of resources by the poor."[177]

The foundation was established more than fifty years ago in 1969, as fourteen civil rights and local community organizations came together under a single umbrella. The goal was to leverage their combined resources by pulling in the same direction. One of these organizations was the community center that was built in McComb after the sixteen bombings and four church burnings during the Freedom Summer of 1964.[178] It was led by Spencer Nash, who has served on the Delta Foundation's board of directors ever since and in 2010 became the president and CEO.[179]

Nash explained that the foundation and its predecessor organizations have supported many different types of projects throughout its more than fifty-year history. One was Freedom Village in the late 1960s, a self-sufficient community of families who were out of work because of agricultural automation: "And at that time, you know, we didn't know how to do anything but plant the cotton, scrape the cotton, chop the cotton and pick the cotton. So that was a problem. And then, the plantation owners, since they did not need us, decided that, 'Well, we are not going to provide a place for you to live.'" Freedom Village did not last long but served as a temporary place for people to stay until they found somewhere to go.

The foundation's approach today is primarily to help people who cannot get credit start businesses. It has loaned more than $35 million to minority business owners:

> They would get turned down. You know, an old concept is, no credit is as bad as bad credit. . . . We tried to become innovative in how we dealt with it. John Doe wants to go into business. John has no money. He's got a good idea. So we get him help to get a business plan developed and come back. And what we would do sometimes, we would buy equity in that business. If it cost $100,000 to go into business, we would lend him $51,000, and then we would buy $49,000 in equity, and with an option for him to buy it back. And that was the kind of situation.

The foundation has sometimes been in a tricky position as borrowers struggle to repay their loans. There are limits to how flexible it can be, particularly given that it has financial obligations of its own. One way the foundation deals with this risk is by being thoughtful about the collateral required. Another is to provide ongoing technical assistance if the business owners want hands-on help. Sometimes this is to teach people how to do accounting or showing them how best to use their laptops to do the accounting.

Nash lists business after business that has been successful in terms of yielding a return on investment and also in terms of giving minority people in the Delta the opportunity to build better lives for themselves and their families. This is partly why he says he is hopeful about the future and continues to work through his retirement years as the president and CEO of an ambitious organization: "I think when you are optimistic, you work harder. Whether it's going to improve or not, I don't know. . . . I'm optimistic that things are going to get better in the Delta."

The Economic Equity Policy Agenda

Health equity is not possible without economic equity. Financial insecurity is often the underlying reason people struggle to access healthy foods, afford safe housing, and live in neighborhoods conducive to physical activity. This is not a story about people making bad decisions or not trying hard enough, as the path to greater economic security is not readily accessible to everyone. We need to remove these structural barriers by creating and keeping good jobs that are accessible to all and protecting and supporting people so they can become financially secure.

Economic Equity Policy Goal #1: Create and Retain Good Jobs That Are Accessible to All.

Examples of national, state, and local policies:

- Local leaders should prioritize building the infrastructure and amenities described elsewhere in this book—such as grocery stores, parks, safe communities, and schools—as one of the primary approaches to attracting employers and employees to their areas.
- Banks and philanthropic organizations should end discrimination in lending practices and adopt policies that expand services to Black business owners who historically have been marginalized.
    - Use different ways to determine credit and risk, alternative types of collateral, and repayment schedules adapted to the business's anticipated cash flow cycle.
    - Provide loans that are linked with technical assistance to help entrepreneurs develop basic accounting and budgeting skills necessary to successfully run a business.
- Ensure that economic development in a community's downtown is more accessible to Black-owned businesses and extended to nearby historically Black neighborhoods, such as Nelson Street in Greenville.
- Invest in making Black-owned businesses attractive and linked to thriving sections of town. For example, the street signs in the

Chrisman Avenue neighborhood in Cleveland could be replaced to match the attractive street signs along the walking trail, shops, and area surrounding Delta State University to better link this community to the thriving downtown.
- Communities with opportunities to develop tourism should strengthen partnerships with each other to link civil rights and blues across the region so that tourists spread out from the more visited spots and spend more time in the area.
- Target agricultural subsidies to small farmers, particularly those who grow food products, and keep a substantial portion of this output local.
- Do not prioritize gambling—whether through in-person gaming or the state lottery—as a path to economic development.
- Equitably invest the revenue generated by the state from gambling instead of using it to offset costs so that taxes are cut for high-income earners.

Economic Equity Policy Goal #2: Protect and Support People So They Can Become Financially Secure.

Examples of national, state, and local policies:

- Effectively target job training and spend the money that has been appropriated so that people can gain employable skills and have pleasant experiences when accessing services.
- Increase and update the federal minimum wage more often to keep up with inflation and to support a livable wage.
- Federal and state leaders should strengthen policies that support people who are trying to work while caring for dependents. These include paid family leave, childcare subsidies, and refundable child tax credits.
- Banks, philanthropic organizations, and government leaders should prioritize increased access to banking services. This could include the development of mobile technology so that people can bank without having to go to a physical building and the formation of partnerships with local banks so people can use nearby ATMs without paying exorbitant fees. Educational modules could be developed to help customers learn budget management and credit building and include default features that nudge users toward best practices, such as opt-out defined contributions savings plans.

Expanded banking services could also include the elimination of overdraft fees and minimum account balance requirements and provide lower transaction costs for money orders and small loans so that people are less likely to use payday lending.
- Develop additional supports to protect people from problem gambling. This could include greater restrictions on approaches that casinos use to entice customers, such as free alcohol and the cashing of tax refund checks, and limiting government advertising for the lottery in low-income communities.
- Develop greater protections for payday lending customers, such as capping the interest rate that can be charged.
- The IRS should adjust the audit process so that low-income families of color are not targeted disproportionately.

As meaningful as it would be to make progress on all fronts, improving education is arguably the most meaningful thing we can do to improve a region's economy and the health of its population. People with greater educational attainment are more likely to have financial security, which means they will be better able to do all the things that increase the likelihood that they will be healthy, such as eating well, being physically active, and living in safe neighborhoods. A population of well-educated people makes a community more attractive for employers, which increases jobs, amenities, and access to healthy foods, housing, and medical care. All of these factors are mutually reinforcing, and improving any of them makes it easier to improve the others.

4 Education

If I had a magic wand and could improve one social issue because of the effect it would have on health, it would be education. Study after study shows that people with more education have a higher quality of life, have fewer chronic diseases, and are likelier to live longer.[1] In a systematic review of this literature, authors concluded, "The positive association between an individual's educational attainment and their health and longevity is one of the strongest, pervasive, and most robust in the social sciences."[2] Education policy is health policy.

Robert F. Kennedy made a similar argument during his first trip to Mississippi, which was actually one year before his visit to the Delta in 1967. He told a crowd of nearly six thousand at the University of Mississippi, "We must create a society in which Negroes will be as free as other Americans. Free to vote and to learn and to earn their way and to share in the decisions of government, which in turn shapes their lives." Kennedy explained that education was critical to making this vision a reality and that the "privileged minority of educated men and women who are the students of this country" have a special responsibility to "commit their mind and their bodies to the task."[3]

University leaders tried to block his visit, but the law students who invited him persisted. Kennedy was taking a real risk by visiting Oxford, given the resentment over his role in the university's racial integration less than four years earlier. As attorney general, Kennedy had negotiated with Governor Ross Barnett to protect James Meredith, the university's first Black student, whom the courts had ordered be admitted. Thousands of people protested on campus the night Meredith arrived, with many focusing their anger on Kennedy, chanting, "Ask us what we say, it's to hell with Bobby K."[4] Many still blamed him for the escalation of conflict that led to two deaths and many more injuries that night in 1962.[5] Kennedy referenced this lingering contempt in the opening of his 1966 speech and joked that some in Mississippi saw his presence as inviting the fox into the chicken house. To him it was like "putting a chicken in a fox house."[6]

Multiple events in the year following his 1966 speech made it clear that the threat of violence in Mississippi over the racial integration of education was real. Meredith was shot that June as he marched from Memphis to Jackson to commemorate his graduation and draw attention to civil rights. He survived, but leaders such as Dr. Martin Luther King Jr. and Stokely Carmichael resumed the walk in his place.[7] When Senator Edward Kennedy arrived in Jackson for a speech by Dr. King, two escort vehicles were disabled because ten pounds of tacks had been placed on the road from the airport.[8] As Robert F. Kennedy boarded a plane from Jackson to the Delta in February 1967, he was handed a pamphlet with the headline "Bobby Kennedy will be murdered."[9]

Many of the stories Kennedy heard while in the Delta validated his belief that education was critical to changing lives on an individual and societal level. For example, about an hour after receiving the death threat pamphlet, Kennedy was in Greenville talking with a group who had established a temporary farming commune. Among the crowd was Catherine Wilson, an eighteen-year-old who was the second youngest of eight siblings raised by a single mother. Wilson later described how the trajectory of her life changed in 1964 when civil rights workers from the North happened to move in next door.[10] These outsiders were in Mississippi as part of the Freedom Summer to register people to vote for the first time and to establish schools with curricula focused on the rights and responsibilities of citizenship, Black history, and poetry by Black writers such as Langston Hughes.[11]

The Freedom Schools had largely faded by Kennedy's visit in 1967, but they had changed the way Wilson and other former students saw their place in America. She started participating in civil rights protests despite paying a heavy price, which included the loss of her welfare benefits and being jailed for twenty days, when she watched guards beat a pregnant woman to the point of miscarriage.[12] Another former student said that the Freedom School he attended in Clarksdale "was like shining a very bright light into a very dark place for a time, and it just changed my perception about many things for the rest of my life."[13]

Kennedy spoke often about the transformative power of education and sometimes used a similar metaphor of light. During his 1966 speech at the University of Mississippi, he told the nearly six thousand students, faculty, and administrators who attended, "You must use your lamps, the lamps of your learning, to show our people past the forest of stereotypes and slogans into the clear light of reality, and of fact, and of truth. And answers founded on clear and dispassionate thoughts must be matched at the same time by actions rooted in conviction and a passionate desire to reshape the world."[14]

Education and Health

Recent studies show that the importance of education is actually greater now than it used to be when many of the initial studies were done and that the relationship between education and health is causal,[15] not just the manifestation of the advantage that is passed between generations in privileged families.[16] In particularly compelling studies, researchers have examined what happens when children from lower-income nonwhite families are admitted to elite colleges they typically would not have applied or been accepted to because their grades and standardized test scores were low. Not only do they tend to do well, but also the positive effect that this schooling has on their quality of life and long-term health is greater than for the children from privileged backgrounds. The opposite would likely be true if education were simply correlated with health but not causally linked.[17]

There is similarly compelling evidence of the mechanisms that explain why education is so intensely connected to health. One is that people with greater educational attainment feel a greater sense of control over their lives, which in turn leads to doing the types of things that facilitate good health and avoiding risky behaviors that do not.[18] They are more likely to vaccinate their children, go to the doctor, exercise, and eat well. They are also less likely to drink excessively, smoke, and have unprotected sex.[19]

Focusing too much on these individual benefits of education for health runs the risk of blaming people and missing the structural issues involved. Educational attainment increases financial stability, and financial stability removes many of the barriers to making healthy decisions.[20] Someone with a college education can expect to earn anywhere from $600,000 to $1.1 million more than a high school graduate over the course of a forty-year work life.[21] A lifetime of higher income means people are more likely to be able to afford high-quality housing in neighborhoods that are safe and have amenities such as parks, libraries, and grocery stores. They are better able to afford nutritious foods and gym memberships. They are also more likely to have greater access to medical care because they have private health insurance through their employers and do not put off needed care because of deductibles and copays (more on this in the next chapter).

It is not that education is more important than health care, food, neighborhoods, and jobs, but that each of these factors improves with increased education. They are mutually reinforcing in a positive feedback loop that makes it clear that it is good for your health to be educated and to live around other people who are educated. Employers are more likely to come to areas that have a large pool of skilled workers. Business leaders and health professionals are more likely to stay in areas with good schools for their own children.

The link between education and health is so robust in part because the effects go in both directions. In other words, not only does more education lead to better health, but also healthy people are better positioned to do well in school and to reap the benefits of education.[22] For example, children from preschool through college who are overweight and food insecure are more likely to miss days of school and to have diminished memory and cognitive function, which leads to lower scores in math and reading and increased emotional and social struggles.[23]

A skeptic might agree with all of these points and say that the connection between education and health supports a "pull yourself up by your bootstraps" philosophy, that if people want to improve their situations, they should get more education so they are more competitive for better jobs. However, the problem is not that people living in poverty do not value education enough or that their children need to try harder. The presence of many layers of systemic barriers means that many people do not have equitable access to educational opportunities. And even if they did, the same level of educational attainment does not necessarily translate to the same level of financial security and health given a multitude of structural barriers that affect who gets jobs and who can pass on wealth to subsequent generations.[24]

Gaps and Root Causes

Many of the people I interviewed said that focusing on education is one of the most important ways to improve health in the Mississippi Delta, if not the most important. A woman in Cleveland said,

> Education and health go hand in hand. . . . Health and education issues contribute to a workforce and not being insured or whatever the problem is there. And so that contributes to then sort of this vicious cycle of people don't seek health care early, either because they're not educated or they don't have the insurance or the money or whatever it is to get that health care. And so whatever is wrong

with them gets exacerbated. And once it gets exacerbated, they get much, much sicker. So when they get sicker, health care becomes more expensive. And so a lot of the places that might hire people don't tend to come to this area of the country because health care is so expensive. And so, therefore, they're economically disadvantaged because they can't get a job. And so it goes back into the, you know, it just continues. And there are not a lot of ways out of that loop except to die or to move.

A community leader in Greenville echoed this point: "Education is one of the key factors of our success. If you don't have education, then we are just a lost generation. . . . What do you do to improve [conditions]? You've got to start with education." People hoped and believed that their children would use school as the path to a better life.

High school graduation rates—one of the most common measures of an educational system—suggest that Mississippi is strikingly average for a state that is at the bottom of many other rankings. The state's graduation rate has been climbing to a record high of 88 percent,[25] which makes it one of the top ten in the nation, not far off the national rate of 89 percent.[26] The Black-white graduation gap is narrower in Mississippi (82 percent to 88 percent) than in the United States as a whole (80 percent to 89 percent).[27] However, it does not take much digging beyond these high-level statistics to see evidence of deep struggles and serious racial inequity. Some places in the Delta have dramatically lower graduation rates. For example, 65.2 percent of the eligible cohort in Coahoma County (where 56 of the 66 students are Black) and 70.8 percent in the city of Greenville (where 322 of the 329 students are Black) graduated from high school in 2019.[28]

The reading proficiency of fourth graders is an even more compelling measure than graduation rates because it captures inequities at an early stage and predicts success in high school and beyond. The good news is that Mississippi saw the largest improvement in the country in fourth-grade reading levels between 2017 and 2019.[29] The bad news is that this is largely because the starting point was so bad, and Mississippi was last in the nation ten years earlier.[30] Even with the statewide increases, only 17 percent, 18 percent, and 19 percent of fourth-grade children are proficient in reading in the three most populated counties in the Delta (Bolivar, Coahoma, and Washington Counties, respectively).[31] Even more alarming is that these numbers mask disparities because they represent children from all races and income levels. One estimate suggests that 14 percent of Black fourth graders in Mississippi are reading at grade level,[32] a rate well below the 31.2 percent of children statewide and 51.0 percent of children nationally.[33]

The Mississippi Department of Education aggregates these numbers along with math, science, and other scores to develop a composite grade for every school and every district each year. A handful of individual schools in the Delta, including some that are predominantly Black, received a grade of A in recent ratings. However, at the district level, most parts of the Delta received a D or F, and no district received better than a C.[34] Only one majority-Black district in the state—Clinton Public Schools in the Jackson suburbs—has received an A in recent years.[35]

These differences epitomize the idea that health is not just a product of people making good choices. Doing well in school and taking advantage of a good education requires hard work and perseverance, but it is shortsighted and incorrect to point to these statistics of disparities as evidence that members of particular populations are not working hard enough. The problems are structural and therefore require structural solutions. As Ibram X. Kendi writes, "The lack of resources leads directly to diminished opportunities for learning. In other words, the racial problem is the opportunity gap, as antiracist reformers call it, not the achievement gap."[36]

Four sets of interrelated factors shape everything administrators, teachers, and parents try to do to educate children in the Mississippi Delta: the de facto racial segregation of schools, the state's formula for funding districts, a school rating system largely based on standardized testing, and teacher shortages.

An education policy agenda should focus on eliminating five barriers:

(1) **Segregation.** Are policies and programs in place to eliminate racial segregation in schools at every level?
(2) **Funding levels.** Are adequate funds available, and are the funds equitably obtained and equitably distributed?
(3) **Standardized tests.** Are standardized test scores used as the primary method of determining how schools and districts are evaluated? Are other evaluation methods used?
(4) **Recruiting and retaining teachers.** Do teacher salaries, especially in low-income areas, demonstrate that education is a priority for the state?
(5) **The social, emotional, and academic needs of students.** Are the social, emotional, and academic needs of every student met at each step of the educational experience, including higher education?

White Flight

It has been more than sixty years since the US Supreme Court held in *Brown v. Board of Education* and other landmark cases that educating children of different races in separate schools is inherently unequal. Even so, schools in the Delta are overwhelmingly segregated by race. Districts and schools that have a majority of Black students tend to be located in overwhelmingly Black communities. For example, in the school year 2021–22, 93 percent (*n* = 226) of the student body at West Bolivar High School, 100 percent (*n* = 46) of the student body at Coahoma Early College High School, and 96.4 percent (*n* = 2,157) of the student body at Clarksdale Municipal School District were reported to be Black, non-Hispanic.[37] Many students I interviewed in Clarksdale said that not a single white student is in the graduating class.

Large numbers of white parents responded to *Brown v. Board of Education* by pulling their children out of public schools. This "white flight" was particularly prevalent in the South, where, by 1958, enrollment in private schools increased by 250,000 and by 1965 increased to nearly 1 million.[38] Enrollment in private schools increased another 200,000 from the mid-1960s to 1980.[39] The shift had begun even earlier, as private school enrollment in the South increased 43 percent in response to a pre-*Brown* Supreme Court ruling that outlawed segregation in higher education but that many white parents took as a warning that further desegregation might be coming. Nearly 450 laws were passed by the legislatures of southern states in the decade following *Brown* to block desegregation and allow for the transfer of public funds to these private schools.[40] Mississippi was the epicenter of this movement toward de facto segregation. There were only 3 non-church-run private schools in the state in 1954, but by 1966 there were 121. This number almost doubled to 236 in 1970.[41]

White flight is not an exclusively southern phenomenon. Parents in northern cities such as Boston responded to racial integration by pulling their kids from public schools or moving to nearby suburbs.[42] A history of segregation or "redlining" often meant that these surrounding communities were racially homogeneous. Seemingly colorblind policies kept out most Black families because it was harder for them to get educations that would allow them to find jobs with high enough incomes to afford buying homes, which inflated further as the disparity in schools increased. Black families that could afford to move to affluent suburbs with better schools were kept out through unfair treatment by realtors and lenders. White flight schools—typically officially called academies—remain an important part of Mississippi's educational landscape today. The state does not track private school enrollment, but one estimate suggests that about 8 percent of children across the state attend private schools.[43] This proportion may be increasing, as the decrease in public school enrollment between 2012 and 2019 (4.5 percent) was larger than would be expected because people moved away. Greenville—the largest school district in the Delta—saw a decrease of 22 percent during this period.[44] Only 3 percent of students in Greenville's public schools are white.[45]

Tuition at a typical private academy such as Lee Academy in Clarksdale was $6,403 for the 2020-21 school year, plus a registration fee of $200, a building fee of $215, and a technology fee of $215.[46] The school's website advertises that financial assistance is available, but interviews with people in the community suggest that the scope and magnitude of the help is not large. An academy leader said they do not systematically include money in the budget for aid, but that alumni periodically provide donations and tell them to "apply it to whoever needs some help."

The movement toward private schools in the Delta is particularly striking given that these academies are not renowned for academic excellence. As a teenager from Greenville described, "The education I got, I paid for it. And there's people in Madison and Jackson, they got a better education than me, and they went to school for free. Why should I have to do all this, and I'm still not getting a good education?" The facilities at these schools are not necessarily much nicer, even though the word *academy* conjures images of a stately campus. They tend to have nice football fields but not enough students to fill teams in all the sports they offer unless the most athletic kids play multiple sports.

The leader of a private academy in the Delta disputed this perception and said that class sizes are smaller and graduation rates are higher in private schools than their public counterparts. It is hard to objectively assess the disparity given differences in reporting, but surveys of parents and anecdotal evidence suggest that differences in achievement might stem from the benefits of the privilege these kids bring with them rather than what is given to them at schools.[47]

Many white parents say they took their kids out of public school because of concerns about violence, but in an independent content analysis, crime was just as common in Mississippi private schools even though these incidents received far less media coverage than crime in the nearby public schools.[48] But even this academy leader's description of why she was sent to a private school as a child suggests it has as much to do with cultural prejudice as academics: "[My mother] didn't want me to be around girls who are pregnant in high school because that's not something that we teach in our house. There's just certain things that you don't want your children exposed to. They grew up totally different. I'm talking Black kids raised totally different than I raise my children, and I don't want them exposed to things like ugly language, and pregnant girls in ninth grade, and girls in twelfth grade who have three kids. It's just not—anyway, so I understand why they were created."

White flight segregation leaves school districts depleted of valuable resources. Entire communities suffer as test scores and school ratings decrease, fewer people want to move to an area, employers leave because of a lack of skilled workers, property values drop, local government cannot keep up with the budget needs of its school district, school infrastructure deteriorates, salaries for teachers and administrators become uncompetitive, the teacher shortage grows worse, student performance suffers, the district's rating stagnates or drops further, parents who can afford to pull their kids out do so, property values continue to drop, and the cycle continues. Everything a community can do to improve population health and quality of life intersects with education.

Charter Schools

The growth of charter schools in the United States is one of the most divisive topics in education. These schools receive government funding on a per-pupil basis but are exempt from many of the regulations and expectations surrounding public education. Between school years 2010–11 and 2021–22, the number of public charter schools increased from approximately 5,300 to 7,800 and enrollment more than doubled from 1.8 million to 3.7 million students. Similarly, the number of children in public charter schools increased from 400,000 to 3.1 million, or from 1 percent to 6 percent of public school students.[49] This may be another form of white flight, as more than one thousand of the charter schools have student populations that are at least 99 percent white.[50]

Some parents and educators are excited by this growth and believe that the autonomy from government regulations frees these schools to innovate rather than teach to the test. The argument is that a marketplace of competition will lead to the good schools becoming popular and the bad schools dying out. Many supporters view these schools as a place where children of Black, Hispanic, immigrant, or other nonwhite backgrounds can get the opportunities they need in the public education system. Opponents argue that education should not be subject to market forces because the negative effects of failure are too great for the affected children. They worry that these schools divert money from existing public schools. In this view, they exacerbate the challenges felt by the most vulnerable communities and worsen the racial opportunity gap. The National Conference of State Legislatures reviewed the evidence on charter schools and concluded the following: "The most rigorous studies conducted to date have found that charter schools are not, on average, better or worse in student performance than the traditional public school counterparts. . . . This average result, however, obscures tremendous variation between individual charter schools and charter schools in different states."[51]

People on all sides of the issue have data to support their arguments. In a commonly cited study, 17 percent of charters led to academic gains, 46 percent were neutral, and 37 percent were significantly worse.[52] But more nuance is needed, as the results vary substantially by state policy and demographic factors. In another study, schools that served more disadvantaged students had a positive effect on math scores, whereas schools with students with prior achievement from higher-income families did worse.[53] Economists have estimated that children leaving charter schools cost the public system they are leaving between $1,500 and $3,500 in the short term, but this does not cause long-term harm to school budgets because administrators are able to equilibrate.[54] Similarly, charter schools have increased racial division in some communities, but researchers estimate that 95 percent of the segregation would still exist if all charter schools were eliminated.[55]

Desegregation in Cleveland

Tension over racial equity in Mississippi's schools boiled over in 2017 when a federal judge affirmed an order from one year earlier for the Cleveland schools to desegregate.[56] Cleveland High School was required to merge with the nearly 100 percent Black East Side High School to create a unified school that was named Cleveland Central. Local leaders decided that one of the old schools would become the site for the new consolidated high school and the other for a new consolidated middle school. The district had been on the US Justice Department's radar for decades, and Assistant Attorney General Thomas Perez said, "Cases like this should really be in the history books, not in the courtroom. . . . It is intolerable for districts to continue operating schools that retain their racial identity from the Jim Crow era."[57]

Cleveland's story is a bit more complicated because the judge's order broke up Cleveland High School, which in 1965 was the first public school in the Delta to admit Black students through a freedom-of-choice plan that allowed students to transfer to any school in the district.[58] Before the desegregation order in 2017, 47 percent of the 560 students were Black and 47 percent were white.[59] The demographics of the new high school were expected to be 75 percent Black, and many worried this would lead to white flight, which Cleveland hadn't experienced to the same degree as Clarksdale and Greenville. In other words, the effect of the court's decision might be to eliminate one of the few racially diverse schools in the region and more fully segregate the schools.

The story attracted attention from major national and international media outlets. Some reporters focused on the real challenges faced by the new school, including lawsuits alleging that white students received preferential treatment that made it less likely for Black students to be chosen for prestigious honors such as salutatorian and valedictorian.[60] A resident worried that "what we are starting to see in Cleveland is [that] Cleveland is starting to look more like the rest of the Delta," with white kids in private schools and Black kids in public schools.

But many Cleveland youth stressed that they were pleased with how the unification has gone and that they did not see a lot of tension. A young Black woman said, "A lot of people see it as it was a big change for us. But actually, I think it was a change for the better because there is slightly more stuff available for us than it's ever been." Her peers added, "It still feels like I'm going to school, like nothing's different," and, "You just have more friends." Another person said, "It's never really been a problem between the kids. It is more the adults." Some parents on both sides are disappointed they cannot share traditional aspects of their high school experience with their children, such as the mascot, colors, homecoming, and prom. But many were eager to move on. A Black man explained that "East Side wanted to preserve East Side. That was frustrating to me because the way I was thinking about it was, you're not going to change those mindsets until we have generations that are educated together, that can learn that they're just people with different skin color. Because if they continue to isolate and build those walls, then they don't have to come into contact with any information that disrupts their stereotypes that they already have in their head, or disrupts any of their way of life, period."

Football played an important role in bringing the two sides of town together during that first year. Ricky Smither, a young Black man who became coach of the new Cleveland Central team, asked the principal of the new school for a list of families he thought were opposed to the consolidation. He then went to each of their homes to hear their concerns and try to build relationships. The response was strong, and many showed up to games that fall wearing shirts saying "United in Purple" to celebrate the new school colors.[61] It helped that the new team was immediately successful and was undefeated during its first season.[62] But not everyone was on board. *Mississippi Today* reported that 224 students transferred out of the district between May 2017 when the order was confirmed and the start of the school year that fall. Most of the students who left were white and went to private schools.[63] A more conservative estimate suggests that the number of students who left because of the unification is closer to 100. Even so, this drop has important financial implications for the district given that the state provides about $5,000 per student.[64]

Many leaders and community members feel that the drop is not as big as feared and are proud of how their community has navigated this difficult situation. As a young Black person put it, "I feel like it's going pretty well, but I always imagine that if there's one place that it could go well, it would be Cleveland, mainly because of the university and the type of people that are in Cleveland because of the university. I feel like Cleveland's a little bit more progressive than most areas. But it's a little bit different in Winona and Montgomery County." A leader in Greenville echoed this point and worried that his community was next and things would not go as well: "You're talking about a school district that has a total population of about 20,000 people and you have two high schools. One, O'Bannon, which is 99 percent Black, they say, but it's 100 percent Black. And then you have Riverside, which is predominantly white. A consent decree was ordered way back but has not been followed as of this date. And you know, the Justice Department still come in and try to work with them, but they still have not made any progress."

Funding

The racial segregation of schools in the Delta contributes to and is exacerbated by inadequate funding. Mississippi schools are among the most poorly funded in the nation no matter what metric is used. If all federal, state, and local funding is combined, Mississippi spent $8,771 per K–12 student in 2017, the most recent year that comparable state-by-state data are available. This is far less than the national average of $12,201, the least among states in the Deep South, and less than all but four other states in the country. The state ranks tenth for lowest amount of spending per student from state general funds and fifth for lowest amount of local spending per student. The proportion of spending on Mississippi students that comes from federal funds is the second highest in the nation, second only to New Mexico.[65] These rankings are even more dramatic when considering that Mississippi has experienced a 230 percent increase in the ratio of spending on prisons to spending on education between 1980 and 2013, the seventh-highest increase in the nation.[66]

Gaps in funding push school leaders in the Delta to cut corners to make ends meet. Billy Joe Ferguson—the superintendent of schools in Carroll County—told a reporter the following:

> If I hire a teacher, I'm looking to hire a teacher with the least amount of experience because I can't hire a teacher that costs twice what a beginning teacher would cost. Last year we had 10 or 11 people that retired or left. And so I replaced them with lower-paid people. Textbooks are so high. I've got expenses on school buses and teacher salaries, those are things that have to be there [in the budget] when it comes down to it. The teachers make do. They find things on the Internet and we try to buy up to date workbooks and things like that so the kids don't get short-changed. But it would be better if we just had money.[67]

Ferguson balanced the district's budget by officially retiring but then staying in his role while being paid benefits rather than a salary. This reduced the portion of the budget for his salary from about $80,000 per year to $18,000. A teacher in the district explained, "I was able to get textbooks and to do educational field trips from him taking a pay cut. Honestly. Because, if he didn't there wouldn't be a budget for that."[68]

People in the Delta described a host of ways these funding gaps affected their educational experiences. Some schools have been relatively successful at getting grants to bring technology to the classroom, but this masks the dearth of other resources. A teenager in Clarksdale said, "We have a cart of Chromebooks—like little laptops—in almost every classroom" because of grants. Another said, "We don't even have textbooks." The mother of a third grader in Cleveland said, "I think it's just ridiculous—they don't have math textbooks!" A high school student in Clarksdale said he has textbooks, but they are almost unusable because someone made a point of ripping out the corner of every page, which means that he cannot find the homework exercises that are assigned by page number. Teachers said they navigate the lack of adequate supplies by spending money out of their own pockets.[69]

When asked what they would most like to change about their schools, a teenager in Cleveland responded without hesitation, "I'd say the bathrooms" because they are old and dirty. Another said the cafeteria: "It's like really small and cramped. And the workers, we have like four workers. And we don't have enough lunch time to just sit down and enjoy our food because the line is out the door, and you have twenty minutes to eat." Others said their buildings lacked climate control. They can wear coats in the classroom during the winter, but they can do little for relief on hot days. Research shows a strong relationship between academic performance and extreme heat, which may account for as much as 5 percent of the difference in educational outcomes between racial and ethnic groups.[70]

Scholars and policymakers debate whether the problems with education can be solved with more spending. Some argue that the key question should not be how much more funding is needed, but how funding is used.[71] This is a false dichotomy because both questions are critically important. But the debate over how money should be spent should not distract from making sure there is enough to work with. Schools that operate in a perpetual state of financial crisis cannot afford to attract the best administrators and teachers, to maintain and update infrastructure, or to provide teachers and students with adequate materials. Long-term planning is impossible, which gives them little room to decide how to spend their money beyond crisis management.

Research shows that when school districts around the country have been forced by the courts to spend more, the educational performance of children from low-income families increases.[72] For example, in one study it was estimated that a 10 percent increase in spending per pupil each year for all twelve years of elementary and secondary education would lead to 0.31 more years of school completed, 7 percent higher wages when the pupil reaches the workforce, and a 3.2 percent reduction in the annual incidence of adult poverty.[73]

Quitman County Experiment

An experiment of sorts in Quitman County—where sixty years earlier Dr. King launched the Poor People's Campaign—illustrates the connection between funding, leadership, and educational outcomes. When Michael

Cormack took over as principal of Quitman County Elementary School in Lambert, the school had been through four principals in the previous five years and was consistently rated D or F. Principal Cormack was hand-selected by Jim Barksdale, a Mississippi native who was putting the fortune he made as the former CEO of AT&T Wireless and Netscape toward various philanthropic endeavors.[74] The Barksdale Reading Institute had been supporting small-scale projects to increase literacy but ultimately concluded that real change would not be possible without new leadership. The Quitman County School District let him select the next principal and vice principal in exchange for his paying a salary that would be competitive enough to attract someone to the region.

Barksdale and Cormack made it clear that their strategy was not to fire most of the staff but to empower and better support the teachers who were there.[75] The progress was rapid and dramatic. The percentage of children reading and doing math at grade level quickly improved from 38 percent to 59 percent and from 30 percent to 89 percent, respectively. The school rating soon rose from F to C. In his memoir of living in Mississippi, Richard Grant wrote that he believes this story is an example that shows that the combination of money and pain can transform a school in the Delta.[76] Cormack eventually left Quitman County Elementary School to be the CEO of the Barksdale Reading Institute and later the chief of staff to the superintendent of the Jackson Public School District.[77] The elementary school has maintained high test scores since his departure and now has an A rating, while the rest of the schools in the district are at C and D.[78]

As encouraging as this progress is, not every district has a philanthropist willing to invest significant amounts of money. However, this story supports the argument that the challenges facing education in the Delta are structural and that increased funding is an important part of the equation.

The Mississippi Adequate Education Program

Changing the formula that determines how state funds are allocated to school districts is one of the most hotly discussed issues in Jackson. The legislature created the Mississippi Adequate Education Program (MAEP) in 1994 to calculate how much a district would need to run schools at an "adequate" level. The relatively unambitious definition for this standard was that they would have enough to achieve a rating of C, although the formula was designed to provide additional funds to lower-income districts. Then

Governor Kirk Fordice vetoed the bill to create the MAEP, but a bipartisan coalition of legislators mobilized the necessary two-thirds to override his veto.[79] In the more than twenty years since the MAEP went into effect, the legislature has mostly ignored the statutory funding requirement it created. The budget passed by the legislature and governor each year has only twice fully funded schools at the level determined by the MAEP formula. The amount appropriated is typically 11 percent to 13 percent less than the amount considered to be adequate,[80] which has resulted in a budget shortfall of approximately $2 billion over the last decade.[81]

Some leaders advocate for changing the MAEP. Others say that the formula itself is not the problem, but that it is not followed. In November 2015, a ballot question known as Initiative 42 was used to ask voters to pass a constitutional amendment mandating the legislature and governor to increase school funding to comply with the MAEP.[82] The question narrowly failed, in part perhaps because voters were confused by an ambiguous option added by the legislature known as Alternative 42a, which did not mention the formula or require anything specific: "The Legislature shall, by general law, provide for the establishment, maintenance and support of an effective system of free public schools."[83]

Twenty-one school districts—about one-third of which were in the Delta—have since sued the state for not complying with the MAEP formula. These districts were represented by former governor Ronnie Musgrove, who asked the state to repay money that would have been allocated to them had the formula been followed.[84] The courts ultimately ruled that decisions made by the legislature in the past did not constrain the legislature in the future from deciding how much to appropriate.[85] The Mississippi Supreme Court upheld the ruling in October 2017 when the districts appealed.[86] Legislative leaders tried to revise the formula in 2017 but were blocked by a bipartisan coalition of senators because school leaders in their districts were worried it would lead to even less funding in the long run.[87] The new formula would have established a base funding rate of $4,800 per student with additional money for specific learning needs. The resulting increase in state spending would have been $107 million over seven years, still far short of the $157 million if MAEP were fully funded.

Some leaders have tried to make up budget shortfalls by asking for more local funding. But this is not easy because the districts that most need the additional money are located in communities without property tax bases to support increased funding. Some have tried but failed to raise additional local taxes. For example, the city of Leland—where the median income is barely above $30,000—tried to pass a bond issue to help make up the gap of more than $4.6 million that did not come from the legislature between 2007 and 2018. The initiative was supported by 58 percent of voters, but this was 2 points short of the needed threshold of 60 percent.[88]

Some districts around the country make up gaps through donations from parents and others, but this is not a viable option in most parts of the Delta. I am not aware of any systematic data on private donations to pay for materials and resources used in the public schools, but clear evidence from around the country shows that this practice exacerbates inequities such that the schools that are already better off get that much more.[89] This contributes to a cycle in which schools in wealthier communities perform better, parents with resources move to these communities so their children get the best schools, they, in turn, contribute through property taxes and private donations, the schools continue to thrive, and so on.

Testing, Rating, and Curriculum

How schools are evaluated and compared is another factor in this cycle. The Elementary and Secondary Education Act of 1965 enacted by the US Congress was a transformative law for many reasons, including a provision—authored by Senator Robert F. Kennedy—to standardize expectations so that schools across the country could be accountable and compared in a systematic way.[90] Robert F. Kennedy's brother Senator Edward Kennedy was instrumental in working with President George W. Bush to develop No Child Left Behind, which went a step further to require all schools to be tested.[91] No Child Left Behind had mixed results. Some studies showed positive gains for children in disadvantaged communities,[92] and others showed that the improvement was not real since educators were simply teaching to the test.[93]

No Child Left Behind was replaced in 2015 with the Every Student Succeeds Act. At the bill signing ceremony, President Barack Obama said that the goals of No Child Left Behind "were the right ones: High standards. Accountability. Closing the achievement gap. But in practice, it often fell short. It didn't always consider the specific needs of each community. It led to too much testing during classroom time. It often forced schools and school districts into cookie-cutter reforms that didn't always produce the kinds of results that we wanted to see."[94] Many think that President Obama did not go far enough. They see standardized testing as rooted in the eugenics movement, incapable of truly measuring achievement, and inherently biased against nonwhite and lower-income populations. Ibram X. Kendi argues,

"The use of standardized tests to measure aptitude and intelligence is one of the most effective racist policies ever devised to degrade Black minds and legally exclude Black bodies. We degrade Black minds every time we speak of an 'academic-achievement gap' based on these numbers."[95]

The Every Student Succeeds Act gave states more flexibility to design their own standards and systems of accountability.[96] Mississippi's plan—approved by the US Department of Education in March 2018—kept the state's system of rating schools A through F but now allows schools to be compared with themselves rather than to a statewide standard and more heavily weighs the scores of the previous year's lowest-performing students.[97] The COVID-19 pandemic disrupted full implementation of these revisions, although some people are cautiously optimistic the new approach will be an improvement. Even so, many feel that the act of rating schools—especially through standardized testing—is an excessively blunt approach that is biased against schools in places like the Delta given the host of additional barriers these children, parents, and schools face. These ratings implicitly blame the schools and their leaders for not doing well enough rather than identifying and addressing structural challenges. They also make it hard for struggling schools to break the cycle because they keep property values low and scare off potential employers from moving to the area.

Perpetually struggling districts face the looming threat that they will be taken over by the state. A law passed by the legislature in 2016 determined that any district with an F rating in two consecutive years or twice in a three-year period would become part of a new Achievement School District in which the state hires a new superintendent and the elected local school board is dissolved and replaced by the state Board of Education. The state has the discretion to return the district back to local control once it has achieved a C rating for five consecutive years.[98] Districts in Yazoo City and Humphreys County—both in the Delta—were the first to become part of the state's new Achievement School District. Jermall Wright, Ed.D., who was hired in April 2019 as the superintendent, is not new to this type of situation, having recently worked to turn around schools in the cities of Denver, Colorado, and Birmingham, Alabama.[99] The position was attractive to Wright, in part because he would not have to navigate the tricky and sometimes distracting politics of working with a locally elected school board. Even so, he says he is careful not to use the term *takeover* because "it has such a negative connotation. . . . It's not a state takeover in the sense that there's not a whole bunch of outside folks coming to descend upon the district and blow things up and do things differently. I'm new, but my team has deep roots both in Humphreys and Yazoo. And those who are new joining us still have deep roots within the Mississippi Delta and the state in general."[100]

He warns that progress will not be easy or immediate: "The Mississippi Achievement School District [ASD] wasn't created because things have been going well in these districts for at least the past decade. So if it took us a decade to get to the point where we are now, then one year in the ASD, two years in the ASD, three years in the ASD isn't going to 100 percent fix and address all of those issues that happened over the decade to get to where we are now."[101]

Sometimes the pressure of testing and rating gets the best of school administrators. One of the most talked about stories in Clarksdale is of an elementary school principal who was caught helping students cheat on the state tests. Teachers were instructed to use codes such as mentioning the name of an animal that started with the letter corresponding to the right answer and walking around the room tapping on the desks of students who were answering questions incorrectly. A teenager said she had been a student at that elementary school and was in the room when some of this happened. When she came back from a bathroom break during a test, she saw a teacher had written words on the board starting with the letter they should answer for certain questions: "When I came back like, 'I was like what?' It was, 'Abraham, Blockade,' like that. That's how she wrote the answer, like she was taking attendance. And like I was confused, but I just like dismissed it." She adds that when she realized what had happened, she initially laughed, "I know all those answers anyway," but then she challenged the teacher: "And I asked the teacher, like, 'What's that on the board?' like to see if she was going to tell me. She was like, 'Nothing.' I was like, 'Oh, okay.' Like really?" The principal is said to have then threatened teachers who might be whistleblowers with warnings that "if you make me look bad, you will not work for me."[102]

This story struck such an intense chord with people for two reasons. First, it served as a reminder of just how far behind people feel that the schools are in Clarksdale. Many were understanding about the principal's intention to improve the school's scores, feeling that even artificially higher scores now would bring more resources that would make the schools better in the long term. But for others, the episode reinforced cynicism about the whole system. The student who challenged the teacher after noticing the cheating said, "What's the point in doing this? They're still going to fail." Second, they are frustrated by what they see as corruption that allowed the principal to still work in the district after such an egregious violation. A person in Clarksdale laughed as he said, "Instead of firing her, they relocated her into the superintendent's office. They created a job for her!" It did not help public perception that this incident took place on the heels of the Clarksdale school board president being arrested in 2013 for a history of stealing air fresheners from the Fred's Super Dollar.[103] The state ultimately stepped in, and the principal received a record twenty-year ban from teaching.

Common Core

One approach to addressing inequities between districts is to require all schools to follow the same curriculum or to at least work toward the same competencies. No Child Left Behind catalyzed a movement toward a standardized curriculum across the country. A nonpartisan collaboration through the National Governors Association created what became known as the Common Core. One of the most important aspects of this curriculum is that it is designed with the standards of the college admissions tests, such as the ACT and the SAT, in mind. No Child Left Behind did not require any particular curriculum be used, but leaders in Mississippi adopted the Common Core in 2010 believing that it would position the state to be competitive in applications for federal education grants.[104]

The Common Core was adopted by forty-one states but has remained controversial.[105] The Every Student Succeeds Act specifically clarifies that although states can adopt the Common Core, the US Department of Education "shall not attempt to influence, incentivize, or coerce State adoption of the Common Core State Standards developed under the Common Core State Standards Initiative or any other academic standards common to a significant number of states, or assessments tied to such standards."[106] Some of the frustration people describe is not about the Common Core itself but over the culture of needing to teach to a test with material developed centrally. In one survey, 25 percent of teachers who left the profession said that dissatisfaction over testing and accountability pressures was the major factor.[107] A leader in Greenville was frustrated that so much of the emphasis of education in the struggling schools in his community is on passing tests designed around the Common Core: "What's more important? Getting them to a point where they can have a good quality of life or passing the test? Which is more important? And the test was more important, and that's kind of a problem."

Mississippi's most recent governors—Phil Bryant between 2012 and 2020 and Tate Reeves since January 2020—have called for a repeal of the Common Core.[108] Legislators introduce bills every year to eliminate the Common Core, but none have been enacted. A bill in 2015 came very close and made it through both chambers on a somewhat bipartisan basis (passing eighty-eight to twenty-nine in the House and forty-six to six in the Senate) only to be vetoed by Governor Bryant.[109] The bill's scope had been limited during negotiations such that all it would do was create an independent study group to propose which standards to eliminate and keep but not require the state's Department of Education to act accordingly. Governor Bryant explained, "I am steadfast in my belief that Common Core must be abandoned," but this bill "would do nothing to realistically accomplish that."[110]

Some people say that one of the appeals of private schools and the white flight academies is that they are not subject to the same Common Core standards and can use whatever textbooks and curricula they want. As the leader of a private school explained, "I don't limit my teachers, like there's no, 'You have to teach this. You have to teach it in this time period.' We do what's best for kids, which I think is something that the public schools, they think they do that, but they put them all in a box, and you have to pass this test." Even so, this leader clarified that, in effect, the school does use the Common Core because its standards are aligned with the ACT, which its students take to get into college: "We don't call it the Common Core; we just teach to the ACT standards."

Seven districts in Mississippi—including two on the edge of the Delta in Grenada and Vicksburg—have been granted waivers to disregard the Common Core curriculum and to use a different approach.[111] It is too soon to evaluate the effect of these "Districts of Innovation," as none of the waivers is more than a few years old. Corinth—a city of fourteen thousand people about two and half hours east of the Delta—now uses a curriculum developed by Cambridge University in England. A test occurs at the end of the year; it is designed by Cambridge and is more focused on critical thinking skills than on predictable content questions.[112]

District leaders in Corinth understood that they would be exempt from the state's standardized testing, which drives the Mississippi Department of Education rating. It was not until the end of the school year that the state clarified that their students needed to take the state test, and the district's rating would be based on these results. The district rushed to offer the test at the end of the school year after all other instruction was complete and without any specific preparation. As a result, the high school received an

F rating even though the district had previously improved its rating from C to B. Its students scored a full point higher on the ACT than the state average, and 95 percent of its seniors graduated high school. Leaders in Corinth worry that this F rating will scare people and employers away from the area.[113] This story epitomizes the challenges of using a standardized test built around a standardized curriculum to compare educational quality in districts across the state and county.

Third-Grade Gate

Standardized testing is used not only to rate schools but also to determine whether children are allowed to advance between third and fourth grade. Mississippi is one of sixteen states that requires students to be proficient in reading before they move to fourth grade.[114] Proficiency is determined entirely by their performance on an exam at the end of the year, which is nicknamed the "third-grade gate," rather than in combination with an assessment by their teachers. This approach has been controversial. Supporters say the pressure and accountability of this test is one of the main reasons why reading scores have risen faster in Mississippi than anywhere else in the country in recent years, improving the state's ranking from forty-ninth in 2013 to twenty-ninth in 2019.[115]

But many people are worried and upset by this approach. Lisa Darling-Hammond, Ed.D., a researcher who has studied the effects of similar reading requirements says, "We have had dozens and dozens of studies on this topic. The findings are about as consistent as any findings are in education research: the use of testing is counterproductive, it does not improve achievement over the long run, but it does dramatically increase dropout rates. Almost every place that has put this kind of policy in place since the 1970s has eventually found it counterproductive and has eliminated the policy." She predicted there would be early gains, but the negatives would ultimately outweigh any positives and would be disproportionately felt by children who are Black, immigrants, and from low-income families.[116]

The Mississippi Department of Education responded to the initial improvements in reading scores by raising the standards further.[117] This led to 8,941 children across the state failing the exam in the spring of 2019, more than one-fourth of all third graders.[118] Districts were encouraged to hire reading coaches to work closely with these children,[119] but the money that was allocated meant that fewer than one hundred reading coaches could be hired by the more than four hundred school districts across the state.[120] About one-third of these students passed the second attempt in May.[121] The remaining six thousand children—still 18 percent of all third graders—were offered free eye exams by the Mississippi Optometric Association and encouraged to attend summer school programs focused on preparing for the final round of the reading test.[122] Ultimately, 10 percent of children in Mississippi were required to repeat third grade during the 2019–20 school year.[123]

The numbers are particularly striking in the Delta. Fewer than two-thirds (63 percent) of children in the Coahoma County district passed the test on the first try. In the Clarksdale Municipal district, it was only 40 percent. Both districts have experienced intense teacher shortages, and a leader in one district said that each of the children who needed to retake the test had a permanent sub as a teacher all year in both first and second grades.[124] In other words, the real issue is not just whether individual children can read but the presence of systemic gaps that have prevented these children from being adequately prepared. The Mississippi State Board of Education decided to waive the requirement that the children finishing third grade during the pandemic-disrupted 2020–21 school year pass the test to graduate to fourth grade. The tests were still administered, but children who did not pass will be given additional resources the following year rather than be held back.[125]

Teachers

A wide body of evidence suggests that teacher quality is one of the most important factors to shape student learning.[126] The positive effect of good teachers was reflected in the glowing comments of many teenagers in the Delta. For example, a ninth grader in Clarksdale said his favorite teacher's influence extends beyond the classroom: "When I have a problem, I go to her, and she helps me build myself up and keep myself up. And she's also like a godmother to me. But I'm telling you, she's amazing." A young woman from Clarksdale said that she struggled during elementary school because classmates made fun of her for trying hard and knowing the answers: "I just kind of stopped raising my hand and just let others because they made me feel bad about myself, you know?" She credits her teachers for encouraging her to continue striving for excellence and said this was crucial for her to stay on a path to successfully complete high school and college and land a well-paying job in the Delta that she is excited about.

Others described the harmful effects of bad teaching. They found it discouraging when their teachers seemed disinterested or out of their depth.

A young woman from Shaw said, "We have teachers that are like, 'I don't like coming to work.'" When asked what she meant, one of her friends explained that some are doing little more than reciting from a book: "Some teachers, they teach, and some teachers don't. Like they sit down but don't teach at all. They read from this and this and this when we can read on our own." Teenagers described teachers who created environments that did not make them feel safe or comfortable. In some cases, this seemed inadvertent, such as a teacher who asked a ninth grader where he was from because his vocabulary and clothes seemed different: "Sometimes the teacher asks me where I'm from. I say, 'I'm from the Delta. Clarksdale. I'm from here.' They said, 'You just don't, you talk and act so sophisticated.'" This young man was discouraged from making an effort, and everyone in the class received the message that being from Clarksdale means not being sophisticated or articulate.

Some even described teachers as actively antagonistic. One person said a young man she knew was traumatized by his teacher regularly telling him to "sit his fat ass down" or "get his fat ass over there." She explained that "when his mom found out, she confronted the teacher about it. Of course, nothing happened to that teacher except that then the next day, he made fun of him again and was like, 'Yeah, so this crybaby went and told his mom.'"

Teacher Shortages

As inspiring as these good stories are and as upsetting as these bad stories are, we should look beyond specific instances and specific teachers to consider how hard it is to work in education and the structural factors that make it that much harder in the Delta. Studies show that places with the most intense need are most likely to be served by the least experienced teachers and to be exposed to the most disruptions in long-term development and consistency in the curriculum, and they are at greatest risk of future turnover problems because less experienced teachers are very likely to move soon.[127] Mississippi is one of twenty-one states that do not publish data on teacher hiring, but those data we do have suggest that the shortage in the Delta is particularly severe. For example, the percentage of teachers who are not fully certified has increased sixfold in the last two decades, and classes are being led by permanent substitute teachers.[128] In many school districts in the Delta, the proportion of teachers who lack certification quickly doubled and is now between 19 percent and 34 percent of all teachers.[129]

A recent nationwide analysis was conducted to look at the number of vacancies and undercertified teachers, and the conclusion was that "the teacher shortage is real, large and growing, and worse than we thought."[130] One reason for the worsening shortage is that fewer people are choosing to go into teaching. Between 2009 and 2015 there was a nationwide drop of 15.4 percent fewer education degrees awarded and 27.4 percent fewer people completing teacher preparation programs.[131] Since 2015, the number of students enrolling in education and teacher preparation programs in Mississippi has dropped 40 percent.[132] At the same time, schools across the nation experienced 16 percent turnover,[133] and 90 percent of vacancies are caused by people leaving the profession altogether.[134] These nationwide and statewide trends hit low-income communities hardest because teachers are nearly twice as likely to leave schools in low-income communities than those in affluent communities.[135]

The dynamics of who goes into teaching and who stays in the field create a racial gap that makes it unlikely that students will have nonwhite teachers. Only 27 percent of teachers in Mississippi are Black compared with 48 percent of students, and Louisiana is the only one other state that has such a large gap in diversity between teachers and students.[136] The gender differences among teachers add to this disparity, and only 6 percent of teachers in Mississippi are Black men.[137] A leader explained why this is important: "I don't think you have to come from that type of background in order to relate, but it helps. It definitely helps. . . . There's been so much recent research coming out lately about the impact that teachers of color have not just on students of color, but on all students."[138]

Students in Mississippi districts are also more likely to be taught using an online platform such as Edgenuity or Edmentum. These are not just used as supplements, complements, or a way to manage disruption caused by COVID-19; in many cases they are the main mode of instruction. As one person described, "It's basically like a computer screen and you have an instructor on there." The district hires a facilitator to stand at the front and guide students through the modules. But there is no way to ask questions since the facilitators rarely have any content expertise.[139] As one student in the Delta described to a *Mississippi Today* reporter, "It's hard because ain't nobody really teaching. We're just going over some of the facts that we should know and it's kind of difficult. If I've got a question to ask, how you do that? I can't ask the computer and the teacher that up in there, she don't know it." Another student added, "You go to school and see these people that's supposed to give you this emotional support, this educational support and they don't. They don't give you either and now you're like, 'Why leave my house? I don't have any purpose.'"[140] A number of districts in the Delta remained fully remote throughout the entire 2020–21 school year, and leaders and parents say the effects of being taught exclusively online are serious and will be felt for years to come.[141]

Certification

The teaching shortage in the Delta is exacerbated by the obstacles people face to becoming certified. Candidates are required to score 21 or higher on the ACT, pass the Praxis Core test, and pass additional Praxis tests relevant to their subjects.[142] Many people struggle to satisfy these requirements, even after doing well in a teacher training program and even after succeeding in their initial classroom experiences, in part because what is on these tests is not closely aligned with what they are taught in their programs.[143] Nonwhite candidates from lower-income backgrounds are significantly less likely to pass certification exams by a difference of nearly 40 percentage points (75 percent vs. 38 percent).[144] Retaking the test is expensive since the Praxis Core costs $150 and the subject tests cost $120.[145] The financial effect of this situation is compounded by the state-mandated salary of $14,000 for teachers' assistants, people who are not certified but are effectively permanent subs with their own classrooms for the entire year.[146] They cannot afford to take the tests that will allow them to be better paid for the work they are doing. Many people who want to be teachers give up even after investing significant time and money in preparing for a career in teaching.

The state developed a new pilot program in November 2017 to certify 110 people on a provisional basis and allow them a temporary one-year license while they work on passing the Praxis exams. This is not a long-term solution but means that these people can receive a full salary and better afford to take the certification tests. The state's Department of Education created a position whose full-time role is to work on the teacher shortage, including building relationships between high schools and colleges. In January 2019, more than one thousand people signed up for the free Praxis training that was offered for the first time.[147] Early evidence suggests these efforts are helping. The Jackson school district, which is not in the Delta but faces many of the same struggles, saw the number of teachers without full certification drop from 184 in 2018 to 29 in 2021 and the number of unfilled positions over the same period drop from 246 to 75.[148]

Teacher Salaries

These steps are encouraging but do little to address the even more fundamental challenge of how low the salaries are for full-time teachers who are certified. Mississippi has some of if not the lowest teacher salaries in the nation. Starting teachers who are certified make about $35,000 per year. The average salary across all levels is $42,925, well below the national average of approximately $60,000.[149] The very highest point on the state's salary schedule in 2020 for people with doctorates and at least thirty-five years of experience is $68,870.[150]

Comparing teacher salaries in Mississippi with those of other states across the country might be misleading given the huge difference in cost of living. A teacher in New York with comparable experience makes $40,000 more, but life there is more expensive.[151] Yet teacher salaries in Mississippi are low compared even with those of neighboring states. After taking cost of living into consideration, teachers would need to make at least $4,000 more per year to match what they would earn in Alabama, Arkansas, or Tennessee.[152] These differences make it very hard for administrators in Mississippi to attract and retain teachers.

The legislature has rarely increased teacher pay in recent decades. When it does, it is typically as increases of $1,000 or $1,500.[153] Many say this is not enough, as it barely amounts to anything after inflation and taxes. Teachers describe a host of challenges stemming from this very low pay. A woman in Clarksdale said she teaches summer school in Chicago, where she stays with relatives, "because they cut summer school here. I always have to get a supplement so I can make it through the year." Another woman said, "The pay is terrible. I'm supposed to be retired eight years and I cannot live off of my retirement."

School districts can use their own funds to increase salaries beyond the state's schedule, but the intense connection between school funding and property taxes means that few districts in the Delta are financially positioned to compete with districts elsewhere in Mississippi or across state lines. For example, DeSoto County, which borders the Delta but is effectively a suburb of Memphis, has higher rates of home ownership and higher property values, which means greater property tax revenue and more money for the school system. The DeSoto County School District paid teachers an additional $4,204 beyond the state minimum in 2018. By comparison, teachers in the nearby East Tallahatchie Consolidated District in the Delta received just $9.72 extra.[154] Decentralizing school funding and tying it to local property taxes means that low-income communities will never be able to compete for the most experienced teachers.

Teach for America

One way schools in low-income communities deal with teacher and budget shortages is by hiring people through the Teach for America (TFA) program, which places recent college graduates with an interest in education equity in high-need districts for two years in exchange for salary, benefits, experience teaching, and in many cases help to pay off student loans.[155] TFA has been sending young adults to the Mississippi Delta since 1993. However, these numbers decreased in recent years from 272 in 2015 to 196 in 2016 and 131 in 2017.[156] TFA elicited strong feelings from students, parents, teachers, and administrators in the Delta. A woman in Cleveland said, "They're well-meaning people. I mean, 90 percent of them mean well," to which another woman in Cleveland responded,

> Yes. But you throw them in these classrooms in a culture that they don't understand with behaviors that they're not used to, and you're asking them to manage these kids where there's still a cultural disconnect. . . . And that's where my love/hate relationship falls in with TFA because in my line of work, I interact with them quite often. And there are some who have come here and who have started freedom schools and who are doing great work. But then you have those that come here that feel as if they know it all; they have their cape on.

An education leader in Clarkdale made a similar point about what she referred to as "the white savior complex" of some TFA participants. She described the emotional effect on the community of relying too heavily on outsiders to fill the need and the importance of strengthening homegrown talent: "There's a lot of TFA people here, and I think that that can be genuinely destructive, even if the need is high. That's the opposite of what needs to happen, is for people to feel more powerless and more like the only people who could, this is the only path out or whatever."

Many stressed they were not opposed to TFA, but that they wished that these young teachers were better trained,[157] had more mentorship, and were more often from Mississippi, and that more stayed in Mississippi when their two years were over. A young man in Clarksdale described how disruptive this turnover is: "We have a lot of teachers that kids can kind of get connected to their first year. But their second year, they come back to school, the teacher's gone and they have a new teacher, and so it's a different learning style and they don't understand what's going on in the classroom. And there's nothing that they really can do to kind of build up to where they need to be." A white teacher who moved to the region even though she is not part of TFA said that students hold back from getting too attached to her because they assume she is leaving in a year or two: "They keep asking, 'This is your last year?' to which I reply, 'No it isn't. I live here!'"

Some people also worried that TFA was a bandage or even a distraction from deeper issues that need addressing. As one education leader put it, TFA is a "mixed blessing" because it fills teaching spots but does not solve the fundamental problems. We need to get at the root of the teacher shortages.

Supporting Students

The relationship between teachers and students is critical. We have already seen that structural issues can affect the likelihood that teachers are at their best because they are qualified, have the resources they need, and are happy in their jobs. Unfortunately, the broader systemic issues that make work harder for teachers in the Delta also make learning harder for students. We need to identify and address barriers from the child's point of view. Some of the structures that need to be improved include emotional support for children with adverse childhood experiences and learning disabilities; universal preschool; a healthy, nonphysical approach to discipline; and comprehensive sex education that includes easy access to contraception.

Emotional Support

Children do not show up to school as blank slates. Their readiness and ability to learn are shaped by their lives at home and in their communities. Approximately 45 percent of all children in the United States and 61 percent of Black children have experienced at least one adverse childhood experience.[158] These experiences include being abused or witnessing violence and any form of economic or familial instability, such as moving frequently or parents getting divorced, leaving, or going to prison. The number of children who experience at least one adverse childhood experience is likely much higher in the Delta, where nearly two-thirds of children live in single-parent households,[159] the violent crime rate in many communities is high (see chapter 2), and more than 60 percent of Black children live below the federal poverty level of $26,200 for a family of four.[160] The median household income in most Delta counties is lower or barely higher than the federal poverty level, which suggests that the number of children who grow up in severe poverty is actually much higher.

Children who deal with these traumatic experiences are more likely to suffer from delayed language development, chronic absenteeism, bullying, and other major challenges at school.[161] Adverse childhood events have a cumulative effect, which means that the likelihood and intensity of negative outcomes increases for each additional adverse event a child experiences.[162] These children carry an intense burden, and many worry about what sacrifices they need to make to help put food on the table and care for family members.[163]

Adolescents face unique pressures because they can and sometimes are expected to get jobs to supplement the family income. A young woman in Cleveland whose mom works long and difficult hours described how the difficulty of juggling these responsibilities makes it that much harder to do well in school: "I have to, like clean up around the house because she's not there to do it anymore." This young woman tries to get to bed by 11:45 P.M., but "if I have a test the next day, which I usually do because of my math teacher, she usually gives them on Wednesdays, and I work on Tuesdays, and I get off at like, 10:00, 10:30 or something, then I'll study up until like 1." She said she is trying to cope, but "there's just days that it's good and days that it's not. And I just like, try to like breathe in and take it one step at a time. Sometimes it isn't that easy."

Many teenagers said that maintaining good mental health is one of the most intense challenges they face and that this is exacerbated by not having anyone to ask for help. The adults in their lives sometimes do not model good coping mechanisms, turn to alcohol and drugs, or simply do not deal with issues. When they ask parents, grandparents, or other caregivers for support, a young woman said, "you're told, suck it up, pray about it, and you gotta keep pushing. Who cares? The world doesn't care about you. You got to keep it moving and do what you gotta do." She explained this approach is not working for her and is getting in the way of school and life: "I care. It's bothering me. It's affecting me. And as I cover that up, what happens to it? It doesn't go away. Well, people kept telling me to suck it up and pray about it. I believe in prayer. I'm a Christian, but you sometimes need to talk things out. You need to seek professional help. It may be out of the realm of just what goes on in this house stays in the house. It never gets healed if it don't leave the house, right?"

Some youth said that the lack of emotional support from teachers and other adults in their lives adds to their burden as they become the support systems for their friends, siblings, and cousins. For example, a young man described how he recently talked his ninth-grade classmate through suicidal thoughts. He was worried when this friend did not show up to school or respond to any phone calls or texts, so he turned up unannounced at his house around midnight: "He was so surprised. He was crying, and I sat there and talked. We had a whole conversation until late in the morning." It is hard to imagine either of them focusing at school the next day.

Word has spread that he is a safe person to talk with and so others have sought his guidance on everything from depression to bullying and how to come out to their family as gay: "Even the seniors come to me. . . . The parents don't accept it. They don't want that for their child. They see it as it's not right. And they have the teens terrified. It has them literally terrified to see how their parents think of them. And they get treated like less of a person." This young man said it is incredibly gratifying to support his peers, but it is also exhausting. "I have my breakdowns. . . . I get bullied every day [because some people] take my kindness for weakness." He hit an emotional tipping point of his own while supporting an eleventh-grade friend who had been kicked out of the house after coming out to his parents as gay: "It was so hard for me to get through that. And with me having my emotional instability, I also broke down because it was really sad to see that the parents, someone that's supposed to be there for you, not even doing their job. . . . What am I supposed to do? What am I supposed to do? And I can't help all of these people. Like, how am I supposed to be there for them once I have to do things for myself, too?" For this young man and many like him, going to school is as much about the emotional work of dealing with intense adversity he and others face as it is about educational achievement.

Intense unmet need is likely, as the rates of autism spectrum disorder and mental health diagnoses are much lower in Mississippi than the rest of the nation,[164] which likely reflects underdiagnosis and undertreatment for children with learning differences as opposed to a lower prevalence of these conditions.[165] Children with autism spectrum disorder are more likely to struggle with verbal and nonverbal communication, social interactions, and environments that are chaotic or unpredictable. They can thrive academically, socially, and emotionally if given the proper support,[166] but even when children in the Delta receive timely autism diagnoses, schools struggle to provide adequate services. These schools struggle to hire enough teachers as it is, let alone teachers with appropriate qualifications for students with special needs. Many people also described that a stigma surrounds mental health in small communities because of a perception that everyone knows everything about everyone.[167]

Behavioral and emotional challenges among students are a primary reason many teachers leave the profession. For example, a woman in Clarksdale told a story about her daughter-in-law: "My baby boy's wife, this was her first year to teach, and she was like spit on and had people running out of the classroom. . . . It was just tough on her. She is expecting, and she is on bedrest, and she swears she would never teach again." The geographic concentration of poverty means that teachers in the Delta are more likely to have multiple children in their classrooms who deal with adverse childhood events and learning disabilities, and the teachers have inadequate resources to support these children. These needs have intensified in recent years as the COVID-19 pandemic hit families in the Delta particularly hard and children here struggle to process the national conversations around racism.[168] This is a perfect storm in which the places with the greatest needs face the greatest gaps, resulting in teachers who are burnt out. Adequate funding will help schools hire enough well-qualified teachers and train everyone to support the large numbers of children who deal with learning, social, and emotional difficulties. Administrators and teachers need to be given the space and the tools to talk about racism in America. Schools can also institute trauma-informed policies and programs to help children develop emotional and social skills to build resilience.[169]

School-Based Health Centers

Some districts are using school-based health centers (SBHCs) to address the physical and emotional needs of their students, particularly those in communities with severe gaps in access to health care (see the next chapter for more on these gaps). SBHCs are clinics that operate on or near school grounds as partnerships between the school and a community health center, hospital, or local health department.[170] Mississippi is not one of the sixteen states that appropriates money to SBHCs from the state's general funds,[171] but the state's Division of Medicaid has developed a program to allow schools to be reimbursed for health care services outside the traditional fee-for-service program.[172] Mississippi is home to seventy-three SBHCs, more than many large states such as Colorado and Massachusetts, although in those places children tend to already have access to care.[173]

Children who participate in SBHCs experience a variety of positive outcomes, including increased immunization rates, more physical activity, better nutritional habits, reduced barriers to mental health services, decreased absenteeism, increased graduation rates, reduced dropout rates, and increased grade point averages.[174] The SBHC provides an entry point for a child's entire family to access medical services at a local community health center. A new program developed in 2021 used federal money through the Coronavirus Aid, Relief, and Economic Security Act, a COVID-19 relief bill passed by Congress, to establish a pilot in which schools will virtually connect children to health care services. These telehealth visits are meant to help with issues like diabetes and to provide emotional and behavioral support.[175]

Universal Preschool

Preschool or prekindergarten (pre-K) has been called "the most important grade" because of the many benefits for children, families, and society as a whole.[176] Children who participate in pre-K have greater language development, literacy, problem-solving skills, and self-control than those who do not, all of which leads to fewer behavioral challenges and greater educational outcomes in kindergarten and first grade. This then snowballs to greater achievement throughout their entire school career, decreased likelihood of needing child welfare services or being involved in criminal activity, and higher incomes as adults, which in turn leads to greater taxes paid back to society, greater financial security, and better overall health.[177] Children who do not participate in preschool do better if more of their classmates were in pre-K because their teachers' attention is less focused on the disruptive behavior of others who have not yet been taught the emotional skills needed to do well in a school setting.[178] Mississippi was at the center of the creation of Head Start in the 1960s, a nationally funded preschool program for disadvantaged children. Today, the state ranks well below the national average for the percentage of four-year-olds enrolled in preschool (34.4 percent compared with 44.2 percent nationally). The disparity is even greater for three-year-olds (10 percent compared with 37.4 percent nationally).[179]

Large cities and states such as New York City and Florida have shown that universal pre-K is possible but expensive. An intermediate approach is to prioritize developing programs for children in low-income families. In one study, it was estimated that providing preschool to the poorest 25 percent of children in the country would cost about $13.2 billion, but the net economic effect would be positive by the ninth year due primarily to savings from crime reduction and increased wages and benefits. "Within 44 years, the offsetting budget benefits alone would total $83 billion, more than three times the costs of the program. Thus, by 2050, every tax dollar spent on the program would be offset by $3.18 in budget savings and governments collectively would be experiencing $57 billion in surpluses due to the prekindergarten investment."[180] Some states would see even greater savings per every dollar spent.

Mississippi policymakers have adopted this incremental approach and have taken important steps to increase the availability of preschool to many of the most vulnerable children in the state. In 2013, the legislature passed the Early Learning Collaborative Act to help individual communities establish pre-K programs that are voluntary but universal.[181] The state is not running schools or building facilities, but it is matching local spending of city and county general funds, philanthropy, tuition, and in-kind donations from churches and other organizations. The goal is to establish a network of public and private partnerships that together provide preschool access to every child.

The legislature initially appropriated $3 million for eleven communities but has increased this amount three times so that the funding level is now more than double the original level. An estimated three thousand four-year-olds in nineteen communities across the state benefited from this program in 2019.[182] One-third of these programs are in the Delta, but the funding model places some of them at a disadvantage because many have struggled to raise money locally. The Tallahatchie Early Learning Alliance is an impressive outlier, which in 2016 raised $340,000. This was the second-highest amount in the state and approximately five times more than the next highest collaborative in the Delta.[183]

These are encouraging steps but are far from enough. As journalist John Merrow writes, "We can, and should, be creating a preschool system that would be good enough for everyone. Public preschools should be built the same way we constructed our highway system: the same road available to all Americans, rich and poor."[184] And even then, universal access to high-quality preschool is only a solid foundation if children also have access to high-quality schools in first grade and beyond.[185]

Teenagers in the Delta who made it to college described how important preschool was to put them on the track to success. They said that looking back, they can see that they were singled out by their teachers at a very young age and given more opportunities than their peers. As a young man described, "Preschool probably was the start. And then I think that this is when it like, I started separating. And then you get to high school, and you see a very clear separation." Another young man told a similar story: "If you showed a little bit of potential, they had this gifted program. And starting in first grade, if you tested gifted, you could be put in this program. Essentially for one day a week they'd take you out of class and they would work on you with stuff that was much higher level. So I mean, in first grade, I was reading at a third-grade level."

An adult from Clarksdale said that very early on she also was put in a class with other gifted kids who were taken on field trips and given other extra opportunities. She went on to graduate from college and get a graduate degree. She says that most of the other kids who were singled out with her early in elementary school have had similarly successful careers that have taken them out of the Delta. The rest have stayed behind and are now the parents of the kids in the same schools they attended. She says they are frustrated and cynical: "They don't come to the parent teacher conferences. Why should they? We have completely devoured the trust factor. There is no reason for them to trust the public school system to work for their children." High-quality, universal pre-K would be an important step to preparing children for success in school. But as these stories illustrate, it is not enough, and the benefits diminish if children are not continually supported as they age through the system. All students should receive the same level of attention as these teens who said they felt singled out at a very young age.

Corporal Punishment

Unfortunately, many children experience school as a place of trauma rather than as a refuge and place of support. Mississippi is one of nineteen states in which corporal punishment of children is legal from preschool through high school. Corporal punishment is the use of physical force with the intent to cause a child to experience pain in order to correct misbehavior.[186] This is typically done with a paddle or large wooden board.

No state relies on physical violence in school as heavily as Mississippi. More than one-fourth of the reported instances of corporal punishment in the 2015–16 school year (the most recent year for which data are available) across the United States were in Mississippi. The twenty-three thousand reported instances here were seven thousand more than in Texas, where the state's population is ten times as large. Alabama and Arkansas were the only other states with more than ten thousand cases. Corporal punishment—in Mississippi and in the rest of the country—is disproportionately used on Black boys and children with disabilities.[187] Nearly 85 percent of schools in Mississippi report using corporal punishment.[188] No evidence supports corporal punishment as an effective approach to discipline. In fact, ample evidence shows its use causes serious problems. Students are less likely to be engaged in their schoolwork and more likely to be isolated from their peers.[189] Studies have shown decreases in cognitive ability, lower academic performance, worse parent-child relationships, and greater risk for physical abuse.[190]

The effect of this approach extends far beyond the kids who are directly beaten because the other children worry about classmates who are hit and are scared they could be next. One person said that rather than safe spaces, "schools are run like prisons, and you have no bodily autonomy over yourself." Children with disabilities, such as autism spectrum disorder, face a particularly steep battle to recover from the trauma of receiving or witnessing paddling. Parents say that these children come home crying and are afraid to go back to school because of the constant triggers that cause them to relive the experience.[191] Many students, parents, and even teachers said that the culture and policies surrounding discipline create a toxic environment that makes a hard situation even harder.

The leader of an after-school program said that they do not allow corporal punishment, but 100 percent of the children who come to them have been paddled, some many times, often in front of the whole class, and many times for very minor offenses: "Our kindergarteners, first graders, second graders, you throw a pencil, that's literally it, for being late, for being tardy. . . . In high school, usually you can get the choice. Do you want three licks, or do you want three days out of school suspension? And a lot times, people will be like, 'I don't want to miss school for three days because I actually care about my grades. So I'll take the three licks.'" Physical punishment in school is described by the Human Rights Watch as a major human rights violation and has been proved to be counterproductive, harmful, and ineffective.[192] Corporal punishment can cause serious injuries and is associated with depression, anger, increased dropout rates, and disengagement from educational opportunities; it can also adversely affect a child's self-image, contribute to disruptive and violent behavior, adversely affect academic achievement, aggravate medical conditions, and lead to developmental regression.[193] Corporal punishment is harmful to educational progress, even if there is no significant physical injury. Mississippi has been described as experiencing "an extreme school discipline crisis" given the frequent and widespread use of corporal punishment.[194]

People regularly mentioned an incident in which a teacher in Greenville became frustrated when a middle school student on the autism spectrum refused to go where she was told, and the teacher responded by dragging her across the gym floor by her hair. The school's principal tried to fire the teacher, but the superintendent insisted she receive a relatively minor suspension instead. It was only after video of the episode surfaced online and the broader community watched the teacher drag the girl that the teacher was fired and charged with abuse of a vulnerable person. She was then banned from teaching for twelve years,[195] and the superintendent was fired.[196]

Paddling is not technically allowed unless a parent signs a consent form at the beginning of the year. This suggests that many people condone and even support the use of corporal punishment on their children. In fact, some parents told me that schools are having more discipline problems now because they are not paddling as much as they used to. A woman in Clarksdale said, "Now you can't whup them at school and the kids know it." But other parents feel powerless to protect their children from corporal punishment. One person in Clarksdale described how children on the no-paddle list sometimes still get paddled: "And then they go up to the school and they become the angry parent," which further strains an already difficult dynamic. Even when teachers and administrators respect the lack of consent, these children are still witnesses to violence against their classmates.

Some leaders establish cultures in their schools that are more geared toward positive reinforcement than corporal punishment. A woman in Charleston described, "If your child has a problem or he has a discipline problem and they put him with another teacher, he or she is going to end up in my room. And what I do is I listen to the child. They have a voice in my classroom." Sometimes this strategy requires tuning out what other teachers and even parents say about these children: "I don't just go by the other teacher's word or even I've had some parents come in my classroom and [talk] down [about] their child. I said, 'Well, I'm going to get to know that child.' And I get to know him or her. And some of them, they are not developmentally where they will learn, but I'm going to teach them all I can, and if I see them come to a stopping point, I try to move them forward. I encourage them." She described how excited and proud these children are when they then do well: "Like when they took their test this year my class came out of that test and they said, 'I know I did good. I know I did good on that test!'"

The evidence is clear that this approach to discipline is better than physical violence, which should be banned. Students would be less likely to need discipline if their emotional needs were better addressed. Teachers are more likely to come to these interactions with patience and perspective when they are well supported and their job satisfaction is high.

Sex Education

Sexual health is another critical issue in which children's lives outside the classroom affect their ability to do well in school and in which schools can better prepare children to make healthy decisions. Mississippi ranks second in the nation in teen pregnancies, second in teen births, second in gonorrhea infections, second in chlamydia infections, seventh in syphilis infections, and seventh in HIV infections.[197] More than one-eighth of all births in Mississippi are to women under the age of nineteen, and one in five teen births is a repeat birth.[198] These high rates of pregnancy and disease were the result of risky behavior; 61 percent of Mississippi youth (ninth–twelfth grade) have engaged in sexual intercourse (compared with the national level of 46 percent), and 24 percent of Mississippi youth have had four or more sexual partners (twice the national average). Among those who engaged in sexual intercourse, 34 percent did not use condoms, and 86 percent did not use birth control pills.[199] Research shows that teenagers are significantly less likely to engage in these risky behaviors if they have been educated by parents or educators.[200]

A young man in Clarksdale identified this as one of the major barriers to improving physical and financial health in the Delta: "Teenage mothers who are already living in poverty-restricted areas get pregnant, and now the child statistically has a high chance of living in poverty. And it's just being repeated as a cycle. It's just affecting us as a whole." He added that one of the biggest challenges is that parents are uneducated and unwilling to talk to their children: "It's that the parents are too afraid to talk about sex because it's like they be afraid because they don't think that they'll do it so young. But without the proper knowledge of sex, not knowing what it is, it's just going to make the child anxious to know what it is."

A controversial law passed by the Mississippi legislature in 2011 (House Bill 999) requires school districts to implement a sex education curriculum. A major compromise gave districts power to choose between two approaches: abstinence-only or abstinence-plus. Both are required to emphasize that abstinence from sexual activity before marriage and fidelity within marriage are the only certain ways to avoid out-of-wedlock pregnancy, sexually transmitted diseases, and related health problems. Only districts that choose the abstinence-plus approach are allowed to discuss the cause, effects, and prevention of sexually transmitted diseases. The law explicitly states that regardless of which approach they adopt, "in no case shall the instruction or program include any demonstration of how condoms or other contraceptives are applied" and "there shall be no effort in either an abstinence-only or an abstinence-plus curriculum to teach that abortion can be used to prevent the birth of a baby." Finally, the law requires that in all cases, "sex-related education instruction may not be conducted when boys and girls are in the company of any students of the opposite gender." Students need to be separated by gender into different classrooms and taught separately.[201] At best, this approach is a missed opportunity to build a shared language and knowledge base among all youth. At worse, this approach is harmful to people who do not conform to binary gender categories or identities.

More than one-fifth of Mississippi's high schools did not adopt a sex education curriculum by the June 30, 2012, deadline. By the first year, a slight majority of districts (eighty-one) had chosen abstinence-only over abstinence-plus (seventy-one). School districts with the greatest need—that is, the highest rates of teenage pregnancy and sexually transmitted disease—tended to choose abstinence-plus.[202] Virtually every district in the Delta chose the (slightly) more comprehensive approach.[203]

In a survey of 3,600 parents across the state, 90 percent supported sex education that addressed the transmission and prevention of HIV and other sexually transmitted infections, more than 80 percent endorsed discussion of where to obtain birth control, and more than 70 percent endorsed demonstration of correct condom use.[204] The vast majority of principals said they consulted with parents, and in some cases, it seems that a vocal minority played an important role.[205] The decision-making process was also tilted by the state's approach of leveraging federal grant programs to provide $1.2 million to help districts that chose the abstinence-only approach compared with $520,000 to help those that chose abstinence-plus.[206]

A nonprofit organization called Mississippi First tried to fill this gap by developing a more comprehensive evidence-based curriculum called "abstinence-plus CHART" (Creating Healthy and Responsible Teens) for use in districts that chose the abstinence-plus approach and by securing funding from a variety of sources to support these districts with implementation.[207] Mississippi First leaders visited every district in the state to advocate for the CHART approach. They made a video called "How to Put on a Sock" that demonstrates how to apply a condom despite never using the words *condom, penis,* or *sex*.[208] The video went viral and was covered by media across the country. About half of the districts that chose abstinence-plus also adopted the CHART curriculum.[209]

The full effects of the sex education law are difficult to evaluate because it is hard to know exactly how it has been implemented. So much of what children learn during these sessions is a function of the norms that are subtly validated or discouraged by educators. Discussions of female sexuality almost never mentioned pleasure but instead focused only on "plumbing."[210] In one study of the implementation of HB 999, most teachers surveyed went off script in some way because they disagreed with what they were supposed to teach or didn't find it functional given their setting.[211] For example, the law's only direction about how to deal with nonheterosexuality was to teach "the current state law related to sexual conduct, including forcible rape, statutory rape, paternity establishment, child support and homosexual activity."[212] The state law referenced here forbids "unnatural intercourse," which is defined as the "detestable and abominable crime against nature committed with mankind or with a beast."[213] This statute has been interpreted to include consensual heterosexual oral and anal sex[214] and carries a punishment of ten years in prison and twenty-five years on the state registry of sex offenders.[215]

Teachers used one of three strategies to deal with questions from students about homosexuality: avoidance, overt homophobia, or subversive inclusion and normalizing.[216] A number of teachers and students described to me the bizarre situation of being required to role-play heterosexual marriages while also being required to separate by gender, which effectively mandated that students act out gay weddings. This experience was described by some as amusingly ironic given resistance across the state to gay marriage. The experience was also likely traumatic to children who do not identify with stereotypical heterosexual cisgender norms.

The evidence we have regarding the law's effects suggests that districts that chose the abstinence-plus curriculum supplemented by CHART saw the biggest drops in teen pregnancy rates.[217] Students in these programs had higher levels of self-efficacy and were more likely to abstain from sexual activity than those in the districts that chose the abstinence-only approach.[218] For example, the teen pregnancy rate in Coahoma County, where Clarksdale is located, decreased 60 percent between 2010 and 2016. These improvements in the Delta are even more striking given the many factors that counteract the positive effects of comprehensive sex education, such as poverty and lack of access to contraception. Much work remains to be done, as the rate here is still higher than the state's, which is still dramatically higher than the nation's; more recent numbers suggest the rate is climbing again.[219]

Other programs have been developed to provide additional support. For example, the Delta Health Alliance was one of eighty-four organizations in the United States to receive a sex education grant from the US Department of Health and Human Services in 2015. They developed a three-year program that reached eleven school districts, five private school districts, five local rural health clinics, and three dozen community and faith-based organizations.[220] Their goals were to reduce the rate of teen pregnancies by 10 percent, reduce the rate of sexually transmitted infections by 20 percent, and increase condom use by 30 percent.[221] However, this funding was eliminated by the federal government in 2017.[222]

Higher Education

Children in the Mississippi Delta face many obstacles to obtaining a high-quality education, including higher levels of adverse childhood events, learning disabilities that are undiagnosed or inadequately supported, teacher shortages, underpaid teachers, inadequate district funding, and the trauma of corporal punishment. If children can navigate these barriers from preschool through high school and get to college, they are better positioned to have higher incomes throughout their lives, to live longer, and to be happier.

However, ongoing challenges make it much harder to get a degree and to reap the benefits when they finish college. Getting to college is not enough. This is an emotionally demanding experience for anyone but particularly for children from low-income families and/or those who are among the first in their families to pursue higher education. They are more likely to be food insecure.[223] They are also more likely to suffer from depression and anxiety, which places them at greater risk of having lower grade point averages or dropping out.[224] Teenagers from the Delta who made it to college said they quickly recognized the gaps in their educations. A woman from Cleveland said, "I didn't know I never learned some things until I got there. And then I started on my remedial classes, and I was like, 'Wow,' you know? I said, 'We are so far behind.' There's so many kids that had come from other areas. They were helping me, and they were like, 'Oh, this is easy. This is easy, I already know how to do this.' And I had never even been introduced to a lot of things because we weren't taught those things. They weren't part of our curriculum in high school for us to graduate." Another young woman said, "The education level is very, very low. Like when I came from Mound Bayou to here, I was behind majorly. Like I was failing all my classes because I was a year behind in the education level." These students explained that it was not just that they were underprepared academically; they had the sense that there were unspoken social skills they lacked and subtle cultural cues they were missing. A young man from Clarksdale said, "I went to a training program at Ole Miss [the University of Mississippi] and while being there, I was around 23 other young people my age. And I could kind of see the separation between me being from the Delta." A young woman from Clarksdale described this separation: "It's just a lot of things that you don't think about. I think one of the things that I tell a lot of younger people that I learned through college was the power of networking and actually getting yourself out there to meet people and potentially job opportunities, or whatever it was. I don't think the school system I was brought [up] in adequately prepared me for that."

Mississippi ranks second to worst in the country for the share of the population with a bachelor's degree.[225] The gap is particularly severe for Black students. An important indicator of this racial divide is how many attend the University of Mississippi, the state system's flagship school. In recent years about one-eighth of the freshman class has been Black even though more than one-third of the state's population is Black. A 40-percentage-point difference exists between the share of high school graduates who are Black compared with the share of University of Mississippi freshman who are Black, which represents the largest gap for a state's flagship university in the nation.[226]

Colleges and universities across the state—including the University of Mississippi—have offices and programs to help students navigate the difficult transition from high school to college. Many students do very well, get good grades, and secure internships and jobs that put them in strong positions to build successful careers. But they still face barriers to leveraging their educations because they face greater pressure to return home and help care for family members, even if it means taking a job that pays less and is less satisfying. A young woman from Greenville explained the generational and geographical pull:

> I have a love-hate relationship with the Delta. The Delta has given me so much, like I'm so grateful that I'm from Greenville, and it has taught me so much, and has made me a stronger person for living there because there are certain obstacles and things you have to overcome if you live in the Delta, because of the education, and because of the poverty, and because of the racism that still exists there. But at the same [time] like they say, I just can't see continuing to be there. But it's just like I feel like adults sometimes try to make you feel guilty, like if you don't want to come back. And I'm like, I don't know, it kind of tears me up on the inside. I'm like, I want to help, but like, do I have to sacrifice that also? I want to do better [than] the community I came from.

A young woman from Clarksdale echoed this sentiment and pointed out that the quality of the education system where she grew up was a barrier not only to getting to college but also to coming back and raising her family: "I would love for my kids to be in a community like Clarksdale, but I don't want them to have to be educated through that system. . . . I want to help the Delta and where I come from, but I don't want to drain me and stop like the potential that I have." A young man from Clarksdale who was a freshman at the University of Mississippi said something similar: "I wouldn't want my child to experience the educational system like I did. I feel like that's a disservice to them. And it's just like when you become a parent, you have to think about the broader picture, and it's you like subjecting them to a poor educational system just because you want to better it? I don't know. Like, it's just hard to just think about. I don't know though, I'm pretty sure that at the end of the day I will come back and try to better it."

Ripples of Hope

The challenges to improving education in the Mississippi Delta are profound. The fundamental issues of funding can only truly be solved by the government leaders who set budgets. But others can pursue many actions to address structural barriers to ensure that administrators, teachers, parents, and students have the resources they need to succeed. The leaders of the following four organizations are doing heroic work to address the needs they see in their communities.

Regional Initiatives for Sustainable Education (RISE)

Adrienne Hudson says that her education at Coahoma County High School in Clarksdale was adequate, but she had to overcome a lot of challenges on her way to getting a bachelor's degree in English and a master's degree in guidance education and reading. In particular, she remembers that her eleventh-grade English teacher was an emergency hire to fill a gap, despite having no credentials or experience. Her most recent job had been working at a nearby casino: "She was a nice person, but she didn't know how to teach. That impacted my life and the lives of my classmates."[227] Hudson came back to the Coahoma County School District to become a teacher and then an assistant principal for four years. She was frustrated by the need to hire people like her eleventh-grade emergency licensed teacher because there were not enough people with the proper certification: "As a teacher and administrator, I wanted to improve the things I thought should have been better when I was a student, but the teacher shortage crisis has caused much of our community's progress to deteriorate over the last two decades."[228]

Hudson eventually transitioned to Delta State University to pursue a Ed.D. and build on the research about teacher shortages. There she gained a deeper appreciation that the teacher shortages she experienced as a student, teacher, and administrator were a systemic issue that in Mississippi was six times worse than it had been two decades earlier. She was surprised to realize that there was not already an organization in the Delta focused on issues such as the teacher shortage. So she started one: "I felt like I had to become a revolutionary—the Fannie Lou Hamer for education in the Mississippi Delta."[229]

In 2017, she created a nonprofit to focus on strengthening education in high-poverty areas like the Mississippi Delta: Regional Initiatives for Sustainable Education (RISE). The organization began small with a $25,000 grant that did not allow any of the three-person staff or twelve volunteers to be paid. One of the first things they did was host a conference at Delta State University in May 2017 named iRISE. Teachers, principals, and other administrators from around the Delta came together to talk about the structural issues driving the challenges they faced.

RISE emerged from this conference with a clearer sense of what it would do to address the teacher shortage. Hudson is convinced that the main driver of the teacher shortage is not that there are too few people in the area who could be great teachers or even too few people who want to be teachers. The problem is that there are too many barriers to becoming certified. As described earlier in the chapter, people are stuck being paid $14,000 per year until they pass the Praxis certification exams. However, the exams are not closely aligned with how teachers are trained. Hudson concluded, "There is a teacher pool in our community, but we have to remove the obstacles to their success."[230]

RISE has focused on creating a positive and nurturing environment for teachers and people seeking certification, recognizing that "so much of the barrier is the fear of failing again."[231] It created a training program named Successful Educators Equals Successful Students (SE = SS), and the main goal is increasing the percentage of teachers working in schools in Coahoma County and throughout the Delta who are fully certified. Participants receive free test preparation for the Praxis exams, Pearson's Foundations of Reading exam, or the ACT. These sessions focus on content, strategies for taking standardized tests, and coping with anxiety.

By the end of the program's first year, twenty-one educators had worked together as a cohort and completed all the requirements to be fully licensed.[232] Most of these people were already teaching as permanent subs but now are more likely to stay in their jobs and stay in the field as their salaries tripled almost overnight. Nearly a dozen other teachers have passed at least one Praxis exam and are on their way to being fully certified.[233]

Hudson is passionate about helping teachers in the Delta feel supported, that they are part of something big, and that they have the tools to succeed. She is deliberate in calling everyone who engages with her organization's programs part of a family and refers to the RISE annual conference as "a family reunion."[234] This effort to empower teachers and leaders of the RISE family is so powerful because it is combined with a deliberate focus on overcoming and removing the structural barriers they face.

Clarksdale Collegiate Public Charter School

It is against the backdrop of potential controversy discussed earlier that Amanda Johnson created Clarksdale Collegiate, the first public charter school in the Mississippi Delta. The legislature enacted a law in 2013 that gave a state board authority to authorize the creation of new charter schools but initially included a restriction that new schools could only pull from a single school district. This made sense in Jackson or in other large cities, but it effectively prevented charters from opening in rural communities. This restriction was lifted in 2016.[235]

At this point, Johnson was living in Clarksdale, where her husband, Sanford, was working to educate school districts on the benefits of choosing a comprehensive approach to sex education (he is the person mentioned earlier who made a viral video about how to put on a condom while only talking about socks and feet). She had been teaching in the area for many years but always on the other side of the Mississippi River in Arkansas, first as a TFA corps member and then helping to create and lead the KIPP Delta Elementary Literacy Academy.[236] She and Sanford wanted to continue building a life in Clarksdale but did not want to have to keep bringing their children to her school in Arkansas, nor did they want to put their kids in the Clarksdale public schools or in the private academy.

Johnson began having conversations about opening a charter school with community members soon after the new law took effect in 2016, and these conversations culminated in a public hearing in August 2017. Many people spoke in favor of the charter school, but many were opposed. They were worried that the district would lose money because it would not have as many students. Others were concerned that Johnson would make the existing schools worse by taking the best teachers and the students who were doing well. As one person argued, "If all of these highly active things that we say we can do to get these children ready and give them this public education, why don't we volunteer and do it inside of Coahoma County [public schools]?" Or as another person put it, as "we talk about support for a charter school and support for 150 children because parents have to have a choice for a good public school, I say to you, am I not my brother's keeper? How do we choose which children we save of Clarksdale?"[237]

Local leaders asked Johnson about each of these concerns. She reassured them her school would welcome everyone and fully support kids who struggled or needed disability services. She told them that discipline would focus on positive reinforcement and keeping children in school and also that paddling or any other form of corporal punishment would not be allowed. Leaders were reassured by these responses and said, "Let's be honest, if the teachers were happy where they were and felt supported or whatever they wouldn't leave. It's not like Amanda is offering them $10,000 more."

Johnson's application was approved in September 2017, and Clarksdale Collegiate opened its doors one year later for the 2018–19 school year. The school was approved to have 675 children in grades K–8 but started small with 50 children each in kindergarten, first grade, and second grade. The goal is to add a new grade each year. A lawsuit against a charter school in Jackson threatened to derail these plans, but the courts ruled in September 2019 that it is consistent with the state constitution and state law to use public dollars for charter schools.[238] Johnson has a healthy relationship with the superintendent of the local school district, but the two systems work independently of each other. This can be a little awkward given that Clarksdale Collegiate is located in St. Paul's Methodist Church, which is adjacent to Kirkpatrick Elementary, one of the higher-rated elementary schools in town. About half of the classrooms are in the old Sunday School rooms within the church building, and the rest are in prefab trailers that sit in the parking lot near Kirkpatrick Elementary. Ground was broken in October 2020 for new facilities that will house labs, a cafeteria, and more classrooms.

Testing for the state's public accountability and rating system was supposed to begin during the 2019–20 school year but was put off because of the COVID-19 pandemic. It is therefore too early to point to any concrete data on academic outcomes, but there are many reasons some feel the school is a hopeful presence in the community. One is that so many parents took the leap of faith, registered their children for a new school, and decided to stay. Word spread, and there was soon a waiting list. There was enough interest from parents and teachers that a new class was added, and third grade was added at the start of the 2019–20 year, which brought the total number of students to 247. Students come from as far as forty-five minutes away. Most of the students are Black, but the school is more racially diverse than most public schools in the region.

Parents and community members like the school's rigorous approach in which students are there longer (7:30 A.M. until 4:00 P.M.) and the school year lasts longer (184 days). All children have breakfast and a morning reflection together under the high ceilings and stained-glass windows of what was once the church's sanctuary. Parents like the intense emphasis on college: each school bus has the phrase "College Bound" printed across the back, and the hallways and classrooms are decorated with banners of the alma maters of each teacher, from Mississippi State University to the University of North Carolina. Every room has air-conditioning and a SMART board. Some have Chrome Books, and one has a 3-D printer. The school has a jungle-themed library in which children independently read under giant palm leaves or in bunkbeds that look like safari hideouts.

This model is spreading. In September 2019, the state approved the creation of a new charter school in Greenwood. This is the ninth in the state and the second in the Delta. The school, which will be known as Leflore Academy, will begin with a sixth-grade cohort and then expand to be a middle school with grades 6–8 by 2023.[239] At least five other charter school applications are making their way through the approval process. Johnson is careful to emphasize that public charters are not the solution to replace public education but can play an important role by giving some families other options. She feels that "the opposition voice will always be the loudest in the room, but my families are excited. They understand and have bought into what we are trying to accomplish."[240]

Spring Initiative

The Spring Initiative is another nonprofit organization in Clarksdale focused on helping a relatively small number of people, believing that changes in their lives will ripple to the entire community and beyond. Like RISE, the Spring Initiative began with individuals who noticed a need and stepped up to address it. An interesting difference is that in this case, the people initiating change are outsiders to the Delta.

Anja Thiessen first came to Mississippi in 2001 as a high school exchange student from Germany. Her host family in Illinois participated in a trip to build houses with Habitat for Humanity. She returned home to Germany but kept in touch with the people she met in Mississippi and even came back to visit. Bianca Zaharescu was born in Romania but moved to the United States as a child as her dad went to graduate school and ultimately got a faculty job at the University of Illinois. Zaharescu also first came to Mississippi on a Habitat for Humanity trip and could not stop thinking about the people she met. She returned multiple times and even took a gap year between high school and college to live in Clarksdale and work as a volunteer teacher. A few years later, as Zaharescu was about to graduate from the University of Illinois, Thiessen was living in Germany, where she worked for Procter and Gamble and ran a nonprofit organization. They had not been on the same trips but knew of each other and began connecting. They were both inspired by the Sunflower County Freedom Project, which provided after-school programs and a variety of comprehensive services to children in another part of the Delta.[241] They decided they would start their own organization to adapt this model in Clarksdale.

The Spring Initiative is built on a philosophy of the "transformational power of education and caring relationships" to "empower students to live out their full potential; break the cycle of poverty; lead happy, healthy, secure, and fully engaged lives; and give back to their community."[242] Thiessen and Zaharescu started with twelve middle-school-age children, some of whom they had known since their earlier trips and others who came to the program when they asked principals to suggest children who would most benefit. They experienced very little resistance and said that the typical parent response was, "You're going to do something cool with my kid and teach them stuff that right now they're not really experiencing? Yes, please do it if I feel like I can trust you."

In some ways it helped that Thiessen and Zaharescu are European because they are from so far outside the Delta that they are not part of Mississippi's historical racial and economic dynamic. Zaharescu explains, "We were very aware that it's not ideal to start anything as two outsiders. Basically, two white women coming in from the outside. But we also, I think, felt like there's kind of this need, and we kind of felt like we are equipped enough that we've got to do something, but be very intentional about really trying to really partner and try to make it be as community-led as possible, even though clearly we are right now starting it."

At the heart of Spring is an after-school program in which a cohort of students comes together for three hours every afternoon, including during school breaks and over the summer. These children have unstructured time at the playground to get out some energy and structured academic instruction to teach concepts and help with homework. But the most important part of their time at Spring might be the sharing that happens early each afternoon. This is effectively a family meal in which children are given a healthy snack, and everyone describes a good thing that happened that day, a bad thing that happened, and a hope they have. These exchanges help leaders know how everyone is doing and why. They give the children an opportunity to learn to empathize and support others while also feeling that people care about them. The teachers also serve as the bus drivers who pick up all the children, which gives them another opportunity at the start and end of every day to touch base. Many children ask to be dropped off last, so they have as much time with their teachers as possible.

Thiessen and Zaharescu decided to provide a fully comprehensive program for a smaller number of children and their families rather than a narrow set of services for a large number of children. The need is so great, and the challenges are so severe, they felt that providing intensive support would be the most effective way to structure their program. There are now four active cohorts in addition to the original group that aged out. The program technically only runs for three hours in the afternoon, but the staff are all paid as full-time employees because they provide comprehensive support that affects all aspects of the children's lives. Some children are eligible for Medicaid, but the parents do not apply because they do not have a birth certificate and they do not want to go back to the state office because workers were rude to them. Spring's staff helps families gather documents and fill out the application forms. They help parents navigate the health care system. They go to doctors' appointments, help make sure physicians understand the families' needs, and help the families understand and follow the recommendations. They help intervene with school leaders and go to youth court with children who have gotten in trouble.

Spring provides individual and group therapy to help children process everything they are going through. Zaharescu explains, "If you really want to work with students who literally have had family members be killed, are in some cases orphans, have gone through crazy physical, sexual trauma, whatever—you can't really be there and also help someone really achieve the kind of transformational results in their life that they can, that they're totally capable of it—that's just not going to happen unless you can be that intensely supportive." The group takes trips to visit cultural sites across the United States, including Memphis, New York City, the Grand Canyon, and Washington, DC, so that children gain a better sense of the opportunities that are out there in the wider world beyond Clarksdale. They have visited campuses in Starkville and Oxford, home of Mississippi State University and the University of Mississippi, so that the youth can picture themselves at college.

All of this is expensive, but parents are not asked to pay anything. Thiessen and Zaharescu no longer run the programming directly because they are focused on managing the organization and fundraising. Much of their funding comes from state and federal governments and foundations, but they have also built a substantial donor base that gives $5,500 every month. Some of these donations are from individuals and churches giving $100–$500 per month as a tithing, and one family donates $1,000 every month.

Thiessen and Zaharescu are proud of how the organization has grown, but they say nothing pleases them more than watching the children grow. For each child that means something different. For example, there have been children who have been put on nondiploma tracks at school because of behavioral issues. Even as early as second or third grade, they have been moved to special education classes for children on whom the school system has effectively given up. Rather than being in intellectually stimulating classrooms, they are changing the diapers of classmates with more severe physical disabilities. Their parents were not happy about this situation but did not know they have the right to challenge the school system or did not know how to do so. Spring worked with these parents to advocate to have their children moved back to their classrooms. After fourteen to fifteen months of intensive services at Spring, they are reading and advancing grade levels in the regular classes.

One of the biggest indicators of Spring's success is that all but three of the youth (11 out of 14) in the initial cohort attended college. Some are juniors on the verge of graduating with bachelor's degrees. Most of these children and their families say they almost definitely would not have made it this far without the supportive peers and leaders at Spring. Many of them come back to Clarksdale in the summer, work at Spring as interns, and help the next generation. Some say they do not want to come back to the Delta now that they see the opportunity elsewhere. Spring does not push anyone to come back. The mission is to help these people and their families, not to help Clarksdale, the Delta, Mississippi, or the South as a whole.

Participating in the Spring Initiative does not guarantee that a child will make it through school and be successful. Unfortunately, one person in the initial cohort is now serving a life sentence in prison for murder, and another is homeless and struggling with drugs. Both tried to stick with the program but dealt with extreme trauma at an early age. These stories are heartbreaking for Thiessen and Zaharescu, who have known these people almost their entire lives, but they are still motivated to never give up on anyone. As Zaharescu describes, "Significantly less than half of our students most likely would graduate high school without Spring, in their own words, for the older ones, and barely any would be attending college anywhere. And from the beginning, we really wanted to work with the students who are really struggling the most and are the most behind, knowing that those same students are literally just as brilliant and capable as anybody who's gotten the most investment in the richest neighborhood in the United States."

Indianola Promise Community

The Delta Health Alliance (DHA) is one of the largest nonprofit organizations in Mississippi. It was formed in 2001 and for its first decade worked on a variety of projects to improve health and well-being throughout the Mississippi Delta. In 2010, DHA became one of twenty-one organizations to receive a grant from the US Department of Health and Human Services to establish a Promise Neighborhood modeled after the Harlem Children's Zone in New York City. This was a highly competitive process: more than three hundred organizations applied, and only one other rural organization was selected.[243] The Harlem Children's Zone launched in 1990 as an antitruancy program but evolved to be a fully comprehensive approach to neighborhood revitalization. More than twenty-seven thousand people throughout one hundred blocks receive a variety of services to increase the opportunities available for children from cradle to grave, including efforts to improve birth outcomes; preschool, after-school, college, and career prep services; tax preparation; family outreach; and health education.[244] DHA wanted to do something similar in a rural setting but was reluctant to require applications or a lottery to decide who gets to participate, as was done in Harlem. A team at Mathematica helped them calculate how many children they could serve in a comprehensive way and then looked to identify a community with about that number of children. They quickly landed on Indianola.

Indianola, in Sunflower County, is the childhood home of blues legend B. B. King. Today it is a city of about ten thousand people located thirty minutes east of Greenville and thirty minutes southeast of Cleveland. Indianola has been through some rough times, with a median income of $27,000 and an unemployment rate consistently above 11 percent even before the COVID-19 pandemic. Nearly half of the three thousand children live in poverty, and 30 percent of youth between the ages of sixteen and twenty-four are out of school and not working.[245] Approximately 80 percent of Indianola's residents are Black, and the railroad tracks still divide the community between the large, stately homes on the north side and the smaller, dilapidated homes on the south side. At the same time that DHA received the federal grant, Indianola was reeling from the closure of Delta Pride, a catfish processing plant that had provided many jobs in the community.[246] The schools had also just been taken over by the state and consolidated after years of poor performance.[247]

DHA initially received $330,000 to begin planning. In 2012, it received more than $6 million to establish the Indianola Promise Community (IPC). The initiative has since expanded to an annual budget of nearly $8 million and encompasses thirty programs run in collaboration with twenty-two partner organizations, including health care, education, government, community, and faith-based organizations. The goal is to develop "a pipeline of academic, family, and community resources, from prenatal care through high school graduation, creating a path for students to gain meaningful careers and earn financial independence."[248]

More than nine hundred children up to age five are mailed a free book each month to read with their parents. Three dozen high school students participate in ACT prep every semester. Families are taught about nutrition and physical activity. Teachers engage in professional development courses, and teenagers participate in a youth council to get more involved in city government.[249] Young children participate in preschools and summer camps whose curricula have been aligned to focus on kindergarten readiness.[250] A handful of former TFA corps members have stayed to help run the IPC Literacy Fellows program, which is focused on helping elementary school–age children prepare for the third-grade reading test.[251]

A DHA leader explains that data collection and monitoring have played a critical role in everything IPC does: "A lot of people wanted to come to the Delta and do some really good things. And I'm not saying that they did or they didn't. It's just that we don't really know the effect because the idea of tracking and measuring those things were very foreign to this area of the country. . . . If you don't measure it, you didn't do it. That's kind of our mantra." This data collection is more focused on real-time learning and adaptation than on long-term evaluation and academic publication. Every child has a digital passport that allows their parents, teachers, and other program leaders to see how they are doing in an integrated way. The Linking Individuals, Neighborhoods, and Kids to Services program provides case management led by trained community members to help connect specific children and families to social services as needs arise.[252] This data collection effort, along with an annual door-to-door survey of 350 community members, has also allowed leaders to examine trends across the entire population.[253]

The willingness to adapt in real time has made it a little more difficult to rigorously evaluate the programs to pinpoint the exact effects of specific components, but the overall results have been striking. Three-fourths of Indianola's children now have medical homes as regular sources of health care. Their heart rates and blood pressures went from abnormal and highly varied to stable and regular. Kindergarten readiness increased from 25 percent in 2013 to 48 percent in 2016, far exceeding the initial target of 37 percent.[254] The percentage of first and second graders reading at grade level increased to 70 percent. Of the third graders who could not pass the third-grade gate reading test in the fall of 2015, 59 percent passed it the following spring, a jump of 23 percentage points from the previous year.[255] The high school graduation rate rose 10 points in one year, from 61 percent in 2014 to 71 percent in 2015.[256]

These gains are even more impressive given that IPC leaders have not been able to tap into donations to the same degree as the leaders of other Promise Communities. The Harlem Children's Zone's annual budget in 2013 was $101 million, 70 percent of which came from private contributions. The Harlem program is therefore able to spend $5,000 on each child per year. By comparison, the Indianola budget is one-thirteenth as large, and 89 percent of funding comes from the federal government. It spends less than $1,000 per child.[257]

IPC has not been perfect, and the work is not yet done. For example, a program focused on nutrition and physical activity for third through sixth graders did not result in substantial improvements. Some programs have struggled with attrition as students and teachers drop out over the course of the school year. Leaders of other nonprofit organizations in the Delta are frustrated that DHA has become a magnet for philanthropy in the region, which makes it harder for others to attract funding to address the issues in their communities. Some are alarmed over allegations that DHA leaders misused funds in the past,[258] over the salaries paid to DHA's employees,[259] and about DHA's historical involvement with the Delta Council, an organization of business leaders that throughout its history has perpetuated structural racism.[260] Others are concerned about whether the Promise Community model is sustainable, particularly if grant money dries up.

DHA leaders say they are aware of these concerns and are focused on long-term sustainability. One person explained that if something does not seem to be working, they try not to view it as a failure but instead use the data to understand why and what to change. Another said, "When we're saying that we're making a promise, the promise is not fulfilled after five years. When you start looking at the changes that have to be made and the problems that have existed for generations and generations and generations, it takes a lot to change."[261] The good news is that the program is being extended and becoming a model for other rural communities, including elsewhere in the Delta. The Deer Creek Promise Community was created in 2017 to focus on the 1,500 children in the Hollandale and Leland school districts. Just as in Indianola, this Promise Community is meant to be a comprehensive approach to helping children from prenatal care to high school and beyond. More than thirty programs are focused on case management, literacy, behavioral support, summer camps, and college prep.[262]

IPC and its successors are compelling demonstrations that dramatic improvement is possible. Children, parents, teachers, and leaders will do better if they have more resources. At the same time, no single intervention is a panacea or can single-handedly improve educational and health outcomes.

The Education Equity Policy Agenda

Overwhelming evidence suggests that education is one of the most important factors that shape the opportunities that young people will have for a healthy life, if not *the* most important factor. People with good educations are better off financially, are more stable in their relationships, are more likely to do the things that promote health, such as eating well, exercising, and going to the doctor, and are less likely to do risky and unhealthy things, such as having unprotected sex. Individuals who are well educated are also more likely to live in the same neighborhoods as other well-educated people who experience these same benefits. As a result, the effects of education ripple across populations and neighborhoods so that property values go up, companies bring jobs, grocery stores stay open, and communities have tax dollars to provide amenities such as sidewalks, parks, schools, and appropriate policing. Children raised in these neighborhoods are more likely to inherit wealth and to have access to educations that position them to pass down all these benefits to the next generation and beyond.

To achieve equity in education, we need to eliminate segregation in schools, increase and balance funding across districts, improve standardized assessments and their implementation, pour resources into recruiting and retaining teachers, and address students' social, emotional, and academic needs at every step of the educational experience.

Education Equity Policy Goal #1: Eliminate Racial Segregation in Schools.

Examples of national, state, and local policies:

- Immediately implement policies and programs that eliminate racial segregation in schools.
- Decentralize school funding from property taxes and community wealth to address de facto segregation.

Education Equity Policy Goal #2: Increase and Balance Funding across Districts.

Examples of national, state, and local policies:

- Increase funding for education and resources for districts based on identified need and ensure funding is sufficient to provide comfortable buildings, educational materials, and the ability to recruit the most qualified teachers and administrators. Districts with the greatest needs will need additional resources. This is one of the most important investments states can make, though it will likely require additional financial support from the federal government.
- Balance funding between districts to ensure quality education in all schools, not just those in wealthy areas. The connection between property taxes, home values, parent contributions, and the quality of schools is a powerful mechanism of de facto segregation that ensures that the quality of education is intensely connected to the wealth of a community.

Education Equity Policy Goal #3: Improve Standardized Assessments and Their Implementation and De-Emphasize the Importance of Standardized Testing.

Examples of national, state, and local policies:

- Build assessments that more accurately reflect student strengths, measure growth in a meaningful way, and can be used by educators to support learning.
- Ensure that assessments are rigorous, tied to high standards such as the Common Core, are free from bias, and reflect performance-based tasks.
- Implement standardized testing in a way that is more supportive and less punitive.
- Identify schools in need of more structured support, mentoring, and resources in an effort to mitigate the perverse incentives that encourage corruption and cheating.
- States should use multiple measures, not just a "gate" at any given grade, to determine if students are prepared to advance to the next grade level.

- Colleges and universities should place less emphasis on a student's performance on the SAT or ACT and work to eliminate this requirement altogether.

Education Equity Policy Goal #4: Increase Resources Directed toward Recruiting and Retaining Teachers.

Examples of national, state, and local policies:

- Dramatically increase the salaries of teachers and administrators—particularly in low-income areas—to reflect the central roles they play in shaping community health and wealth. Increasing pay for teachers should be one of the most important aspects of increasing and leveling education budgets across districts.
- Thoughtfully revise certification requirements so they are not overly burdensome, particularly for nonwhite candidates. This could include providing free training for licensing exams, better aligning the curriculum of education degrees and licensing exams, and revising the licensing process so people can receive full salaries while working toward full licenses.

Education Equity Policy Goal #5: Address Students' Social, Emotional, and Academic Needs at Every Step of the Educational Experience.

Examples of national, state, and local policies:

- Increase funding for mental health support—for example, ensure the availability of sufficient school guidance counselors and develop trauma-informed approaches to provide a full range of emotional and social support. This includes training teachers on trauma-informed practices, such as how to help children with adverse childhood experiences and other issues they are likely to encounter.
- Schools should be equipped with the resources and staffing to properly identify, support, and educate students with a wide range of disabilities, including autism spectrum disorder.
- Schools should provide evidence-based, nonheteronormative, comprehensive sex education; provide easy access to contraceptives; and adopt and enforce policies so that all youth are safe and supported.

- Use school-based health centers to connect students with resources for physical, emotional, and sexual health.
- Give every child access to free preschool and full-day kindergarten.
- Ban corporal punishment.
- Schools should be required to promote a college-going mindset beginning in elementary school to help students envision what a path to and through college could look like.
- Provide students with personalized, comprehensive, and supportive "high-touch" college counseling at least by the start of high school. This should extend to include academic support to help students prepare for the full college experience.
- Colleges and universities should make it a higher priority to recruit students from historically underrepresented and low-income communities and to provide additional resources to support them throughout their experiences in higher education.

Simply put, being educated and living near people who are well educated is good for your health. But too few people have equitable opportunities to receive high-quality educations. Supposedly colorblind policies connecting school funding with property taxes and community wealth act as mechanisms to enable de facto racial segregation and limit who has access to opportunity. Attempts to increase equity are resisted as overreach that infringes on local control. Although local discretion has some advantages and provides a venue for residents in underserved communities to make their voices heard,[263] we cannot let this be an excuse for not making the structural changes needed so that all children and all communities have the opportunity to thrive. We can and must do better.

5 Health Care

The health reform debate in the United States in the past century has almost exclusively been about insurance for medical care. This focus is too narrow and needs to be broadened so that the goal of health reform is health. This paradigm shift would push us toward solutions more likely to address the fact that so many people need a lot of health care. When policymakers, journalists, and others talk about health in broader terms, they usually focus on whether people make good decisions, such as whether they exercise or smoke. We have seen on issue after issue that systemic barriers make it harder for some people to make the healthiest decisions about food and physical activity. For those barriers to truly be removed, we need to improve access to economic security and educational opportunity. Indeed, as previously stated, there is probably nothing better that we can do to improve population health than work toward equity in education.

But it is a mistake to think of medical care and population health as opposing goals, that one should be prioritized at the expense of the other. Even when people make all the best decisions about eating and physical activity, some will inevitably get cancer or have other medical needs. Primary care can help detect problems before they become severe, and specialists can treat the complicated issues that arise. Health equity cannot be achieved without ensuring that everyone has access to high-quality medical care.

The caravan that carried Senator Robert F. Kennedy and Senator Joseph Clark through the Mississippi Delta did not stop in the city of Mound Bayou even though it is right next to Highway 61 directly between the last two scheduled stops in Cleveland and Clarksdale. This omission is surprising, because the city of fewer than two thousand people is notable for two major reasons. First, Mound Bayou was founded in 1877 by Isaiah T. Montgomery and Benjamin T. Green, two cousins who were former slaves to the brother of Confederate president Jefferson Davis, with the vision that its all-Black population would be economically and politically self-sufficient. This meant that nearly all the land, farms, schools, health care, and businesses were Black owned and that all the city government leaders were Black. Leading figures in the national civil rights movement such as

Booker T. Washington and Medgar Evers spent time in Mound Bayou and saw it as a model community. In addition, the citizens in this area provided protection for witnesses and Emmett Till's mother, Mamie Till-Mobley, who were testifying and attending Till's 1955 trial. Many of the journalists who wrote about Till's murder also resided in this community. The town thrived for a time but was struggling by the late 1960s as the price of cotton fell, and large numbers of people moved to northern cities in search of work.

Second, Mound Bayou was noteworthy as the site of a new health care clinic that opened in 1966, a year before Kennedy's visit. The money for the facility largely came from the Office of Economic Opportunity, a new federal agency created as part of President Lyndon Johnson's War on Poverty and run by Kennedy's brother-in-law Sargent Shriver. The idea and the energy for the clinic came from two young doctors in the Boston area—John Hatch at Tufts University and Jack Geiger at Harvard University—who saw medicine as a critical front in the battle for civil rights. Geiger first came to Mississippi with the wave of northern volunteers during the Freedom Summer of 1964. He returned to the Deep South regularly and marched in Selma, Alabama, with Dr. Martin Luther King Jr. in 1965.

Geiger was stunned to see that the poverty, poor health outcomes, and lack of infrastructure in the Delta were comparable to the conditions he witnessed a few years earlier during a medical school trip in Africa. He responded by working with Hatch and many others to build a community health center (CHC) inspired by the clinics he helped establish in the rural outskirts of Durban, South Africa. The Delta Health Center would become the model for the CHCs that provide care to an estimated thirty million patients in over 14,000 communities around the country today. Geiger may have selected Mound Bayou as the site for the health clinic because the community had opened Taborian Hospital in 1942, which led to the arrival of the "dynamic and resourceful" civil rights leader and surgeon Theordore Roosevelt Mason Howard.[1]

Long before the term *social determinants of health* was widely used, Howard and other leaders of the Delta Health Center recognized that its patients could not be healthy if they did not have a safe place to live and did not have enough food to eat. A community farm was developed so people could pick fresh vegetables, and community boards were created to empower residents to advocate for issues such as better sanitation in their communities. This approach was similar to that of the farming and livestock cooperatives developed by local leaders such as L. C. Dorsey and Fannie Lou Hamer.[2] These programs were difficult to sustain as federal funding diminished in the early 1970s, but the center has continued to provide a wide range of health care services to thousands of patients each year.

Gaps and Root Causes

By looking closely at the Mississippi Delta it is apparent that many people face multiple, compounding challenges to achieving good health and that overcoming these obstacles is not simply a matter of making better choices. This chapter explores the reasons why Black residents who tested positive for COVID-19 were more likely to die of the virus than their white neighbors. While upstream factors addressed elsewhere in this book, such as housing, education, and safety, are critical to a healthy life, an adequately functioning and high-quality health care delivery system is essential to eliminating health disparities when illness inevitably arises. A health care equity policy agenda should focus on eliminating five barriers:

(1) **Geographic accessibility.** Are there enough providers and health care facilities close enough to be accessed by the population in the region?
(2) **Affordability.** Is cost a barrier to getting care?
(3) **Availability.** Do providers have the resources to deliver the best care?
(4) **Accommodation.** Do health care systems adapt to the schedules and needs of their patients?
(5) **Acceptability.** Are providers responsive to the racial, gender, ethnic, cultural, and linguistic context of the populations they serve?

Any one of these Five A's of Access on its own imposes a significant barrier to receiving medical care.[3]

Geographic Accessibility

Mississippi is the most medically underserved state in the country, and an estimated 57 percent of the state's population lives in a community that lacks an adequate number of primary care providers.[4] The ratio of population to primary care providers in Mississippi (1,890 to 1)[5] is double the ratio in states with the best access, such as Massachusetts (970 to 1).[6] Mississippi is the only state in which more than half of the population lives in health professional shortage areas.

These statistics are alarming given the clear evidence that routine primary care is a critical factor that affects whether people get the right health care when they need it. But these aggregate statewide numbers mask even deeper gaps in the most rural parts of the Delta where the ratios are two or three times worse. Quitman and Tunica Counties, at the northern tip of the Delta, for example, have one provider each. Issaquena County does not have a single primary care provider. Community health workers and nurse practitioners fill some of this gap in rural communities like the Delta, but they are not particularly well supported.[7]

It is not easy to attract physicians to the area. The CEO of a CHC said in recent years she has had the budget to employ ten physicians but has only been able to hire three: "And we interviewed a lot. It came down to no American-born physicians want to live in rural America. Once they graduate, they want to seek the city. They want to know where they can get that Starbucks coffee." Administrators in the Delta have tried at least four strategies to recruit and retain physicians. The CEO who has struggled to hire enough doctors works with a recruiter who, for a fee of $25,000, connects doctors with openings: "Every physician is now signed up with a recruiter. . . . They look at who's graduating from the schools of medicine, and they just send out contacts. And then they know what our vacancies are, so they'll contact a physician and say, 'Hey, I know where there's some vacancies. You sign up with me.' And they do us the same way, 'I know some physicians who might be available. You sign up with me.'" This is a high price to pay every few years for providers who are not likely to stay.

Another approach is loan forgiveness programs such as the University of Mississippi School of Medicine's Rural Physicians Scholarship Program. Participants receive $30,000 toward their college debts for practicing in an underserved area for two years.[8] This has brought some providers to the region, but few stay. As one leader put it, "It's an extremely big challenge trying to recruit someone back who's not . . . used to being from such a small place."[9] This insight motivates the third strategy of targeting people who are originally from the Delta. However, many former residents are reluctant to return after attending medical school in a larger city. As one physician who returned home to the Delta described, "A way of life we have grown accustomed to, we would not be able to maintain that in the Delta. And I think that is the deterrent for new people who would have offers in that area. It's the lack of resources, just for everyday living."[10]

One person explained further that one of the biggest barriers is the quality of the local schools: "You could change the job, you could change what's happening in your work environment, but you can't change the school" where you send your kids.[11] Those who do come often leave by the time their children finish elementary school. In other words, improving the quality of education is not only crucial for helping people make decisions that lead them to being healthier and needing less medical care, it is also one of the most important things that can be done to address the health care workforce shortage in the Mississippi Delta.

The fourth strategy is to target international medical graduates, typically someone from another country who is hoping to obtain permanent resident status (commonly known as a green card) after completing a medical residency. The J1 visa for international doctors requires them to return to their countries of origin for two years before coming back to the United States. Doctors can be exempted from this requirement if they commit to practicing primary care for forty hours per week for three years in a medically underserved area. Every state's department of health is allowed to request thirty waivers to the J1 visa requirement. The Delta is so underserved that it is allowed a virtually unlimited number of such positions through the Delta Regional Authority, which processed thirty-one applications for the Mississippi Delta in 2018.[12]

Although successful at temporarily bringing some providers to the Delta, this program is little more than a stopgap with some unpleasant side effects. Physicians rarely stay longer than three to five years, and one administrator said the longest they could remember was seven years. Frequent turnover makes it hard for patients to develop relationships with their health care providers. As one person in Clarksdale described, "I go back a couple of times [to the CHC] and I have a different one. And I say, 'What happened to so and so?' 'Well . . .' They give me an excuse so they can go ahead. So I've seen three different doctors within the last probably year and a half." This problem is compounded by the cultural gap between providers and patients, which both parties say can be a barrier to optimal care. Cultural barriers are discussed in greater depth later in this chapter.

Other kinds of providers are also needed. For example, midwives could help address the projected shortage of obstetricians and gynecologists in the Delta.[13] In 2014–15, only 2.2 percent of births in Mississippi were attended by midwives compared with the US average of 10.3 percent.[14] One major barrier to increasing the number of midwives in Mississippi is that there is only one accredited certified nurse-midwifery program serving Tennessee,

Arkansas, and Mississippi. Further, the program is housed at a private university where the tuition costs are higher than the tuition at a public university. In addition to midwives, nurse practitioners can also expand access to preventive health care services in rural settings, particularly nurse practitioners with clinical experience in rural communities.[15] Hiring and licensing practices in Mississippi also limit the types of jobs midwives and nurse practitioners can get.

Health Facility Closures

CHCs are under constant financial stress. It is hard to obtain statistics specific to the Delta, but more than one-third (35 percent) of CHC patients across Mississippi do not have insurance, and 93 percent have household incomes less than 200 percent of the federal poverty level (FPL).[16] As a result, Mississippi's CHCs are particularly dependent on federal funds. Only Alabama and Wyoming have CHCs with higher proportions of their operating revenues coming from the federal government.[17] The main source of this federal money, known as the Community Health Center Fund, is operating on a temporary extension after it expired in September 2017. According to one estimate, without a permanent appropriation by Congress, Mississippi's CHCs would lose $32 million, with an indirect effect on the state's economy of $19 million.[18] CHC leaders described being frustrated and exhausted because much of their time is spent advocating for continued funding, a never-ending treadmill of grant applications and contingency planning.

Even before the COVID-19 pandemic hit in 2020, there was a looming threat that access barriers in the Delta could soon be much worse because 2019 was the single worst year for rural hospital closures in the United States. Five rural hospitals had already closed in Mississippi in the last decade, including two that served the Delta (Belzoni and Marks) and one just outside the Delta (Kilmichael). The list may grow longer, as researchers at Mississippi State University found that half of the state's rural hospitals (48 percent) are at "high financial risk" of closing.[19] This rate is higher than any other state's in the country and more than double the national level of 21 percent (map 5.1).[20] More than half of the rural hospitals in Mississippi spend more than they make each year.[21] Many of the most financially vulnerable hospitals in Mississippi are in the Delta, such as Bolivar Medical Center in Cleveland and the University of Mississippi Medical Center–Grenada. This is alarming, given that both of these were also noted as

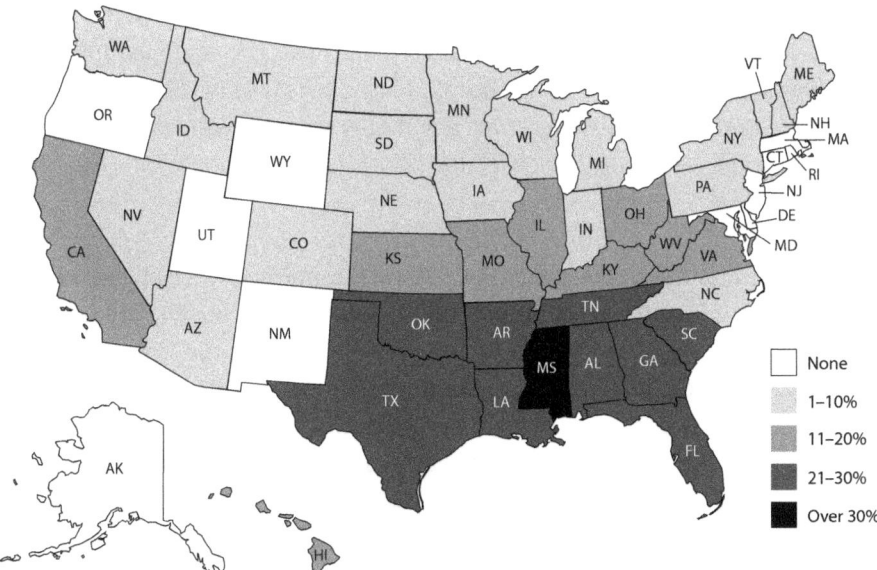

MAP 5.1 Percentage of rural hospitals classified as "vulnerable" by state, 2015. From M. Maya McDoom et al., "Rural Hospitals: Economic and Health Implications in Mississippi" (issue brief, Center for Mississippi Health Policy, November 2015), 2, https://scholarsjunction.msstate.edu/cgi/viewcontent.cgi?article=1000&context=ssrc-publications. Used with permission from Center for Mississippi Health Policy.

being "critically essential"[22] to their communities because of the level of services provided at each place and the lack of available options for patients should they close.[23] Map 5.1 highlights the many hospitals across the United States that are also at risk of being closed.

Northwest Mississippi Regional Medical Center plays a similar role for the residents of Clarksdale, but it nearly closed in 2018. The 181-bed, nonprofit hospital was owned by Community Health Systems until November 2017, when it and three other hospitals were sold to Curae Health, which is based in Knoxville, Tennessee. Community Health Systems chairman and CEO Wayne Smith cited dramatic declines in revenue and suggested, "These four hospitals will benefit from alignment with a smaller organization specializing in the operation of rural hospitals."[24] Curae seemed to regret its decision almost immediately and filed for Chapter 11 bankruptcy for the Clarksdale hospital in August 2018. A spokesperson for Curae said that the hospital significantly underperformed projections and faced $57 million in liabilities compared with $12.6 million in assets.[25] A letter was sent to the 484 employees in October announcing that a closure was imminent. A few weeks later, Community Health Systems announced it would buy back the hospital that one year earlier it said it was not equipped to run. Although locals are relieved the hospital has been saved in the short term, they are understandably concerned about how long this will last.

Transportation

Most communities in the Delta lack public transportation, which makes it very difficult for people who live in rural areas to get to health care facilities. Consider Issaquena County, one of seven counties in the state without a hospital[26] and one of forty-nine counties without a single intensive care unit bed.[27] As already mentioned, no primary care providers practice in the county. The nearest places to access health care are forty-five minutes north in Greenville, sixty minutes east in Yazoo City, and sixty minutes south in Vicksburg, meaning that people must drive between one and a half and two hours for every appointment. These distances would be hard in any circumstance but are virtually impossible for many residents of the Delta given that a startlingly high 17 percent of households in Issaquena County do not have cars. Half of the households in the county include two people, 44 percent of whom had one or no cars.[28] Many people are stuck.

A comparatively low 9 percent of all households in Tunica—another Delta county without a hospital—do not have vehicles. This suggests that the isolation here is not quite as severe, especially given that the hospitals in Clarksdale and Southaven are each a manageable drive of thirty minutes away, and Memphis is not much farther. However, in 2020, 40.7 percent of all households in Tunica County reported having only one car.[29] It is hard to get to a doctor's appointment without a car or if someone in your family is using the household's only car to get to work. The income from that job is likely crucial to the family economy, which makes it very difficult to justify taking time off until a medical concern becomes serious. By that point, the care that is required is often more intensive in terms of costs and the number of trips required to see a health care provider.

Some health care facilities have taken matters into their own hands to help patients overcome transportation barriers. For example, the CEO of the Aaron Henry Community Health Center in Clarksdale described how frustrating it is to watch members of the local community receive referrals for specialty care but then not be able to get to appointments. The center used grant money to buy two vans to take people to providers in Memphis and

Greenville. Word quickly spread to the point at which they regularly received calls from people asking to use seats for purposes other than health care. Additional grant money was received to establish Delta Rides, a program with a $2 million budget whose mission statement is "Moving Mississippi Forward."[30] The system operates a small number of set lines throughout the area, including stops for major employers in the region such as the state penitentiary in Parchman and the casinos in Tunica County. As helpful as this service is, the cost of seven dollars per ride makes it hard for anyone to rely on it as a routine source of transportation.

Needing to drive long distances is a barrier to care for many, but ironically, some people with money and flexible work hours choose to drive farther to Memphis or Jackson for their routine visits because they believe they are likely to receive a higher quality of care. As a gentleman in Greenville described, "Once a year I go to an annual check up to a cardiologist and once a year I go to a check up with a urologist. Those physicians are in Jackson . . . they are associated with the University [of Mississippi] Medical Center. I have this belief in my head that teaching hospitals are the best in the state. I don't care what state you're in, I think they are going to be the better hospitals."

Affordability

Not enough health care providers are located in the Mississippi Delta, and not everyone can travel to the clinicians who are there. But even if physical access is possible, medical services are not accessible if they are too expensive. Many people struggle to get care because they lack insurance coverage or because the insurance they have does not provide much coverage.

Uninsured

Mississippi had the sixth-highest uninsured rate in the country in 2018 at 11.9 percent.[31] This gap in coverage is driven in part by the dearth of good jobs (see chapter 3). As a result, fewer than half of Mississippians (49 percent) receive insurance as an employment benefit, the second-lowest rate in the country.[32] In 2020, 14.2 percent of adults in Mississippi less than sixty-five years of age did not have insurance. This is an important cut point because sixty-five is the age at which everyone becomes eligible for Medicare. Tunica County's uninsurance rate was the best in the region at 13.6 percent, and the rates in the rest ranged from 14.6 percent to

19.2 percent compared with the statewide rate of 14.2 percent.[33] The percentage of children who lack insurance is comparatively low in the Delta because the state has generous eligibility thresholds to qualify for government-financed health insurance through the Children's Health Insurance Program. In 2017, most counties in the Delta were at 3 percent or 4 percent uninsured children compared with the statewide rate of 5 percent.[34] People can get help obtaining health insurance if they do not have employer-sponsored insurance benefits. The path to public or commercial coverage varies and depends on factors such as state of residence, household income, number of people living in a household, age, and being a parent. Differences according to these variables are the product of a patchwork of federal and state decisions made over time that reflect who policymakers feel is deserving of government help.

Consider the options for someone in Mississippi who is younger than sixty-five, does not have children, and has an income less than 100 percent of the FPL. In 2022, the FPL was $13,590 for an individual and $4,720 for each additional person in a household.[35] It does not matter if their income drops lower, they will not qualify for government help because nonelderly adults without children are not eligible for Mississippi's Medicaid program. Under the Affordable Care Act (ACA), eligibility for Medicaid was expanded to childless, nonelderly adults earning up to 138 percent of the FPL, but ten states, including Mississippi, have not expanded Medicaid eligibility as of publication, which creates a coverage gap for millions of people living primarily in the Deep South.

If our hypothetical person's income increases to or exceeds 100 percent of the FPL, they become eligible for an ACA program that provides federal tax credits to help pay for private insurance purchased through an online platform known as a health insurance exchange or marketplace. The amount of the tax credit decreases as income increases. Circumstances change once children enter the picture. During pregnancy, a woman in Mississippi qualifies for Medicaid if the household income is double the FPL.[36] But when pregnancy ends, different eligibility rules apply to children and parents. Children continue to receive government-sponsored insurance through Medicaid or the Children's Health Insurance Program until the age of eighteen if their family income is less than 214 percent of the FPL (about $49,500 for a family of three),[37] but many mothers lose Medicaid coverage sixty days after giving birth.

The 2021 American Rescue Plan Act included an option for states to receive federal funding to extend Medicaid eligibility for all pregnant enrollees from sixty days to one year after giving birth. This option became permanent through the Consolidated Appropriations Act of 2023. On April 1, 2023, Mississippi began providing twelve months of postpartum coverage to nearly every person who gives birth while on Medicaid. Parents in Mississippi only qualify for Medicaid for longer than one year after giving birth if the household income is at or less than 26 percent of the FPL. A family's income must be less than $5,400 per year to be eligible for Medicaid after the postpartum year.[38] Again, that is only if they have children; otherwise adults in Mississippi do not qualify for Medicaid, no matter how low their income. Medicaid expansion would provide coverage for adults with incomes at or below 138 percent of the FPL at little cost to Mississippi, which already receives a high federal matching rate for state money spent on Medicaid, and the federal government would pay 90 percent of the cost of coverage for adults covered through the ACA expansion.

Many people in the Delta struggle to understand the categories and thresholds that govern Medicaid eligibility. Teenagers in Clarksdale said they worried about losing insurance once they turn eighteen and graduate from high school because age nineteen is the cutoff for eligibility for Medicaid or the Children's Health Insurance Program through the child eligibility pathway. The patchwork nature of health insurance in the United States leads to confusion regarding the coverage options for which young adults qualify. Teenagers reported advice from grandparents, older siblings, and cousins that the provision of the ACA that enables young adults to be covered through a parent's or family member's commercial health insurance plan through age twenty-six also applies to Medicaid if the young adult is enrolled in college, which it does not. Medicaid eligibility is individually determined. These young adults can obtain coverage if their parents get jobs with insurance benefits, they qualify for federal tax credits by getting jobs that provide an income of at least the federal level, or they become parents.

Underinsured

Having inadequate insurance coverage is also a major driver of high health care costs and a barrier to accessing care. Nationwide, health insurance plans have higher and higher deductibles, which means that the amount subscribers must pay out of pocket before insurance kicks in is getting larger and larger.[39] Mississippi is being hit especially hard by this development, but how someone is affected depends on how they get insurance. Three statistics paint the picture of just how expensive and weak health insurance is for people in Mississippi who get coverage through their work. First, employees pay one-third of their premiums out of their paychecks, the fifth-highest share in the nation. Second, the median income is so low in Mississippi that even though the actual dollar amount of premiums is less than the national average, the share of an employee's income that goes toward premiums is the highest in the nation at 9 percent. Third, Mississippi employees pay an additional 5.4 percent of their incomes toward deductibles, also the highest rate in the nation. In other words, people who obtain insurance through their employers still must pay 14.4 percent of their income for insurance.[40]

Reliable county-level data on premiums and deductibles for employer-sponsored insurance are not readily available, so it is hard to know exactly how this is playing out in the Delta. However, the median income here is dramatically lower than in the rest of the state, suggesting that people are paying an even higher percentage of their income toward premiums and deductibles. And again, these are the people who are able to have insurance through an employer. The situation is not too different for those who do not get insurance through an employer but have an income that allows them to buy subsidized insurance through the health insurance exchange. However, buying insurance this way is an overwhelming experience that only helps people with certain incomes.

Sacrifices and Trade-Offs

HealthCare.gov made the health insurance shopping experience smoother than it otherwise would have been, but it is still very hard to know how to balance the pros and cons of the available options. Even with a PhD in health policy, I struggled to feel confident that I understood all implications and which options would be best in each situation. It is estimated that Mississippi has the second-lowest level of health literacy in the country and that health literacy in the Delta is the poorest in the state.[41] The people who need help the most are therefore least likely to understand terms like *premiums*, *deductibles*, and *coinsurance* let alone the trade-offs. A health care administrator in Cleveland said she has seen this countless times, that poor health literacy in the region perpetuates a cycle of bad insurance, high costs, and bad health: "You sign up for things that you don't understand because someone calls you and tells you to. A lot of older people from this area, they don't have family. They don't know how to read and write. So if someone calls as a health care representative and says, 'Hey, Miss Smith, this is what we're offering. You need to do this,' they do it. When you come in to see us as a health care provider, it costs you a lot of money out of pocket. Well, in turn, they don't come. They don't get their medicines filled."

A woman in Clarksdale told a story that is in some ways even more frustrating because she understood the terms of the insurance she was buying but did not have other options. She had insurance through her employer, but the $2,000 deductible kept her from seeking care: "I never, ever, ever meet my deductible. . . . I can't speak for everyone, but I'm on a very strict budget where my check is gone before it comes. So anything outside the realm of the basic necessities like rent and everything like that, and there go that word, necessity. My health care should be a necessity, but sometimes it's just not." Health care is out of reach for her even though she lives near a hospital and even though she has insurance. But as a woman in Cleveland asked, "How are we supposed to be healthy with the worst health insurance?"

Many others described the difficult financial trade-offs they must make because they cannot afford medical care. For example, a woman in her fifties with congestive heart failure, diabetes, asthma, and stenosis said that finding a doctor or getting to their office is not a problem. She has insurance and lives in Cleveland, not far from the hospital and the row of private practice offices nearby. However, money is very tight because she, her husband, and their adopted eight-year-old son live on a monthly income of about $1,100. Two adult children also live at home and barely make enough to cover their own expenses: "I have to pay a house note, car note, utilities, everything, out of our income that we have. So anything that exceeds that, then I have to rely on my family to help me."

She struggles to cover the copays for her visits. She owes a lot of money for services and equipment such as an oxygen machine, which she needs but are not covered and she cannot afford. She is enrolled in Medicare and Medicaid, neither of which covers many of her medications. When asked how she balances the competing pressures of paying her medical bills and everything else her family needs, she responded, "If I'm at my worst in my health, then I decide okay, why don't you go ahead and get this medication because I'm suffering at this time, and I really need the medication. And if I'm doing okay and have been to the doctor lately and had some shots, I had some medication, I feel like it could take me through for this period of time, then I decide, okay, I'll pay these [nonmedical bills]. . . . This is like a normal routine you're in; not just for me, but for everybody."

She is right that she is not alone in facing difficult choices because of health care costs. More than one-third of Mississippians (37.4 percent) have past-due medical debt. This is a staggeringly high figure, which not only is the worst in the nation but also is nearly 10 percentage points higher than the next-highest state (Florida at 28.1 percent).[42] There are no reliable data on medical debt specifically in the Delta, but it is reasonable to suspect that the trend consistent with other statistics applies here as well, and that things are even worse.

Affordable Care Act

The ACA, or Obamacare, is the most comprehensive national health reform law since the creation of Medicare and Medicaid in 1965. The hope was that it would alleviate and maybe even eliminate many of the problems of uninsurance and underinsurance. What has the law meant for Mississippi?

In 2020, 8.6 percent of the US population, or twenty-eight million people, were without health insurance at some point during the year.[43] The number of people in Mississippi without insurance has declined dramatically since implementation of the ACA, but many other states, particularly those that opted to expand Medicaid under the ACA, experienced larger drops in uninsurance,[44] and Mississippi still has the sixth-worst uninsured rate in the country.[45] This partly explains why, according to a 2018 survey, only 17 percent of Mississippians say they are better off as a result of the ACA, 47 percent say they are unaffected,[46] and people say that Obamacare passed by the Delta, helping people up north or in other parts of the country but not them. In many ways they are right. Even the provision that children can stay on their parents' plans until age twenty-six has a particularly limited effect in Mississippi because the state has one of the lowest percentages of people with employer-sponsored insurance.[47]

Decisions made by Mississippi's leaders about how to implement the ACA weakened the law's reach. For example, as the earlier hypothetical example illustrated, the options available to people in the Delta through Health Care.gov were limited by the fact that only one company was selling plans. The underlying logic of the individual health insurance marketplace was that market pressure would drive down costs. But that cannot happen if one company has a monopoly. Other companies indicated that they would have been willing to sell plans on the marketplace when it looked like the Mississippi Department of Insurance would be in charge. However, they pulled out when Governor Phil Bryant blocked the establishment of a state-run marketplace and gave control instead to the federal government via the HealthCare.gov platform.[48]

Some people saw the Medicaid expansion as a major missed opportunity for expanding coverage in the Delta. A community leader in Greenville said, "The exchange has made a real difference, but expanding Medicaid would have put us in holy heaven." Complying with this part of the ACA would eliminate the categorical rules for eligibility such that childless adults could be covered, and income thresholds for parent eligibility would increase from 26 percent to 138 percent of the FPL. Many more people would be covered, leading to fewer hospitals not being paid for services and fewer individuals going into medical debt. The Obama administration tried to convince holdout states like Mississippi to expand Medicaid. The Biden administration resumed these efforts in 2021, including by providing financial carrots in COVID-19 relief legislation passed by Congress. During the 2024 legislative session, the Mississippi Legislature has come the closest to enacting Medicaid expansion it has in a decade, so hope exists.

Mississippi's leaders staunchly opposed Medicaid expansion even though 52 percent of Mississippians supported expansion according to a 2018 survey.[49] State leaders expressed concern that the federal government will not follow through with promises to cover most of the expansion and that the state's share of 10 percent is still a lot of money. However, evidence from other states that have expanded Medicaid suggests that this spending would likely be more than offset by the many ways it boosts the state's economy.[50] According to one estimate, expanding Medicaid would have brought more than $1 billion to the state each year.[51]

People in the Delta described being concerned and confused about what the fight over the ACA means for them. One person went as far as to say that the political fight in Jackson, combined with the election of Donald Trump in 2016, and the threat of congressional attempts at repealing the ACA were enough to convince her to buy coverage directly from an insurance company even though it meant missing out on the tax credit she could receive through HealthCare.gov: "With the election last year [in 2016], it kind of made me a little bit nervous, and I decided not to do Obamacare. I didn't know what it would be like depending on who won. I didn't want to just go from having Obamacare to having nothing. When you think about the politics, I mean, politically they might literally screw millions of people's insurance. And I just didn't want to risk it."

Doctors and administrators were similarly frustrated about the state's decision to reject the Medicaid expansion. In one study, researchers estimated that 72 percent of all rural hospital closures are in states that rejected the Medicaid expansion, a trend that has continued as states like Mississippi hold out more than ten years after the ACA's enactment.[52] The additional money flowing into the Delta's health care system could help to keep struggling hospitals and CHCs financially viable. But these leaders were hardly in love with Medicaid and warned that expansion would not be a panacea because many doctors do not accept this insurance. The program has an intense administrative burden and reimburses at a fraction of what private insurance and Medicare pay. Many say it is not enough to cover their costs.

The director of a CHC in an isolated rural community said, "If the governor would expand Medicaid, then I would have a whole different looking picture here. . . . We might survive if we had expanded Medicaid." At the same time, she sometimes allowed the clinic to absorb the costs of care because dealing with the state's Medicaid department was such an administrative headache: "I didn't want to do the paperwork. I would rather treat the people for free than deal with the paperwork. It's not even about the low reimbursement." Her insight highlights the mutually reinforcing nature of the problems of accessibility and affordability. Hospitals, clinics, and providers struggle to remain financially viable when their patients cannot pay. People struggle to get care when there are not enough providers and facilities. This results in a population in which major health problems often go unaddressed.

Availability

The challenge of running a financially viable health care facility contributes to the third dimension of access for patients: the availability of medical services that are high quality. The issue here is not the geographic distribution of doctors but whether they have the resources to deliver the best care. Are the facilities and equipment up to date? Are systems in place to coordinate care between providers? Too often in the Delta, the answer is no.

Equipment and Facilities

There are pockets of modernity in the Mississippi Delta's health care delivery system, but much of the technology and buildings used today are old. It is hard to systematically evaluate the state of the facilities and equipment across the Delta, but the people I spoke with were frustrated. Just as the woman in the Cleveland focus group asked how people in the Delta are supposed to be healthy given the insurance options available to them, doctors often asked how they are supposed to provide optimal care with outdated equipment.

This issue epitomizes the degree to which the problems of health care in the Delta are difficult to disentangle. Administrators are sympathetic to the preferences and needs of doctors but question how to afford new technology when there are not enough patients with insurance to bring in revenue or enough doctors to fully staff their clinics. Doctors respond that they will not be able to recruit or retain enough providers unless the technology is up to date. For example, a doctor who considered moving to the Delta said the salary would have been lucrative and the reality of living in a small community was not a major drawback because they had relatives in the region. The biggest deterrent was the number of people who warned, "If you go down to that country town, they don't have any of the equipment. You're not going to be able to do what you need to do."

A specialist said that the administrators in the region "are very shortsighted" because they are not investing in the technology to keep people like him practicing in their hospitals. His procedures are an important source of income for the local hospital, but the available equipment is from 1999. "If I were in a different setting, oh my gosh, it's like you're God. Like 'whatever you say, we're going to do it by tomorrow. We're going to need new equipment.' That's what happens. If I'm in Memphis and I say, 'I need a new cath [catheter] lab.' 'Sure, we'll build it for you. You're bringing the revenue.' But no, not here." It is very difficult to know what new technologies are worth the investment as clinics and hospitals struggle to make ends meet. Sometimes new machines were purchased with grants or received as gifts but go unused because they are too expensive to operate. For example, when Quentin Whitwell and his team of investors bought Panola Medical Center in Batesville in 2018, they were surprised to find two hyperbaric chambers that were bought years ago but never taken out of their protective wrapping because it would cost $100,000 to get them up and running.[53]

Taborian Hospital in Mound Bayou is the most dramatic example of unused medical technology in the Delta. The hospital opened in 1942 in this all-Black city and became a center of health care for Black people across the entire Delta. The hospital struggled to stay financially viable as desegregation and the creation of the Delta Health Center and other CHCs meant that people had other places to go. The doors closed in 1983, but the community has worked to revive the hospital. The federal government provided a $2.9 million grant in 2011 that gave local leaders the start to restore the building and buy cutting-edge technology. The hospital reopened for a few months as an urgent care facility but was forced to close because of legal and financial challenges.[54] The building is beautiful but sits unoccupied. It is an eerie experience to walk the halls of Taborian Hospital and see expensive equipment sitting unused in room after room.

Care Coordination

The coordination of care between primary care providers and specialists is a critical dimension of high-quality health care. It is not fair under any circumstances to expect patients to take the lead role in relaying critical information between providers. The low level of health literacy in the Delta raises the stakes even higher. The use of electronic health records is an important part of care coordination and is one way that Mississippi is a national leader in health care. All critical access hospitals and 89 percent of small rural hospitals in Mississippi are reported to have adopted certified electronic health records.[55] In 2013, the most recent year when a report specific to Mississippi was issued, overall adoption of basic electronic health records among office-based providers in Mississippi was a little less than the national adoption rate (40 percent compared with 48 percent).[56] In 2021 the national data showed four in five office-based physicians (78 percent) and nearly all non-federal acute care hospitals (96 percent) had adopted electronic health records.[57] There are still gaps in how the electronic records are used, but the struggles in Mississippi are typical of the challenges faced by hospitals and doctors across the country.

One of the most common care coordination problems and barriers to providing risk-appropriate care (having the care delivered by the provider with the appropriate level of education and skills matched to the type of health condition that needs to be treated) in the Delta is tension between physicians. Many people told stories about being referred to specialists forty-five miles away because their primary care providers had bad relationships with the specialists in the town where they lived and were receiving care. Patients are frustrated by the expensive inconvenience but often do not feel they have options. As someone in Clarksdale put it, "They got to take it. They don't ask questions." The leader of a CHC confirmed the edge between some providers: "There's a competitiveness about the area in that there are so few resources. And if I'm going to practice in a community, then I need to compete with you for that Medicaid patient or I need to compete with you for this so that I can survive. It's a matter of survival." This mentality is particularly striking given that primary care providers and specialists are not actually competing to provide the same services but are mutually interdependent.

Accommodation

You might expect that a health care system vying for every patient would be geared toward anticipating and meeting their needs and that hospitals, clinics, and doctors would compete to provide the best user experience possible. Accommodation, or the degree to which health care is organized around the constraints and preferences of patients, is an important dimension of access. Unfortunately, this is another gap in health care in the Delta.

Hours

Some people are not affected by the major access barriers of geography or affordability. They have an established relationship with a primary care provider who lives near them and who accepts their insurance. Their deductible is not a major obstacle because they have a stable income from a good job. However, they still struggle to receive care because their doctor works the same hours as they do. As a woman in Cleveland explained, "I've been going to my doctor for a while. Love her to death, but at five she's gone because she has a life. . . . We can't take off work because most of the time, we use all our vacation time, and we need to save it for something very important." It is hard to justify missing work for a doctor's visit, especially for routine care. This becomes another reason why people wait to seek care until they are worried enough by their conditions. As described earlier, these visits have domino effects through a person's social network given that so many households in the Delta have only one car or none at all. It is hard to get to an appointment unless a friend or relative takes time off to provide a ride.

A search of the list of providers in the Magnolia Health Plan network reveals that of the twenty-eight doctors and nurse practitioners in Clarksdale, twenty-eight in Cleveland, and forty in Greenville, only five see patients on weekends (none in Clarksdale, three in Cleveland, and two in Greenville).[58] In most cases this is only for a few hours on Saturday morning. The Aaron Henry clinic in Clarksdale stays open until seven o'clock in the evening one day each week, as do its subsidiary clinics in Tunica, Batesville, and Coldwater. Henry also runs three school-based clinics to provide care to children during school hours.[59]

An Emergency-Based Culture of Health

When people seek care, the actual experience of visiting a provider is often slow and full of delays, which reinforces the feeling that the system does not accommodate their needs. As one person in Greenville put it, "If you go there in the morning, you might as well take your lunch because you're going to be there for a while." This person deals with the long delays by trying to get appointments in the late afternoon when the clinic is quieter. Others choose to forgo visits altogether and only seek care when a concern becomes particularly alarming. At this point, the most likely option is to visit the emergency room. Hence, a leader in Clarksdale described her community as having an "ER culture of health." The emergency department (ED) is the least desirable place for someone to receive care for something that is not truly an emergency. It is more expensive for the patient and allows little ability to follow up or track someone over time. It may be appealing that the ED is always open and has to treat patients regardless of their insurance status, but the experience hardly accommodates patient needs.

Wait time is an imperfect measure but provides some sense of a patient's experience in an ED. The average wait time to be seen by a doctor at Bolivar Medical Center in Cleveland is only six minutes, but someone can expect to be there about two hours before going home. Northwest Mississippi Medical Center in Clarksdale has similar wait times, and both are typical for the rest of the state. Someone visiting Delta Regional Medical Center in Greenville, on the other hand, would wait an average of forty-eight minutes before being seen by a doctor and nearly three hours before going home. These numbers are the second and third worst in their categories in the state.[60]

These averages suggest many people wait much longer. A gentleman in Greenville described a trip to the local ED as "dying in the waiting room" because his experiences are consistently bad. Unless something very serious is happening such as a stroke or a heart attack, he would rather drive an hour or two to an ED in Greenwood, Vicksburg, Jackson, or Memphis. Although the wait times in other parts of the Delta are better than in Greenville, nobody had anything good to say about their visits to the ED. A woman in Cleveland said, "I pray as I pack [my nine-year-old son] up, put him in the car, and drive to Bolivar Medical because I don't know what I'm walking into. Sometimes it's a great experience, and sometimes it's a horrible experience."

People told stories about nearly every ED in the Delta in which waiting was more than just an inconvenience and very nearly resulted in a fatal episode. For example, a woman in Clarksdale described a time she brought in her twin brother just hours after having come home from the ED because he was not reacting well to the treatment. When they arrived, the brother was conscious but "spaced out." The sister said "they never did call him" from the waiting room and his condition worsened the longer they waited. "He was just going in and out, rolling [his eyes] like this, just going in and out of it." They sought help but were told to sit down. The ED was busy because there had just been a code-blue situation. "We went back and sat down. And he just fell down. And guess what? Code blue." His blood pressure dropped dramatically, and the medical staff rushed to revive him. "They didn't even take him to the back. They worked on him right there." This traumatic experience is also inefficient for the health care system, which could not keep up with the patients' needs because it was constantly responding to a code-blue crisis.

Patient Experience

An important detail to this story epitomizes another aspect of accommodation. When the woman brought in her twin, she braced herself for dealing with the staff: "They going to be nasty, you know this. Well, you don't know it, but we know it, they be nasty at the desk." She chose to return even though she anticipated being challenged by the ED staff, but rudeness was nonetheless an important consideration when deciding to seek care. Another person in Clarksdale elaborated: "When you go to the emergency room on a regular basis for pain especially, they tired of you. I'll tell you, they are tired of you. I had a doctor tell me this. They will get rid of you. And especially the older patients, this is something that happens, not just lately, this been going on for years. They get tired of seeing you. And they treat you like anything."

Most people had wonderful things to say about the doctors and nurse practitioners who take care of them. Words like *compassionate*, *kind*, and *patient* were common. However, health care is an experience much broader than the few minutes someone spends with a provider. As a woman in Cleveland explained, "It starts from the bottom up. It starts from when you walk in the door, and you go to the registration desk. It starts there. It starts with his or her nurse. That doctor him or herself may be excellent, but if their nurse is not, if that woman out in the lobby isn't, I mean, that whole experience just . . . If that X-ray tech sucks, then that whole experience is something completely different." Another person in the same focus group added, "It makes you sicker."

This point applies to health care in any setting, not just the ED. A woman in her sixties who lived in Greenville said she stopped going to her doctor for more than a decade because the person at the desk was rude to her. She followed through on her vow never to return until a new person was hired. In the meantime, she developed chronic health conditions that should have been monitored. People said they perceived a direct relationship between ability to pay and the degree to which they were treated with kindness and respect by staff. As someone in Clarksdale put it, "You know like sometimes if you go to the hospital, once they find out you don't have insurance, it's like whoop, the whole experience is going to turn all the way around. Insurance plays a part on what type of care you can afford and how they're going to treat you." Another person in Clarksdale added that "the Jesus touch" level of health care is not available to people who "don't have the money to get that kind of treatment."

Acceptability

The fifth dimension of access suggests that patients are more likely to receive high-quality health care from providers who respect their sex, gender identity, and their racial, cultural, and linguistic backgrounds. Some providers attributed this to beliefs and practices that they saw as impeding care. For example, a doctor in Cleveland explained that many of their patients rely on home remedies to treat the symptoms of diabetes rather than seek care: "I have patients who have poor circulation who soak their feet in alcohol, rubbing alcohol, and Epsom salts. So it's how do you teach them to go away from that alcohol and Epsom salt as therapy for your neuropathy or that numbness you're feeling to, 'Oh, I might have a blockage. I need to go see a doctor'? It's just something that mom did, that grandma did. And grandma and mom had their limbs amputated, and that's what they foresee as their future."

Younger residents of the Delta expressed similar frustrations about the mindset some members of their family bring to health care. For example, many Black women said they have been taught that they should not bathe or wash their hair while having their period.[61] A woman in Cleveland explained, "So the way that they think is being infused into how their grandchildren think. So if they say, 'Well, girl, I ain't going to that doctor. I'm going to soak my feet in some Epsom salts, and I'll be fine.' So as that child gets older, they're going to see, too, well, there's really no relevance in me going to the doctor because Grandmama said it's not necessary for me to go. So why should I even bother to go?" Some people said that the most common approach to health problems from older members of their family is to "pray about it" or rub olive oil on the forehead as Jesus did in the scriptures.[62] "I am a religious person and I believe in the power of God, but you cannot pray about everything. You can pray about anything, but you need help sometimes." Others added that the deep levels of religiosity in the Delta created a stigma against someone who is not well, particularly those with mental health issues: "I feel like the Delta, especially among Black churches, it's very prosperity Gospel-driven. And I think that hinders, especially the Black community, because you have these preachers and these religious leaders that are actively preaching, 'pray about it, God will heal you.' And basically, if you believe enough, it'll happen. So what happens when you do have depression and you have anxiety, you're having all these thoughts, but yet the people that you go to for advice are telling you it's just because you're not praying enough."

Structural Racism in Health Care

These insights, echoed by providers and patients, suggest that lack of health literacy and education are major issues that affect who gets care in the Mississippi Delta. But framing this problem as the fault of patients misses the mark and incorrectly absolves the health care system for its failures in treating everyone with respect. Nonwhite populations in the Delta are systematically more vulnerable to each of the access gaps discussed so far. Many studies have also documented profound degrees of racism in health care in which people of color are treated very differently even when they have the same physical and financial situations as white people.[63] Black women face an additional layer of not being heard, which partially explains why they are three times more likely to die of pregnancy-related causes than white women, even after controlling for income and education.[64] The disparities in Mississippi are even worse, the 2017–19 pregnancy-related death ratio in Mississippi for non-Hispanic Black people was 65.1 deaths per 100,000 live births, which is approximately four times higher than 16.2 deaths per 100,000 live births for white, non-Hispanic people.[65] Racism is also partly why Black women are 40 percent more likely to die of breast cancer even though they are screened at the same level as their white counterparts and have a lower incidence of testing positive.[66]

Many people in the Delta described a deep level of mistrust in the medical establishment. They remember the era of "Mississippi appendectomies" in which thousands of Black women in the mid-twentieth century were sterilized without their consent. They had tubal ligations while being told they were having surgery for something else.[67] They remember the Tuskegee experiments in Alabama in which Black men with syphilis were left untreated for forty years without their consent so that researchers could study the disease's full progression.[68] A Black doctor in Cleveland described how this history casts a shadow over the medical community in the Delta today. Some doctors overcompensate by being so sensitive that they won't perform a hysterectomy even when it is requested.

Black residents of the Delta—particularly women—do not need to hearken back to Tuskegee or the mid-twentieth century to explain why they do not feel seen or heard by the health care system. They are told countless stories of being ignored and disrespected, and they have had their own personal experiences. For example, a young Black woman described the frustration and shame she felt when her physician, an older white woman, denied her request for birth control, saying, "No, I'm not going to give you the pill. But I will pray for you." A Black woman in Clarksdale described how a series of traumatic encounters made a scary health situation much worse. Her story epitomizes so many of the access barriers highlighted throughout this chapter. One experience was with an eighty-five-year-old nephrologist in Cleveland, forty miles from her home, who was concerned about "spilled protein in the urine" during a recent pregnancy. He did a biopsy but never informed her of the result. She figured no news was good news and did not follow up. When she found out a couple of months later that she was pregnant again—this time unplanned—her primary care provider wanted her to again see a nephrologist to investigate the reemerging high levels of protein in her urine. She insisted this time that the visit was with someone closer to home and closer in age. The second specialist chastised her for getting pregnant while having 23 percent kidney function, saying, "Why the hell did you go and get pregnant? That was very stupid!" She was stunned and responded that the original nephrologist never told her about the state of her kidneys. He did not believe her and said the results were clearly written in her medical record: "I'm looking at it right here, it's in black and white. That was the stupidest thing you could have ever done!"

The news was devastating, but so was the nature of the interaction. "I'm just crying. You know, just tears coming down my face. I was in shock that he was talking to me like that. I was in shock." She was informed that her life was in danger and that if her daughter was born alive there would likely be permanent complications. She was humiliated and felt little confidence in this doctor's ability to guide her through the pregnancy to preserve her life and the life of her yet-to-be-born daughter. She felt stuck since she also did not want to go back to the original specialist in Cleveland. She managed to get a referral to a specialist at the University of Mississippi Medical Center in Jackson. She was pleased with the care she received, but driving 150 miles each way so often took an intense toll on her family. Her husband and two young children occasionally made the trip with her, and sometimes they stayed overnight so they did not have to do the three-hour return drive after having already driven three hours down. They sent one of the children to live with relatives in Atlanta for a little while. This helped, but it was traumatic for her and her young child to be separated. "Needless to say, it was a very tedious and discouraging pregnancy."

Her daughter was born without major complications and has no resulting psychological or physical abnormalities. She continued receiving dialysis after the pregnancy but switched to the local Clarksdale hospital when the situation was not as complicated. She was glad to be close to home with her new baby but was alarmed by the quality of care she received. She taught herself to understand and work the machines after watching two people die while receiving dialysis. That's how she recognized that her technician set the machine to drain enough fluid for a person three times her size. She explained the error to the technician and then adjusted the machine herself. "I don't know when she came behind me and changed it, but she did. I must have dozed off. But after I woke up, I couldn't move. I was trying to move and heard people in my section saying, 'Oh, look at her. She's passing out.'" She tried to raise her hand to tell someone she was struggling to breathe, but the best she could do was kick her foot. "This might sound so strange, but I knew I was dying. I knew it instinctively, and I couldn't do anything about it. I began praying and asked God to intervene." Someone noticed what was happening, ran over, unhooked the machine, and revived her.

Four months after this traumatic incident, she learned she would soon receive a pair of kidneys. She was only 120 pounds at that point with a frame so small that "they gave me both kidneys from a cadaver child." The surgery was a success, but now her fight to be heard and understood is with insurance companies. She said the private insurance she has through work "recently kicked out all my claims for the last four years" because they felt more services should be billed to Medicare, which covered her because of her kidney disease. The two insurances "go back and forth saying, 'I'm not paying, you have to pay. I'm not paying, you have to pay.' I had to call and do coordination of benefits myself, and they're still like, 'I'm not paying.' And so I have to call relentlessly."

Some months her pharmacy does not fill her prescriptions because of the confusion between the insurance companies: "I have to beg for my medicine every month. I have to figure out what's wrong." She says she never backs down but worries about the people who probably do. "What hurt my heart was what about the fifty, sixty-year-old uneducated person that doesn't know what to do or what to say or what to demand? What about the person that just says, 'Well, they didn't send my medicine this month. I'll just wait to next month and die in the process.'"

Demographic Characteristics of the Health Care Team

The cultural acceptability of health care does not necessarily require that the demographic characteristics of clinicians match those of patients, but research shows greater understanding and trust in both directions when the two come from similar backgrounds.[69] There are no systematic data about the demographic characteristics of health care workers at the local level, so it is hard to make definitive statements about the racial makeup of clinicians. However, there is reason to believe that the medical workforce in the Delta is more racially diverse than in other parts of the country, but it is far from a reflection of the region's population. Of the 139 doctors who graduated from medical school in Mississippi in 2017, 8 percent were Black. This rate is a little higher than the national average of 5.8 percent.[70] But this does not tell us who stayed in the state or where they chose to settle.

Many pioneers have blazed a trail, such as Peggy Wells, the first Black woman to graduate from the University of Mississippi School of Medicine in 1969 and the founder of the Children's Clinic, the first Black-white medical partnership in the state;[71] Helen Barnes, the first board-certified Black woman to practice obstetrics-gynecology in Mississippi;[72] and Mary Williams, a young Black woman who owns, runs, and practices at what she describes as the first urgent and primary care clinic in Coahoma County. She was recognized as one of the top fifty leading businesswomen in the state, and Congressman Bennie Thompson praised her on the floor of the US House of Representatives in March 2019.[73]

However, many Black providers in the Delta continue to struggle. One said that "medicine is still very much a white man's world. I mean, no one has said to me, 'You're not welcome,' or 'You don't deserve to be here.'

No one has verbalized that to me, but there's always these undertones." Another Black physician described something similar but added that he felt a responsibility and loyalty to the people of the Delta: "I don't see myself packing my bags because it took me two years to build this. . . . I've invested a lot into this place. But most importantly, I care about these people because they look like me and I treat every patient as if they're a family member."

As described earlier, international medical graduates play an important role in the Delta's health care delivery system and fill positions that in many cases would go unoccupied. But they are in a delicate position as outsiders. A report on the medical workforce in Mississippi noted that "most IMG [international medical graduate] physicians we interviewed were carefully respectful of the communities and patients they served, portrayed their appreciation of the opportunities that working in the United States presented to them and their families, and were generally quite reluctant to be critical." Some described subtle forms of discrimination such as patients choosing en masse to be seen by a new American doctor who moved into town. Some felt that their status as outsiders in the Deep South strengthened their bond with Black patients. As one foreign doctor put it, "[My community here] is not far off from [where I come from] in terms of the problems that we, we see. . . . I do have an accent . . . but it's very strange that a lot of the patients here, they understand me better than . . . a Yankee doctor."[74]

Ripples of Hope

This look at the Five A's of Access makes it clear that the Mississippi Delta is one of the hardest places in the United States to obtain high-quality health care. This is a discouraging prognosis, but there are many people and organizations working to improve access to health care in the Delta. They embody the spirit of Robert F. Kennedy's vision that "each time a [person] stands up for an ideal, or acts to improve the lot of others, or strikes out against injustice, he sends forth a tiny ripple of hope, and crossing each other from a million different centers of energy and daring, those ripples build a current which can sweep down the mightiest walls of oppression and resistance."[75]

Preventing Amputations Related to Diabetes

Dr. Foluso Fakorede's goal is to reduce the amputation rate among people with diabetes in the Mississippi Delta by 25 percent by 2025. National research shows that foot amputations related to diabetes occur in intense geographic clusters.[76] Rates are highest in places where deep poverty exists,[77] and health care is segregated along class lines such that hospitals see a higher proportion of patients who have lower income.[78] Compton, California, for example, has been described as "a war zone" because of the number of people with missing limbs.[79] The risk of amputation is even higher in places like the Delta because people in nonurban areas are shown to have 51.3 percent higher odds of a major amputation.[80] An administrator in the region called the Delta the "amputation capital of the country" because the procedure is so common.

Fakorede moved to the area in 2015. He borrowed money from friends and spent a lot of his own savings to open a practice in Cleveland because four banks denied him a loan. There was no other cardiologist in Bolivar County and no endocrinologist within one hundred miles. He views reducing the rate of amputations related to diabetes as a battle against racial oppression and notes that the map of where this procedure is most common is almost identical to the pre–Civil War map of slavery.

This outcome is particularly tragic given that it is almost entirely avoidable. The tools for managing diabetes are available to people with resources and education, and the warning signs would be caught by someone with regular access to health care. Fakorede says a procedure called an angiography takes thirty minutes and could prevent 92 percent of all amputations. He describes going into the leg like a plumber with a Roto-Rooter: "I go in and I can shave off the plaque in your legs, put a balloon and open it up and if some patients need stents, we put stents in there. And their legs and their arteries and their circulation is restored." Fakorede adds that he is "very pissed," as he believes "75 to 80 percent of all amputations in the Mississippi Delta are patients who never had a doctor like me take them to the lab and just shoot contrast down their leg to see if we can prevent their amputation."

One of the main drivers of this problem is that providers are paid by the number of procedures and are rewarded for having higher volume, regardless of the appropriateness of the procedure. The administrator who described the Delta as the "amputation capital of the country" elaborated that there are surgeons in the area "who make it their bread and butter to do this extreme and irreversible procedure. We have surgeons who will do amputations without checking if there is blood flow to that leg." Convincing primary care providers and other physicians to pay attention and refer patients to Fakorede has been a major challenge. Some are put off by what they view as the northern arrogance of an outsider. Others just do not understand or do not have the time to think about changing how they practice. Fakorede spent a lot of time in his first year texting and emailing photos of what he was seeing to other physicians. He likens this approach to the decision by Emmett Till's mother to leave the casket open at her son's funeral so the world could see the violent effects of racial inequity.[81]

Insurance is a major barrier. In this case, the problem is not that people lack coverage but that their insurance company requires prior authorization (explicit permission in advance) for this procedure, or a high chance exists it will not be covered.[82] Fakorede goes on to explain, "An angio procedure will be much more effective, but we have to jump through hoops to get it approved. But no prior authorization is needed for amputation. They will chop your leg off and not bat an eye." The hospital is struggling financially and so regularly turns away people for the procedure because they cannot pay. Fakorede finds this incredibly frustrating, "But a for-profit hospital is the only game in town in one of the most underserved areas. So what happens when a patient comes in and can't afford a procedure that's limb salvage? They eventually lose their limbs. They'll present back to the emergency room with a rotten foot."[83] The result is that a surgeon would have no choice but to amputate.

Fakorede says he does angiography procedure about fifteen times per week. The results have yet to be published in a peer-reviewed journal, but a ProPublica reporter looked into the records at Bolivar Medical Center and found that major amputations decreased 75 percent from twenty-four in 2014 to six in 2017.[84] Fakorede is doing everything he can to spread the word. He testified before Congress and convinced a Democrat from New Jersey and a Republican from Florida to establish the Congressional Peripheral Artery Disease Caucus.[85] He has billboards around the Delta advertising for an Amputation Prevention Institute. He regularly visits health fairs and churches to educate people that they can decrease the likelihood of an amputation by changing their lifestyle and seeking a second opinion if a doctor recommends the procedure. "It's going to take an effort of not only engaging researchers in different facets of the political spectrum, the educational spectrum, but also the community; faith-based is key down here. The number one target should be faith-based because that's where like a day like today, every single person is at church." His efforts are helping break down the barriers to healthy eating outlined in chapter 1.

"Take Me to Ruleville"

The North Sunflower Medical Center in Ruleville is a leader in changing the health care landscape in the Mississippi Delta. Ruleville is a small town of about three thousand people in Sunflower County, which is fifteen miles from the legendary state penitentiary in Parchman. The median income is $31,300, and 73 percent of the population is Black.[86] The major point of pride for Ruleville is that it was the home of civil rights activist Fannie Lou Hamer, who achieved national prominence for a speech at the 1964 Democratic National Convention in which she challenged the all-white Mississippi delegation.

People all over the Delta praise the quality of health care available in Ruleville. Almost everyone who mentioned the North Sunflower Medical Center quoted the marketing slogan that the answer to any medical care question is "Take me to Ruleville." People heard the same thing from their friends and relatives, and one person said they know people who drive two hours each way from Jackson to get their primary care in Ruleville. Another said that when they moved to the Delta and asked around about health care options, everyone said to go to Ruleville.

The irony is that many of the doctors at North Sunflower also practice in Cleveland and the other surrounding communities. In other words, people could theoretically see many of the same providers closer to home. But this clinic does several things differently to address the most common barriers to accessing care. For example, the clinic is open seven days a week from eight o'clock in the morning to midnight. People can be seen without an appointment many hours after all the primary care providers in their town have closed for the day. People also say the experience and interactions at North Sunflower are so much more pleasant than they often encounter in other health care settings. The wait times are shorter, and they feel that they are treated with kindness. As one person put it, "The one word to describe Ruleville: hospitality. Kind of like when you go to a hotel, right? Hospitality. You treat people nice, and they want to come back. So that's something that you see in Ruleville." Others said, "They hired people who treat people with respect and they get it," and "They're more welcoming to us."

The broader health care community has taken notice. In 2017, the Mississippi Nurses Association recognized the North Sunflower Medical Center as the hospital of the year.[87] This distinction is remarkable given that fifteen years earlier it was on the verge of financial collapse and only ever had enough money to operate for the next eight hours. Nurses clocked out many hours early each day but continued to work for free, hoping that saving the hospital some money would preserve their jobs.[88]

North Sunflower's major turning point came in 2004 when local businessman Billy Marlow was asked to chair the board of directors and serve as the interim administrator even though he had no experience in health care, having spent a career in real estate and farming. One of the first things Marlow did was invest in renovating the facilities: "When you have a hospital that's dirty or has a bad image, you can't recruit." One way he paid for expensive renovations was by expanding hours so more patients could be seen and revenues could be higher. He also converted North Sunflower to a "critical access hospital,"[89] which allowed for higher reimbursements for Medicare services.[90]

The website for the North Sunflower Medical Center says there are now more than five hundred employees.[91] Taken together, these changes have allowed for volume to increase from 120 patients per month to 3,500.[92] This dramatic turnaround gives hope to others that providing health care is financially viable in the Mississippi Delta.

Marlow is trying to export his success to other health care facilities in the Delta. In 2010, he created a consulting firm, Sunflower Management Group, "to provide expert advice and leadership to critical access hospitals."[93] His vision and skills were put to the test immediately at Tallahatchie General Hospital, a struggling facility in Charleston, a town of about two thousand people one hour northeast of Ruleville.[94] This was a particularly tall order given that Tallahatchie County was ranked as the third least healthy in the state.[95] Marlow brought the hospital's CEO into the leadership of Sunflower Management Group and adopted many of the same approaches that have been so successful in Ruleville.[96] The outcome has been similar. After being on the edge of closing just a few years earlier, the hospital experienced four consecutive years of profitability. Tallahatchie General's debt has been reduced dramatically, and two hundred jobs have been added.

The clinic in Tutwiler, on the other side of Tallahatchie County from Charleston, will be a major test of Marlow's ability to make health care financially viable in rural Mississippi. Tutwiler is similar to Ruleville in that it is small and poor, and more than 80 percent of its population is Black. Before being acquired by Tallahatchie General in 2016, the

Tutwiler Clinic survived thanks to the faith and energy of Sister Anne Brooks, a Catholic nun who told me she had been called by God in the late 1970s to go to medical school. After graduating from the Michigan State University College of Osteopathic Medicine, she participated in a program that sent her to underserved communities across the country. She fell in love with Mississippi and wanted to return. She wrote the mayors of little towns in the Delta asking if they would be interested in having a physician. "Tutwiler was the only town that answered me. I didn't tell them I was a nun." They had a building for a clinic but no physician. A stream of people had come through on three-year stints to pay off their loans but then left. One shot himself to death in the woods behind the clinic.

When Brooks arrived in Tutwiler in 1983, there were still separate waiting rooms for Black and white patients. She immediately closed the Black waiting room and worked tirelessly to seek charitable donations to supplement the lost revenue from the large amount of free care given to people who could not afford to pay anything. When I asked Brooks what the financial model has been for the clinic, she responded, "Please give us money." She writes more than one thousand cards at Christmas to thank donors and ask for more money. "Without donations, we couldn't pay the staff because we pay decent wages."

Brooks has held this clinic together and has been a major part of the Tutwiler community for more than three decades. She worked full time into her late seventies despite having a brain aneurysm. This was obviously not a sustainable situation. Becoming part of a larger system would likely be the best hope for her clinic, but she was not sure how this would play out. "Because of the nature of what we do and to take donations, it's going to be extremely hard for a hospital to keep a clinic like this going. They would face the same story. Medicaid and Medicare, transportation problems. We're not exactly sure what's going to happen." It is too early to tell whether this will be a success, but the turnarounds in Ruleville and Charleston provide reasons for optimism.

The improvements in health outcomes across the county provide another reason to be optimistic. Tallahatchie County improved by twenty spots in the state's rankings of healthiest counties between 2011 and 2018.[97] It is hard to know which specific factors played the biggest role in driving this improvement, but the takeaway is that negative trends are not inevitable and can be reversed.

Telehealth

The improved infrastructure and financing of the North Sunflower Medical Center has opened the door to opportunities that likely would not have been possible otherwise. One of the most consequential is the ability to engage with the telemedicine program at the University of Mississippi Medical Center (UMMC) in Jackson. Mississippi has been regarded as a national leader in telehealth,[98] one of only nine states in the nation to receive a grade A from the American Telemedicine Association.[99]

UMMC was at the fore of this technology and developed its first telehealth program in 2003.[100] The Mississippi Legislature supported these efforts by enacting a parity law in 2013 to allow Medicaid to reimburse for services provided remotely.[101] This has allowed the UMMC Center for Telehealth to provide services for thirty-five medical specialties in 165 sites in fifty-two of Mississippi's eighty-two counties, including in community hospitals and clinics, mental health facilities, community health centers, schools, colleges, mobile health vans, corporations, prisons, and patients' homes.[102] UMMC was recently recognized by the Health Resources and Services Administration as one of two telehealth Centers of Excellence in the nation.[103] This designation came with an award of $600,000 to develop telemedicine further and the possibility of receiving another $2 million.[104]

One of the ways UMMC expanded services was by partnering with the North Sunflower Medical Center in 2014 to develop the Diabetes Telehealth Network in Ruleville. The program gives tablets to patients to help them manage their diabetes and allows providers to receive alerts in real time. People can talk to providers remotely, which allows them to receive guidance without having to find a ride to the clinic. The lack of connectivity in the rural Delta was a major barrier, so UMMC and North Sunflower collaborated with the office of Governor Phil Bryant and C Spire, the area's major telecommunications provider, to substantially improve the internet infrastructure in the region.[105]

The program is relatively new, but it seems to have been successful. More than one hundred people participated in a pilot study lasting one year. They experienced a statistically and substantively significant drop in their A1C levels from 9.5 percent at baseline to 7.7 percent just three months later. Even more impressive is that these improvements were sustained during the remaining nine months of the study.[106] Participants were compliant with medication 96 percent of the time and were spared driving a combined total of 9,400 miles during the twelve months of the study. Virtually all participants (93 percent) said someone was available to help if they had a problem.[107] The program has resulted in nearly $700,000 in annual savings "due to reductions in hospital readmissions alone."[108] In an op-ed, US Senator Roger Wicker (R-MS) and Brendan Carr (commissioner at the US Federal Communications Commission) said, "If just 20 percent of the state's diabetic population were to enroll in this type of remote patient monitoring, Medicaid savings for Mississippi could be $189 million per year.[109] However, these programs are limited in scope, in part because they are dependent on reliable and accessible broadband internet. This infrastructure is not available in all regions of the Delta, particularly in deeply rural areas.

The Health Care Equity Policy Agenda

Residents of the Mississippi Delta face enormous barriers to accessing high-quality health care. There are not enough doctors. Lack of transportation makes it difficult for people to keep appointments, let alone see specialists who are hours away in Memphis or Jackson. Large numbers of people do not have insurance, and those who do have it struggle to afford copayments and deductibles. When people seek care, the experience is often frustrating for all involved. Patients are unlikely to be seen by a provider who looks like them. They have long waits and feel they are not treated with respect by staff. Providers lament that they do not have up-to-date technology. These barriers are often mutually reinforcing such that people who are the hardest hit in one dimension are likely to be among the hardest hit in another.

Some of these barriers are rooted in personal or institutional racism. Others are the product of a complicated set of factors that work together to create incentives and constraints that make it hard for well-intentioned people to make decisions that benefit the overall system. The high rate of diabetes-related foot amputations is a great example. The issue has been called a "mega-disparity" because poor people are more likely to have diabetes in the first place, and some racial and ethnic groups are more likely to be poor, and as discussed in chapter 1, access to healthy food that could help with diabetes is challenging. People living in poverty are less likely to manage chronic illnesses such as diabetes once they have a diagnosis and are more likely to receive care in a health care setting that is struggling for money and workforce. They are also more likely to have insurance that requires prior authorization for foot-saving procedures but that reimburses for amputations without question.

No panacea can solve these problems, and no single change will address all of these factors. Our focus should be on multiple changes across each of these dimensions. The health care equity policy agenda should expand geographic access to doctors and hospitals, make health care services affordable for all, improve the quality of care so that the best and most cost-efficient services are available and well coordinated, accommodate the preferences and needs of patients, and provide care that is accepting and responsive to cultural differences.

Health Care Equity Policy Goal #1: Expand Geographic Access to Health Professionals and Hospitals.

Examples of national, state, and local policies:

- Continue and strengthen financial incentives to recruit health care professionals—for example, physicians, midwives, nurse practitioners, and registered nurses—to health professional shortage areas, including loan forgiveness and visa opportunities. These programs should be revised to encourage providers to stay in these communities even longer.
- Encourage Black, Hispanic, and Indigenous youth, and youth from other historically underrepresented groups, to consider careers in health services. This should include targeted services to support students in middle school, high school, and college who express interest, including scholarships for historically underrepresented students.
- Expand scope of practice and reimbursement policies to enable nurse practitioners, midwives, physician assistants, allied dental professionals, and community health workers to provide more services to more people so that patients have more options and to reduce the number of areas with health professional shortages.
- Local leaders should invest in developing robust transportation systems so that residents can get to health care facilities and other important locations such as grocery stores and parks.
- Expand broadband coverage to support more mobile clinics and technology-based options, such as smartphone applications and telehealth, to increase geographic access to health care services.

Health Care Equity Policy Goal #2: Make Health Care Services Affordable for All.

Examples of national, state, and local policies:

- National policymakers should work toward decoupling the link between health insurance and employment to help increase access to coverage in places like the Mississippi Delta where unemployment is high and the most common jobs are in retail.
- States should expand Medicaid so that their residents, hospitals, and providers can use these federal funds to increase access to care. This should include not only expanding Medicaid to childless adults through the ACA but also increasing on a permanent basis the length of time women are eligible for coverage after giving birth.
- Policymakers, the insurance industry, health care facilities, and consumer advocacy groups should work together to increase outreach and support to help people understand their options and sign up for health insurance.
- Health insurance plans should have lower caps on the maximum amount of money that people spend on out-of-pocket expenses such as deductibles, copayments, and coinsurance.

Health Care Equity Policy Goal #3: Improve the Quality of Care So That the Best and Most Cost-Efficient Services Are Available and Include Well-Coordinated and Risk-Appropriate Care.

Examples of national, state, and local policies:

- Prioritize coordination of care so that patients do not receive too few or too many services, and that services are consistent and efficient and provided by appropriately skilled clinicians. The medical home model is one example of a promising way to strengthen connections between types of providers.
- Health care facilities should be supported to strengthen their electronic health records systems. Health data should be secure but compatible so that information can be shared as patients receive care in different settings.
- Connect people with a variety of services, including initiatives that target specific populations that navigate specific situations, such as Centering Pregnancy programs or Baby Cafés.

- Track structures, processes, and outcomes by race and ethnicity.
- Review and report data through a health equity lens.

Health Care Equity Policy Goal #4: Accommodate the Preferences and Needs of Patients.

Examples of national, state, and local policies:

- Health care providers and facilities should expand hours so that patients can access services at convenient times.
- The entire patient experience should be a priority so that people feel heard and valued when they set appointments, check in, receive care, and navigate billing.
- Health care leaders should proactively focus on increasing health care literacy and streamlining complicated situations so that patients can understand and remember key details. This could include strategies as simple as providing a printout or audio recording of discharge instructions rather than relying on patients to remember everything.

Health Care Equity Policy Goal #5: Provide Care That Is Responsive to Cultural Differences.

Examples of national, state, and local policies:

- Track health care quality and health outcomes by race and ethnicity to identify and target health disparities with specific interventions to promote equity.
- Invest in training and retaining providers originally from underserved areas to increase the likelihood that patients are treated by people who look like them, speak their language, and relate to their cultural preferences.
- Medical schools and other training programs should place greater emphasis on cultural humility and address how cultural and racial divides between providers and patients can be acknowledged and overcome.
- Grand rounds and other continuing education efforts should focus on how to provide equitable health care, recognize conscious and unconscious biases, and emphasize that race is a social construct rather than an inherent genetic or biological risk factor.
- Ensure that all health professionals know that racism is the risk factor, not race.

Addressing each of these policy goals would improve access to high-quality health care in the Mississippi Delta. It should also be clear by now that a robust health care system is only part of what is needed to improve a population's health. John Hatch and Jack Geiger learned this while establishing the nation's first community health center in Mound Bayou in the mid-1960s, right around the time that Robert F. Kennedy made his iconic trip to the region. Geiger said that as he and Hatch conducted listening sessions across the Delta, "there were two or three other priorities that came ahead of health as we ordinarily define it. There were food, jobs, housing, and then maybe education. Health was fourth, or fifth on the list."[110]

These issues are not mutually exclusive. The most effective way to improve the health of a population is arguably to invest in food, jobs, housing, and education, but access to high-quality, equitable health care remains critical.

Conclusion
Advancing the Health Equity Agenda

By now it should be clear that good health is not just the result of an individual's willpower to eat well, exercise regularly, and go to the doctor when needed. While people are more likely to be healthy if they make good decisions, story after story of the people in the Mississippi Delta illustrates that it is significantly harder to make good choices when you do not have good options or when the best choices are not the most intuitive or accessible.

Residents of the Mississippi Delta are not less interested in being healthy or any less capable of making healthy decisions, all things being equal. The problem is that all things are not equal. Race and class intensely shape who has the best opportunities to make the healthiest decisions, and these differences are largely driven by policies made by governments at the national, state, and local levels and by businesses and other organizations. Achieving health equity—or ensuring that everyone has an opportunity to lead their best life—requires new policies to remove the underlying structural barriers.

Eating well is challenging when few grocery stores are nearby, fresh foods are not affordable, and time to prepare wholesome foods is limited. An active lifestyle is nearly impossible when parks are not nearby, sidewalks do not connect, and safety is an overriding issue. Generational wealth cannot be built when well-paying jobs are scarce, banks do not give mortgage loans, and available housing is low quality and unsafe. A great education is a path to a better life but hard to obtain if too few teachers, inadequate resources, and improper and disproportionate discipline are the norm. Access to medical care is limited when primary care providers are scarce, each visit to a specialist requires three hours of driving, and high deductibles and other out-of-pocket costs consume a large share of one's annual income.

This negative feedback loop can work in the other direction. Improving educational opportunity for all increases the likelihood that children from the Delta will become doctors and get other good jobs and that employers will come to the area. This leads to more grocery stores, better housing, and increased amenities. A community with all of these resources makes it more attractive for doctors and employers to come, which coincides with greater investment in schools and so on.

The COVID-19 pandemic clarified the interconnectedness of health, health care, race, and class. People of color and people living in poverty were disproportionately more likely to contract the virus, to die of it if they test positive, and to suffer the consequences of the broader economic downturn.[1] It is not that they are genetically predisposed to illness but that they are more likely to have underlying issues such as obesity and asthma that make them more vulnerable. It is unfair to view these conditions as the result of a lifetime of unhealthy decisions because these populations have not benefited from the privileges that facilitate healthy decision-making.

The COVID-19 pandemic should also be a wake-up call to public health leaders who have been writing and talking about social determinants of health for so long that they have failed to appreciate just how far outside the mainstream of American discourse this idea still is. Even as health has been one of the dominant issues in US politics over the past fifteen years, the focus has almost exclusively been on improving access to insurance and medical care. The highly partisan and polarized response to the COVID-19 pandemic has hardened public divisions on these issues rather than brought us together. The health reform debate in America needs to be reformed so that the goal is population health.

Anyone reading this book will have missed the point if they come away thinking of the Delta as a third-world country or grateful they do not have similar problems in their community. Northerners should not be dismissive of these issues by viewing them as endemic to the South. Some of these problems are indeed particularly acute in Mississippi and other parts of the Deep South, but most are *not* unique to this region. The extremes of the Delta help us more clearly see the complex relationships between class, race, and health that make achieving health equity across the nation so difficult. We should emerge from a focus on the Delta awake to the inequities around us.

For example, my home state of Massachusetts is regularly ranked as the healthiest in the country. The high level of population health in Massachusetts is driven by relatively low rates of undesirable outcomes such as cancer and by high rankings in the drivers of health, such as low levels of obesity and smoking, lower air pollution, high rates of childhood vaccinations, good health insurance, and a sufficient number of dentists and mental health providers.[2] But these statewide rankings obscure deep inequities along racial, ethnic, class, and other lines. Residents in the more rural, western part of the state face many of the same geographical barriers to food, physical activity, schools, and health care as people in the Delta. Boston has been described as "the most racist city in America,"[3] in part because of the historically intense degree of de facto segregation between neighborhoods.

The specific dynamics here are a little different from those in the Mississippi Delta, but the factors are the same. Education is intensely linked to community wealth, meaning that those who can afford it move to neighboring suburbs. This drives up property values and the tax base in these outlying communities and drains the city of resources to improve schools. Access to food, safe housing, amenities, and good jobs all decrease as a result, and the cycle is perpetuated. The policies driving these trends are officially considered colorblind, but they disproportionately affect Black populations.

Next Steps

How do we address all these inequities? The complex interrelated nature of these issues makes it clear that there will never be a single solution for every problem. A place-based understanding of complex root causes points to place-based solutions that allow for adapting to local needs. This context-oriented approach to solutions also makes it easier to adopt an asset-rich mindset in which communities are viewed not just for what they are lacking but also for their strengths and resources.

The answer to the question of where to start is "everywhere." We should address it all. Food insecurity. Walkable neighborhoods. Crime. Housing. Jobs. Education. Access to health care. It is all necessary and it all adds up. These issues are interrelated to such an intense degree that we cannot fully improve any of them unless we improve all of them, and anything we do to improve one of these dimensions will ripple to the others.

That said, I would start with education. Research clearly shows that education is a powerful way—perhaps the most effective single thing—for individuals and communities to catalyze the positive feedback loop that leads to more jobs, better housing, safer neighborhoods, healthier food options, and access to great medical care. Improving education is easier said than done but is possible through budgets and policies that prioritize education, support teachers, and ensure that local districts have equitable access to the resources they need. Short-term solutions will not work because solving generational problems requires sustained investment. For starters, we should pay teachers A LOT more.

In each chapter, I highlighted the root causes that need to be addressed and ended with the principles and goals that should guide national, state, and local policy change. These were kept deliberately broad so that they would be applicable in a wide variety of settings. The specific strategies that should be adopted are highly dependent on the context of how a problem is manifested in a particular place, the history that led to this problem, and the dynamics that shape who decides. These lists are also not exhaustive of every policy change needed to address all types of inequities.

Policy discussions about inequities inevitably turn to debates about redistribution of resources. Yes, we need to develop policies that target populations that are the most vulnerable and most underserved, but this does not necessarily mean we need to take away from one group to help another. Solutions focused on improving each of these issues should not be framed as a zero-sum game. With the exception of maybe the very richest who might have to give up a marginal degree of their privilege, helping vulnerable groups is not likely to disadvantage others. In fact, groups—whether defined in terms of race, ethnicity, class, or something else—that cling to the idea of protecting themselves from losing something are inadvertently supporting policies that harm their health and financial security.

Resources are not as limited as we might think but reflect our values. We should decide as a society that nothing is more valuable than our children's education not only because it is good for their long-term economic security and health but also because it is so integral to facilitating the cyclical effects of a strong economy and population health.

Political Determinants of Health

If I could pick one other issue to focus on to achieve health equity, it would be voting rights. Elected officials are more likely to feel responsible for improving conditions for all people if they are democratically accountable to all people. This is why the World Health Organization places all of the factors that shape health—access to health care, food security, neighborhood safety, housing, economic freedom, and education—within a broader framework that acknowledges that each of these is shaped by political processes and power. Political scientist Ilona Kickbusch explains that "looking at health through the lens of political determinants means analyzing how different power constellations, institutions, processes, interests, and ideological positions affect health within different political systems and cultures and at different levels of governance."[4]

In theory, people elect politicians who see these disparities and promise to change the policies driving them, replace leaders who fail to deliver, and reward those who do with reelection. However, abundant political science research documents countless ways this simplistic understanding of democratic representation fails to promote the interests of the most marginalized, often while simultaneously blaming them for not doing more to change their circumstances. For example, Martin Gilens found a relationship between what Americans say they want and the policies government pursues, but public opinion among the wealthy seems to matter the most. As he and Benjamin Page later wrote in the *Washington Post,* "Americans who are less well-off have essentially no influence over what their government does."[5]

Relatively little research has been done on the role of politics and power in shaping population health. Public health is "still commonly caught in a naïve, idealistic, and narrow view of public policy."[6] Public health professor and researcher Scott L. Greer and colleagues agree and suggest that the political nature of public health "makes the enduring paucity of political science informed analysis and strategy in mainstream public health professional culture all the more puzzling."[7] Public health leaders and scholars are likely to be frustrated by a lack of policy change until they develop a fuller understanding of political forces. Calls to action and calls for political change will run the risk of going unheard if driven by a weak understanding of politics.

There is no question that voting rights are central to determining who has power and access to resources in the Mississippi Delta. I did not make voting the theme of focus group conversations, but it came up often. People regularly said voting is pointless because it is so unlikely to make a difference. As one person in Greenville said, "I don't care [about politics]. They're going to do what they're going to do anyway. My vote is not going to count. They're going to do what they want to do."

This dynamic is a backward version of the "What's the Matter with Kansas" dilemma often talked about by scholars and pundits in which people supposedly vote against their self-interest. In this case, people are not voting because the candidates aligned with their preferences go on to win but are outnumbered to such a large degree by legislators from elsewhere in the state—most of whom are white—that they have very little ability to shape state policy to improve conditions in the Delta. Voting is not likely to be a mechanism for achieving health equity unless districts are redrawn, Black voters across Mississippi turn out in large numbers in statewide elections, and a greater share of white voters support candidates who promote equity.

Hope

This is a hopeful book, even if it did not always feel like it. But hope for hope's sake is empty. We cannot achieve health and racial equity unless we name the past and present injustices, identify their root causes, and confront them through policy change. As Mississippi-based poet Derrick Harriell says, it's not just that the past informs the present and future, but that the present can change the past.[8] Similarly, Ibram X. Kendi writes, "There is nothing I see in our world today, in our history, giving me hope that one day antiracists will win the fight, that one day the flag of antiracism will fly over a world of equity. What gives me hope is a simple truism. Once we lose hope, we are guaranteed to lose. But if we ignore the odds and fight to create an antiracist world, then we give humanity a chance to one day survive, a chance to live in communion, a chance to be forever free."[9] When asked at the end of a focus group to write a short statement about what he wished policymakers and others knew about his life, a teenager in Clarksdale wrote the following:

> I want you to know that we are affected. We're the future that sees no future due to past mistakes. We seek change but change is so high up and no one is willing to build that ladder of success. We know about hope but we can't keep putting hope in your hands and you just washing it away before you eat up our goals and success because you're well paid. Our meals don't consist of money greens and sweet salary tea, but hope. Hope that one day it'll be another day. Hope that one day those bites are full of chance, full of change, full of reasons to wake up again. We want to be full because this hunger of oppression is eating us all up whether you know it or not. One day you will know and one day you will say that we were the future that made it a better day.

Notes

Preface

1. Morgan Parker, "Now More Than Ever," in *Magical Negro* (Portland, OR: Tin House Books, 2019), 32.
2. Akilah Johnson et al., "Boston. Racism. Image. Reality. The Spotlight Team Takes On Our Hardest Question," *Boston Globe*, December 10, 2017, https://apps.bostonglobe.com/spotlight/boston-racism-image-reality/series/image/.
3. This approach was vetted by the Boston University Medical Center Institutional Review Board and considered exempt.
4. Teju Cole, "The White-Savior Industrial Complex," *Atlantic*, March 21, 2012, https://www.theatlantic.com/international/archive/2012/03/the-white-savior-industrial-complex/254843/.
5. Melvin Delgado, *Urban Youth and Photovoice: Visual Ethnography in Action* (New York: Oxford University Press, 2015).

Prologue

1. "Constitution of the World Health Organization," World Health Organization, accessed September 1, 2022, https://apps.who.int/gb/bd/PDF/bd47/EN/constitution-en.pdf?ua=1. The constitution was adopted by the International Health Conference, New York, June 19–July 22, 1946. It was signed July 22, 1946, by the representatives of sixty-one states and entered into force on April 7, 1948. The definition has not been amended since 1948.
2. James Davis et al., "Prevalence of Single and Multiple Leading Causes of Death by Race/Ethnicity among People Aged 60 to 70 Years," *Preventing Chronic Disease* 14 (2017): 160241, http://dx.doi.org/10.5888/pcd14.160241.
3. "The South Is Likely to Have America's Highest Death Rate from COVID-19," *Economist*, April 25, 2020, https://www.economist.com/graphic-detail/2020/04/25/the-south-is-likely-to-have-americas-highest-death-rate-from-covid-19; Caitlin Owens, "The South Is Vulnerable to a Coronavirus Nightmare," Axios, April 24, 2020, https://www.axios.com/south-coronavirus-vulnerability-d6efaef2-9331-449c-ba05-f6effa78afe5.html; Isaac Chotiner, "How Racism Is Shaping the Coronavirus Pandemic," *New Yorker*, May 7, 2020, https://www.newyorker.com/news/q-and-a/how-racism-is-shaping-the-coronavirus-pandemic; Youyou Zhou and Julia Belluz, "Who Has Died from Covid-19 in the US?," Vox, updated July 21, 2021, https://www.vox.com/22252693/covid-19-deaths-us-who-died.

4. Centers for Disease Control and Prevention, "150th Anniversary of John Snow and the Pump Handle," *Morbidity and Mortality Weekly Report* 53, no. 34 (2004): 783, https://www.cdc.gov/mmwr/preview/mmwrhtml/mm5334a1.htm.

5. Julie Sweetland, "Framing and Shifting the Narrative about Health in the United States" (presentation at US Health Care Expenditures: Costs, Lessons, and Opportunities—a Virtual Workshop, meeting of the National Academies of Science, Engineering, and Medicine, March 16, 2021).

6. Ross C. Brownson et al., "Reimagining Public Health in the Aftermath of a Pandemic," *American Journal of Public Health* 110, no. 11 (2020): 1605-10, https://ajph.aphapublications.org/doi/10.2105/AJPH.2020.305861.

7. Jamie Ducharme and Elijah Wolfson, "Your ZIP Code Might Determine How Long You Live—and the Difference Could Be Decades," *Time*, June 17, 2019, https://time.com/5608268/zip-code-health/.

8. "Where You Live Impacts Your Health," *Forbes*, June 26, 2017, https://www.forbes.com/sites/quora/2017/06/26/where-you-live-impacts-your-health/#59cf753f45df.

9. There are some exceptions, such as Linda Villarosa, "Black Lives Are Shorter in Chicago. My Family's History Shows Why," *New York Times Magazine*, April 28, 2021, https://www.nytimes.com/2021/04/27/magazine/life-expectancy-racial-gap.html; Anne Case and Angus Deaton, *Deaths of Despair and the Future of Capitalism* (Princeton, NJ: Princeton University Press, 2020); and Isabel Wilkerson, *The Warmth of Other Suns: The Epic Story of America's Great Migration* (New York: Random House, 2010).

10. Paula Braveman and Laura Gottlieb, "The Social Determinants of Health: It's Time to Consider the Causes of the Causes," *Public Health Reports* 129 (2014): 19-31, https://doi.org/10.1177/00333549141291S206.

11. Sandro Galea, *Well: What We Need to Talk about When We Talk about Health* (New York: Oxford University Press, 2019).

12. Shervin Assari, "Blacks' Diminished Return of Education Attainment on Subjective Health; Mediating Effect of Income," *Brain Science* 8, no. 9 (2018): 176, https://doi.org/10.3390/brainsci8090176.

13. Geoff B. Dougherty et al., "Measuring Structural Racism and Its Association with BMI," *American Journal of Preventive Medicine* 59, no. 4 (2020): 530-37, https://doi.org/10.1016/j.amepre.2020.05.019.

14. "New AMA Policies Recognize Race as a Social, Not Biological, Construct," American Medical Association, November 16, 2020, https://www.ama-assn.org/press-center/press-releases/new-ama-policies-recognize-race-social-not-biological-construct.

15. Zinzi D. Bailey et al., "Structural Racism and Health Inequities in the USA: Evidence and Interventions," *Lancet* 389, no. 10077 (2017): 1453-63, https://doi.org/10.1016/S0140-6736(17)30569-X.

16. Ibram X. Kendi, *How to Be an Antiracist* (New York: One World, 2019).

17. Ibram X. Kendi, *Stamped from the Beginning: The Definitive History of Racist Ideas in America* (New York: Bold Type Books, 2017); Kendi, *How to Be*.

18. Kendi, *How to Be*, 24.

19. Kendi, 11.

20. For example, during the 2020 vice presidential debate against Senator Kamala Harris, Vice President Mike Pence said that systemic racism does not exist. Nicquel Terry Ellis, "Pence Denies Systemic Racism, Harris Decries Trump Administration 'Pattern' of Racism in Historic Debate," *USA Today*, October 8, 2020, https://www.usatoday.com/story/news/nation/2020/10/07/pence-haris-spar-over-systemic-racism-breonna-taylor-vp-debate/5919398002/. Governor Tate Reeves said that systemic racism does not exist in Mississippi's criminal justice system. Adam Ganucheau, "Gov. Reeves Says There Is No Systemic Racism in the Justice System. The Numbers Say Otherwise," *Mississippi Today*, April 30, 2021, https://mississippitoday.org/2021/04/30/gov-reeves-says-there-is-no-systemic-racism-in-the-justice-system-the-numbers-say-otherwise/.

21. Jonathan M. Metzl, *Dying of Whiteness: How the Politics of Racial Resentment Is Killing America's Heartland* (New York: Basic Books, 2019), 11.

22. See John J. Green, Kate M. Centellas, and Emma Willoughby, "Epistemic Prejudice and Geographies of Innovation: Health Disparities and Unrecognized Interventions in Mississippi," *Medicine Anthropology Theory* 6, no. 4 (2019): 1–28, https://doi.org/10.17157/mat.6.4.646; and James M. Ferris and Elwood Hopkins, "Place-Based Initiatives: Lessons from Five Decades of Experimentation and Experience," *Foundation Review* 7, no. 4 (2015): 97–109, https://scholarworks.gvsu.edu/cgi/viewcontent.cgi?article=1269&context=tfr.

23. "U.S. Life Expectancy by State and Sex for 2019," National Center for Health Statistics, last reviewed February 10, 2022, https://www.cdc.gov/nchs/data-visualization/state-life-expectancy/index_2019.htm.

24. Joint Center for Political and Economic Studies, *Place Matters for Health in the South Delta: Ensuring Opportunities for Good Health for All* (Washington, DC: Joint Center for Political and Economic Studies, November 2012), https://www.nationalcollaborative.org/wp-content/uploads/2016/02/PLACE-MATTERS-for-Health-in-South-Delta.pdf.

25. "Mississippi: Low Birthweight," County Health Rankings, accessed January 2, 2024, https://www.countyhealthrankings.org/explore-health-rankings/mississippi?year=2022&measure=Low+Birthweight&tab.

26. "Birthweight and Gestation," Centers for Disease Control and Prevention, last reviewed January 2, 2024, https://www.cdc.gov/nchs/pressroom/sosmap/lbw_births/lbw.htm.

27. See the 2023 March of Dimes Report Card for Mississippi, accessed April 26, 2024, https://www.marchofdimes.org/peristats/reports/mississippi/report-card.

28. "Coahoma County Health Profile," Mississippi State Department of Health, accessed October 10, 2022.

29. World Health Organization, *Global Nutrition Targets 2025: Low Birth Weight Policy Brief* (Geneva: World Health Organization, 2014), https://iris.who.int/bitstream/handle/10665/149020/WHO_NMH_NHD_14.5_eng.pdf?sequence=2.

30. Kenneth Johnson, "Where Is 'Rural America,' and What Does It Look Like?," The Conversation, February 20, 2017, https://theconversation.com/where-is-rural-america-and-what-does-it-look-like-72045. See also Jessica D. Ulrich-Schad and Cynthia M. Duncan, "People and Places Left Behind: Work, Culture and Politics in

the Rural United States," *Journal of Peasant Studies* 45, no. 1 (2018): 59–79, https://doi.org/10.1080/03066150.2017.1410702; and Richard Florida, "The 3 Rural Americas," Bloomberg, June 1, 2018, https://www.citylab.com/equity/2018/06/the-three-rural-americas/561791/.

31. Kim Parker, "What Unites and Divides Urban, Suburban and Rural Communities," Pew Research Center, May 22, 2018, https://www.pewsocialtrends.org/2018/05/22/what-unites-and-divides-urban-suburban-and-rural-communities/.

32. Kenneth Johnson, "Rural America Broadens Our Economic, Intellectual, Cultural Diversity: We Can't Ignore Its Residents," Salon, February 26, 2017, https://www.salon.com/2017/02/26/rural-america-broadens-our-economic-intellectual-cultural-diversity-we-cant-ignore-its-residents_partner/.

33. Arthur G. Cosby et al., "Growth and Persistence of Place-Based Mortality in the United States: The Rural Mortality Penalty," *American Journal of Public Health* 109, no. 1 (2019): 155–62, https://ajph.aphapublications.org/doi/10.2105/AJPH.2018.304787.

34. Arthur G. Cosby et al., "Preliminary Evidence for an Emerging Nonmetropolitan Mortality Penalty in the United States," *American Journal of Public Health* 98, no. 5 (2008): 1470–72, https://doi.org/10.2105/AJPH.2007.123778.

35. Stan L. Albrecht, Leslie L. Clarke, and Michael K. Miller, "Community, Family, and Race/Ethic Differences in Health Status in Rural Areas," *Rural Sociology* 63, no. 2 (1998): 235–52, https://doi.org/10.1111/j.1549-0831.1998.tb00673.x; Cosby et al., "Preliminary Evidence"; Jeralynn S. Cossman et al., "Underlying Causes of the Emerging Nonmetropolitan Mortality Penalty," *American Journal of Public Health* 100, no. 8 (2010): 1417–19, https://doi.org/10.2105/AJPH.2009.174185; Wesley James and Jeralynn S. Cossman, "Long-Term Trends in Black and White Mortality in the Rural United States: Evidence of a Race-Specific Rural Mortality Penalty," *Journal of Rural Health* 33, no. 1 (2017): 21–31, https://doi.org/10.1111/jrh.12181; Timothy J. Anderson et al., "A Cross-Sectional Study on the Difference between Rural and Nonrural US Counties Using the County Health Rankings," *BMC Health Services Research* 15 (2015): 441, https://doi.org/10.1186/s12913-015-1053-3.

36. Steven A. Cohen, "A Closer Look at Rural-Urban Health Disparities: Associations between Obesity and Rurality Vary by Geospatial and Sociodemographic Factors," *Journal of Rural Health* 33, no. 2 (2017): 167–79, https://doi.org/10.1111/jrh.12207.

37. Ulrich-Schad and Duncan, "People and Places"; Johnson, "Where Is 'Rural America'?"

38. "About Delta Regional Authority," Delta Regional Authority, accessed September 2, 2022, https://dra.gov/about-dra/about-delta-regional-authority/.

39. "Yazoo River Basin," Mississippi Department of Environmental Quality, accessed September 2, 2022, https://www.mdeq.ms.gov/water/surface-water/watershed-management/basin-management-approach/basin-listing/yazoo-river/.

40. David Cohn, "Where I Was Born and Raised: The Delta Land," accessed September 2, 2022, http://users.soc.umn.edu/~samaha/cases/cohn_delta.html; James C. Cobb, *The Most Southern Place on Earth: The Mississippi Delta and the Roots of Regional Authority* (New York: Oxford University Press, 1992).

41. "Mississippi: DeSoto (DE)," County Health Rankings, accessed September 2, 2022, https://www.countyhealthrankings.org/app/mississippi/2020/rankings/desoto/county/outcomes/overall/snapshot.

42. "Mississippi: Tunica (TU)," County Health Rankings, accessed September 2, 2022, https://www.countyhealthrankings.org/app/mississippi/2020/rankings/tunica/county/outcomes/overall/snapshot.

43. Scott L. Greer et al., "Policy, Politics, and Public Health," *European Journal of Public Health* 27, Suppl. 4 (2017): 40–43, https://doi.org/10.1093/eurpub/ckx152.

44. Thomas Oliver, "The Politics of Public Health Policy," *Annual Review of Public Health* 27 (2006): 195–233, https://doi.org/10.1146/annurev.publhealth.25.101802.123126; Johan P. Mackenbach, "Political Determinants of Health," *European Journal of Public Health* 24, no. 2 (2014): 2, https://doi.org/10.1093/eurpub/ckt183; Ilona Kickbusch, "The Political Determinants of Health—10 Years On," *British Medical Journal* 350 (2015): h81, https://doi.org/10.1136/bmj.h81; Daniel Dawes, *The Political Determinants of Health* (Baltimore: Johns Hopkins University Press, 2020).

45. Greer et al., "Policy, Politics."

46. World Health Organization, *A Conceptual Framework for Action on the Social Determinants of Health* (Geneva: World Health Organization, 2010), https://apps.who.int/iris/handle/10665/44489.

47. Nicole Bernier and Carole Clavier, "Public Health Policy Research: Making the Case for a Political Science Approach," *Health Promotion International* 26, no. 1 (2011): 109, https://doi.org/10.1093/heapro/daq079.

48. V. O. Key Jr., *Southern Politics in State and Nation* (New York: Alfred A. Knopf, 1949); Cobb, *Most Southern Place*; Robert Mickey, *Paths Out of Dixie: The Democratization of Authoritarian Enclaves in America's Deep South, 1944–1972* (Princeton, NJ: Princeton University Press, 2015); Avidit Acharya, Matthew Blackwell, and Maya Sen, *Deep Roots: How Slavery Still Shapes Southern Politics* (Princeton, NJ: Princeton University Press, 2018).

49. Meghan A. Navarro, "Signing the Treaty of Dancing Rabbit Creek," Smithsonian National Postal Museum, accessed September 2, 2022, https://postalmuseum.si.edu/exhibition/indians-at-the-post-office-murals-treaties/signing-of-the-treaty-of-dancing-rabbit-creek.

50. "Mississippi American Indian and Alaska Native Population Percentage by County," Index Mundi, accessed September 2, 2022, https://www.indexmundi.com/facts/united-states/quick-facts/mississippi/american-indian-and-alaskan-native-population-percentage#map.

51. Bo Petersen, "Buried in History: Secrecy Protects Local Indian Mounds," *Post and Courier*, updated November 2, 2016, https://www.postandcourier.com/news/buried-in-history-secrecy-protects-local-indian-mounds/article_89319e6e-843f-57f5-98f4-3da6ec7f48cc.html#newsletter-popup.

52. Edward Ball, "Retracing Slavery's Trail of Tears," *Smithsonian Magazine*, November 2015, https://www.smithsonianmag.com/history/slavery-trail-of-tears-180956968/.

53. "Issaquena County," Mississippi Encyclopedia, last updated April 14, 2018, https://mississippiencyclopedia.org/entries/issaquena-county/.

54. Michael Maciag, "2017 State Population by Race, Ethnicity Data," Governing, July 2, 2015, https://www.governing.com/gov-data/census/state-minority-population-data-estimates.html.

55. "Mississippi: % Non-Hispanic African American," County Health Rankings, accessed September 2, 2022, https://www.countyhealthrankings.org/app/mississippi/2016/measure/factors/54/data?sort=desc-3.

56. "QuickFacts: Tunica County, Mississippi; Leflore County, Mississippi; Quitman County, Mississippi; Coahoma County, Mississippi; Bolivar County, Mississippi," US Census Bureau, accessed October 24, 2022, https://www.census.gov/quickfacts/fact/table/tunicacountymississippi,leflorecountymississippi,quitmancountymississippi,coahomacountymississippi,bolivarcountymississippi/RHI725221.

57. Acharya, Blackwell, and Sen, *Deep Roots*.

58. Byron D'Andra Orey, "Black Legislative Politics in Mississippi," *Journal of Black Studies* 30, no. 6 (2000): 791–814, https://doi.org/10.1177/002193470003000605.

59. Mickey, *Paths Out of Dixie*.

60. Michael Perman, *The Southern Political Tradition* (Baton Rouge: Louisiana State University Press, 2012), 18.

61. Cobb, *Most Southern Place*.

62. Orey, "Black Legislative Politics."

63. Cobb, *Most Southern Place*.

64. Mickey, *Paths Out of Dixie*.

65. Nancy Krieger et al., "Jim Crow and Premature Mortality among US Black and White Population, 1960–2009: An Age-Period-Cohort Analysis," *Epidemiology* 25, no. 4 (2014): 494–504, https://doi.org/10.1097/EDE.0000000000000104.

66. Mickey, *Paths Out of Dixie*.

67. Mickey.

68. Mickey.

69. Mickey.

70. Frank Parker, *Black Votes Count: Political Empowerment in Mississippi after 1965* (Chapel Hill: University of North Carolina Press, 1990).

71. Charles Menifeld, Stephen Shaffer, and Charles E. Jones, "Voting Behavior among African-Americans in Southern Legislatures" (paper delivered at the annual meeting of the American Political Science Association, 2000).

72. Menifeld, Shaffer, and Jones.

73. Orey, "Black Legislative Politics," 807.

74. Orey, 809.

75. David K. Jones, "Political Participation in the Least Healthy Place in America: Examining the Political Determinants of Health in the Mississippi Delta," *Journal of Health Politics, Policy and Law* 44, no. 3 (2019): 505–31, https://doi.org/10.1215/03616878-7367048.

76. Eyder Peralta, "After Snafu, Mississippi Ratifies Amendment Abolishing Slavery," NPR, February 19, 2013, https://www.npr.org/sections/thetwo-way/2013/02/19/172432523/after-snafu-mississippi-ratifies-amendment-abolishing-slavery.

77. For example, in his 2021 budget, Governor Tate Reeves called for the creation of a "Patriotic Education Fund" to limit the ways the history of racism and slavery could

be taught in Mississippi schools. Tal Axelrod, "Mississippi Governor Calls for Spending $3 Million on 'Patriotic Education Fund,'" The Hill, November 17, 2020, https://thehill.com/homenews/state-watch/526441-mississippi-governor-calls-for-spending-3-million-on-patriotic-education?rl=1. The Trump administration's 1776 Commission released a report in January 2021 criticizing attempts to talk in schools about the role of racism in the country's creation. President's Advisory 1776 Commission, *The 1776 Report* (January 2021), https://trumpwhitehouse.archives.gov/wp-content/uploads/2021/01/The-Presidents-Advisory-1776-Commission-Final-Report.pdf.

78. Robert F. Kennedy, "Day of Affirmation Address, University of Capetown, Capetown, South Africa, June 6, 1966," John F. Kennedy Presidential Library and Museum, accessed March 7, 2024, https://www.jfklibrary.org/learn/about-jfk/the-kennedy-family/robert-f-kennedy/robert-f-kennedy-speeches/day-of-affirmation-address-university-of-capetown-capetown-south-africa-june-6-1966.

79. The University of Wisconsin Population Health Institute describes five steps to improve community health. "Work Together," County Health Rankings, accessed March 7, 2024, https://www.countyhealthrankings.org/take-action-improve-health/action-center/work-together. It also contains a searchable database of more than four hundred policy ideas across multiple domains, from health care to education and economic development. "Strategies," County Health Rankings, accessed March 7, 2024, https://www.countyhealthrankings.org/take-action-to-improve-health/what-works-for-health/strategies.

Chapter 1

1. Tiffani Grant et al., *Mississippi Obesity Action Plan: The Vision, Goal and Call to Action, 2018* (Jackson: Mississippi State Department of Health, February 2018), https://msdh.ms.gov/msdhsite/_static/resources/6164.pdf.

2. Edward A. Frongillo et al., "Food Insecurity Is More Strongly Associated with Poor Subjective Well-Being in More-Developed Countries Than in Less-Developed Countries," *Journal of Nutrition* 149, no. 2 (2018): 330–35, https://doi.org/10.1093/jn/nxy261.

3. Ron Friedman, "What You Eat Affects Your Productivity," *Harvard Business Review*, October 17, 2014, https://hbr.org/2014/10/what-you-eat-affects-your-productivity; Tamlin S. Conner, "On Carrots and Curiosity: Eating Fruit and Vegetables Is Associated with Greater Flourishing in Daily Life," *British Journal of Health Psychology* 20, no. 2 (2015): 413–27, https://doi.org/10.1111/bjhp.12113.

4. Ellen B. Meacham, *Delta Epiphany: Robert F. Kennedy in Mississippi* (Jackson: University Press of Mississippi, 2018), 16.

5. Meacham, 84.

6. Meacham, 131, 134.

7. Meacham, 132.

8. Meacham, 133.

9. Henry Hampton, Steve Fayer, and Sarah Flynn, *Voices of Freedom: An Oral History of the Civil Rights Movement from the 1950s through the 1980s* (New York: Bantam Books, 1990), 453.

10. Meacham, *Delta Epiphany*, 173.

11. Meacham, 173.

12. Meacham, 177.

13. Meacham, 181.

14. "Policy Basics: The Supplemental Nutrition Assistance Program (SNAP)," Center on Budget and Policy Priorities, updated June 9, 2022, https://www.cbpp.org/research/food-assistance/the-supplemental-nutrition-assistance-program-snap.

15. Grant et al., *Mississippi Obesity Action Plan*.

16. Jeffrey Levy et al., *F as in Fat: How Obesity Threatens America's Future, 2013* (Trust for America's Health and Robert Wood Johnson Foundation, August 16, 2013), https://www.rwjf.org/en/insights/our-research/2013/08/f-as-in-fat--how-obesity-threatens-america-s-future-2013.html

17. Grant et al., *Mississippi Obesity Action Plan*; Levy et al., *F as in Fat*.

18. "Mississippi: Adult Obesity," County Health Rankings, accessed September 3, 2022, https://www.countyhealthrankings.org/app/mississippi/2020/measure/factors/11/map.

19. Sabrina Strings, *Fearing the Black Body: The Racial Origins of Fat Phobia* (New York: New York University Press, 2019).

20. Ingrid K. Richards Adams et al., "An Examination of Demographic and Psychosocial Factors, Barriers to Healthy Eating, and Diet Quality among African American Adults," *Nutrients* 11, no. 3 (2019): 519, https://doi.org/10.3390/nu11030519; Beverly J. McCabe-Sellers et al., "Assessment of the Diet Quality of US Adults in the Lower Mississippi Delta," *American Journal of Clinical Nutrition* 86, no. 3 (2007): 697–706, https://doi.org/10.1093/ajcn/86.3.697; Katherine L. Tucker et al., "A Regional Food-Frequency Questionnaire for the US Mississippi Delta," *Public Health Nutrition* 8, no. 1 (2005): 87–96, https://doi.org/10.1079/PHN2004663; G. Pagliai et al., "Consumption of Ultra-processed Foods and Health Status: A Systematic Review and Meta-analysis," *British Journal of Nutrition* 125, no. 3 (2021): 308–18, https://doi.org/10.1017/S0007114520002688.

21. Grant et al., *Mississippi Obesity Action Plan*.

22. Grant et al.

23. Vincent L. Mendy et al., "Overweight, Obesity, and Extreme Obesity among Mississippi Adults, 2001–2010 and 2011–2015," Centers for Disease Control and Prevention, June 22, 2017, https://www.cdc.gov/pcd/issues/2017/16_0554.htm.

24. Grant et al., *Mississippi Obesity Action Plan*.

25. "Definitions of Food Security," US Department of Agriculture, last updated April 22, 2022, https://www.ers.usda.gov/topics/food-nutrition-assistance/food-security-in-the-us/definitions-of-food-security.aspx.

26. Jessica L. Thomson et al., "A Simulation Study of the Potential Effects of Healthy Food and Beverage Substitutions on Diet Quality and Total Energy Intake in Lower Mississippi Delta Adults," *Journal of Nutrition* 141, no. 12 (2011): 2191–97, https://doi.org/10.3945/jn.111.144659; Tammy Leonard et al., "Overlapping Geographic Clusters of Food Security and Health: Where Do Social Determinants and Health Outcomes Converge in the U.S.?," *SSM-Population Health* 5 (2018): 160–70,

https://doi.org/10.1016/j.ssmph.2018.06.006; Angela Odoms-Young and Marino A. Bruce, "Examining the Impact of Structural Racism on Food Insecurity Implications for Addressing Racial/Ethnic Disparities," *Family and Community Health* 41 (2018): S3–S6, https://doi.org/10.1097/FCH.0000000000000183; "Hunger Runs Deep in the Communities Working Hardest to Feed Us," Feeding America, accessed September 3, 2022, https://www.feedingamerica.org/hunger-in-america/rural-hunger-facts.

27. Jennifer M. Poti et al., "Is the Degree of Food Processing and Convenience Linked with the Nutritional Quality of Foods Purchased by US Households?," *American Journal of Clinical Nutrition* 101, no. 6 (2015): 1251–62, https://doi.org/10.3945/ajcn.114.100925; Alyssa J. Moran et al., "What Factors Influence Ultra-processed Food Purchases and Consumption in Households with Children? A Comparison between Participants and Non-participants in the Supplemental Nutrition Assistance Program (SNAP)," *Appetite* 134 (2019): 1–8, https://doi.org/10.1016/j.appet.2018.12.009.

28. Larissa Galastri Baraldi et al., "Consumption of Ultra-processed Foods and Associated Sociodemographic Factors in the USA between 2007 and 2012: Evidence from a National Representative Cross-Sectional Study," *BMJ Open* 8, no. 3 (2018): e020574, https://doi.org/10.1136/bmjopen-2017-020574; Ingrid Laukeland Djupegot et al., "The Association between Time Scarcity, Sociodemographic Correlates and Consumption of Ultra-processed Foods among Parents in Norway: A Cross-Sectional Study," *BMC Public Health* 17 (2017): 447, https://bmcpublichealth.biomedcentral.com/articles/10.1186/s12889-017-4408-3; Tamara Dubowitz et al., "Lifecourse, Immigrant Status and Acculturation in Food Purchasing and Preparation among Low-Income Mothers," *Public Health Nutrition* 10, no. 4 (2007): 396–404, https://doi.org/10.1017/S1368980007334058; Victoria Inglis, Kylie Ball, and David Crawford, "Why Do Women of Low Socioeconomic Status Have Poorer Dietary Behaviours Than Women of Higher Socioeconomic Status? A Qualitative Exploration," *Appetite* 45, no. 3 (2005): 334–43, https://doi.org/10.1016/j.appet.2005.05.003; Jennifer Jabs and Carol M. Devine, "Time Scarcity and Food Choices: An Overview," *Appetite* 47, no. 2 (2006): 196–204, https://doi.org/10.1016/j.appet.2006.02.014; Bernestine B. McGee et al., "Food Shopping Perceptions, Behaviors, and Ability to Purchase Healthful Food Items in the Lower Mississippi Delta," *Journal of Nutrition Education and Behavior* 43, no. 5 (2011): 339–48, https://doi.org/10.1016/j.jneb.2010.10.007; Kristen Wiig and Chery Smith, "The Art of Grocery Shopping on a Food Stamp Budget: Factors Influencing the Food Choices of Low-Income Women as They Try to Make Ends Meet," *Public Health Nutrition* 12, no. 10 (2009): 1726–34, https://doi.org/10.1017/S1368980008004102.

29. Moran et al., "What Factors?," 1.

30. Pagliai et al., "Consumption of Ultra-processed Foods."

31. Ross C. Brownson, Debra Haire-Joshu, and Douglas A. Luke, "Shaping the Context of Health: A Review of Environmental and Policy Approaches in the Prevention of Chronic Diseases," *Annual Review of Public Health* 27 (2006): 341–70, https://doi.org/10.1146/annurev.publhealth.27.021405.102137; Lila J. Finney Rutten et al., "Poverty, Food Insecurity, and Obesity: A Conceptual Framework for Research, Practice, and Policy," *Journal of Hunger and Environmental Nutrition* 5, no. 4

(2010): 403–15, https://doi.org/10.1080/19320248.2010.527275; Joseph Awetori Yaro, "Theorizing Food Insecurity: Building a Livelihood Vulnerability Framework for Researching Food Insecurity," *Norwegian Journal of Geography* 58, no. 1 (2004): 23–37, https://doi.org/10.1080/00291950410004375; Food and Agriculture Organization of the United Nations et al., *The State of Food Security and Nutrition in the World 2018: Building Climate Resilience for Food Security and Nutrition* (Rome: Food and Agriculture Organization of the United Nations, 2018), http://www.fao.org/3/I9553EN/i9553en.pdf.

32. "Food Insecurity among Overall (All Ages) Population in the United States," Feeding America, accessed September 3, 2022, https://map.feedingamerica.org/; Janice E. Stuff et al., "High Prevalence of Food Insecurity and Hunger in Households in the Rural Lower Mississippi Delta," *Journal of Rural Health* 20, no. 2 (2004): 173–80, https://doi.org/10.1111/j.1748-0361.2004.tb00025.x; Alex Rozier, "Mississippi Still the Hungriest State," *Mississippi Today*, May 4, 2018, https://mississippitoday.org/2018/05/04/mississippi-still-the-hungriest-state/?mc_cid=9d10ec2dcb&mc_eid=df26913b5e.

33. "Understand Food Insecurity," Feeding America, accessed September 3, 2022, https://hungerandhealth.feedingamerica.org/understand-food-insecurity/.

34. David L. Pelletier, Christine M. Olson, and Edward A. Frongillo, "Food Insecurity, Hunger, and Undernutrition," in *Present Knowledge in Nutrition*, 10th ed., ed. John W. Erdman Jr., Ian A. Macdonald, and Steven H. Zeisel (Washington, DC: International Life Sciences Institute, 2012), 1165–81; "Hunger Deprives Our Kids of More Than Just Food," Feeding America, accessed September 3, 2022, https://www.feedingamerica.org/hunger-in-america/child-hunger-facts.

35. Rozier, "Mississippi Still the Hungriest."

36. "Hunger Hits African American Communities Harder," Feeding America, accessed September 3, 2022, https://www.feedingamerica.org/hunger-in-america/african-american.

37. "Mississippi: Food Insecurity," County Health Rankings, accessed September 3, 2022, https://www.countyhealthrankings.org/app/mississippi/2018/measure/factors/139/data?sort=desc-3.

38. "States Are Using Much-Needed Temporary Flexibility in SNAP to Respond to COVID-19 Challenges," Center on Budget and Policy Priorities, accessed September 3, 2022, https://www.cbpp.org/sites/default/files/atoms/files/3-31-20fa.pdf.

39. By my count as of 2019.

40. Aallyah Wright, "Clarksdale Grocery Store Closing: What Does It Mean for the Delta Community?," *Mississippi Today*, January 8, 2018, https://mississippitoday.org/2018/01/08/long-time-clarksdale-grocery-store-closing-what-does-it-mean-for-delta-community/.

41. "Food Deserts in the United States," Annie E. Casey Foundation, February 13, 2021, https://www.aecf.org/blog/exploring-americas-food-deserts.

42. Anna Bengston et al., *Food Access in West Tallahatchie: A Community Partnership Working to Improve Food Futures* (University of Michigan, n.d.), accessed September 3, 2022, http://graham.umich.edu/media/files/dow/Dow-Masters-2016-Food-Access-West-Tallahatchie.pdf.

43. McGee et al., "Food Shopping."

44. Sarah Elton, "Please Don't Call It a Food Swamp," The Conversation, September 3, 2018, https://theconversation.com/please-dont-call-it-a-food-swamp-97219.

45. Erin R. Hager et al., "Food Swamps and Food Deserts in Baltimore City, MD, USA: Associations with Dietary Behaviours among Urban Adolescent Girls," *Public Health Nutrition* 20, no. 14 (2017): 2598–607, https://doi.org/10.1017/S1368980016002123; Kristen Cooksey-Stowers, Marlene B. Schwartz, and Kelly D. Brownell, "Food Swamps Predict Obesity Rates Better Than Food Deserts in the United States," *International Journal of Environmental Research and Public Health* 14, no. 11 (2017): 1366, https://www.ncbi.nlm.nih.gov/pmc/articles/PMC5708005/.

46. Aaron Marquis, "The Advantages of Opening a Fast-Food Restaurant in Rural Places," Chron, accessed September 3, 2022, https://smallbusiness.chron.com/advantages-opening-fastfood-restaurant-rural-places-34152.html.

47. Marquis.

48. J. Nicholas Bodor et al., "Disparities in Food Access: Does Aggregate Availability of Key Foods from Other Stores Offset the Relative Lack of Supermarkets in African-American Neighborhoods?," *Preventive Medicine* 51, no. 1 (2010): 63–67, https://doi.org/10.1016/j.ypmed.2010.04.009; Carol R. Horowitz et al., "Barriers to Buying Healthy Foods for People with Diabetes: Evidence of Environmental Disparities," *American Journal of Public Health* 94, no. 9 (2004): 1549–54, https://doi.org/10.2105/AJPH.94.9.1549; Paul L. Hutchinson et al., "Neighbourhood Food Environments and Obesity in Southeast Louisiana," *Health and Place* 18, no. 4 (2012): 854–60, https://doi.org/10.1016/j.healthplace.2012.03.006; Shannon N. Zenk et al., "Relative and Absolute Availability of Healthier Food and Beverage Alternatives across Communities in the United States," *American Journal of Public Health* 104, no. 11 (2014): 2170–78, https://doi.org/10.2105/AJPH.2014.302113.

49. McGee et al., "Food Shopping."

50. Karen Washington, "Food Apartheid: The Root of the Problem with America's Groceries," interview by Anna Brones, *Guardian*, May 15, 2018, https://www.theguardian.com/society/2018/may/15/food-apartheid-food-deserts-racism-inequality-america-karen-washington-interview.

51. Michael J. Widener, "Spatial Access to Food: Retiring the Food Desert Metaphor," *Physiology and Behavior* 193 (2018): 257–60, https://doi.org/10.1016/j.physbeh.2018.02.032; Steven Cummins, Ellen Flint, and Stephen A. Matthews, "New Neighborhood Grocery Store Increased Awareness of Food Access but Did Not Alter Dietary Habits or Obesity," *Health Affairs* 33, no. 2 (2014): 283–91, https://www.healthaffairs.org/doi/full/10.1377/hlthaff.2013.0512.

52. Christine Anne Vaughan and Tamara Dubowitz, "Fixing America's Food Deserts Alone Won't Fix Our Terrible Diets," *The RAND Blog*, December 11, 2017, https://www.rand.org/blog/2017/12/fixing-americas-food-deserts-alone-wont-fix-our-terrible.html.

53. Priya Fielding-Singh, "Why Do Poor Americans Eat So Unhealthfully? Because Junk Food Is the Only Indulgence They Can Afford," *Los Angeles Times*, February 7, 2018, https://www.latimes.com/opinion/op-ed/la-oe-singh-food-deserts-nutritional-disparities-20180207-story.html.

54. Kiarri N. Kershaw et al., "Assessment of the Influence of Food Attributes on Meal Choice Selection by Socioeconomic Status and Race/Ethnicity among Women Living in Chicago, USA: A Discrete Choice Experiment," *Appetite* 139 (2019): 19–25, https://doi.org/10.1016/j.appet.2019.04.003.

55. "Food Prices and Spending," US Department of Agriculture Economic Research Service, last updated February 14, 2024, https://www.ers.usda.gov/data-products/ag-and-food-statistics-charting-the-essentials/food-prices-and-spending/.

56. The other part of the country with similar levels of disparities is Appalachia. See Anne Cafer et al., "National Food Affordability: A County-Level Analysis," *Preventing Chronic Disease* 15, no. 9 (2018): 180079, https://doi.org/10.5888/pcd15.180079.

57. McGee et al., "Food Shopping," 342.

58. Janelle Fritts, "How Does Your State Treat Groceries, Candy, and Soda?," Tax Foundation, October 30, 2019, https://taxfoundation.org/grocery-tax-candy-tax-soda-tax-2019/.

59. Bobby Harrison, "Some See Grocery Tax as 'Cruel.' Others, Including Top State Leaders, Believe It Is Fair," *Mississippi Today*, December 13, 2020, https://mississippitoday.org/2020/12/13/some-see-grocery-tax-as-cruel-others-including-top-state-leaders-believe-it-is-fair/.

60. Moran et al., "What Factors?"

61. Moran et al., 5.

62. Carol L. Connell et al., "Energy Density, Nutrient Adequacy, and Cost per Serving Can Provide Insight into Food Choices in the Lower Mississippi Delta," *Journal of Nutrition Education and Behavior* 44, no. 2 (2012): 148–53, https://doi.org/10.1016/j.jneb.2011.02.003.

63. "Mississippi Supplement Nutrition Assistance Program (SNAP)," Benefits.gov, accessed September 3, 2022, https://www.benefits.gov/benefit/1288.

64. Lauren Hall and Catlin Nchako, "A Closer Look at Who Benefits from SNAP: State-by-State Fact Sheets," Center on Budget and Policy Priorities, March 16, 2020, https://www.cbpp.org/research/food-assistance/a-closer-look-at-who-benefits-from-snap-state-by-state-fact-sheets#Mississippi.

65. Anthony Warren, "Families Will Receive Additional SNAP Benefits as Part of $1.9T Stimulus Package," WLBT Jackson, updated March 22, 2021, https://www.wlbt.com/2021/03/22/familes-will-receive-additional-snap-benefits-part-t-stimulus-package/.

66. Hall and Nchako, "Closer Look."

67. "Food Stamp Revamp Would Have Heavy Impact in Delta," Delta News, updated November 8, 2018, https://www.deltanews.tv/news/food-stamp-revamp-would-have-heavy-impact-in-delta/article_707157fa-1112-11e8-8a7f-fffaee42e193.html.

68. Tim Marema, "The Geography of Food Stamps," *Daily Yonder*, December 31, 2018, https://www.dailyyonder.com/geography-food-stamps/2018/12/31/25422/; Tim Marema, "Top 100 Counties, SNAP Participants as Percent of Population," *Daily Yonder*, May 7, 2018, https://www.dailyyonder.com/top-100-counties-snap-participants-percent-population/2018/05/07/25314/.

69. "Foods Typically Purchased by Supplemental Nutrition Assistance Program (SNAP) Households," US Department of Agriculture, November 18, 2016, https://www.fns.usda.gov/snap/foods-typically-purchased-supplemental-nutrition-assistance-program-snap-households.

70. "Foods Typically Purchased"; Binh T. Nguyen et al., "The Supplemental Nutrition Assistance Program and Dietary Quality among US Adults: Findings from a Nationally Representative Survey," *Mayo Clinic Proceedings* 89, no. 9 (2014): 1211–19, https://doi.org/10.1016/j.mayocp.2014.05.010; Tatiana Andreyeva, Amanda S. Tripp, and Marlene B. Schwartz, "Dietary Quality of Americans by Supplemental Nutrition Assistance Program Participation Status: A Systematic Review," *American Journal of Preventive Medicine* 49, no. 4 (2015): 594–604, https://doi.org/10.1016/j.amepre.2015.04.035; Cindy W. Leung et al., "Associations of Food Stamp Participation with Dietary Quality and Obesity in Children," *Pediatrics* 131, no. 3 (2013): 463–72, https://doi.org/10.1542/peds.2012-0889.

71. Katelin M. Hudak and Elizabeth F. Racine, "The Supplemental Nutrition Assistance Program and Child Weight Status: A Review," *American Journal of Preventive Medicine* 56, no. 6 (2019): 882–93, https://doi.org/10.1016/j.amepre.2019.01.006; Charles L. Baum, "The Effects of Food Stamps on Obesity," *Southern Economic Journal* 77, no. 3 (2011): 623–51, https://doi.org/10.4284/sej.2011.77.3.623; Leung et al., "Associations."

72. Lorenzo Almada, Ian McCarthy, and Rusty Tchernis, "What Can We Learn about the Effects of Food Stamps on Obesity in the Presence of Misreporting?," *American Journal of Agricultural Economics* 98, no. 4 (2016): 997–1017, https://doi.org/10.1093/ajae/aaw017; Joseph Rigdon et al., "Re-evaluating Associations between the Supplemental Nutrition Assistance Program Participation and Body Mass Index in the Context of Unmeasured Confounders," *Social Science and Medicine* 192 (2017): 112–24, https://doi.org/10.1016/j.socscimed.2017.09.020; Nathaniel L. DeBono, Nancy A. Ross, and Lea Berrang-Ford, "Does the Food Stamp Program Cause Obesity? A Realist Review and a Call for Place-Based Research," *Health and Place* 18, no. 40 (2012): 747–56, https://doi.org/10.1016/j.healthplace.2012.03.002.

73. Corti Lorts et al., "Participation in the Supplemental Nutrition Assistance Program and Dietary Behaviors: Role of Community Food Environment," *Journal of the Academy of Nutrition and Dietetics* 119, no. 6 (2019): 932–43, https://doi.org/10.1016/j.jand.2018.11.021.

74. Jiyoon Kim, "Do SNAP Participants Expand Non-food Spending When They Receive More SNAP Benefits?—Evidence from the 2009 SNAP Benefits Increase," *Food Policy* 65 (2016): 9–20, https://doi.org/10.1016/j.foodpol.2016.10.002.

75. Diane Whitmore Schanzenbach, "Testimony: Pros and Cons of Restricting SNAP Purchases," Brookings, February 16, 2017, https://www.brookings.edu/testimonies/pros-and-cons-of-restricting-snap-purchases/.

76. Mississippi did not take full advantage of federal money and flexibility given to states to use SNAP to help families. It was one of nine states that chose not to extend the school meal replacement known as P-EBT through the 2020–21 school year. "States Are Using."

77. "House Bill No. 1090 (as Sent to Governor)," Mississippi Legislature, Regular Session 2017, http://billstatus.ls.state.ms.us/documents/2017/pdf/HB/1000-1099/HB1090SG.pdf.

78. Randy Alison Aussenberg, *Errors and Fraud in the Supplemental Nutrition Assistance Program (SNAP) Specialist in Nutrition Assistance Policy*, R45147 (Washington, DC: Congressional Research Service), updated September 28, 2018, https://sgp.fas.org/crs/misc/R45147.pdf.

79. Anna Wolfe, "'Food Stamps' Fraud Investigator Extorted Convenience Stores, Authorities Say," *Mississippi Today*, October 8, 2018, https://mississippitoday.org/2018/10/08/food-stamps-fraud-investigator-extorted-convenience-stores-authorities-say/.

80. "Food Stamp Investigator Gets 39 Months for Extortion Plea," *U.S. News & World Report*, April 16, 2019, https://www.usnews.com/news/best-states/mississippi/articles/2019-04-16/food-stamp-investigator-gets-39-months-for-extortion-plea.

81. Moran et al., "What Factors?"

82. Margaret Brown and Sara Imperiale, "States Can Leverage SNAP for Healthy Food and Strong Economies," *Natural Resources Defense Council* blog, June 8, 2020, https://www.nrdc.org/experts/sara-imperiale/states-can-leverage-snap-healthy-food-strong-economies.

83. Alyssa Moran et al., "Increases in Sugary Drink Marketing during Supplemental Nutrition Assistance Program Benefit Issuance in New York," *American Journal of Preventive Medicine* 55, no. 1 (2018): 55–62, https://doi.org/10.1016/j.amepre.2018.03.012.

84. Sanjay Basu et al., "Ending SNAP Subsidies for Sugar-Sweetened Beverages Could Reduce Obesity and Type 2 Diabetes," *Health Affairs* 33, no. 6 (2014): 1032–39, https://doi.org/10.1377/hlthaff.2013.1246.

85. Schanzenbach, "Testimony."

86. Basu et al., "Ending SNAP Subsidies."

87. "Massachusetts Healthy Incentives Program (HIP)," Mass.gov, accessed September 4, 2022, https://www.mass.gov/service-details/healthy-incentives-program-hip-for-clients.

88. "What Is a Farmers Market?," Farmers Market Coalition, accessed September 4, 2022, https://farmersmarketcoalition.org/education/qanda/.

89. Darcy A. Freedman et al., "A Farmers' Market at a Federally Qualified Health Center Improves Fruit and Vegetable Intake among Low-Income Diabetics," *Preventive Medicine* 56, no. 5 (2013): 288–92, https://doi.org/10.1016/j.ypmed.2013.01.018; Alexandra E. Evans et al., "Introduction of Farm Stands in Low-Income Communities Increases Fruit and Vegetable among Community Residents," *Health and Place* 18, no. 5 (2012): 1137–43, https://doi.org/10.1016/j.healthplace.2012.04.007; "Farmers Markets," County Health Rankings, last updated February 16, 2018, https://www.countyhealthrankings.org/take-action-to-improve-health/what-works-for-health/strategies/farmers-markets; Chelsea R. Singleton et al., "Farm-to-Consumer Retail Outlet Use, Fruit and Vegetable Intake, and Obesity Status among WIC Program Participants in Alabama," *American Journal of Health Behavior* 40, no. 4 (2016): 446–54, https://doi.org/10.5993/AJHB.40.4.6.

90. Stephanie B. Jilcott Pitts et al., "Farmers' Market Use Is Associated with Fruit and Vegetable Consumption in Diverse Southern Rural Communities," *Nutrition Journal* 13 (2014): 1, https://nutritionj.biomedcentral.com/articles/10.1186/1475-2891-13-1.

91. "Farmers Markets in Mississippi," Mississippi Department of Agriculture and Commerce, accessed September 4, 2022, https://www.mdac.ms.gov/bureaus-departments/farmers-market/markets-mississippi/.

92. Stephanie B. Jilcott Pitts et al., "Farmers' Market Shopping and Dietary Behaviours among Supplemental Nutrition Assistance Program Participants," *Sustainability and Public Health Nutrition* 18, no. 13 (2015): 2407–14, https://doi.org/10.1017/S1368980015001111.

93. Darcy A. Freedman et al., "Systematic Review of Factors Influencing Farmers' Market Use Overall and among Low-Income Populations," *Journal of the Academy of Nutrition and Dietetics* 117, no. 7 (2016): 1136–55, https://doi.org/10.1016/j.jand.2016.02.010.

94. Emily Broad et al., *Increasing Federal Food Assistance Access at Farmers Markets in Mississippi: Analysis and Recommendations* (Harvard Law School Mississippi Delta Project, May 2010), http://www.chlpi.org/wp-content/uploads/2013/12/Mississippi-Farmers-Markets-Food-Assistance-Benefits-FORMATTED.pdf.

95. Broad et al.

96. "Mississippi Farmers Markets with Access for SNAP/EBT Participants," Mississippi Department of Agriculture and Commerce, revised August 2018, https://www.mdac.ms.gov/agency-info/programs/mississippi-farmers-market-nutrition-program/markets-accepting-ebt-in-mississippi/.

97. Scott Lincicome, "Examining America's Farm Subsidy Problem," CATO Institute, December 18, 2020, https://www.cato.org/commentary/examining-americas-farm-subsidy-problem.

98. Mark A. Perelman, "USDA Squeezes the Food Industry with Outdated Subsidies," Yale Center for Business and the Environment, May 14, 2018, https://cbey.yale.edu/our-stories/usda-squeezes-the-food-industry-with-outdated-subsidies.

99. "Mississippi: Children Eligible for Free or Reduced Price Lunch," County Health Rankings, accessed September 4, 2022, https://www.countyhealthrankings.org/app/mississippi/2019/measure/factors/65/data?sort=desc-2.

100. "Serving Healthy School Meals: Despite Challenges, Schools Meet USDA Meal Requirements," Pew Charitable Trusts, September 30, 2013, https://www.pewtrusts.org/en/research-and-analysis/reports/2013/09/30/serving-healthy-school-meals.

101. Lauren E. Au et al., "Eating School Lunch Is Associated with Higher Diet Quality among Elementary School Students," *Journal of the Academy of Nutrition and Dietetics* 116, no. 11 (2016): 1817–24, https://doi.org/10.1016/j.jand.2016.04.010; Lauren E. Au et al., "Eating School Meals Daily Is Associated with Healthier Dietary Intakes: The Healthy Communities Study," *Journal of the Academy of Nutrition and Dietetics* 118, no. 8 (2018): 1474–81, https://doi.org/10.1016/j.jand.2018.01.010.

102. "USDA Approves Program to Feed Kids in Mississippi: Pandemic EBT to Feed Children during COVID-19 National Emergency," press release, Food and Nutrition

Service, US Department of Agriculture, June 2, 2020, https://www.fns.usda.gov/news-item/usda-027920.

103. "LIST: Summer Feeding Programs in South Mississippi," WLOX, June 1, 2020, https://www.wlox.com/2020/06/01/list-summer-feeding-programs-south-mississippi/; Jackie Mader, "In Mississippi, Food Gap Widens during Summer," *Washington Monthly*, July 7, 2014, https://washingtonmonthly.com/2014/07/07/in-mississippi-food-gap-widens-during-summer/.

104. Chiquikta Fountain, "Experiences with the Summer Food Service Program," Delta Hands for Hope, June 6, 2017, https://www.deltahandsforhope.org/blog/2017/6/6/experiences-with-the-summer-food-service-program.

105. Jamie Zoellner et al., "Nutrition Literacy Status and Preferred Nutrition Communication Channels among Adults in the Lower Mississippi Delta," *Preventing Chronic Disease* 6, no. 4 (2009): A128, https://www.ncbi.nlm.nih.gov/pmc/articles/PMC2774642/.

106. "Flashin' Fruit Punch," Hi-C, accessed September 4, 2022, https://www.hi-c.com/products/flashin-fruit-punch.

107. Samantha Thomas et al., "'The Solution Needs to Be Complex': Obese Adults' Attitudes about the Effectiveness of Individual and Population Based Interventions for Obesity," *BMC Public Health* 10 (2010): 420, https://bmcpublichealth.biomedcentral.com/track/pdf/10.1186/1471-2458-10-420.

108. Bengston et al., *Food Access*.

109. Eldar Shafir as quoted in Derek Thompson, "Your Brain in Poverty: Why Poor People Seem to Make Bad Decisions," *Atlantic*, November 22, 2013, https://www.theatlantic.com/business/archive/2013/11/your-brain-on-poverty-why-poor-people-seem-to-make-bad-decisions/281780/.

110. Moran et al., "What Factors?," 4.

111. Anuj K. Shah, Sendhil Mullainathanand, and Eldar Shafir, "Some Consequences of Having Too Little," *Science* 338, no. 6107 (2012): 682–85, https://doi.org/10.1126/science.1222426; Adele Diamond, "Executive Functions," *Annual Review of Psychology* 64 (2013): 135–68, https://doi.org/10.1146/annurev-psych-113011-143750.

112. Anandi Mani et al., "Poverty Impedes Cognitive Function," *Science* 341, no. 6149 (2013): 976–80, https://doi.org/10.1126/science.1238041.

113. Fielding-Singh, "Why Do Poor Americans?"

114. Fielding-Singh.

115. Fielding-Singh.

116. "Maternal, Infant, and Child Health, Healthy People 2020," HealthyPeople.gov, archived content, last updated February 6, 2022, https://wayback.archive-it.org/5774/20220414032744/https://www.healthypeople.gov/2020/topics-objectives/topic/maternal-infant-and-child-health/objectives.

117. "Rates of Any and Exclusive Breastfeeding by State among Children Born in 2016," Centers for Disease Controls and Prevention, accessed September 4, 2022, https://www.cdc.gov/breastfeeding/data/nis_data/rates-any-exclusive-bf-state-2016.htm.

118. "About Baby Café USA," Baby Café USA, accessed September 4, 2022, http://www.babycafeusa.org/your-nearest-baby-cafe/us-baby-cafes-2.html.

119. "Mississippi CHAMPS Communities," Center for Health Equity, Education, and Research, accessed September 4, 2022, https://www.cheerequity.org/mississippi-champs-communities.html.

120. Presley talked about her experience at the Delta Directions Regional Forum, July 2017.

121. "About Us," Delta Fresh Foods, accessed September 4, 2022, http://www.deltafreshfoods.org/attorneys.html.

122. Deborah Moore, Judy Belue, and Brooke Smith, *Social Justice for Lunch: Delta Fresh Foods Initiative at the National Farm to Cafeteria Conference* (WhyHunger, 2015), 2, https://whyhunger.org/wp-content/uploads/2015/05/Food_Justice_Voices_Social_Justice_for_Lunch_DFFI_WhyHunger%20.pdf.

123. Phillip Waller, "The Delta: Growing in the Food Desert," hottytoddy.com, December 12, 2013, https://hottytoddy.com/2013/12/12/the-delta-growing-in-the-food-desert/.

124. Moore, Belue, and Smith, *Social Justice for Lunch*.

125. David Bennett, "Delta Fresh Foods Initiative Links Health Food and Delta Schools, Farm Progress," October 3, 2012, https://www.farmprogress.com/management/delta-fresh-foods-initiative-links-healthy-food-and-delta-schools.

126. Leslie Hossfeld, Laura Jean Kerr, and Judy Belue, "The Good Food Revolution: Building Community Resiliency in the Mississippi Delta," *Social Sciences* 8, no. 57 (2019): 1–10, http://nebula.wsimg.com/b7ea659ad58c69643ca7eea7dd5e14c4?AccessKeyId=B3F998F49D2DF20954AE&disposition=0&alloworigin=1.

127. Hossfeld, Kerr, and Belue.

128. Hossfeld, Kerr, and Belue.

129. "Community Gardens Flyer," Delta Health Alliance, accessed September 4, 2022, https://deltahealthalliance.org/project/school-gardens-delta-eats/.

130. "Community Gardens Flyer"; "Mississippi: Tallahatchie (TA): Health Outcomes," County Health Rankings, accessed September 4, 2022, https://www.countyhealthrankings.org/app/mississippi/2018/rankings/tallahatchie/county/outcomes/overall/snapshot.

131. "Mississippi: Tallahatchie (TA)"; "East Tallahatchie School District, MS," Census Reporter, accessed September 4, 2022, https://censusreporter.org/profiles/97000US2801410-east-tallahatchie-school-district-ms/.

132. "Kennedy Wellness Center Opens with Unique Mission to Improve Health in Mississippi Delta," hottytoddy.com, January 18, 2016, https://hottytoddy.com/2016/01/18/kennedy-wellness-center-opens-with-unique-mission-to-improve-health-in-mississippi-delta/.

133. "Mississippi: Overall Rank," County Health Rankings, accessed September 4, 2022, https://www.countyhealthrankings.org/app/mississippi/2018/rankings/outcomes/overall.

134. Esther Thatcher et al., "Retail Food Store Access in Rural Appalachia: A Mixed Methods Study," *Public Health Nursing* 34, no. 3 (2017): 245–55, https://doi.org/10.1111/phn.12302; Finney Rutten et al., "Poverty, Food Insecurity"; McGee et al., "Food Shopping."

Chapter 2

1. Thomas J. Ward Jr., *Out in the Rural: A Mississippi Health Center and Its War on Poverty* (Oxford: Oxford University Press, 2016), 103.
2. Ward, 96.
3. Ward, 103.
4. "Mississippi: Severe Housing Problems 2016," County Health Rankings, accessed September 24, 2022, https://www.countyhealthrankings.org/app/mississippi/2016/measure/factors/136/map.
5. "Counties in Mississippi," *U.S. News and World Report*, accessed September 24, 2022, https://www.usnews.com/news/healthiest-communities/mississippi.
6. Lauren Taylor, "Housing and Health: An Overview of the Literature," *Health Affairs*, June 7, 2018, https://doi.org/10.1377/hpb20180313.396577; Craig Evan Pollack, Beth Ann Griffin, and Julia Lynch, "Housing Affordability and Health among Homeowners and Renters," *American Journal of Preventive Medicine* 39, no. 6 (2010): 515–21, https://doi.org/10.1016/j.amepre.2010.08.002.
7. Lauren Taylor, "Housing and Health."
8. "Counties in Mississippi."
9. Erica Hensley, "'System Doesn't Work for Anybody': Repeat Evictions Take Toll on Tenants, Courts and Landlords," *Mississippi Today*, September 28, 2018, https://mississippitoday.org/2018/09/28/system-doesnt-work-for-anybody-repeat-evictions-take-toll-on-tenants-justice-courts-and-landlords/.
10. James R. Dunn and Tania Kyle, *Effects of Housing Circumstances on Health, Quality of Life and Health Care Use for People with Severe Mental Illness: A Review* (Wellesley Institute, April 2007), https://www.wellesleyinstitute.com/wp-content/uploads/2014/05/Effects-of-Housing-Mental-Health.pdf; Rebekah Levine Coley et al., "Relations between Housing Characteristics and the Well-Being of Low-Income Children and Adolescents," *Developmental Psychology* 49, no. 9 (2013): 1775–89, https://doi.org/10.1037/a0031033; Julie Robison et al., "Mental Health in Senior Housing: Racial/Ethnic Patterns and Correlates of Major Depressive Disorder," *Aging and Mental Health* 13, no. 50 (2009): 659–73, https://doi.org/10.1080/13607860802607298.
11. Lauren Taylor, "Housing and Health"; Janet Ford, Roger Burrows, and Sarah Nettleton, *Home Ownership in a Risk Society: A Social Analysis of Mortgage Arrears and Possessions* (Bristol: Policy, 2001); Sarah Nettleton and Roger Burrows, "Mortgage Debt, Insecure Home Ownership and Health: An Exploratory Analysis," *Sociology of Health and Illness* 20, no. 5 (1998): 731–53, https://onlinelibrary.wiley.com/doi/pdf/10.1111/1467-9566.00127; William M. Rohe, Shannon Van Zandt, and George McCarthy, "The Social Benefits and Costs of Homeownership: A Critical Assessment of the Research" (Low-Income Homeownership Working Paper Series No. LIHO-01.12, Joint Center for Housing Studies of Harvard University, 2001), https://www.jchs.harvard.edu/sites/default/files/liho01-12.pdf; Susan J. Smith et al., "Housing as Health Capital: How Health Trajectories and Housing Paths Are Linked," *Journal of Social Issues* 59, no. 3 (2003): 501–25, https://doi.org/10.1111/1540-4560.00075; Mark P. Taylor, David J. Pevalin, and Jennifer Todd, "The Psy-

chological Costs of Unsustainable Housing Commitments," *Psychological Medicine* 37, no. 7 (2007): 1027–36, https://doi.org/10.1017/S0033291706009767; Scott Weich and Glyn Lewis, "Poverty, Unemployment, and Common Mental Disorders: Population-Based Cohort Study," *BMJ* 317, no. 7151 (1998): 115–19, https://doi.org/10.1136/bmj.317.7151.115.

12. Lauren Taylor, "Housing and Health"; Barbara Alexander et al., *The State of the Nation's Housing, 2014* (Cambridge, MA: Joint Center for Housing Studies of Harvard University, 2014), https://www.jchs.harvard.edu/sites/default/files/sonhr14-color-full_0.pdf; Jason M. Fletcher, Tatiana Andreyeva, and Susan H. Busch, "Assessing the Effect of Increasing Housing Costs on Food Insecurity," *Journal of Children and Poverty* 15, no. 2 (2009): 79–93, https://doi.org/10.1080/10796120903310541; Craig Evan Pollack, Beth Ann Griffin, and Julia Lynch, "Housing Affordability and Health among Homeowners and Renters," *American Journal of Preventive Medicine* 39, no. 6 (2010): 515–21, https://doi.org/10.1016/j.amepre.2010.08.002.

13. Dunn and Kyle, *Effects of Housing Circumstances*; Coley et al., "Relations between Housing Characteristics"; Robison et al., "Mental Health"; Lauren Taylor, "Housing and Health"; Ford, Burrows, and Nettleton, *Home Ownership*; Nettleton and Burrows, "Mortgage Debt"; Rohe, Van Zandt, and McCarthy, "Social Benefits and Costs"; Smith et al., "Housing as Health Capital"; Mark Taylor, Pevalin, and Todd, "Psychological Costs"; Weich and Lewis, "Poverty, Unemployment."

14. Kirsten Beyer et al., "Housing Discrimination and Racial Cancer Disparities among the 100 Largest US Metropolitan Areas," *Cancer* 125, no. 21 (2019): 3818–27, https://doi.org/10.1002/cncr.32358.

15. "Counties in Mississippi."

16. Jung Hyun Choi, Amalie Zinn, and Aniket Mehrotra, "Black Homeownership Increased Slightly during the Pandemic, but High Interest Rates Threaten to Further Widen Racial Homeownership Gaps," *Urban Institute* (February 21, 2024), https://www.urban.org/urban-wire/black-homeownership-increased-slightly-during-pandemic-high-interest-rates-threaten.

17. Paul Taylor et al., *Wealth Gaps Rise to Record Highs between Whites, Blacks and Hispanics* (Washington, DC: Pew Research Center, July 26, 2011), https://www.pewresearch.org/wp-content/uploads/sites/3/2011/07/SDT-Wealth-Report_7-26-11_FINAL.pdf.

18. Ellen B. Meacham, *Delta Epiphany: Robert F. Kennedy in Mississippi* (Jackson: University Press of Mississippi, 2018), 102.

19. Giacomo Bologna, "Black Mississippians Twice as Likely to Be Denied a Home Loan as Whites, Data Show," *Clarion-Ledger*, April 22, 2019, https://www.clarionledger.com/story/news/politics/2019/04/22/homes-sale-black-mississippians-denied-loans-more-often/3496801002/.

20. "The Race-Based Mortgage Penalty," *New York Times*, March 7, 2018, https://www.nytimes.com/2018/03/07/opinion/mortage-minority-income.html; Beyer et al., "Housing Discrimination."

21. Bologna, "Black Mississippians."

22. "Race-Based Mortgage Penalty."

23. Ben Lane, "CFPB Study Shows Alternative Credit Models Lead to More Loans, Cheaper Loans," HousingWire, August 8, 2019, https://www.housingwire.com/articles/49810-cfpb-study-shows-alternative-credit-models-lead-to-more-loans-cheaper-loans/.

24. Jacob William Faber, "Segregation and the Geography of Creditworthiness: Racial Inequality in a Recovered Mortgage Market," *Housing Policy Debate* 28, no. 2 (2018): 215–47, https://doi.org/10.1080/10511482.2017.1341944.

25. This includes the Depository Institutions Deregulation and Monetary Control Act (1980), the Alternative Mortgage Transaction Parity Act (1982), the Secondary Mortgage Market Enhancement Act (1984), the Financial Institutions Reform, Recovery and Enforcement Act (1989), and the Federal Housing Enterprises Safety and Soundness Act (1992).

26. Justin P. Steil et al., "The Social Structure of Mortgage Discrimination," *Housing Studies* 33, no. 5 (2018): 759–76, https://doi.org/10.1080/02673037.2017.1390076.

27. Faber, "Segregation and the Geography"; Jacob S. Rugh and Douglas S. Massey, "Racial Segregation and the American Foreclosure Crisis," *American Sociological Review* 75, no. 5 (2010): 629–51, https://doi.org/10.1177/0003122410380868.

28. Eric P. Baumer et al., "Illuminating a Dark Side of the American Dream: Assessing the Prevalence and Predictors of Mortgage Fraud across US Counties," *American Journal of Sociology* 123, no. 2 (2018): 549–603, https://doi.org/10.1086/692719.

29. Nick Noel et al., "The Economic Impact of Closing the Racial Wealth Gap," McKinsey & Company, August 13, 2019, https://www.mckinsey.com/industries/public-sector/our-insights/the-economic-impact-of-closing-the-racial-wealth-gap#.

30. Paul Taylor et al., *Wealth Gaps*.

31. Kelsey Ott, "Clarksdale Police Officer Shot in Head While Investigating Robbery," WREG Memphis, February 13, 2016, https://wreg.com/news/clarksdale-police-officer-shot-in-head-while-investigating-robbery/.

32. Mike Suriani, "Nun Beaten and Stabbed Hoping to Return Soon to Jonestown Mississippi," WREG Memphis, June 7, 2012, https://wreg.com/news/nun-beaten-and-stabbed-hoping-to-return-soon-to-jonestown-mississippi/.

33. "Clarksdale Attorney Shot, Killed at Law Firm," *Clarion-Ledger*, June 27, 2015, https://www.clarionledger.com/story/news/2015/06/26/attorney-shot-law-firm/29373543/.

34. Jeri Borst, "Murder Suicide Rocks Community," *Delta Democrat-Times*, May 2, 2019, https://www.ddtonline.com/front-page-slideshow-news-breaking-news/murder-suicide-rocks-community#sthash.SE4dwqJA.OsvEgHCY.dpbs; Adam Leith Gollner, "Inside One Police Chief's Hunt for Justice in a Pair of Unsolved Mississippi Murders," *Vanity Fair*, September 10, 2018, https://www.vanityfair.com/style/2018/09/inside-one-police-chiefs-hunt-for-justice-unsolved-mississippi-murders; Rod McCullom, "Murder in the Mississippi Delta," *Ebony*, March 4, 2013, https://www.ebony.com/news/murder-in-the-mississippi-delta-459/; William Browning, "Death in the Delta," *Hazlitt*, November 21, 2018, https://hazlitt.net/longreads/death-delta; "Mississippi—Locked and Lost!," True Crime and Mysteries Podcast, Podtail, February 9, 2017, https://podtail.com/podcast/true-crime-and-mysteries/episode-19-mississippi-locked-lost/.

35. "Mississippi: Homicides 2018," County Health Rankings, accessed September 24, 2022, https://www.countyhealthrankings.org/app/mississippi/2018/measure/factors/15/data?sort=desc-2.

36. Alex Bryant, "10 U.S. Counties with the Highest Murder Rate," Police1, June 5, 2017, https://www.policeone.com/ambush/articles/10-us-counties-with-the-highest-murder-rate-kerWgaEUmxJkn74J/.

37. For the purposes of these statistics, violent crime is defined as murder, manslaughter, rape, robbery, or aggravated assault. "Federal Bureau of Investigation Crime Data Explorer," Federal Bureau of Investigation, accessed September 24, 2022, https://crime-data-explorer.fr.cloud.gov/explorer/state/mississippi/crime; "FBI Releases 2018 Crime Statistics," press release, Federal Bureau of Investigation, September 30, 2019, https://www.fbi.gov/news/pressrel/press-releases/fbi-releases-2018-crime-statistics.

38. Bryant, "10 U.S. Counties."

39. "FBI Releases 2018 Crime Statistics."

40. Dahleen Glanton, "Chicago Gangs Find New Turf in Rural South," *Chicago Tribune*, June 1, 2004, https://www.chicagotribune.com/news/ct-xpm-2004-06-01-0406010200-story.html.

41. Mississippi Analysis and Information Center, *State Gang Threat Assessment 2017* (Mississippi Analysis and Information Center, December 22, 2017), https://www.supertalk.fm/wp-content/uploads/2018/02/STATE-GANG-THREAT-ASSESSMENT-2017.pdf.

42. Glanton, "Chicago Gangs."

43. "Mapping Police Violence," Campaign Zero, accessed September 24, 2022, https://mappingpoliceviolence.org/states.

44. Courtney Anderson and Nina Harrelson, "Man Killed in Officer-Involved Shooting in Clarksdale," WREG Memphis, November 11, 2018, https://wreg.com/news/man-killed-in-clarksdale-officer-involved-shooting/.

45. Tom Dees, "Mississippi Man Killed by Police While Walking with His Son, Mother Speaks Out," FOX 13 Memphis, November 12, 2018, https://www.fox13memphis.com/top-stories/family-mississippi-man-killed-by-police-while-walking-with-his-son-mother-speaks-out/871602986/.

46. "Press Release: Officer Involved in Fatal Shooting of Unarmed Man Indicted in Bolivar County," Mississippi NAACP, March 27, 2015, http://naacpms.org/officer-involved-in-fatal-shooting-of-unarmed-man-indicted-in-bolivar-county/.

47. Jeff Amy, "Judge Ends Evidence-Tampering Case against Ailing Ex-Deputy," AP News, March 22, 2019, https://apnews.com/560427dcc9f04ed49b965a6840e6b8b6.

48. "MBI Investigating the Third Officer-Involved Shooting in 3 Days in North Mississippi," WMC Action News 5, January 27, 2020, https://www.wmcactionnews5.com/2020/01/27/mbi-investigating-third-officer-involved-shooting-days-north-mississippi/; WTVA 9 News, "Coahoma County Sheriff's Office: One Person Injured in Officer-Involved Shooting," YouTube video, 0:24, March 9, 2020, https://www.youtube.com/watch?reload=9&v=UQCknPzCMpU; "Greenville: Police Release Name of Officer Involved in Deadly Tuesday Shooting," WITN, July 9, 2019, https://www.witn.com/content/news/BREAKING-OVERNIGHT-Shooting

-under-investigation-512458491.html; "Arkansas Man Shot, Killed by Deputy Near Mississippi Delta Casino; State Investigating," THV 11, March 6, 2019, https://www.thv11.com/article/news/crime/arkansas-man-shot-killed-by-deputy-near-mississippi-delta-casino-state-investigating/91-e1b58d38-1bdd-43de-a89b-45a32bec9dd7.

49. "Police Officer, Suspect Hospitalized after Shooting," WMC Action News 5, February 13, 2018, https://www.wmcactionnews5.com/story/37489112/police-officer-suspect-hospitalized-after-shooting/; "Bank Robbery Suspect Shot by Police after Chase into Tunica," WMC Action News 5, January 10, 2018, https://www.wmcactionnews5.com/story/37237430/tunica-highway-reopens-after-officer-involved-shooting/.

50. Kayleigh Skinner, Kelsey Davis Betz, and Aallyah Wright, "'Fed the F—Up': Why Young Activists Are Organizing Protests across Mississippi," *Mississippi Today*, June 5, 2020, https://mississippitoday.org/2020/06/05/fed-the-f-up-why-young-activists-are-organizing-protests-across-mississippi/.

51. Richard Bolen, "Is the Clarksdale Police Force Really Corrupt?," *Clarksdale News*, November 12, 2018, https://clarksdalenews.com/is-the-clarksdale-police-force-really-corrupt/.

52. Aallyah Wright, "Homicide Rate Climbs as Clarksdale Police Tackle Internal Issues, Staff Shortage," *Mississippi Today*, November 26, 2018, https://mississippitoday.org/2018/11/26/homicide-rate-climbs-as-clarksdale-police-tackle-internal-issues-staff-shortage/.

53. Aallyah Wright, "Clarksdale Mayor Pledges $10,000 For 'Drug Dealers, Gang Members' to Get out of Town," *Mississippi Today*, May 20, 2019, https://mississippitoday.org/2019/05/20/clarksdale-mayor-pledges-10000-for-drug-dealers-gang-members-to-get-out-of-town/.

54. Ewan Palmer, "Mississippi Mayor Will Pay Drug Dealers and Gang Members $10,000 to Leave His City," *Newsweek*, May 21, 2019, https://www.newsweek.com/mississippi-mayor-clarksdale-chuck-espy-10000-1431347.

55. James A. Levine, "Poverty and Obesity in the US," *Diabetes* 60, no. 11 (2011): 2667–68, https://diabetes.diabetesjournals.org/content/60/11/2667; Patricia A. Hageman, Carol H. Pullen, and Michael Yoerger, "Physical Function and Health-Related Quality of Life in Overweight and Obese Rural Women Who Meet Physical Activity Recommendations," *Journal of Aging and Physical Activity* 26, no. 3 (2018): 438–44, https://doi.org/10.1123/japa.2017-0117; Physical Activity Guidelines Advisory Committee, *2018 Physical Activity Guidelines Advisory Committee Scientific Report* (Washington, DC: US Department of Health and Human Services, February 2018), https://health.gov/our-work/physical-activity/current-guidelines/scientific-report.

56. US Department of Health and Human Services, *Physical Activity Guidelines for Americans*, 2nd ed. (Washington, DC: US Department of Health and Human Services, 2018), https://health.gov/sites/default/files/2019-09/Physical_Activity_Guidelines_2nd_edition.pdf.

57. National experts recommend that adults do at least 150 minutes of moderate physical activity or 75 minutes of vigorous activity throughout the week, including some form of muscle-strengthening activity two times per week. Elementary school–age youth should have an hour of physical activity every day, with vigorous activity

at least three times per week. Children three to five years of age should get at least three hours of active play every day. US Department of Health and Human Services, *Physical Activity Guidelines*; "CDC Healthy Schools: Physical Activity Facts," Centers for Disease Control and Prevention, last reviewed July 26, 2022, https://www.cdc.gov/healthyschools/physicalactivity/facts.htm.

58. Debra L. Blackwell and Tainya C. Clarke, "State Variation in Meeting the 2008 Federal Guidelines for Both Aerobic and Muscle-Strengthening Activities through Leisure-Time Physical Activity among Adults Aged 18–64: United States, 2010–2015," *National Health Statistics Reports* 2018, no. 112 (2018): 1–22, https://www.cdc.gov/nchs/data/nhsr/nhsr112.pdf.

59. Blackwell and Clarke.

60. "Mississippi: Physical Inactivity," County Health Rankings, accessed September 24, 2022, https://www.countyhealthrankings.org/app/mississippi/2018/measure/factors/70/map; Anush Yousefian et al., "Active Living for Rural Youth: Addressing Physical Inactivity in Rural Communities," *Journal of Public Health Management and Practice* 15, no. 3 (2009): 223–31, https://doi.org/10.1097/PHH.0b013e3181a11822.

61. Umstattd Meyer et al., "Rural Active Living: A Call to Action," *Journal of Public Health Management and Practice* 22, no. 5 (2016): E11–E20, https://doi.org/10.1097/PHH.0000000000000333; Yousefian et al., "Active Living"; Brittney N. Dixon et al., "A Social-Ecological Review of the Rural versus Urban Obesity Disparity," *Health Behavior and Policy Review* 6, no. 4 (2019): 378–94, https://doi.org/10.14485/HBPR.6.4.6; Brian K. Lo et al., "Examining the Associations between Walk Score, Perceived Built Environment, and Physical Activity Behaviors among Women Participating in a Community-Randomized Lifestyle Change Intervention Trial: Strong Hearts, Healthy Communities," *International Journal of Environmental Research and Public Health* 16, no. 5 (2019): 849, https://doi.org/10.3390/ijerph16050849; Candace I. J. Nykiforuk et al., "Universal Design for the Rural Walks of Life: Operationalizing Walkability in Bonnyville, Alberta, Canada," *Critical Public Health* 28, no. 2 (2018): 213–24, https://doi.org/10.1080/09581596.2017.1311009; Verity Cleland et al., "A Qualitative Study of Environmental Factors Important for Physical Activity in Rural Adults," *PLoS ONE* 10, no. 11 (2015): e0140659, https://doi.org/10.1371/journal.pone.0140659; Jessie X. Fan, Ming Wen, and Neng Wan, "Built Environment and Active Commuting: Rural-Urban Differences in the U.S.," *SSM—Population Health* 3 (2017): 435–41, https://doi.org/10.1016/j.ssmph.2017.05.007; Michael C. Robertson et al., "Urban-Rural Differences in Aerobic Physical Activity, Muscle Strengthening Exercise, and Screen-Time Sedentary Behavior," *Journal of Rural Health* 34, no. 4 (2018): 401–10, https://doi.org/10.1111/jrh.12295; Geoffrey Whitfield et al., "National-Level Environmental Perceptions and Walking among Urban and Rural Residents: Informing Surveillance of Walkability," *Preventive Medicine* 123 (2019): 101–8, https://doi.org/10.1016/j.ypmed.2019.03.019; Elaine M. Murtagh, Martin Dempster, and Marie H. Murphy, "Determinants of Uptake and Maintenance of Active Commuting to School," *Health and Place* 40 (2016): 9–14, https://doi.org/10.1016/j.healthplace.2016.04.009; Carolyn McAndrews, Kenta Okuyama, and Jill S. Litt, "The Reach of Bicycling in Rural, Small, and Low-Density Places," *Transportation Research Record* 2662 (2017): 134–42, https://doi.org/10.3141/2662-15; Calvin P.

Tribby and Doug S. Tharp, "Examining Urban and Rural Bicycling in the United States: Early Findings from the 2017 National Household Travel Survey," *Journal of Transport and Health* 13 (2019): 143–49, https://doi.org/10.1016/j.jth.2019.03.015; Matthew Chrisman et al., "Environmental Influences on Physical Activity in Rural Midwestern Adults: A Qualitative Approach," *Health Promotion Practice* 16, no. 1 (2015): 142–48, https://doi.org/10.1177/1524839914524958; Anush Yousefian Hansen et al., "Built Environments and Active Living in Rural and Remote Areas: A Review of the Literature," *Current Obesity Reports* 4, no. 4 (2015): 484–93, https://doi.org/10.1007/s13679-015-0180-9; Adrian E. Bauman et al., "Correlates of Physical Activity: Why Are Some People Physically Active and Others Not?," *Lancet* 380, no. 9838 (2012): 258–71, https://doi.org/10.1016/S0140-6736(12)60735-1; Paul Daniel Patterson et al., "Obesity and Physical Inactivity in Rural America," *Journal of Rural Health* 20, no. 2 (2006): 151–59, https://doi.org/10.1111/j.1748-0361.2004.tb00022.x.

62. Jennie L. Hill et al., "Do the Features, Amenities, and Quality of Physical Activity Resources Differ between City and County Areas of a Large Rural Region?," *Family and Community Health* 39, no. 4 (2016): 273–82, https://doi.org/10.1097/FCH.0000000000000119; Amanda S. Gilbert et al., "A Qualitative Study Identifying Barriers and Facilitators of Physical Activity in Rural Communities," *Journal of Environmental and Public Health* 2019 (2019): 7298692, https://doi.org/10.1155/2019/7298692.

63. Jessica L. Thomson, Melissa H. Goodman, and Alicia S. Landry, "Assessment of Neighborhood Street Characteristics Related to Physical Activity in the Lower Mississippi Delta," *Health Promotion Perspectives* 9, no. 1 (2019): 24–30, https://doi.org/10.15171/hpp.2019.03.

64. "U.S. Census Gazetteer 2017," US Census Bureau, accessed September 24, 2022, https://www2.census.gov/geo/docs/maps-data/data/gazetteer/2017_Gazetteer/2017_gaz_place_28.txt.

65. "Tunica, Mississippi Means of Transportation to Work by Selected Characteristics," US Census Bureau, accessed October 18, 2022, https://data.census.gov/cedsci/table?q=vehicles%20tunica%20mississippi&tid=ACSST5Y2020.S0802.

66. Yousefian et al., "Active Living."

67. Akihiko Michimi and Michael C. Wimberly, "Natural Environments, Obesity, and Physical Activity in Nonmetropolitan Areas of the United States," *Journal of Rural Health* 28, no. 4 (2012): 398–407, https://doi.org/10.1111/j.1748-0361.2012.00413.x.

68. "Physical Inactivity," America's Health Rankings, accessed September 24, 2022, https://www.americashealthrankings.org/explore/annual/measure/Sedentary/state/CO.

69. "Counties in Mississippi."

70. "The Best Time to Visit Clarksdale, MS, US for Weather, Safety, and Tourism," Champion Traveler, accessed September 24, 2022, https://championtraveler.com/dates/best-time-to-visit-clarksdale-ms-us/.

71. Kara James and Angela Williams, "Yazoo County Reports Second Heat-Related Death in 3 Weeks," WAPT 16, July 20, 2017, https://www.wapt.com/article/dangerous-heat-continues-to-scorch-mississippi/10334677#; Mark Giannotto, "Dennis Mitchell's Death Raises the Question: Why Wasn't an Athletic Trainer

There?," *USA Today*, August 29, 2018, https://usatodayhss.com/2018/dennis-mitchells-death-raises-the-question-why-wasnt-an-athletic-trainer-there; Stephanie K. Baer, "A 32-Year-Old Former NFL Player Died of Heatstroke as a Heat Wave Grips the US," Buzzfeed News, July 19, 2019, https://www.buzzfeednews.com/article/skbaer/nfl-player-dies-heat-stroke-heat-wave.

72. "Motor-Vehicle Deaths by State," National Safety Council, accessed September 24, 2022, https://injuryfacts.nsc.org/state-data/motor-vehicle-deaths-by-state/.

73. Larrison Campbell, "Why Mississippi Is the Deadliest Place to Drive a Car," *Mississippi Today*, July 3, 2018, https://mississippitoday.org/2018/07/03/why-mississippi-is-the-deadliest-place-to-drive-a-car/.

74. Stephanie S. Frost et al., "Effects of the Built Environment on Physical Activity of Adults Living in Rural Settings," *American Journal of Health Promotion* 24, no. 4 (2010): 267–83, https://doi.org/10.4278/ajhp.08040532; Devajyoti Dekaa, Charles T. Brown, and James Sinclair, "Exploration of the Effect of Violent Crime on Recreational and Transportation Walking by Path and Structural Equation Models," *Health and Place* 52 (2018): 34–45, https://doi.org/10.1016/j.healthplace.2018.05.004.

75. Yousefian et al., "Active Living"; Nicole E. Rader et al., "We Never See Children in Parks: A Qualitative Examination of the Role of Safety Concerns on Physical Activity among Children," *Journal of Physical Activity and Health* 12, no. 7 (2015): 1010–16, https://doi.org/10.1123/jpah.2014-0053.

76. HOPE Credit Union, *HOPE 2018 Impact Report* (HOPE Credit Union, n.d.), accessed September 25, 2022, https://hopecu.org/manage/media/Hope_2018-Impact-Report_V3_Final.pdf.

77. Willy Foote, "Lifting the Poor: What the Mississippi Delta Can Teach the Congo," *Forbes*, December 19, 2013, https://www.forbes.com/sites/willyfoote/2013/12/19/lifting-the-poor-what-the-mississippi-delta-can-teach-the-congo/#7ea452856e7e.

78. Foote.

79. "HOPE Receives Housing Visionary Award from the National Housing Conference," HOPE Credit Union, June 7, 2019, https://hopecu.org/2019/06/hope-receives-housing-visionary-award-from-the-national-housing-conference/.

80. Foote, "Lifting the Poor."

81. "Eastmoor," HOPE Credit Union, accessed September 25, 2022, https://hopecu.org/manage/media/Eastmoor-One-pager.pdf.

82. HOPE Credit Union, *HOPE 2017 Impact Report* (HOPE Credit Union, n.d.), accessed September 25, 2022, https://hopecu.org/manage/media/2017-HOPE-Impact-Report.pdf.

83. HOPE Credit Union.

84. "Magnolia Crossing, in Yazoo City, on a Renaissance Path," US Department of Housing and Urban Development, archived August 15, 2016, https://archives.hud.gov/local/ms/goodstories/2014-01-26.cfm.

85. Foote, "Lifting the Poor."

86. "Parks and Trails Health Impact Assessment Toolkit," Centers for Disease Control and Prevention, archived content, last reviewed November 27, 2013, https://www.cdc.gov/healthyplaces/parks_trails.

87. Philip J. Troped et al., "Associations between Self-Reported and Objective Physical Environmental Factors and Use of a Community Rail-Trail," *Preventive Medicine* 32, no. 2 (2001): 191–200, https://doi.org/10.1006/pmed.2000.0788.

88. "About the Museum," Martin and Sue King Railroad Heritage Museum, accessed September 25, 2022, https://clevelandtrainmuseum.com/about-the-museum/.

89. Active Living Research, *The Power of Trails for Promoting Physical Activity in Communities* (San Diego, CA: Active Living Research, January 2011), https://activelivingresearch.org/sites/activelivingresearch.sdsc.edu/files/ALR_Brief_PowerofTrails_0.pdf.

90. Kourtney Williams, "Greenville Walking Trail Looking to Improve Safety Precautions," Delta News, March 28, 2018, https://www.deltanews.tv/news/greenville-walking-trail-looking-to-improve-safety-precautions/article_9c95c7d2-32d5-11e8-b7f5-c7eb429185b0.html.

91. "Mississippi River Flood of 1927," *Britannica*, last updated September 3, 2022, https://www.britannica.com/event/Mississippi-River-flood-of-1927.

Chapter 3

1. Ellen B. Meacham, *Delta Epiphany: Robert F. Kennedy in Mississippi* (Jackson: University Press of Mississippi, 2018); Rachel Fradette and Donna Ladd, "Interrupting the Poverty Cycle: Looking Back to Move Forward in Mississippi," *Jackson Free Press*, December 20, 2017, https://www.jacksonfreepress.com/news/2017/dec/20/interrupting-poverty-cycle-looking-back-move-forwa/.

2. Henry Hampton, Steve Fayer, and Sarah Flynn, *Voices of Freedom: An Oral History of the Civil Rights Movement from the 1950s through the 1980s* (New York: Bantam Books, 1990), 453.

3. Drew Dellinger, "The Last March of Martin Luther King Jr.," *Atlantic*, April 4, 2018, https://www.theatlantic.com/politics/archive/2018/04/mlk-last-march/555953/.

4. Dellinger, "Last March."

5. "Poor People's Campaign, Event May 12, 1968 to June 24, 1968," Martin Luther King, Jr. Research and Education Institute, accessed September 29, 2022, https://kinginstitute.stanford.edu/encyclopedia/poor-peoples-campaign.

6. "Poor People's Campaign."

7. Erik Ortiz, "Fifty Years after the Poor People's Campaign, America's Once-Poorest Town Still Struggles," NBC News, June 22, 2018, https://www.nbcnews.com/news/nbcblk/fifty-years-after-poor-people-s-campaign-america-s-once-n885451.

8. "Poor People's Campaign."

9. Katina Rankin, "The Mule Train: Poor People's Campaign Continued," YouTube video, 30:00, February 4, 2020, https://www.youtube.com/watch?v=W2lL6G6YosI&t=3s.

10. Irv Randolph, "Remembering Robert Kennedy's Legacy," AP News, June 16, 2018, https://apnews.com/0777d47d1a8142ce8ef66d6520e6185a (no longer available).

11. Bruce P. Kennedy et al., "Income Distribution, Socioeconomic Status, and Self-Rated Health in the United States: A Multilevel Analysis," *BMJ* 317, no. 7163 (1998): 917–21, https://doi.org/10.1136/bmj.317.7163.917; John Lynch et al., "Is Income Inequality a Determinant of Population Health? Part 1. A Systematic Review," *Milbank Quarterly* 84, no. 1 (2004): 5–99, https://doi.org/10.1111/j.0887-378X.2004.00302.x; Richard G. Wilkinson and Kate E. Pickett, "Income Inequality and Population Health: A Review and Explanation of the Evidence," *Social Science and Medicine* 62, no. 7 (2006): 1768–84, https://doi.org/10.1016/j.socscimed.2005.08.036.

12. Kate E. Pickett and Richard G. Wilkinson, "Income Inequality and Health: A Causal Review," *Social Science and Medicine* 128 (2015): 316–26, https://doi.org/10.1016/j.socscimed.2014.12.031.

13. Raj Chetty et al., "The Association between Income and Life Expectancy in the United States, 2001–2014," *Journal of the American Medical Association* 315, no. 16 (2016): 1750–66, https://doi.org/10.1001/jama.2016.4226.

14. Atheendar S. Venktaremani et al., "Economic Opportunity, Health Behaviors, and Mortality in the United States," *American Journal of Public Health* 106, no. 3 (2016): 478–84, https://doi.org/10.2105/AJPH.2015.302941; Laura Dwyer-Lindgren et al., "Inequalities in Life Expectancy among US Counties, 1980 to 2014 Temporal Trends and Key Drivers," *JAMA Internal Medicine* 177, no. 7 (2017): 1003–11, https://doi.org/10.1001/jamainternmed.2017.0918; Jacob Bor, Gregory H. Cohen, and Sandro Galea, "Population Health in an Era of Rising Income Inequality: USA, 1980–2015," *Lancet* 389, no. 10077 (2017): 1475–90, https://doi.org/10.1016/S0140-6736(17)30571-8; Frank J. Elgar et al., "Early-Life Income Inequality and Adolescent Health and Well-Being," *Social Science and Medicine* 174 (2017): 197–208, https://doi.org/10.1016/j.socscimed.2016.10.014; Steven H. Woolf and Heidi Schoomaker, "Life Expectancy and Mortality Rates in the United States, 1959–2017," *Journal of the American Medical Association* 322, no. 10 (2019): 1996–2016, https://doi.org/10.1001/jama.2019.16932; Dovile Vilda et al., "Income Inequality and Racial Disparities in Pregnancy-Related Mortality in the US," *SSM—Population Health* 9 (2019): 100477, https://doi.org/10.1016/j.ssmph.2019.100477; Erik T. Nesson and Joshua J. Robinson, "On the Measurement of Health and Its Effect on the Measurement of Health Inequality," *Economics and Human Biology* 35 (2019): 207–21, https://doi.org/10.1016/j.ehb.2019.07.003.

15. Paula A. Braveman et al., "Socioeconomic Disparities in Health in the United States: What the Patterns Tell Us," *American Journal of Public Health* 100 (2010): S186–96, https://doi.org/10.2105/AJPH.2009.166082.

16. Arthur G. Cosby et al., "Growth and Persistence of Place-Based Mortality in the United States: The Rural Mortality Penalty," *American Journal of Public Health* 109, no. 1 (2019): 155–62, https://doi.org/10.2105/AJPH.2018.304787.

17. David E. Bloom and David Canning, "The Health and Wealth of Nations," *Science* 287, no. 5456 (2000): 1207–9, https://doi.org/10.1126/science.287.5456.1207; Alok Bhargava et al., "Modeling the Effects of Health on Economic Growth," *Journal of Health Economics* 20, no. 3 (2001): 423–40, https://doi.org/10.1016/S0167-6296(01)00073-X; Angus Deaton, "Health, Inequality, and Economic Development," *Journal of Economic Literature* 41, no. 1 (2003): 113–58, https://doi.org/10.1257

/0022051033215447l0; David E. Bloom, David Canning, and Jaypee Sevilla, "The Effect of Health on Economic Growth: A Production Function Approach," *World Development* 32, no. 1 (2004): 1–13, https://doi.org/10.1016/j.worlddev.2003.07.002; David M. Mirvis and Joy A. Clay, "The Critical Role of Health in the Economic Development of the Lower Mississippi Delta," *Business Perspectives* 20, no. 1 (2009): 16–23, https://www.proquest.com/openview/5b25d5623735265c966594c2dc65fbd3/1?pq-origsite=gscholar&cbl=37173; Inas R. Kelly, Nadia Doytch, and Dhaval Dave, "How Does Body Mass Index Affect Economic Growth? A Comparative Analysis of Countries by Levels of Economic Development," *Economics and Human Biology* 24 (2019): 58–73, https://doi.org/10.1016/j.ehb.2019.03.004.

18. "Overview of Mississippi," *U.S. News and World Report*, accessed September 29, 2022, https://www.usnews.com/news/best-states/mississippi; "Business Environment Rankings," *U.S. News and World Report*, accessed September 29, 2022, https://www.usnews.com/news/best-states/rankings/economy/business-environment; "Employment Rankings," *U.S. News and World Report*, accessed September 29, 2022, https://www.usnews.com/news/best-states/rankings/economy/employment; "Growth Rankings," *U.S. News and World Report*, accessed September 29, 2022, https://www.usnews.com/news/best-states/rankings/economy/growth; "Economic Opportunity Rankings," *U.S. News and World Report*, accessed September 29, 2022, https://www.usnews.com/news/best-states/rankings/opportunity/economic-opportunity.

19. Adam Ganucheau, "Mississippians Worried about State Economy," *Mississippi Today*, April 12, 2018, https://mississippitoday.org/2018/04/12/nbc-news-survey-monkey-poll-mississippians-worried-about-state-economy/?mc_cid=77f2724df8&mc_eid=df26913b5e.

20. Brett Kittredge, "Mississippi's Economy Grows Slowly," Mississippi Center for Public Policy, February 1, 2019, https://mspolicy.org/mississippis-economy-grows-slowly/.

21. Kittredge.

22. "Unemployment Rates by County," Mississippi Department of Employment Security, updated August 2022, https://mdes.ms.gov/media/8651/uratesmap.pdf.

23. "Mississippi Labor Market Data," Mississippi Department of Employment Security, updated August 2022, https://mdes.ms.gov/media/23357/labormarketdata.pdf.

24. Brian Thiede and Shannon Monnat, "The Great Recession and America's Geography of Unemployment," *Demographic Research* 35 (2016): 891–927, https://doi.org/10.4054/DemRes.2016.35.30.

25. Ganucheau, "Mississippians Worried."

26. Anna Wolfe, "Working-Class Mississippians Were Already Living Hand-to-Mouth. Then along Came Coronavirus," *Mississippi Today*, March 22, 2020, https://mississippitoday.org/2020/03/22/working-class-mississippians-were-already-living-hand-to-mouth-then-along-came-coronavirus/.

27. Anna Wolfe, "Mississippi Unemployment Claims Jump Nearly 500% Due to COVID-19," *Mississippi Today*, March 26, 2020, https://mississippitoday.org/2020/03/26/mississippi-unemployment-claims-jump-nearly-500-due-to-covid-19/; Anna Wolfe, "Mississippi's Record-Breaking Unemployment Claims Spike 1700% in Two

Weeks of COVID-19," *Mississippi Today*, April 2, 2020, https://mississippitoday.org/2020/04/02/mississippis-record-breaking-unemployment-claims-spike-1700-in-two-weeks-of-covid-19/.

28. "Local Area Unemployment Statistics," US Bureau of Labor Statistics, accessed June 26, 2020, https://data.bls.gov/timeseries/LASST280000000000003.

29. Sara DiNatale, "Mississippi's Economy Is Rebounding, but Growth Is Expected to Slow," *Mississippi Today*, May 3, 2021, https://mississippitoday.org/2021/05/03/mississippi-economy-growth-rebound-expected-slow/.

30. Melissa M. Farmer and Kenneth F. Ferraro, "Are Racial Disparities in Health Conditional on Socioeconomic Status?," *Social Science and Medicine* 60, no. 1 (2005): 191–204, https://doi.org/10.1016/j.socscimed.2004.04.026; Kim M. Shuey and Andrea E. Wilson, "Cumulative Disadvantage and Black-White Disparities in Life-Course Health Trajectories," *Research on Aging* 30, no. 2 (2008): 200–225, https://doi.org/10.1177/0164027507311151; D. R. Williams, N. Priest, and N. B. Anderson, "Understanding Associations among Race, Socioeconomic Status, and Health: Patterns and Prospects," *Health Psychology* 35, no. 4 (2016): 407–11, https://doi.org/10.1037/hea0000242; Anne Case and Angus Deaton, "Mortality and Morbidity in the 21st Century," *Brookings Papers on Economic Activity* 2017, no. 1 (2017): 397–476, https://doi.org/10.1353/eca.2017.0005; Nesson and Robinson, "On the Measurement."

31. Shervin Assari, "Health Disparities Due to Diminished Return among Black Americans: Public Policy Solutions," *Social Issues and Policy Review* 12, no. 1 (2018): 112–45, https://doi.org/10.1111/sipr.12042; Shervin Assari, "Unequal Gain of Equal Resources across Racial Groups," *International Journal of Health Policy and Management* 7, no. 1 (2018): 1–9, https://doi.org/10.15171/ijhpm.2017.90; Shervin Assari, "The Benefits of Higher Income in Protecting against Chronic Medical Conditions Are Smaller for African Americans Than Whites," *Healthcare* 6, no. 1 (2018): 2, https://doi.org/10.3390/healthcare6010002; Shervin Assari, "High Income Protects White but Not African Americans against Risk of Depression," *Healthcare* 6, no. 2 (2018): 37, https://doi.org/10.3390/healthcare6020037; Shervin Assari et al., "Blacks' Diminished Health Return of Family Structure and Socioeconomic Status; 15 Years of Follow-Up of a National Urban Sample of Youth," *Journal of Urban Health* 95, no. 1 (2018): 21–35, https://doi.org/10.1007/s11524-017-0217-3.

32. Assari, "Unequal Gain," 3.

33. A good place to start for anyone interested in learning more would be James C. Cobb, *The Most Southern Place on Earth: The Mississippi Delta and the Roots of Regional Identity* (New York: Oxford University Press, 1992); Sven Beckert, *Empire of Cotton: A Global History* (New York: Vintage Books, 2015); and Sharon D. Austin Wright, *The Transformation of Plantation Politics: Black Politics, Concentrated Poverty, and Social Capital in the Mississippi Delta* (Albany: State University of New York Press, 2006).

34. "Agribusiness," Mississippi Development Authority, accessed September 29, 2022, https://www.central-mississippi.com/agribusiness/.

35. Cobb, *Most Southern Place*.

36. "Decennial Census of Population and Housing," US Census Bureau, accessed October 16, 2022, https://www.census.gov/programs-surveys/decennial-census.html.

37. Anthony Giancatarino and Simran Noor, *Building the Case for Racial Equity in the Food System* (New York: Center for Social Inclusion, 2014), https://www.raceforward.org/system/files/pdf/reports/2014/Building-the-Case-for-Racial-Equity-in-the-Food-System.pdf.

38. Ronald L. F. Davis, "The U.S. Army and the Origins of Sharecropping in the Natchez District—a Case Study," *Journal of Negro History* 62, no. 1 (1977): 60–80, https://doi.org/10.2307/2717191.

39. Nicholas Lemann, *The Promised Land: The Great Black Migration and How It Changed America* (New York: Vintage Books, 1992), 5.

40. John C. Henshall, *Downtown Revitalisation and the Delta Blues in Clarksdale, Mississippi: Lessons for Small Cities and Towns* (London: Palgrave Macmillan, 2019).

41. Nan Elizabeth Woodruff, "Mississippi Delta Planters and Debates over Mechanization, Labor, and Civil Rights in the 1940s," *Journal of Southern History* 60, no. 2 (1994): 279, https://doi.org/10.2307/2210085.

42. Woodruff, 271.

43. Meacham, *Delta Epiphany*, 108.

44. Isabel Wilkerson, *The Warmth of Other Suns: The Epic Story of America's Great Migration* (New York: Vintage Books, 2011).

45. "The Great Migration, 1910 to 1970," US Census Bureau, September 13, 2012, https://www.census.gov/dataviz/visualizations/020/.

46. Isabel Wilkerson, "The Long-Lasting Legacy of the Great Migration," *Smithsonian Magazine*, September 2016, https://www.smithsonianmag.com/history/long-lasting-legacy-great-migration-180960118/.

47. "Visualizing the Great Migration," Museum of Modern Art, accessed September 29, 2022, https://www.moma.org/interactives/exhibitions/2015/onewayticket/visualizing-the-great-migration/.

48. Meacham, *Delta Epiphany*, 18.

49. Wilkerson, *Warmth of Other Suns*.

50. Becky Gillette, "Loss of Population—Delta Leaders Working to Offset Decline," *Delta Business Journal*, June 28, 2019, https://deltabusinessjournal.com/loss-of-population-delta-leaders-working-to-offset-decline/.

51. Greg Toppo and Paul Overberg, "After Nearly 100 Years, Great Migration Begins Reversal," *USA Today*, February 2, 2015, https://www.usatoday.com/story/news/nation/2015/02/02/census-great-migration-reversal/21818127/.

52. "Mississippi Agriculture Snapshot," Mississippi Department of Agriculture and Commerce, accessed September 29, 2022, https://www.mdac.ms.gov/agency-info/mississippi-agriculture-snapshot/.

53. "Mississippi Census Land Area," US Department of Agriculture National Agricultural Statistics Service, accessed September 29, 2022, https://www.nass.usda.gov/Statistics_by_State/Mississippi/Publications/Economic_and_Demographic_Releases/Census/msfarmnos.pdf.

54. "Mississippi Agriculture Snapshot."

55. "Mississippi Census Land Area."

56. Debbie Elliott, "Mississippi Delta's Economy, Way of Life Fading," NPR, June 6, 2005, https://www.npr.org/templates/story/story.php?storyId=4675562.

57. "Mississippi Census Land Area."

58. "Ag and Food Sectors and the Economy," US Department of Agriculture Economic Research Service, updated February 24, 2022, https://www.ers.usda.gov/data-products/ag-and-food-statistics-charting-the-essentials/ag-and-food-sectors-and-the-economy/; Labor Market Information Department, *2016 Reflections: An In-Depth Look at Mississippi's Economy* (Jackson: Mississippi Department of Employment Security, n.d.), accessed September 29, 2022, https://mdes.ms.gov/media/100392/reflections2016.pdf.

59. Anthony P. Carnevale, Jeff Strohl, and Neil Ridley, *Good Jobs That Pay without a BA: A State-by-State Analysis* (Washington, DC: Georgetown University Center on Education and the Workforce, 2017), https://goodjobsdata.org/wp-content/uploads/Good-Jobs-States.pdf.

60. Anna Wolfe, "Workforce Leaders Spin Key Report, Overstate Mississippi's Role as Leader in Growing Jobs for Workers without College Degrees," *Mississippi Today*, September 16, 2019, https://mississippitoday.org/2019/09/16/workforce-leaders-spin-key-report-overstate-mississippis-role-as-leader-in-growing-jobs-for-workers-without-college-degrees/.

61. Anna Wolfe, "Waging a Living: How Mississippi's Abundant Low-Wage Workers Earn Less Today Than 50 Years Ago," *Mississippi Today*, May 21, 2019, https://mississippitoday.org/2019/05/21/waging-a-living-how-mississippis-abundant-low-wage-workers-earn-less-today-than-50-years-ago/.

62. Wolfe.

63. Wolfe.

64. David Neumark, Junfu Zhang, and Stephen Ciccarell, "The Effects of Wal-Mart on Local Labor Markets," *Journal of Urban Economics* 63, no. 2 (2008): 405–30, https://doi.org/10.1016/j.jue.2007.07.004.

65. "Northwest Community College District Industry Employment Projections, Year 2018 Projected to Year 2028," Mississippi Department of Employment Security, accessed September 29, 2022, https://mdes.ms.gov/media/66068/1northwest_ms_ccd.pdf.

66. Aallyah Wright, "$52 Million Clarksdale Recreation Project Inspires Hope, Raises Questions," *Mississippi Today*, May 9, 2018, https://mississippitoday.org/2018/05/09/clarksdale-project/.

67. Matt Dowd, "Suitable Casino Sites in Mississippi: What Are They? Why? What about the Future?," *Gaming Law Review* 9, no. 4 (2005): 325–32, https://doi.org/10.1089/glr.2005.9.325; Tracy L. Farrigan, "The Tunica Miracle, Sin and Savior in America's Ethiopia: A Poverty and Social Impact Analysis of Casino Gaming in Tunica, MS" (PhD diss., Pennsylvania State University, March 30, 2005), https://etda.libraries.psu.edu/catalog/6603.

68. Farrigan, "Tunica Miracle."

69. Farrigan, 186.

70. Farrigan, 187.

71. Sharon Wright, *Transformation of Plantation Politics*, 73.

72. Farrigan, "Tunica Miracle."

73. Daniel Fromson, "Why Are So Many Casinos in the Mississippi Floodwaters?," *Atlantic*, May 19, 2011, https://www.theatlantic.com/national/archive/2011/05/why-are-so-many-casinos-in-the-mississippi-floodwaters/239149/.

74. Farrigan, "Tunica Miracle."

75. Farrigan.

76. Sharon Wright, *Transformation of Plantation Politics*.

77. Bill Miller, "Casino Industry Has $4 Billion Impact in Mississippi," *Sun Herald*, October 2, 2019, https://www.sunherald.com/opinion/other-voices/article235690877.html.

78. Sharon Wright, *Transformation of Plantation Politics*.

79. Farrigan, "Tunica Miracle."

80. Sharon Wright, *Transformation of Plantation Politics*, 75.

81. Farrigan, "Tunica Miracle."

82. Siew Hoon Lim, "Spotlight on Economics: Do Casinos Have a Positive Effect on Economic Growth?," North Dakota State University Extension and Ag Research News, September 12, 2017, https://www.ag.ndsu.edu/news/columns/spotlight-on-economics/spotlight-on-economics-do-casinos-have-a-positive-effect-on-economic-growth/.

83. Becky Gillette, "Delta Casinos—Using Innovations to Remain Competitive," *Delta Business Journal*, May 29, 2019, https://deltabusinessjournal.com/delta-casinos-using-innovations-to-remain-competitive/.

84. Gillette.

85. Melissa Chadburn, "Why Casino-Driven Development Is a Roll of the Dice," Bloomberg, March 6, 2017, https://www.citylab.com/life/2017/03/why-casino-driven-development-is-a-roll-of-the-dice/518046/.

86. "COVID-19 Drives Commercial Gaming Revenue Down 31% in 2020," American Gaming Association, February 17, 2021, https://www.americangaming.org/new/covid-19-drives-commercial-gaming-revenue-down-31-in-2020/.

87. Howard J. Shaffer, Alexander Blaszczynski, and Robert Ladouceur, "Gambling Control and Public Health: Let's Be Honest," *International Journal of Mental Health and Addiction* 18 (2020): 819–24, https://doi.org/10.1007/s11469-020-00240-0.

88. Tracie O. Afifi et al., "The Relationship of Gambling to Intimate Partner Violence and Child Maltreatment in a Nationally Representative Sample," *Journal of Psychiatric Research* 44, no. 5 (2010): 331–37, https://doi.org/10.1016/j.jpsychires.2009.07.010; Nicki Dowling et al., "Problem Gambling and Intimate Partner Violence: A Systematic Review and Meta-analysis," *Trauma, Violence, and Abuse* 17, no. 1 (2016): 43–61, https://doi.org/10.1177/1524838014561269; Donald W. Black et al., "Pathological Gambling: Relationship to Obesity, Self-Reported Chronic Medical Conditions, Poor Lifestyle Choices, and Impaired Quality of Life," *Comprehensive Psychiatry* 54, no. 2 (2013): 97–104, https://doi.org/10.1016/j.comppsych.2012.07.001.

89. Daniel S. McGrath and Sean P. Barrett, "The Comorbidity of Tobacco Smoking and Gambling: A Review of the Literature," *Drug and Alcohol Review* 28,

no. 6 (2009): 676–81, https://doi.org/10.1111/j.1465-3362.2009.00097.x; Michael A. Tynan, "Attitudes toward Smoke-Free Casino Policies among US Adults, 2017," *Public Health Reports* 134, no. 3 (2019): 234–40, https://doi.org/10.1177/0033354919 834581.

90. Adam Ganucheau and Alex Rozier, "Majority-Black, Democratic Counties Hurt Most by Bridge Closures, Analysis Shows," *Mississippi Today*, August 23, 2018, https://mississippitoday.org/2018/08/23/majority-black-democratic-counties-hurt-most-by-bridge-closures-analysis-shows/.

91. Alex Rozier, "$250 Million Awarded for Emergency Road and Bridge Projects," *Mississippi Today*, January 22, 2019, https://mississippitoday.org/2019/01/22/250-million-awarded-for-emergency-road-and-bridge-projects/.

92. V. Ariyabuddhiphongs, "Lottery Gambling: A Review," *Journal of Gambling Studies* 27 (2011): 15–33, https://doi.org/10.1007/s10899-010-9194-0; Kasey Hendricks, "Who Plays? Who Pays? Education Finance Policy That Supplants Tax Burdens along Lines of Race and Class," *Race Ethnicity and Education* 19, no. 2 (2016): 274–99, https://doi.org/10.1080/13613324.2013.868343.

93. Todd A. Wyett, "State Lotteries: Regressive Taxes in Disguise," *Tax Lawyer* 44, no. 3 (1991): 867–83, https://jstor.org/stable/20771362; Gordon Arbogast, Barry Thornton, and David Szweda, "The Impacts of Wealth Distribution as a Result of State Funded Lotteries," *Journal of Management and Engineering Integration* 9, no. 1 (2016): 82–92, https://search.proquest.com/openview/86ab0e2b9afedcafc77a21f3c1c6345c/1?pq-origsite=gscholar&cbl=716332; Bobby Harrison, "Lottery Exceeding Expectations in Mississippi, Thus Far," *Mississippi Today*, February 13, 2020, https://mississippitoday.org/2020/02/13/lottery-exceeding-expectations-in-mississippi-thus-far/.

94. Charles T. Clotfelter et al., "State Lotteries at the Turn of the Century: Report to the National Gambling Impact Study Commission," Duke University, April 23, 1999, https://govinfo.library.unt.edu/ngisc/reports/lotfinal.pdf.

95. Adam Ganucheau, "To Fix Bridges, Counties Forced to Look at Raising Taxes and Borrowing," *Mississippi Today*, August 13, 2018, https://mississippitoday.org/2018/08/13/to-fix-bridges-counties-forced-to-look-at-raising-taxes-and-borrowing/.

96. Harrison, "Lottery Exceeding Expectations."

97. Jess Bravin, "In Mississippi, a Gray Area between Black and White," *Wall Street Journal*, updated March 28, 2013, https://www.wsj.com/articles/SB10001424127887324096404578354203039290568; Max Galka, "The Lottery Is a Tax—an Inefficient, Regressive and Exploitative Tax," *Huffington Post*, September 3, 2015, https://www.huffpost.com/entry/the-lottery-is-a-tax-an-i_b_8081192.

98. "The Birthplace of the Frog: An Exhibit of Jim Henson's Delta Boyhood," Jim Henson's Delta Boyhood Exhibit, accessed September 30, 2022, https://www.birthplaceofthefrog.com/.

99. "Racial Reconciliation Begins by Telling the Truth," Emmett Till Interpretive Center, accessed September 30, 2022, https://www.emmett-till.org/.

100. Henshall, *Downtown Revitalisation*, 30.

101. "Experience the Blues Where They Were Born," Mississippi Blues Trail, accessed September 30, 2022, http://msbluestrail.org/delta.

102. Caroline Eubanks, "12 Best American 'Music Cities' That Aren't Nashville," Fodor's Travel, accessed September 30, 2022, https://www.fodors.com/news/photos/12-best-american-music-cities-that-arent-nashville.

103. "Experience the Blues."

104. "WROX," Mississippi Blues Trail, accessed September 30, 2022, http://msbluestrail.org/blues-trail-markers/wrox.

105. Henshall, *Downtown Revitalisation*, 93.

106. Henshall, 99.

107. Henshall, 97.

108. Randall Haley, "Bubba O'Keefe—Clarksdale-Coahoma County Tourism Director," *Delta Business Journal*, February 11, 2019, https://deltabusinessjournal.com/bubba-okeefe-clarksdale-coahoma-county-tourism-director/.

109. "Riverside Hotel: Where Blues Gave Birth to 'Rock and Roll,'" Riverside Hotel, accessed September 30, 2022, http://www.riversideclarksdale.com/history.

110. Clark House Inn, homepage, accessed September 30, 2022, https://clarkhouse.info/.

111. Delta Bohemian Tours, homepage, accessed September 30, 2022, https://deltabohemiantours.com/.

112. "Travelers Hotel: At the Crossroads of Creativity and Community," Travelers Hotel, accessed March 8, 2024, https://www.stayattravelers.com/clarksdale-about.

113. Quoted in Alexandra Watts, "How COVID-19 Is Impacting Mississippi Tourism," Mississippi Public Broadcasting, April 22, 2020, https://www.mpbonline.org/blogs/news/how-covid19-is-impacting-mississippi-tourism/.

114. "Sounds around Town in Clarksdale," Delta Bohemian, April 1, 2013, https://deltabohemian.com/sounds-around-town-in-clarksdale/.

115. Haley, "Bubba O'Keefe."

116. Henshall, *Downtown Revitalisation*, 186.

117. Henshall, 53, 112.

118. "Health Effects of Gentrification," Centers for Disease Control and Prevention, archived content, last reviewed October 15, 2009, https://www.cdc.gov/healthyplaces/healthtopics/gentrification.htm.

119. Henshall, *Downtown Revitalisation*, 55.

120. Henshall, 20.

121. Henshall, 78.

122. Henshall, 34.

123. Patrick Sauer, "Shack Up Inn: The Coolest Hotel in America?," *Huffington Post*, August 1, 2011, https://www.huffpost.com/entry/shack-up-inn-coolest-hotel-in-america-bill-talbot-guy-malvezzi_n_915184.

124. "Reservations," Shack Up Inn/Cotton Gin Inn, accessed September 30, 2022, https://convoyant.com/resnexus/reservations/lodging/1B23D08E-47CA-4F07-AA35-0F9F5DF14837?ID=546.

125. Rafael Alvarez, "Shack Chic Down South: Is There Something Wrong about Inviting 'Blues Tourists' to Stay in Shacks Where Slaves and Sharecroppers Once Lived?," *Pittsburgh Post-Gazette*, July 1, 2018, https://www.post-gazette.com/opinion/Op-Ed/2018/07/01/Shack-chic-down-South/stories/201806240009.

126. Robert Fairlie, Alicia Robb, and David T. Robinson, "Black and White: Access to Capital among Minority-Owned Startups" (SIEPR Discussion Paper No. 17-03, Stanford Institute for Economic Policy Research, December 15, 2016), https://siepr.stanford.edu/sites/default/files/publications/17-003.pdf.

127. John Jung, *Chopsticks in the Land of Cotton: Lives of Mississippi Delta Chinese Grocers* (n.p.: Yin and Yang, 2008).

128. "Our Mission," Higher Purpose Co., accessed September 30, 2022, https://higherpurposeco.org/.

129. Shad White, "A Critical Moment for Mississippi's Economy," *Mississippi Business Journal*, January 7, 2020, https://msbusiness.com/2020/01/shad-white-a-critical-moment-for-mississippis-economy/.

130. "WIN Job Centers," Mississippi Department of Employment Security, accessed September 30, 2022, https://mdes.ms.gov/win-job-centers/.

131. "Center for Community and Economic Development (CCED)," Delta State University, accessed September 30, 2022, http://www.deltastate.edu/cced/.

132. "Talent That Knows No Bounds," Mississippi Development Authority, accessed September 30, 2022, https://www.mississippi.org/advantages/workforce/.

133. "New Report: Government Employment and Training Programs: Assessing the Evidence on Their Performance," Economic Justice Program, October 28, 2019, https://maximinlaw.wordpress.com/2019/10/28/new-report-government-employment-and-training-programs-assessing-the-evidence-on-their-performance/.

134. Gregory Ferenstein, "Jobs Training Programs Are Rarely Flexible Enough to Succeed," Brookings, September 16, 2019, https://www.brookings.edu/blog/techtank/2019/09/16/jobs-training-programs-are-rarely-flexible-enough-to-succeed/.

135. Anna Wolfe, "Mississippi Works? Four Years Later, State Has Used Just One-Tenth of $50 Million Work Force Fund," *Mississippi Today*, August 28, 2020, https://mississippitoday.org/2020/08/28/mississippi-works-four-years-later-state-has-used-just-one-tenth-of-50-million-workforce-fund/.

136. James Owen, "Understanding the Underserved: Unbanked and Underbanked Households," Southern Bancorp, November 14, 2019, https://banksouthern.com/blog/understanding-the-underserved-unbanked-and-underbanked-households/.

137. Janell Ross, "A Town with No Bank: How Itta Bena, Mississippi, Became a Banking Desert," NBC News, June 15, 2019, https://www.nbcnews.com/news/nbcblk/how-itta-bena-mississippi-became-banking-desert-n1017686.

138. Drew Dahl and Michelle Franke, "'Banking Deserts' Become a Concern as Branches Dry Up," Federal Reserve Bank of St. Louis, July 25, 2017, https://www.stlouisfed.org/publications/regional-economist/second-quarter-2017/banking-deserts-become-a-concern-as-branches-dry-up.

139. "Frequently Asked Questions," CapWay, accessed September 30, 2022, https://www.capway.co/faq.

140. "Why CapWay Access to Opportunities," CapWay, accessed September 30, 2022, https://www.capway.co/whycapway.

141. Keith Twitchell, "CapWay Creating a New Way," Biz New Orleans, August 1, 2017, https://www.bizneworleans.com/capway-creating-a-new-way/.

142. "Payday Loan Facts and the CFPB's Impact," Pew Charitable Trusts, January 14, 2016, https://www.pewtrusts.org/en/research-and-analysis/fact-sheets/2016/01/payday-loan-facts-and-the-cfpbs-impact.

143. "Consumer Protection," Mississippi Center for Justice, accessed September 30, 2022, https://www.mscenterforjustice.org/our-work/consumer-protection/predatory-lending.

144. Heather Morton, "Payday Lending State Statutes," National Conference of State Legislatures, updated November 12, 2020, https://www.ncsl.org/research/financial-services-and-commerce/payday-lending-state-statutes.aspx.

145. "Pay Advance Fee Schedule," Check into Cash of Mississippi, accessed September 30, 2022, https://checkintocash.com/wp-content/uploads/MS-schedule-rtl-PDL-20231020.pdf.

146. Morton, "Payday Lending State Statutes."

147. Paul Kiel and Hannah Fresques, "Where in the U.S. Are You Most Likely to Be Audited by the IRS?," ProPublica, April 1, 2019, https://projects.propublica.org/graphics/eitc-audit.

148. Kiel and Fresques.

149. Kiel and Fresques.

150. Anna Wolfe, "Tax Preparer from Nation's Poorest County Sentenced to Five Years for $3.5 Million in Tax Fraud," *Mississippi Today*, May 2, 2019, https://mississippitoday.org/2019/05/02/tax-preparer-from-nations-poorest-county-sentenced-to-five-years-for-3-5-million-in-tax-fraud/.

151. Kiel and Fresques, "Most Likely."

152. Anna Wolfe, "'They're the Easiest to Step On': The Real Reason Why Families in the Delta, One of the Nation's Poorest Regions, Are Also the Most Audited by the IRS," *Mississippi Today*, April 17, 2019, https://mississippitoday.org/2019/04/17/theyre-easiest-to-step-on-the-real-reason-why-families-in-the-delta-one-of-the-nations-poorest-regions-are-also-the-most-audited-by-the-irs.

153. Henshall, *Downtown Revitalisation*, 107.

154. The idea was to partner with Dinesh Chawla, an Indian American immigrant who owned a handful of hotels across the Delta, such as the Hampton Inn in Cleveland, who was already planning on building a new luxury hotel just west of DSU's campus. The Trump family ultimately pulled out of the project in 2019 because their involvement brought a lot of extra attention, which was complicated that much further when Chawla was arrested for stealing luggage at the Memphis airport over a long period of time. Bobby Harrison, "Former Trump Hotel Partner Still Eligible for $6 Million State Tax Break Despite Felony Theft Charge," *Mississippi Today*, September 19, 2019, https://mississippitoday.org/2019/09/19/former-trump-hotel-partner-still-eligible-for-6-million-state-tax-break-despite-felony-theft-charge/; Steve Eder and Ben Protess, "Their Father Was a Refugee in India. Now They've Teamed Up with the Trumps," *New York Times*, July 22, 2018, https://www.nytimes.com/2018/07/22/business/trump-hotel-partner-dinesh-chawla.html.

155. "Our Mission," Keep Cleveland Boring, accessed September 30, 2022, https://www.keepclevelandboring.com/keep-cleveland-boring.html.

156. Jacob Threadgill, "Cleveland Music Scene Gets Boost from DMI, Grammy Museum," *Hattiesburg American*, May 3, 2015, https://www.hattiesburgamerican.com/story/news/local/2015/05/03/cleveland-music-gets-boost/26847353/.

157. Brittain Thompson, "Otherfest Is Now a Two Night Stand," *Local Voice*, October 5, 2017, http://www.thelocalvoice.net/oxford/otherfest-is-now-a-two-night-stand/.

158. Threadgill, "Cleveland Music Scene."

159. Octoberfest Mississippi, homepage, accessed October 1, 2022, https://www.octoberfestms.com/.

160. Jacob Threadgill, "Cleveland to Be Indie Epicenter," *Clarion-Ledger*, March 25, 2015, https://www.clarionledger.com/story/life/2015/03/25/cleveland-indie-music-epicenter/70425910/.

161. Threadgill.

162. "2016 Awards," Mississippi Main Street Association, accessed October 1, 2022, http://www.msmainstreet.com/events_news/awards2016/.

163. Brett Shulte, "Down in the Delta, Outsiders Who Arrived to Teach Now Find a Home," *New York Times*, July 21, 2013, https://www.nytimes.com/2013/07/22/us/down-in-the-delta-outsiders-who-arrived-to-teach-now-find-a-home.html; Greg Gandy, "In Mississippi, Art = Community," *Vice*, March 26, 2017, https://www.vice.com/en_us/article/j55vwd/in-mississippi-art-community.

164. Susan Spano, "The 20 Best Small Towns to Visit in 2013," *Smithsonian Magazine*, March 31, 2013, https://www.smithsonianmag.com/travel/the-20-best-small-towns-to-visit-in-2013-1353277/.

165. "2016 Awards."

166. Visit Cleveland Mississippi, homepage, accessed October 1, 2022, https://www.visitclevelandms.com/.

167. "The Chef," Delta Meat Market, accessed October 1, 2022, https://www.deltameatmarket.com/chef.

168. Threadgill, "Cleveland Music Scene."

169. Kyle Peterson, "Rooted in the Delta," Walton Family Foundation, January 24, 2018, https://www.waltonfamilyfoundation.org/stories/foundation/rooted-in-the-delta.

170. "Griot Grit," video, 26:47, PBS, April 7, 2019, https://www.pbs.org/video/griot-grit-ipiwlx/.

171. Meraki Roasting Company, homepage, accessed October 1, 2022, https://merakiroasting.com/.

172. Sheldon Alberts, "Coffee with a Cause: A Mississippi Roastery Serves Youth in Need," Walton Family Foundation, October 17, 2019, https://www.waltonfamilyfoundation.org/stories/home-region/coffee-with-a-cause-a-mississippi-roastery-serves-youth-in-need; "Griot Grit."

173. Henshall, *Downtown Revitalisation*, 134.

174. Alberts, "Coffee with a Cause."

175. Aallyah Wright, "Clarksdale Documentary Ditches 'Poverty Porn' Narrative about the Delta, Spotlights Work and People on the Move," February 11, 2019, https://

mississippitoday.org/2019/02/11/documentary-ditches-poverty-porn-narrative-about-the-delta-spotlights-work-and-people-on-the-move/.

176. "About," Delta Foundation Incorporated, accessed October 1, 2022, https://www.deltafoundationms.org/about/.

177. Delta Foundation Incorporated, homepage, accessed October 1, 2022, https://www.deltafoundationms.org/.

178. "M'Comb Bombings Laid to 3 Whites; Mississippi Jails Suspects—One Has Klan Card," *New York Times,* October 2, 1964, https://www.nytimes.com/1964/10/02/archives/mcomb-bombings-laid-to-3-whites-mississippi-jails-suspectsone-has.html.

179. "About," Delta Foundation Incorporated.

Chapter 4

1. S. Jay Olshansky et al., "Differences in Life Expectancy Due to Race and Educational Differences Are Widening, and Many May Not Catch Up," *Health Affairs* 31, no. 8 (2012): 1803–13, https://doi.org/10.1377/hlthaff.2011.0746; Viju Raghupathi and Wullianallur Raghupathi, "The Influence of Education on Health: An Empirical Assessment of OECD Countries for the Period 1995–2015," *Archives of Public Health* 78, no. 1 (2020): 20, https://doi.org/10.1186/s13690-020-00402-5; Anna Zajacova and Elizabeth M. Lawrence, "The Relationship between Education and Health: Reducing Disparities through a Contextual Approach," *Annual Review of Public Health* 39 (2018): 273–89, https://doi.org/10.1146/annurev-publhealth-031816-044628; Jona Schellekens and Anat Ziv, "The Role of Education in Explaining Trends in Self-Rated Health in the United States, 1972–2018," *Demographic Research* 42 (2020): 383–98, https://doi.org/10.4054/DemRes.2020.42.12; Patrick M. Krueger et al., "Mortality Attributable to Low Levels of Education in the United States," *PLoS ONE* 10, no. 7 (2015): e0131809, https://doi.org/10.1371/journal.pone.0131809; Francisca Rodriguez et al., "Racial and Ethnic Disparities in Dementia Risk among Individuals with Low Education," *American Journal of Geriatric Psychiatry* 26, no. 9 (2018): 966–76, https://doi.org/10.1016/j.jagp.2018.05.011; Isaac Sasson and Mark D. Hayward, "Association between Educational Attainment and Causes of Death among White and Black US Adults, 2010–2017," *Journal of the American Medical Association* 322, no. 8 (2019): 756–63, https://doi.org/10.1001/jama.2019.11330; Catherine E. Ross and Chia-ling Wu, "The Links between Education and Health," *American Sociological Review* 60, no. 5 (1995): 719–45, https://doi.org/10.2307/2096319.

2. Jennifer Karas Montez and Esther M. Friedman, "Educational Attainment and Adult Health: Under What Conditions Is the Association Causal?," *Social Science and Medicine* 127 (2015): 1–7, https://doi.org/10.1016/j.socscimed.2014.12.029.

3. "Robert F. Kennedy Speech at the University of Mississippi (18 March 1966)," audio recording, eGrove, University of Mississippi, accessed October 1, 2022, https://egrove.olemiss.edu/rfkspeech/1/.

4. Hiram Eastland Jr., "A Mississippi Perspective on Robert F. Kennedy," *Clarion-Ledger,* June 15, 2018, https://www.clarionledger.com/story/opinion/columnists/2018/06/15/mississippi-perspective-robert-f-kennedy/705244002/.

5. Ellen B. Meacham, *Delta Epiphany: Robert F. Kennedy in Mississippi* (Jackson: University Press of Mississippi, 2018), 51.

6. "Kennedy Speech."

7. Carolyn Kleiner Butler, "Down in Mississippi: The Shooting of Protester James Meredith 38 Years Ago, Searingly Documented by a Rookie Photographer, Galvanized the Civil Rights Movement," *Smithsonian Magazine*, February 2005, https://www.smithsonianmag.com/history/down-in-mississippi-85827990/.

8. Meacham, *Delta Epiphany*, 34.

9. Meacham, 113.

10. Meacham, 112.

11. "Freedom Schools," Digital SNCC Gateway, accessed October 1, 2022, https://snccdigital.org/inside-sncc/culture-education/freedom-schools/; Jon S. Hale, *The Freedom Schools: Student Activists in the Mississippi Civil Rights Movement* (New York: Columbia University Press, 2016), 196.

12. Meacham, *Delta Epiphany*, 121.

13. Hale, *Freedom Schools*, 196.

14. "Kennedy Speech."

15. Dana Goldman and James P. Smith, "The Increasing Value of Education to Health," *Social Science and Medicine* 72, no. 10 (2011): 1728–37, https://doi.org/10.1016/j.socscimed.2011.02.047; Zajacova and Lawrence, "Relationship between Education"; Krueger et al., "Mortality Attributable"; Ann Goding Sauer et al., "Educational Attainment and Quitting Smoking: A Structural Equation Model Approach," *Preventive Medicine* 116 (2018): 32–39, https://doi.org/10.1016/j.ypmed.2018.08.031; Scott M. Lynch, "Cohort and Life-Course Patterns in the Relationship between Education and Health: A Hierarchical Approach," *Demography* 40, no. 2 (2003): 309–31, https://doi.org/10.2307/3180803; Thijs Bol, "Has Education Become More Positional? Educational Expansion and Labour Market Outcomes, 1985–2007," *Acta Sociologica* 58, no. 2 (2015): 105–20, https://doi.org/10.1177/0001699315570918; Ryan K. Masters, Robert A. Hummer, and Daniel A. Powers, "Educational Differences in U.S. Adult Mortality: A Cohort Perspective," *American Sociological Review* 77, no. 4 (2012): 548–72, https://doi.org/10.1177/0003122412451019.

16. David P. Baker et al., "The Education Effect on Population Health: A Reassessment," *Population and Development Review* 37, no. 2 (2011): 307–32, https://doi.org/10.1111/j.1728-4457.2011.00412.x; Michael Hout, "Social and Economic Returns to College Education in the United States," *Annual Review of Sociology* 38 (2012): 379–400, https://doi.org/10.1146/annurev.soc.012809.102503; Ross and Wu, "Links between Education."

17. Hout, "Social and Economic Returns"; Jennifer Karas Montez and Mark D. Hayward, "Cumulative Childhood Adversity, Educational Attainment, and Active Life Expectancy among U.S. Adults," *Demography* 51, no. 2 (2014): 413–35, https://doi.org/10.1007/s13524-013-0261-x. These experiments also validate the argument that standardized tests such as the SAT contribute to racial inequities rather than blindly measure achievement and predict performance. Richard V. Reeves and Dimitrios Halikias, "Race Gaps in SAT Scores Highlight Inequality and Hinder Upward

Mobility," Brookings, February 1, 2017, https://www.brookings.edu/research/race-gaps-in-sat-scores-highlight-inequality-and-hinder-upward-mobility/.

18. Ross and Wu, "Links between Education"; Crystal L. Park, Dalnim Cho, and Philip J. Moore, "How Does Education Lead to Healthier Behaviours? Testing the Mediational Roles of Perceived Control, Health Literacy and Social Support," *Psychology and Health* 33, no. 11 (2018): 1416–29, https://doi.org/10.1080/08870446.2018.1510932.

19. Raghupathi and Raghupathi, "Influence of Education"; Ross and Wu, "Links between Education"; Shiho Kino, Eduardo Bernabé, and Wael Sabbah, "The Role of Healthcare and Education Systems in Co-occurrence of Health Risk Behaviours in 27 European Countries," *European Journal of Public Health* 28, no. 1 (2018): 186–92, https://doi.org/10.1093/eurpub/ckx071; "Why Education Matters to Health: Exploring the Causes," Virginia Commonwealth University, February 13, 2015, https://societyhealth.vcu.edu/work/the-projects/why-education-matters-to-health-exploring-the-causes.html.

20. Krueger et al., "Mortality Attributable"; Christopher R. Tamborini, Chang Hwan Kim, and Arthur Sakamoto, "Education and Lifetime Earnings in the United States," *Demography* 52, no. 4 (2015): 1383–407, https://doi.org/10.1007/s13524-015-0407-0.

21. Hout, "Social and Economic Returns."

22. Montez and Friedman, "Educational Attainment and Adult Health."'

23. Ashlesha Datar, Roland Sturm, and Jennifer L. Magnabosco, "Childhood Overweight and Academic Performance: National Study of Kindergartners and First-Graders," *Obesity Research* 12, no. 1 (2004): 58–68, https://doi.org/10.1038/oby.2004.9; Katherine Alaimo, Christine M. Olson, and Edward A. Frongillo Jr., "Food Insufficiency and American School-Aged Children's Cognitive, Academic, and Psychosocial Development," *Pediatrics* 108, no. 1 (2001): 44–53, https://pediatrics.aappublications.org/content/108/1/44?download=true; Irene van Woerden, Daniel Hruschka, and Meg Bruening, "Food Insecurity Negatively Impacts Academic Performance," *Journal of Public Affairs* 19, no. 3 (2019): e1864, https://doi.org/10.1002/pa.1864; Gail C. Rampersaud et al., "Breakfast Habits, Nutritional Status, Body Weight, and Academic Performance in Children and Adolescents," *Journal of the American Dietetic Association* 105, no. 5 (2005): 743–60, https://doi.org/10.1016/j.jada.2005.02.007; Maryah Stella Fram et al., "Children Are Aware of Food Insecurity and Take Responsibility for Managing Food Resources," *Journal of Nutrition* 141, no. 6 (2011): 1114–19, https://doi.org/10.3945/jn.110.135988; Meg Bruening et al., "The Struggle Is Real: A Systematic Review of Food Insecurity on Postsecondary Education Campuses," *Journal of the Academy of Nutrition and Dietetics* 117, no. 11 (2017): 1767–91, https://doi.org/10.1016/j.jand.2017.05.022; Daniel Eisenberg, Ezra Golberstein, and Justin B. Hunt, "Mental Health and Academic Success in College," *B.E. Journal of Economic Analysis and Policy* 9, no. 1 (2009), https://doi.org/10.2202/1935-1682.2191.

24. Shervin Assari, "Parental Education Better Helps White Than Black Families Escape Poverty: National Survey of Children's Health," *Economies* 6, no. 2 (2018): 30, https://doi.org/10.3390/economies6020030; Thomas E. Fuller-Rowell et al., "Racial Disparities in the Health Benefits of Educational Attainment: A Study of Inflammatory Trajectories among African American White Adults," *Psychosomatic*

Medicine 77, no. 1 (2015): 33–40, https://doi.org/10.1097/PSY.0000000000000128; John P. Bumpus, Zimife Umeh, and Angel L. Harris, "Social Class and Educational Attainment: Do Blacks Benefit Less from Increases in Parents' Social Class Status?," *Sociology of Race and Ethnicity* 6, no. 2 (2020): 223–41, https://doi.org/10.1177/2332649219854465; Kim M. Shuey and Andrea E. Wilson, "Cumulative Disadvantage and Black-White Disparities in Life-Course Health Trajectories," *Research on Aging* 30, no. 2 (2008): 200–225, https://doi.org/10.1177/0164027507311151.

25. "Mississippi's High School Graduation Rate Highest Ever at 88.4%; Dropout Rate Falls to 8.5%," Mississippi Department of Education, February 17, 2022, https://www.mdek12.org/news/2022/2/17/Mississippis-high-school-graduation-rate-highest-ever-at-88.4-Dropout-rate-falls-to-8.5_20220217.

26. Paula Vanderford, "4-Year Graduation Rates," Mississippi Department of Education, January 2019, https://www.mdek12.org/sites/default/files/Offices/MDE/OEA/OPR/2019/grad-dropout-rates-2019-report.pdf.

27. Vanderford.

28. Vanderford.

29. "State Average Scores," Nation's Report Card, accessed October 1, 2022, https://www.nationsreportcard.gov/reading/states/scores/?grade=4.

30. "Early Warning! Why Reading by the End of Third Grade Matters," Annie E. Casey Foundation, January 1, 2010, https://www.aecf.org/resources/early-warning-why-reading-by-the-end-of-third-grade-matters/.

31. "Counties in Mississippi," *U.S. News and World Report*, accessed October 1, 2022, https://www.usnews.com/news/healthiest-communities/mississippi.

32. Arielle Dreher, "Mississippi's Black Children Face More Barriers Than White Kids," *Jackson Free Press*, October 27, 2017, https://m.jacksonfreepress.com/news/2017/oct/27/report-mississippis-black-children-face-more-barri/.

33. "Counties in Mississippi."

34. "2018 Accountability," Mississippi Department of Education, accessed October 1, 2022, https://www.mdek12.org/OPR/Reporting/Accountability/2018.

35. Sierra Mannie, "The Only A-Rated, Majority-Black District in Mississippi," *Hechinger Report*, June 12, 2017, https://hechingerreport.org/rated-majority-black-district-mississippi/.

36. Ibram X. Kendi, *How to Be an Antiracist* (New York: One World, 2019), 101.

37. "Multi-year Data Download," Mississippi Department of Education, accessed October 25, 2022, https://newreports.mdek12.org/DataDownload.

38. "A History of Private Schools and Race in the American South," Southern Education Foundation, accessed October 1, 2022, https://www.southerneducation.org/publications/historyofprivateschools/.

39. "History of Private Schools."

40. "History of Private Schools."

41. Caleb Smith, "White Flight," *Mississippi Encyclopedia*, accessed October 1, 2022, https://mississippiencyclopedia.org/entries/white-flight/.

42. Thomas Maffai, "A 40-Year Friendship Forged by the Challenges of Busing," *Atlantic*, November 17, 2016, https://www.theatlantic.com/education/archive/2016/11/a-40-year-friendship-forged-by-the-challenges-of-busing/502733/.

43. Brett Kittredge, *Exploring Mississippi's Private Education Sector: The Mississippi Private School Survey* (Ridgeland, MS: Empower Mississippi, August 2017), https://empowerms.org/wp-content/uploads/2017/08/Mississippi-Private-School-Survey.pdf.

44. Brett Kittredge, "Public School Enrollment Declines in Mississippi," Mississippi Center for Public Policy, December 19, 2018, https://mspolicy.org/public-school-enrollment-declines-in-mississippi/.

45. Jess Bravin, "In Mississippi, a Gray Area between Black and White," *Wall Street Journal*, updated March 28, 2013, https://www.wsj.com/articles/SB10001424127887324096404578354203039290568.

46. "Tuition," Lee Academy, accessed October 1, 2022, http://www.leeacademycolts.org/tuition.

47. Suzanne E. Eckes, "The Perceived Barriers to Integration in the Mississippi Delta," *Journal of Negro Education* 74, no. 2 (2005): 159–73, https://www.jstor.org/stable/40034541.

48. Eckes.

49. "Public Charter School Enrollment," National Center for Education Statistics, updated May 2022, https://nces.ed.gov/programs/coe/indicator/cgb/public-charter-enrollment?tid=4.

50. Andre M. Perry, "How Charter Schools Are Prolonging Segregation," *Brookings*, December 11, 2017, https://www.brookings.edu/blog/the-avenue/2017/12/11/how-charter-schools-are-prolonging-segregation/.

51. "Research," National Conference of State Legislatures, accessed October 6, 2022, https://www.ncsl.org/research/education/charter-schools-research-and-report.aspx.

52. Center for Research on Education Outcomes, *Multiple Choice: Charter School Performance in 16 States* (Stanford, CA: Center for Research on Education Outcomes, 2009), https://web.archive.org/web/20120526152943/http://credo.stanford.edu/reports/MULTIPLE_CHOICE_CREDO.pdf.

53. Philip Gleason et al., *The Evaluation of Charter School Impacts: Final Report* (Washington, DC: National Center for Education Evaluation and Regional Assistance, June 2010), https://ies.ed.gov/ncee/pubs/20104029/pdf/20104029.pdf.

54. Paul T. Hill, "Charter Schools: Good or Bad for Students in District Schools?," Brookings, June 7, 2019, https://www.brookings.edu/blog/brown-center-chalkboard/2019/06/07/charter-schools-good-or-bad-for-students-in-district-schools/.

55. Tomás Monarrez, Brian Kisida, and Matthew Chingos, "Charter School Effects on School Segregation," Urban Institute, July 24, 2019, https://www.urban.org/research/publication/charter-school-effects-school-segregation.

56. Aallyah Wright, "Cleveland School Desegregation a Go after Judge's Order," *Mississippi Today*, March 15, 2017, https://mississippitoday.org/2017/03/15/judge-finalizes-cleveland-schools-desegregation-order/.

57. Bravin, "Gray Area."

58. Sharon Lerner, "A School District That Was Never Desegregated," *Atlantic*, February 5, 2015, https://www.theatlantic.com/education/archive/2015/02/a-school-district-that-was-never-desegregated/385184/.

59. Bravin, "Gray Area."

60. Minyvonne Burke, "Black Mississippi Student Says in Lawsuit She Was Denied Graduation Honor Because of Race," NBC News, May 2, 2019, https://www.nbcnews.com/news/nbcblk/black-mississippi-student-says-lawsuit-she-was-denied-graduation-honor-n1001271; Eliot C. McLaughlin, "Black Valedictorian Forced to Share Honor with White Student, Lawsuit Says," CNN, July 5, 2017, https://www.cnn.com/2017/07/03/us/cleveland-mississippi-student-valedictorian-lawsuit/index.html. Similar stories from elsewhere in Mississippi have played out in the national media, such as this case in West Point at the end of the 2021 school year: Stephanie Saul, "Two Black Students Won School Honors. Then Came the Calls for a Recount," *New York Times*, June 11, 2021, https://www.nytimes.com/2021/06/11/us/west-point-high-school-valedictorian.html.

61. Brody Miller, "Cleveland Central Is Trying to Tear Away the Roots of Desegregation in Undefeated Season," *Clarion-Ledger*, October 19, 2017, https://www.clarionledger.com/story/sports/high-school/2017/10/19/cleveland-central-trying-tear-away-roots-desegregation-undefeated-season/775134001/.

62. Miller.

63. Kelsey Davis Betz, "Cleveland School District Releases Breakdown of Enrollment Numbers," *Mississippi Today*, September 12, 2017, https://mississippitoday.org/2017/09/12/cleveland-school-district-releases-breakdown-enrollment-numbers/.

64. Kelsey Davis Betz, "Cleveland School District Considers Layoffs as Enrollment Declines," *Mississippi Today*, February 12, 2018, https://mississippitoday.org/2018/02/12/cleveland-school-district-faces-budget-shortfall-amid-enrollment-decline/.

65. "2017 Public Elementary–Secondary Education Finance Data," US Census Bureau, accessed October 1, 2022, https://www.census.gov/data/tables/2017/econ/school-finances/secondary-education-finance.html. Spending in some parts of the Delta is on par with the rest of the state, but some districts actually spend more. For example, while the district in the city of Cleveland spends $8,791 per student, the districts in Coahoma County and West Tallahatchie County spend $10,280 and $12,131, respectively. Even so, these are still below the national average. "Cleveland School District," Mississippi Department of Education, accessed October 25, 2022, https://msrc.mdek12.org/entity?EntityID=0614-000&SchoolYear=2018; "Coahoma County School District," Mississippi Department of Education, accessed October 25, 2022, https://msrc.mdek12.org/entity?EntityID=1400-000&SchoolYear=2018; "West Tallahatchie School District," Mississippi Department of Education, accessed October 25, 2022, https://msrc.mdek12.org/entity?EntityID=6812-000&SchoolYear=2018.

66. Stephanie Stullich, Ivy Morgan, and Oliver Schak, *State and Local Expenditures on Corrections and Education: A Brief from the U.S. Department of Education, Policy and Program Studies Service* (US Department of Planning, Evaluation, and Policy Development, July 2016), https://www2.ed.gov/rschstat/eval/other/expenditures-corrections-education/brief.pdf.

67. Kayleigh Skinner, "Q & A: Mississippi Superintendent Explains Why He Gave Up His Salary to Help Relieve 'Wretched Conditions' at His Schools," *Hechinger Report*, February 2, 2015, https://hechingerreport.org/q-a-mississippi-superintendent

-explains-why-he-gave-up-his-salary-to-help-relieve-wretched-conditions-at-his-schools/.

68. Alexandra Watts, "A Superintendent Earns $18,000 a Year—by Choice," MPB News, February 27, 2020, https://www.mpbonline.org/blogs/news/a-superintendent-earns-18000-a-year-by-choice/.

69. Aallyah Wright and Kelsey Davis Betz, "After Years of Inaction, Delta Teacher Shortage Reaches 'Crisis' Levels," *Mississippi Today*, https://mississippitoday.org/2019/02/18/after-years-of-inaction-delta-teacher-shortage-reaches-crisis-levels/.

70. Jisung Park et al., "Heat and Learning," *American Economic Journal: Economic Policy* 12, no. 2 (2020): 306–39, https://doi.org/10.1257/pol.20180612.

71. "Money Matters: An Interview with Eric Hanushek," Stanford Hoover Institution, April 26, 2006, http://hanushek.stanford.edu/opinions/education-sector-money-matters-interview-eric-hanushek.

72. Julien Lafortune, Jesse Rothstein, and Diane Whitmore Schanzenbach, "School Finance Reform and the Distribution of Student Achievement" (Working Paper 22011, National Bureau of Economic Research, February 2016), https://www.nber.org/papers/w22011.pdf; Gregory R. Thorson and Sera M. Gearhart, "Do Enhanced Funding Policies Targeting Students in Poverty Close Achievement Gaps? Evidence from the American States, 1996–2015," *Poverty and Public Policy* 11, no. 3 (2019): 205–21, https://doi.org/10.1002/pop4.253.

73. C. Kirabo Jackson, Rucker C. Johnson, and Claudia Persico, "The Effects of School Spending on Educational and Economic Outcomes: Evidence from School Finance Reforms," *Quarterly Journal of Economics* 131, no. 1 (2016): 157–218, https://doi.org/10.1093/qje/qjv036. For more information, see Avence Pittman Jr., "The Relationship between the Mississippi Adequate Education Program and Student Achievement in Mississippi Schools" (PhD diss., University of Mississippi, May 2017, Electronic Theses and Dissertations 516), https://egrove.olemiss.edu/etd/516.

74. "The Barksdales," Barksdale Reading Institute, accessed October 5, 2022, https://msreads.org/about-the-institute/the-barksdales/.

75. Richard Grant, *Dispatches from Pluto: Lost and Found in the Mississippi Delta* (New York: Simon and Schuster, 2015).

76. Grant.

77. "JPS Welcomes New Chief of Staff and Transition Manager to Its Executive Leadership," Forest Hill High School, January 18, 2019, https://www.jackson.k12.ms.us/site/default.aspx?PageType=3&DomainID=60&ModuleInstanceID=779&ViewID=6446EE88-D30C-497E-9316-3F8874B3E108&RenderLoc=0&FlexDataID=22143&PageID=113.

78. "2018 Accountability," Mississippi Department of Education.

79. Anelle Dreher, "MAEP: The Formula and How Politics Got in the Way," *Jackson Free Press*, October 21, 2015, https://www.jacksonfreepress.com/news/2015/oct/21/maep-formula-and-how-politics-got-way/; "Our Opinion: MAEP Funding Data Shows Interesting Reality," *Daily Journal*, February 21, 2018, https://www.djournal.com/opinion/editorials/our-opinion-maep-funding-data-shows-interesting-reality/article_41b66a49-69d0-5498-8bc4-0a0da966dfe2.html.

80. Dreher, "MAEP."

81. Bracey Harris, "Financial Support for Public Schools—and Population—Are Shrinking in Mississippi: Is There an Easy Fix?," *Mississippi Today*, February 26, 2019, https://mississippitoday.org/2019/02/26/financial-support-for-public-schools-and-population-are-shrinking-in-mississippi-is-there-an-easy-fix/.

82. "Public Schools Funding," Secretary of State, accessed October 5, 2022, https://www.sos.ms.gov/elections/initiatives/InitiativeInfo.aspx?IId=42.

83. Mattie Quinn, "In School Funding Fight, Mississippi Voters Choose to Do Nothing," Governing, October 23, 2015, https://www.governing.com/archive/gov-mississippi-school-funding-ballot.html.

84. Kate Royals, "Justices Press Both Sides in School Funding Lawsuit," *Mississippi Today*, May 17, 2017, https://mississippitoday.org/2017/05/17/justices-press-both-sides-in-school-funding-lawsuit/.

85. "Clarksdale Municipal School District v. State of Mississippi, NO. 2015-CA-01227-SCT," Supreme Court of Mississippi, July 14, 2015, https://courts.ms.gov/Images/Opinions/CO124118.pdf.

86. Jimmie E. Gates, "State Supreme Court Says There Is No State Mandate to Fully Fund K–12 Education," *Clarion-Ledger*, October 19, 2017, https://www.clarionledger.com/story/news/politics/2017/10/19/state-supreme-court-says-there-no-state-mandate-fully-fund-k-12-education/781165001/.

87. "House Bill 957," Mississippi Legislature 2018 Regular Session, last updated March 2, 2018, http://billstatus.ls.state.ms.us/2018/pdf/history/HB/HB0957.xml.

88. Kelsey Davis Betz, "'Why Didn't They Vote for Us?': Leland Bond Issue Defeated in a Delta Region Plagued by Crumbling Schools," *Mississippi Today*, September 16, 2019, https://mississippitoday.org/2019/09/16/why-didnt-they-vote-for-us-leland-bond-issue-defeated-in-a-delta-region-plagued-by-crumbling-schools/.

89. Catherine Brown, Scott Sargard, and Meg Benner, "Hidden Money: The Outsized Role of Parent Contributions in School Finances," Center for American Progress, April 8, 2017, https://www.americanprogress.org/issues/education-k-12/reports/2017/04/08/428484/hidden-money/.

90. Milbrey Wallin McLaughlin, *Evaluation and Reform: The Elementary and Secondary Education Act of 1965, Title I* (Santa Monica, CA: Rand, 1974), https://www.rand.org/content/dam/rand/pubs/reports/2009/R1292.pdf.

91. Anthony Rebora, "No Child Left Behind," *Education Week*, September 21, 2004, https://www.edweek.org/ew/issues/no-child-left-behind/index.html.

92. Thomas S. Dee et al., "The Impact of No Child Left Behind on Students, Teachers, and Schools," *Brookings Papers on Economic Activity*, 2010, 149–207, https://www.jstor.org/stable/10.2307/41012846.

93. Neal McClusky, "Has No Child Left Behind Worked?," CATO Institute, February 9, 2015, https://www.cato.org/publications/testimony/has-no-child-left-behind-worked.

94. Gregory Korte, "The Every Student Succeeds Act vs. No Child Left Behind: What's Changed?," *USA Today*, December 10, 2015, https://www.usatoday.com/story/news/politics/2015/12/10/every-student-succeeds-act-vs-no-child-left-behind-whats-changed/77088780/.

95. Kendi, *How to Be*, 101.

96. "Every Student Succeeds Act: Information and Resources," National Conference of State Legislatures, September 26, 2018, https://www.ncsl.org/ncsl-in-dc/standing-committees/education/every-student-succeeds-act-essa-information-and-resources.aspx.

97. "Your School Rating: How It Was Determined, What It Really Means," Parent's Campaign: Research and Education Fund, accessed October 5, 2022, https://1.cdn.edl.io/BpCmnylv3RpmTWfYzxQbjTlMzGQojm4cDvtfC35nqckfSdzn.pdf.

98. "House Bill No. 989 (as Sent to Governor)," Mississippi Legislature Regular Session 2016, http://billstatus.ls.state.ms.us/documents/2016/pdf/HB/0900-0999/HB0989SG.pdf.

99. "Superintendent Dr. Jermall Wright," Little Rock School District, accessed October 5, 2022, https://www.lrsd.org/domain/210.

100. Kayleigh Skinner, "'It's a Matter of Life and Death'—Q&A with New Superintendent of State-Run Achievement School District," *Mississippi Today*, August 7, 2019, https://mississippitoday.org/2019/08/07/its-a-matter-of-life-and-death-qa-with-new-superintendent-of-state-run-achievement-school-district/.

101. Skinner.

102. Bracey Harris, "Clarksdale Principal Barred from License for 20 Years," *Clarion-Ledger*, January 19, 2017, https://www.clarionledger.com/story/news/2017/01/19/clarksdale-principal-given-20-year-license-ban/96774948/.

103. "School Board President Admits to Shoplifting Air Fresheners," WMC5 Action News, August 15, 2013, https://www.wmcactionnews5.com/story/23149859/school-board-president-admits-to-shoplifting-air-fresheners/.

104. Joint Legislative Committee on Performance Evaluation and Expenditure Review, *The Common Core State Standards: Mississippi's Adoption and Implementation*, Report 582 (Jackson: Mississippi Legislature, 2014), https://www.peer.ms.gov/sites/default/files/peer_publications/rpt582.pdf.

105. "Standards in Your State," Common Core State Standards Initiative, accessed March 11, 2024, https://www.thecorestandards.org/standards-in-your-state/.

106. Every Student Succeeds Act, Pub. L. No. 114-95, 129 Stat. 1802, 1852 (2015), https://www.congress.gov/bill/114th-congress/senate-bill/1177/text.

107. Desiree Carver-Thomas and Linda Darling-Hammond, *Teacher Turnover: Why It Matters and What We Can Do about It* (Palo Alto, CA: Learning Policy Institute, August 2017), https://www.edworkingpapers.com/sites/default/files/Teacher_Turnover_REPORT.pdf.

108. Emily Le Coz, "Miss. Withdraws from Common Core Testing," *Clarion-Ledger*, January 16, 2015, https://www.clarionledger.com/story/news/2015/01/16/mississippi-withdraw-parcc/21859553/.

109. "Senate Bill 2161," Mississippi Legislature 2015 Regular Session, last updated April 24, 2015, http://billstatus.ls.state.ms.us/2015/pdf/history/SB/SB2161.xml.

110. Phil Bryant, "Governor's Veto Message for Senate Bill 2161," Mississippi Legislature, April 23, 2015, http://billstatus.ls.state.ms.us/documents/2015/pdf/veto/SB2161.pdf.

111. "Districts of Innovation," Mississippi Department of Education, accessed March 11, 2024, https://www.mdek12.org/ese/districts_of_innovation.

112. Kayleigh Skinner, "Students Flourish at This High School: So Why Is It Labeled an F?," *Mississippi Today*, May 20, 2019, https://mississippitoday.org/2019/05/20/students-flourish-at-this-high-school-so-why-is-it-labeled-an-f/.

113. Skinner.

114. Bracey Harris, "Mississippi Made the Biggest Leap in National Test Scores This Year: Is This Controversial Law the Reason Why?," *Hechinger Report*, November 1, 2019, https://hechingerreport.org/mississippi-made-the-biggest-leap-in-national-test-scores-this-year-is-this-controversial-law-the-reason-why/.

115. Todd Collins, "Mississippi Rising? A Partial Explanation for Its NAEP Improvement Is That It Holds Students Back," Thomas B. Fordham Institute, December 4, 2019, https://fordhaminstitute.org/national/commentary/mississippi-rising-partial-explanation-its-naep-improvement-it-holds-students.

116. Nick Chiles, "As Mississippi Delivers Bad News to 5,600 Third Graders, Stressed-Out Parents Say There Must Be a Better Way," *Hechinger Report*, May 28, 2015, https://hechingerreport.org/as-mississippi-delivers-bad-news-to-5600-third-graders-stressed-out-parents-say-there-must-be-a-better-way/.

117. Collins, "Mississippi Rising?"

118. Kayleigh Skinner and Aallyah Wright, "As Thousands of Third-Graders Prep for Reading Retest, Districts and Literacy Coaches Work to Remove Barriers," *Mississippi Today*, July 9, 2019, https://mississippitoday.org/2019/07/09/as-thousands-of-third-graders-prep-for-reading-retest-districts-and-literacy-coaches-work-to-remove-barriers/.

119. Carey M. Wright, *Mississippi Academic Assessment Program 3rd Grade English Language Arts Assessment Results* (Jackson: Mississippi Department of Education, May 2019), https://www.mdek12.org/sites/default/files/Offices/MDE/OEA/OPR/2019/3rd_grade_maap_ela_results_2019_final.pdf.

120. Chiles, "Mississippi Delivers Bad News."

121. Skinner and Wright, "Thousands of Third-Graders."

122. Skinner and Wright.

123. Harris, "Mississippi Made."

124. Skinner and Wright, "Thousands of Third-Graders."

125. Kate Royals, "Passing Requirements Waived for Some State Tests in 2020–21," *Mississippi Today*, January 21, 2021, https://mississippitoday.org/2021/01/21/passing-requirements-waived-for-some-state-tests-in-2020-21/.

126. Amy Hightower et al., *Improving Student Learning by Supporting Quality Teaching: Key Issues, Effective Strategies* (Bethesda, MD: Editorial Projects in Education, December 2011), https://epe.brightspotcdn.com/96/bd/c7ea3e084ade93466ae02042ba7d/eperc-qualityteaching-12.11.pdf.

127. Lucy Sorensen and Helen F. Ladd, "Teacher Turnover and the Disruption of Teacher Staffing," Brookings, April 29, 2019, https://www.brookings.edu/blog/brown-center-chalkboard/2019/04/29/teacher-turnover-and-the-disruption-of-teacher-staffing/.

128. Kelsey Davis Betz, "Teacher Shortage: State Education Officials, Citing Lack of Data, Don't Know True Teaching Vacancy Numbers," *Mississippi Today*, December 23, 2019, https://mississippitoday.org/2019/12/23/teacher-shortage-state

-education-officials-citing-lack-of-data-dont-know-true-teaching-vacancy-numbers/.

129. Aallyah Wright and Kelsey Davis Betz, "How Grassroots Efforts Are Trying to Solve the Teacher Shortage Crisis," *Mississippi Today*, February 22, 2019, https://mississippitoday.org/2019/02/22/how-grassroots-efforts-are-trying-to-solve-the-teacher-shortage-crisis/.

130. Emma García and Elaine Weiss, *U.S. Schools Struggle to Hire and Retain Teachers* (Washington, DC: Economic Policy Institute, April 16, 2019), 1, https://files.epi.org/pdf/164773.pdf.

131. García and Weiss.

132. Bracey Harris, "Mississippi Teacher Shortage Sparks a New Change in Licensing Some Educators," *Clarion-Ledger*, November 13, 2018, https://www.clarionledger.com/story/news/politics/2018/11/13/mississippi-nix-licensure-exams-some-educators/1932386002/.

133. Rebecca Goldring et al., *Teacher Attrition and Mobility: Results from the 2012–13 Teacher Follow-Up Survey* (Washington, DC: US Department of Education, September 2014), https://nces.ed.gov/pubs2014/2014077.pdf.

134. Carver-Thomas and Darling-Hammond, *Teacher Turnover*.

135. Goldring et al., *Teacher Attrition and Mobility*.

136. Aallyah Wright, "Mississippi's Teacher Prep Pool Is the Second Least Diverse in the Nation," *Mississippi Today*, December 8, 2020, https://mississippitoday.org/2020/12/08/mississippis-teacher-prep-pool-is-not-diverse/.

137. Kayleigh Skinner, "Who's Teaching Mississippi's Children? A Deep Dive into Race, Gender of State's Educators," *Mississippi Today*, September 6, 2019, https://mississippitoday.org/2019/09/06/whos-teaching-mississippis-children-a-deep-dive-into-teacher-demographics/.

138. Skinner, "'Life and Death.'"

139. Aallyah Wright and Kelsey Davis Betz, "Teacher Shortages Force Districts to Use Online Education Programs," *Mississippi Today*, February 20, 2019, https://mississippitoday.org/2019/02/20/teacher-shortages-force-districts-to-use-online-education-programs/.

140. Wright and Davis Betz.

141. Kate Royals, "These Mississippi Schools Never Returned to In-Person Learning: Here's What Happened," *Mississippi Today*, June 9, 2021, https://mississippitoday.org/2021/06/09/these-mississippi-schools-never-returned-to-in-person-learning-heres-what-happened/.

142. Harris, "Teacher Shortage Sparks."

143. Aallyah Wright, "Would-Be Teachers in Mississippi Struggle to Pass Certification Exams, Advocates Call for Evaluation of Prep Programs," *Mississippi Today*, April 1, 2019, https://mississippitoday.org/2019/04/01/would-be-teachers-in-mississippi-struggle-to-pass-certification-exams-advocates-call-for-evaluation-of-prep-programs/.

144. Hannah Putman and Kate Walsh, *A Fair Chance: Simple Steps to Strengthen and Diversify the Teacher Workforce* (National Council on Teacher Quality, February 2019), https://www.nctq.org/dmsView/A_Fair_Chance.

145. Wright and Davis Betz, "Grassroots Efforts."

146. "FY2019–2020 MAEP Salary Schedule," accessed October 5, 2022, https://www.mdek12.org/sites/default/files/documents/OSF/TeacherSalarySchedule/salary-schedule-2019-2020.pdf.

147. Wright and Davis Betz, "Grassroots Efforts."

148. Kate Royals, "How Jackson Public Schools Tackled Its Teacher Shortage," *Mississippi Today*, June 10, 2021, https://mississippitoday.org/2021/06/10/jackson-public-school-teacher-shortage-mississippi/.

149. Aallyah Wright and Kelsey Davis Betz, "After Years of Inaction, Delta Teacher Shortage Reaches 'Crisis' Levels," *Mississippi Today*, February 18, 2019, https://mississippitoday.org/2019/02/18/after-years-of-inaction-delta-teacher-shortage-reaches-crisis-levels/.

150. "FY2019–2020 MAEP Salary Schedule."

151. Madeline Will, "Which States Have the Highest and Lowest Teacher Salaries?," Education Week, April 30, 2019, https://blogs.edweek.org/teachers/teaching_now/2019/04/which_states_have_the_highest_and_lowest_teacher_salaries.html.

152. Bracey Harris, "5 Ways Teacher Pay in Mississippi Falls behind Most States, Including Our Neighbors," *Sun Herald*, April 20, 2018, https://www.sunherald.com/news/local/education/article209462779.html.

153. Kayleigh Skinner, "$1,500 Teacher Pay Raise Approved but Educators Underwhelmed: 'Another Election-Year-Timed Symbolic Gesture,'" *Mississippi Today*, March 28, 2019, https://mississippitoday.org/2019/03/28/1500-teacher-pay-raise-approved-but-educators-underwhelmed-another-election-year-timed-symbolic-gesture/; Bobby Harrison, "Mississippi Lawmakers Pass $1,000 Teacher Pay Raise," *Mississippi Today*, March 18, 2021, https://mississippitoday.org/2021/03/18/mississippi-lawmakers-pass-1000-teacher-pay-raise/.

154. Wright and Davis Betz, "Years of Inaction."

155. "AmeriCorps," Teach for America, accessed October 5, 2022, https://www.teachforamerica.org/life-in-the-corps/salary-and-benefits/americorps.

156. Kelsey Davis Betz, "Teach for America Mississippi and Arkansas to Join Together as One Region," *Mississippi Today*, February 5, 2018, https://mississippitoday.org/2018/02/05/tfa-mississippi-and-arkansas-will-combine-into-one-region/.

157. Olivia Blanchard, "I Quit Teach for America," *Atlantic*, September 23, 2013, https://www.theatlantic.com/education/archive/2013/09/i-quit-teach-for-america/279724/.

158. Vanessa Sacks and David Murphey, "The Prevalence of Adverse Childhood Experiences, Nationally, by State, and by Race or Ethnicity," Child Trends, February 12, 2018, https://www.childtrends.org/publications/prevalence-adverse-childhood-experiences-nationally-state-race-ethnicity.

159. "Mississippi: Children in Single-Parent Households," County Health Rankings, accessed October 5, 2022, https://www.countyhealthrankings.org/app/mississippi/2019/measure/factors/82/data?sort=desc-4.

160. "Mississippi: Children in Poverty," County Health Rankings, accessed October 5, 2022, https://www.countyhealthrankings.org/app/mississippi/2019/measure/factors/24/data?sort=desc-2; "Federal Poverty Level (FPL)," Healthcare

.gov, accessed March 11, 2024, https://www.healthcare.gov/glossary/federal-poverty-level-FPL/.

161. Deborah Fry et al., "The Relationships between Violence in Childhood and Educational Outcomes: A Global Systematic Review and Meta-analysis," *Child Abuse and Neglect* 75 (2018): 6–28, https://doi.org/10.1016/j.chiabu.2017.06.021; Shanta R. Dube, "How Childhood Experiences Contribute to the Education-Health Link," The Conversation, February 7, 2018, https://theconversation.com/how-childhood-experiences-contribute-to-the-education-health-link-89069.

162. Jack P. Shonkoff et al., "The Lifelong Effects of Early Childhood and Toxic Stress," *Pediatrics* 129, no. 1 (2012): E232–46, https://doi.org/10.1542/peds.2011-2663; Vincent J. Felitti et al., "Relationship of Childhood Abuse and Household Dysfunction to Many of the Leading Causes of Death in Adults: The Adverse Childhood Experiences (ACE) Study," *American Journal of Preventive Medicine* 14, no. 4 (1998): 245–58, https://doi.org/10.1016/S0749-3797(98)00017-8.

163. Maryah Stella Fram et al., "Children Are Aware of Food Insecurity and Take Responsibility for Managing Food Resources," *Journal of Nutrition* 141, no. 6 (2011): 1114–19, https://doi.org/10.3945/jn.110.135988.

164. "Data and Statistics on Autism Spectrum Disorder," Centers for Disease Control and Prevention, accessed October 5, 2022, https://www.cdc.gov/ncbddd/autism/data.html.

165. "Data and Statistics."

166. "Education and Autism Spectrum Disorders," Synapse, accessed October 5, 2022, http://www.autism-help.org/autism-education-school-effects.htm.

167. Tessie Rose Bailey and Rebecca Zumeta, *How States Can Help Rural LEAs Meet the Needs of Special Populations* (Edvance Research, May 2015), https://compcenternetwork.org/sites/default/files/archive/HowStatesCanHelpRuralLEAsMeettheNeedsofSpecialPopulations.pdf.

168. Aallyah Wright and Kelsey Davis Betz, "How Teachers Are Dealing with Student Trauma," *Mississippi Today*, August 17, 2020, https://mississippitoday.org/2020/08/17/there-are-a-lot-of-things-happening-in-our-country-that-students-have-feelings-about/.

169. "Trauma-Informed Schools," County Health Rankings, accessed October 5, 2022, https://www.countyhealthrankings.org/take-action-to-improve-health/what-works-for-health/strategies/trauma-informed-schools; David Murphey and Vanessa Sacks, "Supporting Students with Adverse Childhood Experiences: How Educators and Schools Can Help," American Federation of Teachers, accessed October 5, 2022, https://www.aft.org/ae/summer2019/murphey_sacks.

170. Emily Heller, "Improving Access to Care with School-Based Health Centers," *National Conference of State Legislatures* 25, no. 19 (2017): 1–2, https://www.ncsl.org/research/health/improving-access-to-care-with-school-based-health-centers.aspx (no longer available).

171. "Executive Summary State Investment in SBHCs (n=17)," School-Based Health Alliance, accessed October 5, 2022, http://www.sbh4all.org/school-health-care/aboutsbhcs/school-based-health-care-state-policy-survey/ (no longer available).

172. "Health Services: The Medicaid School-Based Administrative Claiming (SBAC) Program," Mississippi Department of Education, accessed October 5, 2022, https://www.mdek12.org/OHS/HS/health-services---school-based-administrative-claiming.

173. "State Investment in SBHCs."

174. "School-Based Health Centers," County Health Rankings, accessed October 5, 2022, https://www.countyhealthrankings.org/take-action-to-improve-health/what-works-for-health/strategies/school-based-health-centers.

175. Kate Royals, "Mississippi Launches Telehealth, Teletherapy Pilot in Schools as 'a Way to Keep Kids Learning,'" *Mississippi Today*, December 29, 2020, https://mississippitoday.org/2020/12/29/mississippi-launches-pilot-telehealth-teletherapy-in-schools-as-a-way-to-keep-kids-learning/.

176. W. Steven Barnett and Jason S. Hustedt, "Preschool: The Most Important Grade," *Educational Leadership* 60, no. 7 (2003): 54–57, https://eric.ed.gov/?id=EJ666030.

177. Richard G. Lynch, *Enriching Children, Enriching the Nation: Public Investment in High-Quality Prekindergarten* (Washington, DC: Economic Policy Institute, 2007), https://www.epi.org/publication/book_enriching/; Suzanne Bouffard, *The Most Important Year: Pre-kindergarten and the Future of Our Children* (New York: Penguin Random House, 2017).

178. Breyon J. Williams, "The Spillover Benefits of Expanding Access to Preschool," *Economics of Education Review* 70 (2019): 127–43, https://doi.org/10.1016/j.econedurev.2019.04.002.

179. Allison H. Friedman-Krauss et al., *The State of Preschool 2019: State Preschool Yearbook* (National Institute for Early Education Research, 2020), https://nieer.org/sites/default/files/2023-09/YB2019_Full_Report.pdf.

180. Lynch, *Enriching Children*, executive summary.

181. Friedman-Krauss et al., *State of Preschool 2019*.

182. "Early Education," Mississippi First, accessed October 5, 2022, https://www.mississippifirst.org/we-support/pre-k/.

183. "Donors Contributed Nearly $1.6 Million to Early Learning Collaboratives in 2016," Mississippi Department of Education, February 7, 2017, https://www.mdek12.org/OCGR/1.6million.

184. Quoted in Barnett and Hustedt, "Preschool."

185. Claudio Sanchez, "Getting the Most Out of Pre-K, 'the Most Important' Year in School," NPR, October 2, 2017, https://www.npr.org/sections/ed/2017/10/02/552868453/getting-the-most-out-of-pre-k-the-most-important-year-in-school.

186. Elizabeth T. Gershoff and Sarah A. Font, "Corporal Punishment in U.S. Public Schools: Prevalence, Disparities in Use, and Status in State and Federal Policy," *Social Policy Report* 30 (2016): 1, https://www.ncbi.nlm.nih.gov/pmc/articles/PMC5766273/.

187. "2015–16 State and National Estimations," Civil Rights Data Collection, accessed October 5, 2022, https://ocrdata.ed.gov/estimations/2015-2016.

188. Gershoff and Font, "Corporal Punishment."

189. Sarah A. Font and Jamie Cage, "Dimensions of Physical Punishment and Their Associations with Children's Cognitive Performance and School Adjustment," *Child Abuse and Neglect* 75 (2018): 29–40, https://doi.org/10.1016/j.chiabu.2017.06.008.

190. Gershoff and Font, "Corporal Punishment."

191. "Impairing Education: Corporal Punishment of Students with Disabilities in US Public Schools," Human Rights Watch, August 10, 2009, https://www.hrw.org/report/2009/08/10/impairing-education/corporal-punishment-students-disabilities-us-public-schools.

192. "Handcuffs on Success: The Extreme School Discipline Crisis in Mississippi Public Schools," Advancement Project, January 17, 2013, https://advancementproject.org/resources/handcuffs-on-success/; "Impairing Education."

193. "Impairing Education."

194. "Handcuffs on Success."

195. "Teacher Barred for 12 Years after Dragging Student by Hair," Fox News, December 7, 2016, https://www.foxnews.com/us/teacher-barred-for-12-years-after-dragging-student-by-hair.

196. Gabriel Austin, "Greenville Superintendent Fired after Disturbing Video of Teacher Dragging Student," *Mississippi Today*, December 1, 2016, https://mississippitoday.org/2016/12/01/greenville-superintendent-fired-after-disturbing-video-of-teacher-dragging-student/.

197. Robert D. Brown and Sara Porcheddu, "Sex Education in Mississippi: A Preliminary Look at the Early Impacts of HB999" (prepared for a presentation at the "Advancing Mississippi: Research for a Better Mississippi for More Mississippians" conference, n.d., accessed October 5, 2022), http://www.mississippi.edu/urc/downloads/160609/presentations/session4_paper2.pdf.

198. Sexuality Information and Education Council, *Sexuality Education in Mississippi: Progress in the Magnolia State* (Sexuality Information and Education Council of the United States, February 2014), https://siecus.org/wp-content/uploads/2018/07/Sexuality-Education-in-Mississippi-Progress-in-the-Magnolia-State.pdf.

199. Colleen McKee et al., *Parental Survey on Sex Education in Mississippi: Implications for House Bill 999, Final Report* (Center for Mississippi Health Policy, November 4, 2011), https://mshealthpolicy.com/wp-content/uploads/2013/02/MSU-HB999-Final-Report-2-9-12.pdf.

200. Colleen McKee, Kathleen Ragsdale, and Linda H. Southward, "What Do Parents in Mississippi Really Think about Sex Education in Schools? Results of a State-Level Survey," *Journal of Health Disparities Research and Practice* 7, no. 1 (2014): 97–119, https://digitalscholarship.unlv.edu/jhdrp/vol7/iss1/9.

201. "House Bill 999 (as Sent to Governor)," Mississippi Legislature 2011 Regular Session, accessed October 5, 2022, http://billstatus.ls.state.ms.us/documents/2011/html/HB/0900-0999/HB0999SG.htm.

202. Sexuality Information and Education Council, *Sexuality Education in Mississippi*.

203. "County Stats," Teen Health Mississippi, accessed October 5, 2022, https://teenhealthms.org/county-stats/.

204. McKee et al., *Parental Survey*.

205. Jerome Kolbo et al., *2012 Implementation of Sex-Related Education Policy in Mississippi* (Center for Mississippi Health Policy, December 2012), https://mshealthpolicy.com/wp-content/uploads/2013/02/2012-ISREP-Report-2013-2-13.pdf.

206. Andy Kopsa, "Sex Ed without Condoms? Welcome to Mississippi," *Atlantic*, March 7, 2013, https://www.theatlantic.com/national/archive/2013/03/sex-ed-without-condoms-welcome-to-mississippi/273802/.

207. "Mississippi Sex Education Law," Teen Health Mississippi, accessed October 5, 2022, https://teenhealthms.org/policy-and-advocacy/mississippi-sex-education-law/.

208. Sanford Johnson, "How to Put on a Sock," YouTube video, 1:51, July 5, 2012, https://www.youtube.com/watch?v=o6kT9yfj7QE.

209. Sexuality Information and Education Council, *Sexuality Education in Mississippi*.

210. Kari Ellis, "Health Educators' Perceptions of Factors Related to the Implementation of School-Based Sexual Education" (honors BA thesis, University of Southern Mississippi, 2016), https://aquila.usm.edu/cgi/viewcontent.cgi?article=1434&context=honors_theses.

211. Ellis.

212. "House Bill 999."

213. MS Code § 97-29-59 (2013), Justia, https://law.justia.com/codes/mississippi/2013/title-97/chapter-29/in-general/section-97-29-59.

214. Larrison Campbell, "Sodomy Ban 'Unconstitutional,'" *Mississippi Today*, November 9, 2016, https://mississippitoday.org/2016/11/09/lawsuit-sodomy-law-unconstitutional/.

215. Mississippi Code Title 45, Chapter 33, Registration of Sex Offenders, accessed October 6, 2022, http://state.sor.dps.ms.gov/so_law.html.

216. Ellis, "Health Educators' Perceptions."

217. Brown and Porcheddu, "Sex Education in Mississippi."

218. Alonzo Jeffery Williams, "A Comparative Analysis of Mississippi Rural Schools' Abstinence-Only and Abstinence Plus Programs" (PhD diss., Walden University, 2015), https://scholarworks.waldenu.edu/cgi/viewcontent.cgi?article=2936&context=dissertations.

219. Aallyah Wright and Erica Hensley, "Teen Pregnancy Rate Declines but Remains High in the Delta; Report Says Social and Economic Factors Key to Further Reduction," *Mississippi Today*, July 31, 2019, https://mississippitoday.org/2019/07/31/teen-pregnancy-rate-declines-but-remains-high-in-delta-region-report-says-socioeconomic-factors-key-to-further-reduction/.

220. "Find a Program," Delta Health Alliance, accessed October 6, 2022, https://deltahealthalliance.org/find-a-program/.

221. "Delta Health Alliance: Delta Futures Teen Pregnancy Prevention Program," Office of Population Affairs, 2017, https://opa.hhs.gov/grant-programs/teen-pregnancy-prevention-program/tpp-successful-strategies/delta-health-alliance.

222. Kate Royals, "Trump Administration Cuts Teen Pregnancy Prevention Efforts in Miss," *Mississippi Today*, July 21, 2017, https://mississippitoday.org/2017/07/21/trump-administration-cuts-teen-pregnancy-prevention-efforts-in-miss/.

223. Van Woerden, Hruschka, and Bruening, "Food Insecurity."

224. Bruening et al., "Struggle Is Real"; Eisenberg, Golberstein, and Hunt, "Mental Health."

225. "Compare the States," *Chronicle of Higher Education*, August 15, 2022, https://www.chronicle.com/interactives/almanac-2018.

226. Meredith Kolodner, "Mississippi's Flagship University Leaves Black Students Behind," *Mississippi Today*, January 29, 2018, https://mississippitoday.org/2018/01/29/mississippis-flagship-university-leaves-black-students-behind/.

227. Kim Davis, "Building a Pipeline of Great Teachers in Rural Mississippi," Walton Family Foundation, November 1, 2019, https://www.waltonfamilyfoundation.org/stories/home-region/building-a-pipeline-of-great-teachers-in-rural-mississippi.

228. Davis.

229. Wright and Davis Betz, "Grassroots Efforts."

230. Davis, "Building a Pipeline."

231. Davis.

232. Davis.

233. Wright and Davis Betz, "Grassroots Efforts."

234. Regional Initiatives for Sustainable Education, homepage, accessed October 6, 2022, https://www.risems.org/conference-flyer.

235. "Senate Bill 2161," Mississippi Legislature 2016 Regular Session, accessed October 6, 2022, http://billstatus.ls.state.ms.us/2016/pdf/history/SB/SB2161.xml.

236. "Who We Are," Clarksdale Collegiate Public Charter School, accessed October 6, 2022, https://www.clarksdalecollegiate.org/about/who-we-are/.

237. Aallyah Wright, "Proposed Charter School Provokes Debate in Clarksdale," *Mississippi Today*, August 15, 2017, https://mississippitoday.org/2017/08/15/proposed-charter-school-provokes-debate-in-clarksdale/.

238. Kayleigh Skinner, "Charter Schools' Use of Tax Dollars Upheld, Mississippi Supreme Court Throws Out SPLC Lawsuit," *Mississippi Today*, September 5, 2019, https://mississippitoday.org/2019/09/05/charter-schools-use-of-tax-dollars-upheld-mississippi-supreme-court-throws-out-splc-lawsuit/.

239. Kayleigh Skinner, "Mississippi Delta to Gain Second Charter School," *Mississippi Today*, September 9, 2019, https://mississippitoday.org/2019/09/09/mississippi-delta-to-gain-second-charter-school/.

240. Aallyah Wright, "Clarksdale Collegiate, the State's First Rural Charter School, Readies for Opening Day," *Mississippi Today*, July 24, 2018, https://mississippitoday.org/2018/07/24/clarksdale-collegiate-the-states-first-rural-charter-school-readies-for-opening-day/.

241. "Who We Are," Sunflower County Freedom Project, accessed October 6, 2022, http://www.sunflowerfreedom.org/who-we-are#contact-us.

242. "About Spring," Spring Initiative, accessed October 6, 2022, https://www.spring-initiative.org/about.

243. "Frequently Asked Questions Regarding the 2010 Promise Neighborhoods Grantees," Promise Neighborhoods, September 21, 2010, https://www2.ed

.gov/programs/promiseneighborhoods/2010/faqs-secretary-announcement.pdf (no longer available).

244. Jackie Mader, "Can a Successful Model from Harlem Deliver 'Promise' to Schools in Rural Mississippi?," *Hechinger Report*, April 28, 2015, https://hechingerreport.org/can-a-successful-model-from-harlem-deliver-promise-to-schools-in-rural-mississippi/.

245. Mader.

246. Matthew Johnson, "Passport to Prosperity, Indianola, Mississippi," Urban, September 6, 2016, http://apps.urban.org/features/promise-neighborhoods/indianola-ms.html.

247. Mader, "Successful Model from Harlem."

248. "Indianola Promise Community," Promise Neighborhoods, accessed October 6, 2022, https://www.promiseneighborhoodsinstitute.org/sites/default/files/PNI_indianola_070615_b.pdf.

249. Mader, "Successful Model from Harlem."

250. Johnson, "Passport to Prosperity."

251. "The Indianola Promise Community Literacy Fellowship: High Expectations and Strong Partnerships Make the Grade," Teach for America, June 2, 2017, https://www.teachforamerica.org/stories/the-indianola-promise-community-literacy-fellowship-high-expectations-and-strong.

252. "Indianola Promise Community," Delta Health Alliance, accessed October 6, 2022, https://deltahealthalliance.org/find-a-program/indianola-promise-community/.

253. Deborah Moore, "Indianola Promise Community: Improving Academic Outcomes in the Delta," Federal Reserve Bank of St. Louis, March 15, 2017, https://www.stlouisfed.org/publications/bridges/winter-2016-2017/indianola-promise-community-improving-academic-outcomes-delta.

254. Moore.

255. Johnson, "Passport to Prosperity."

256. Moore, "Indianola Promise Community."

257. Mader, "Successful Model from Harlem."

258. "Head of Health Alliance under Scrutiny," Greenwood Commonwealth, December 2, 2011, https://www.gwcommonwealth.com/news-state/report-head-health-alliance-under-scrutiny#sthash.BK4zd1uk.dpbs.

259. Steve Wilson, "Large Salaries Dominate Delta Health Alliance," Mississippi Center for Public Policy, May 22, 2019, https://mspolicy.org/large-salaries-dominate-delta-health-alliance/.

260. Bobby J. Smith II, "Mississippi's War against the War on Poverty: Food Power, Hunger, and White Supremacy," *Study the South*, July 1, 2019, https://southernstudies.olemiss.edu/study-the-south/ms-war-against-war-on-poverty/.

261. Johnson, "Passport to Prosperity."

262. "Deer Creek Promise Community," Delta Health Alliance, accessed October 6, 2022, https://deltahealthalliance.org/find-a-program/deer-creek-promise-community/.

263. Raymond Pierce, "Local Control of Schools Is Historically and Politically Important in Black Communities: State Takeovers Disempower Them," The74, November 20, 2018, https://www.the74million.org/article/pierce-local-control-of-schools-is-historically-and-politically-important-in-black-communities-state-takeovers-disempower-them/.

Chapter 5

1. "Mississippi Health Center Fact Sheet: What Are Community Health Centers?," National Association of Community Health Centers, January 2019, https://www.aier.org/article/how-little-mound-bayou-became-a-powerful-engine-for-african-american-civil-rights-and-economic-advancement/.

2. "Our History," Delta Health Center, accessed October 7, 2022, https://deltahealthcenter.org/our-history/; "1969: Fannie Lou Hamer Founds Freedom Farm Cooperative," Digital SNCC Gateway, accessed October 7, 2022, https://snccdigital.org/events/fannie-lou-hamer-founds-freedom-farm-cooperative/.

3. Catherine G. McLaughlin and Leon Wyszewianski, "Access to Care: Remembering Old Lessons," *Health Services Research* 37, no. 6 (2002): 1441–43, https://doi.org/10.1111/1475-6773.12171.

4. Amanda Van Vleet and Julia Paradise, "Tapping Nurse Practitioners to Meet Rising Demand for Primary Care," Kaiser Family Foundation, January 20, 2015, https://www.kff.org/medicaid/issue-brief/tapping-nurse-practitioners-to-meet-rising-demand-for-primary-care/.

5. "Mississippi: Primary Care Physicians," County Health Rankings, accessed October 7, 2022, https://www.countyhealthrankings.org/app/mississippi/2020/measure/factors/4/map.

6. "Massachusetts: Primary Care Physicians," County Health Rankings, accessed October 7, 2022, https://www.countyhealthrankings.org/app/massachusetts/2020/measure/factors/4/map.

7. Jamie Zoellner et al., "Health Literacy Is Associated with Healthy Eating Index Scores and Sugar-Sweetened Beverage Intake: Findings from the Rural Lower Mississippi Delta," *Journal of the American Dietetic Association* 111, no. 7 (2011): 1012–20, https://doi.org/10.1016/j.jada.2011.04.010; Thomas Kippenbrock et al., "The Southern States: NPs Made an Impact in Rural and Healthcare Shortage Areas," *Journal of the American Association of Nurse Practitioners* 27, no. 12 (2015): 707–13, https://doi.org/10.1002/2327-6924.12245.

8. "Mississippi Rural Physicians Scholarship Program," University of Mississippi, accessed October 7, 2022, https://www.umc.edu/Office%20of%20Academic%20Affairs/For-Students/Academic%20Outreach%20Programs/Mississippi%20Rural%20Physicians%20Scholarship%20Program/Mississippi%20Rural%20Physicians%20Scholarship%20Program.html.

9. Jeralynn Cossman and Debra Ann Street, *Rural and Minority MDs in Mississippi: An Overview* (Mississippi Center for Health Workforce, August 2009), 45, https://www.researchgate.net/publication/280568137_Rural_and_Minority_MDs_in_Mississippi_An_Overview.

10. Cossman and Street, 49.

11. Cossman and Street, 48.

12. "Delta Doctors," Delta Regional Authority, accessed October 7, 2022, https://dra.gov/initiatives/promoting-a-healthy-delta/delta-doctors-how-to-apply/.

13. William F. Rayburn et al., "Pursuit of Accredited Subspecialties by Graduating Residents in Obstetrics and Gynecology, 2000–2012," *Obstetrics and Gynecology* 120, no. 3 (2012): 619–25, https://doi.org/10.1097/AOG.0b013e318265ab0a.

14. "Midwives: The Answer to the US Maternity Care Provider Shortage," American College of Nurse-Midwives, 2015, http://www.midwife.org/acnm/files/ccLibraryFiles/Filename/000000005828/DetailedTPsonMaternityCareWorkforce.pdf.

15. Susan M. Skillman, Lisa J. Hager, and Bianca K. Frogner, "Incentives for Nurse Practitioners and Registered Nurses to Work in Rural and Safety Net Settings" (Rapid Turnaround Brief, Center for Health Workforce Studies, University of Washington, November 2015, https://depts.washington.edu/fammed/chws/wp-content/uploads/sites/5/2016/03/CHWS_RTB159_Skillman.pdf); Margaret Brommelsiek and Jane A. Peterson, "Preparing Nurse Practitioner Students to Practice in Rural Primary Care," *Journal of Nursing Education* 59, no. 10 (2020): 581–84, https://doi.org/10.3928/01484834-20200921-08.

16. "Mississippi Health Center Fact Sheet."

17. "How Are Health Centers Responding to the Funding Delay?," Kaiser Family Foundation, February 1, 2018, https://www.kff.org/medicaid/fact-sheet/how-are-health-centers-responding-to-the-funding-delay/.

18. "Economic and Community Impact of Federal Health Center Funding: Mississippi," National Association of Community Health Centers, accessed October 7, 2022, http://www.nachc.org/wp-content/uploads/2016/03/MSEI.pdf (no longer available).

19. *High financial risk* refers to nonaudited operating margin, days' cash on hand, debt-to-capitalization ratio.

20. M. Maya McDoom et al., *The Economic Impact of Potential Closures of Rural Hospitals in Mississippi: A Focus on the Economic and Policy Implications and Alternative Models for Rural Hospitals in Mississippi* (Mississippi State University, August 2015), https://mshealthpolicy.com/wp-content/uploads/2015/11/Economic-Impact-of-Potential-Closures-of-Rural-Hospitals-in-Mississippi_MSU-Aug15.pdf.

21. Michael Topchik et al., *The Rural Safety Net under Pressure: Rural Hospital Vulnerability* (Chartis Center for Rural Health, February 2020), https://www.chartis.com/sites/default/files/documents/Rural%20Hospital%20Vulnerability-The%20Chartis%20Group.pdf; Michael Braga et al., "'Leaving Billions of Dollars on the Table': Rural Hospitals Foundering in States That Declined Obamacare," USA Today Network News, July 28, 2019, https://stories.usatodaynetwork.com/ruralhospitals/financialtroubles/.

22. "Critically essential" is determined by trauma level, the proportion of beds within twenty-five miles as a measure of geographic isolation, the ratio of hospital employees to community residents, and the level of uncompensated care as a measure of the extent to which they cover vulnerable populations.

23. McDoom et al., *Economic Impact*.

24. Jeff Lagasse, "Community Health Systems Sells Off 4 Rural Hospitals to Curae Health," Healthcare Finance, September 29, 2016, https://www.healthcarefinancenews.com/news/community-health-systems-sells-4-rural-hospitals-curae-health.

25. Jeff Amy, "Bankrupt Company Says It Could Close Mississippi Hospital," *Courier Journal*, October 16, 2018, https://www.courier-journal.com/story/news/2018/10/16/bankrupt-company-says-could-close-mississippi-hospital/1658285002/.

26. Mississippi State Department of Health, *2015 Report on Hospitals: Licensed by the Mississippi State Department of Health Division of Health Facilities Licensure and Certification* (Jackson: Mississippi State Department of Health, November 2016), https://msdh.ms.gov/msdhsite/_static/resources/6957.pdf.

27. Anuja Vaidya, "States Ranked by Counties without ICU Beds," Becker's Hospital Review, March 23, 2020, https://www.beckershospitalreview.com/rankings-and-ratings/states-ranked-by-counties-without-icu-beds.html.

28. "Download the Data," Economic Research Service, US Department of Agriculture, accessed October 26, 2022, https://www.ers.usda.gov/data-products/food-access-research-atlas/download-the-data/.

29. "Why We Ask Questions about . . . Vehicles Available," US Census Bureau, accessed October 26, 2022, https://www.census.gov/acs/www/about/why-we-ask-each-question/vehicles/.

30. "Public Transportation in the Mississippi Dela," Community Health Services Center, accessed October 8, 2022, https://www.aehchc.org/darts/delta-rides/.

31. "Annual Report: Uninsured," America's Health Rankings, accessed October 8, 2022, https://www.americashealthrankings.org/explore/annual/measure/HealthInsurance/state/MS.

32. "Health Insurance Coverage of Nonelderly 0–64, Timeframe: 2018," Kaiser Family Foundation, accessed October 8, 2022, https://www.kff.org/other/state-indicator/nonelderly-0-64/?currentTimeframe=0&sortModel=%7B%22colId%22:%22Employer%22,%22sort%22:%22desc%22%7D.

33. "QuickFacts: Bolivar County, Mississippi; Coahoma County, Mississippi; Tunica County, Mississippi; Clarksdale City, Mississippi; Cleveland City, Mississippi," US Census Bureau, accessed October 25, 2022, https://www.census.gov/quickfacts/fact/table/bolivarcountymississippi,coahomacountymississippi,tunicacountymississippi,clarksdalecitymississippi,clevelandcitymississippi,MS#.

34. "Mississippi: Uninsured Children," County Health Rankings, accessed October 8, 2022, https://www.countyhealthrankings.org/app/mississippi/2020/measure/factors/122/data?sort=sc-3.

35. "Federal Poverty Level (FPL)," HealthCare.gov, accessed October 8, 2022, https://www.healthcare.gov/glossary/federal-poverty-level-fpl/.

36. "Medicaid and CHIP Income Eligibility Limits for Pregnant Women as a Percent of the Federal Poverty Level, Timeframe: As of January 1, 2020," Kaiser Family Foundation, accessed October 8, 2022, https://www.kff.org/health-reform/state-indicator/medicaid-and-chip-income-eligibility-limits-for-pregnant-women

-as-a-percent-of-the-federal-poverty-level/?currentTimeframe=0&sortModel=%7B%22colId%22:%22Medicaid%22,%22sort%22:%22desc%22%7D.

37. "Medicaid and CHIP Income Eligibility Limits for Children as a Percent of the Federal Poverty Level, Timeframe: As of January 1, 2020," Kaiser Family Foundation, accessed October 8, 2022, https://www.kff.org/health-reform/state-indicator/medicaid-and-chip-income-eligibility-limits-for-children-as-a-percent-of-the-federal-poverty-level/?currentTimeframe=0&sortModel=%7B%22colId%22:%22Medicaid%20Coverage%20for%20Infants%20Ages%200-1_Medicaid%20Funded%22,%22sort%22:%22desc%22%7D.

38. "Medicaid Income Eligibility Limits for Adults as Percent of the Federal Poverty Level, Timeframe: As of January 1, 2020," Kaiser Family Foundation, accessed October 8, 2022, https://www.kff.org/health-reform/state-indicator/medicaid-income-eligibility-limits-for-adults-as-a-percent-of-the-federal-poverty-level/?currentTimeframe=0&sortModel=%7B%22colId%22:%22Parents%20(in%20a%20family%20of%20three)%22,%22sort%22:%22desc%22%7D.

39. John Tozzi and Zachery Tracer, "Sky-High Deductibles Broke the U.S. Health Insurance System," Bloomberg, June 26, 2018, https://www.bloomberg.com/news/features/2018-06-26/sky-high-deductibles-broke-the-u-s-health-insurance-system.

40. Luke Ramseth, "Mississippi Workers Are Hit Hardest by Rising Health Insurance Costs, Study Finds," *Clarion-Ledger*, December 4, 2019, https://www.clarionledger.com/story/news/politics/2019/12/04/mississippi-workers-pay-highest-share-insurance-costs/4251743002/.

41. Jin Zhang, "The Invisible Barrier: Health Literacy and Its Relationships to Health Factors in Mississippi Counties" (research brief, Mississippi Urban Research Center College of Public Service, January 17, 2018), http://www.jsums.edu/murc/files/2018/01/Jin_Research-Brief.final-1.pdf?x11471.

42. Michael Karpman et al., "Past-Due Medical Debt in America," Urban Institute, March 2016, http://apps.urban.org/features/medical-debt-in-america/.

43. "Health Insurance Coverage in the United States: 2020," US Census Bureau, September 14, 2021, https://www.census.gov/library/publications/2021/demo/p60-274.html.

44. "Health Coverage under the Affordable Care Act: Enrollment Trends and State Estimates" (issue brief, Office of Health Policy, June 5, 2021), https://aspe.hhs.gov/sites/default/files/migrated_legacy_files//200776/ASPE%20Issue%20Brief-ACA-Related%20Coverage%20by%20State.pdf.

45. "Estimates of Uninsured Adults Newly Eligible for Medicaid If Remaining 12 Non-expansion States Expand Medicaid: 2022" (Data Point, Office of Health Policy, February 15, 2022), https://aspe.hhs.gov/sites/default/files/documents/b311f433bae4b25b920aee542c4657e7/medicaid-12-state-expansion-uninsured.pdf.

46. Linda H. Southward et al., *Health Insurance Survey: Knowledge Attitudes and Behaviors of Mississippi Residents* (Mississippi State University Social Science Research Center, November 2017), https://mshealthpolicy.com/wp-content/uploads/2018/08/2017-MS-Health-Insurance-Survey-Final-Report.pdf.

47. "Health Insurance Coverage of the Total Population," Kaiser Family Foundation, accessed October 25, 2022, https://www.kff.org/other/state-indicator/total-population/?currentTimeframe=0&selectedDistributions=employer&sortModel=%7B%22colId%22:%22Location%22,%22sort%22:%22asc%22%7D.

48. David K. Jones, *Exchange Politics: Opposing Obamacare in Battleground States* (New York: Oxford University Press, 2017).

49. "Chism Strategies State of the State Survey Weighted Toplines," Millsaps College, April 9, 2018, http://www.millsaps.edu/_resources/documents/2018-millsaps-college-chism-strategies-survey-results.pdf.

50. Jonathan Gruber and Benjamin D. Sommers, "Paying for Medicaid—State Budgets and the Case for Expansion in the Time of Coronavirus," *New England Journal of Medicine* 382 (2020): 2280–82, https://doi.org/10.1056/NEJMp2007124.

51. Jerry Mitchell, "Mississippi Missed Out on $7 Billion When It Did Not Expand Medicaid: Will That Figure Jump to $20 Billion?," *Mississippi Today*, February 3, 2021, https://mississippitoday.org/2021/02/03/mississippi-missed-out-on-7-billion-when-it-did-not-expand-medicaid-will-that-figure-jump-to-20-billion/.

52. Michael Braga et al., "'Leaving Billions of Dollars on the Table': Rural Hospitals Foundering in States That Declined Obamacare," USA Today Network News, July 28, 2019, https://stories.usatodaynetwork.com/ruralhospitals/financialtroubles/.

53. Giacomo Bologna, "No, They're Not Crazy: But They Did Just Buy a Bankrupt Hospital in Rural Mississippi," *Clarion-Ledger*, April 16, 2019, https://www.clarionledger.com/story/news/politics/2019/04/16/rural-health-investors-buy-bankrupt-mississippi-hospital/3346901002/.

54. "No Hospital Would Serve Them Well—So They Built Their Own," *Clarion-Ledger*, November 30, 2017, https://www.clarionledger.com/story/magnolia/2017/11/28/healthcare-disparities-addressed-historic-miss-hospital/901363001/.

55. *Small rural* refers to those in CBSA nonmetropolitan areas with fewer than one hundred beds. *Critical access* refers to hospitals with fewer than twenty-five beds that are thirty-five miles away from any other general or critical access hospital.

56. "Health IT State Summary," Office of the National Coordinator for Health IT, US Department of Health and Human Services, last updated February 20, 2015, https://dashboard.healthit.gov/quickstats/widget/state-summaries/MS.pdf.

57. "National Trends in Hospital and Physician Adoption of Electronic Health Records," HealthIT.gov, accessed October 26, 2022, https://www.healthit.gov/data/quickstats/national-trends-hospital-and-physician-adoption-electronic-health-records.

58. "Find a Provider," Magnolia Health, accessed October 8, 2022, https://providersearch.magnoliahealthplan.com/search-details.

59. "Locations," Community Health Services Center, accessed October 8, 2022, https://www.aehchc.org/locations/.

60. "Mississippi ER Wait Times and Violations," ER Inspector, ProPublica, updated September 19, 2019, https://projects.propublica.org/emergency/state/MS.

61. Cossman and Street, *Rural and Minority MDs*, 72.

62. Such as James 5:14 in the New Testament.

63. Jehonathan Ben et al., "Racism and Health Service Utilisation: A Systematic Review and Meta-analysis," *PLoS ONE* 12, no. 12 (2017): e0189900, https://doi.org/10.1371/journal.pone.0189900.

64. "Racial and Ethnic Disparities Continue in Pregnancy-Related Deaths: Black, American Indian/Alaska Native Women Most Affected," CDC News Room, September 5, 2019, https://www.cdc.gov/media/releases/2019/p0905-racial-ethnic-disparities-pregnancy-deaths.html.

65. Adam Ganucheau, "Mississippi's Already Troubling Maternal Mortality Rate is Worsening," *Mississippi Today*, January 26, 2023, https://mississippitoday.org/2023/01/26/maternal-mortality-rate-worsens/.

66. Max Blau, "Black Women More Likely to Die of Breast Cancer—Especially in the South," Pew Trusts, May 15, 2019, https://www.pewtrusts.org/en/research-and-analysis/blogs/stateline/2019/05/15/black-women-more-likely-to-die-of-breast-cancer-especially-in-the-south.

67. Thomas J. Ward Jr., *Out in the Rural: A Mississippi Health Center and Its War on Poverty* (Oxford: Oxford University Press, 2016).

68. "The Tuskegee Timeline," Centers for Disease Control and Prevention, last reviewed April 22, 2021, https://www.cdc.gov/tuskegee/timeline.htm.

69. "Cultural Competence in Health Care: Is It Important for People with Chronic Conditions?," Georgetown University Health Policy Institute, accessed October 8, 2022, https://hpi.georgetown.edu/cultural/#.

70. "Distribution of Allopathic Medical School Graduates by Race/Ethnicity, Timeframe: 2018," Kaiser Family Foundation, accessed October 9, 2022, https://www.kff.org/other/state-indicator/allopathic-distribution-by-race-ethnicity/?currentTimeframe=0&sortModel=%7B%22colId%22:%22Location%22,%22sort%22:%22asc%22%7D.

71. "Dr. Peggy Wells MD," Clarksdale, Mississippi, accessed October 9, 2022, https://www.cityofclarksdale.org/leaders/wells/.

72. "Celebrating Dr. Helen Barnes," VC Notes, University of Mississippi Medical Center, February 16, 2018, https://www.umc.edu/news/VCNotes/2018/02/celebrating-dr-helen-barnes.html.

73. "Honoring Dr. Mary Williams Urgent and Primary Care of Clarksdale, MS; Congressional Record Vol. 165, No. 51, 116th Congress, 1st Session," Congress.gov, March 25, 2019, https://www.congress.gov/congressional-record/2019/03/25/extensions-of-remarks-section/article/E341-5.

74. Cossman and Street, *Rural and Minority MDs*, 58.

75. Robert F. Kennedy, "Day of Affirmation Address, University of Capetown, Capetown, South Africa, June 6, 1966," John F. Kennedy Presidential Library and Museum, accessed March 7, 2024, https://www.jfklibrary.org/learn/about-jfk/the-kennedy-family/robert-f-kennedy/robert-f-kennedy-speeches/day-of-affirmation-address-university-of-capetown-capetown-south-africa-june-6-1966.

76. Carl D. Stevens et al., "Geographic Clustering of Diabetic Lower-Extremity Amputations in Low-Income Regions of California," *Health Affairs* 33, no. 8 (2014): 1383–90, https://doi.org/10.1377/hlthaff.2014.0148.

77. Grant H. Skrepnek, Joseph L. Mills Sr., and David G. Armstrong, "A Diabetic Emergency One Million Feet Long: Disparities and Burdens of Illness among Diabetic Foot Ulcer Cases within Emergency Departments in the United States, 2006–2010," *PLoS ONE* 10, no. 8 (2015): e0134914, https://doi.org/10.1371/journal.pone.0134914.

78. Scott E. Regenbogen et al., "Do Differences in Hospital and Surgeon Quality Explain Racial Disparities in Lower-Extremity Vascular Amputations?," *Annals of Surgery* 250, no. 3 (2009): 424–31, https://doi.org/10.1097/SLA.0b013e3181b41d53.

79. Anna Gorman, "Black, Latino Patients Much More Likely Than Whites to Undergo Amputations Related to Diabetes," CNN Health, April 26, 2019, https://www.cnn.com/2019/04/26/health/diabetes-amputation-disparity-partner/index.html.

80. Skrepnek, Mills, and Armstrong, "Diabetic Emergency."

81. Lizzie Presser, "The Black American Amputation Epidemic," ProPublica, May 19, 2020, https://features.propublica.org/diabetes-amputations/black-american-amputation-epidemic/.

82. Presser.

83. Presser.

84. Presser.

85. Presser.

86. "Mississippi: Sunflower (SU)," County Health Rankings, accessed October 9, 2022, https://www.countyhealthrankings.org/app/mississippi/2020/rankings/sunflower/county/outcomes/overall/snapshot.

87. Ben Caxton, "NSMC Hospital of the Year," NSMC News, accessed October 25, 2022, https://northsunflower.com/nsmc-news/nsmc-hospital-year.

88. Tami Lubhy, "This Mississippi Hospital Should Be in Crisis: How It Beat the Odds," CNN Politics, October 2017, https://www.cnn.com/interactive/2017/politics/state/rural-health-care/.

89. Sunflower Management Group, homepage, accessed October 9, 2022, http://sunflowermanagementgroup.com/.

90. "Critical Access Hospitals (CAHs)," Rural Health Information Hub, accessed October 9, 2022, https://www.ruralhealthinfo.org/topics/critical-access-hospitals.

91. "About NSMC," North Sunflower Medical Center, accessed October 9, 2022, http://northsunflower.com/about-nsmc.

92. Lubhy, "Mississippi Hospital."

93. Sunflower Management Group, homepage.

94. "Tallahatchie General Hospital: 5-Star HCAHPs Facility," National Rural Health Resource Center, accessed October 9, 2022, https://www.ruralcenter.org/resource-library/hospital-spotlights/tallahatchie-general-hospital-5-star-hcahps-facility.

95. "Mississippi: Health Outcomes Overall Rank," County Health Rankings, accessed October 9, 2022, https://www.countyhealthrankings.org/app/mississippi/2011/rankings/outcomes/overall.

96. Sunflower Management Group, homepage.

97. "Mississippi: Health Outcomes Overall Rank."

98. "Telemedicine in Mississippi: Defining Boundaries for a New Frontier" (issue brief, Center for Mississippi Health Policy, January 2017), https://mshealthpolicy.com/wp-content/uploads/2017/01/Telemedicine-Issue-Brief-Jan-2017.pdf.

99. Latoya Thomas and Gary Capistrant, "State Telemedicine Gaps Analysis Coverage and Reimbursement," American Telemedicine Association, January 19, 2016, https://mtelehealth.com/state-telemedicine-gaps-analysis-coverage-reimbursement/.

100. Heather Landi, "Lessons Learned from the Mississippi Delta, Tackling Chronic Disease through Remote Monitoring Technology," Healthcare Innovation, October 3, 2016, https://www.hcinnovationgroup.com/population-health-management/article/13026977/lessons-learned-from-the-mississippi-delta-tackling-chronic-disease-through-remote-monitoring-technology.

101. Thomas and Capistrant, "State Telemedicine Gaps Analysis."

102. Kristi Henderson, "Testimony before the United States Senate Committee on Appropriations, Subcommittee on Labor, Health and Human Services, Education, and Related Agencies," US Senate Committee on Appropriations, May 7, 2015, https://www.appropriations.senate.gov/imo/media/doc/hearings/050715%20Henderson%20Testimony%20-%20LaborHHS.pdf.

103. Sara Heath, "Telehealth Closes Patient Care Access Gaps in Rural Mississippi," Patient Engagement HIT, April 23, 2018, https://patientengagementhit.com/news/telehealth-closes-patient-care-access-gaps-in-rural-mississippi.

104. Ruth Cummins, "UMMC Earns National Telehealth Center of Excellence Designation," University of Mississippi Medical Center, October 5, 2017, https://www.umc.edu/news/News_Articles/2017/October/ummc-designated-as-national-telehealth-center-of-excellence.html.

105. Henderson, "Testimony."

106. Tearsanee Carlisle Davis et al., "Mississippi Diabetes Telehealth Network: A Collaborative Approach to Chronic Care Management," *Telemedicine and e-Health* 26, no. 2 (2020): 184–89, https://www.liebertpub.com/doi/full/10.1089/tmj.2018.0334.

107. Michael Adcock, "Leveraging Remote Patient Monitoring to Manage Chronic Disease," *Telehealth and Medicine Today*, November 20, 2018, https://telehealthandmedicinetoday.com/index.php/journal/article/view/109.

108. "Mississippi Telehealth Network Could Be FCC's Model for RPM Expansion," Care Innovations, accessed October 26, 2022, https://news.careinnovations.com/blog/mississippi-telehealth-network-fcc-model-for-remote-patient-management.

109. Roger Wicker and Brendan Carr, "Telehealth Pilot Program Will Improve Health Outcomes, Reduce Costs," *Clarion-Ledger*, July 11, 2018, https://www.clarionledger.com/story/opinion/columnists/2018/07/11/telehealth-pilot-program-improve-health-outcomes-reduce-costs/774782002/.

110. Ward, *Out in the Rural*, 44.

Conclusion

1. Richard A. Oppel Jr. et al., "The Fullest Look Yet at the Racial Inequity of Coronavirus," *New York Times*, July 5, 2020, https://www.nytimes.com/interactive/2020/07/05/us/coronavirus-latinos-african-americans-cdc-data.html.

2. "Massachusetts Named Healthiest State in the Nation," Massachusetts Department of Public Health, December 12, 2017, https://wellbeingindex.sharecare.com/; and this is done with researchers at BU, as reported here: https://www.bu.edu/sph/news/articles/2023/massachusetts-named-healthiest-state-for-third-consecutive-year/.

3. Dart Adams, "Is Boston America's Most Racist City? Ask a Black Bostonian for Once," *Boston Magazine*, September 10, 2021, https://www.bostonmagazine.com/news/2021/09/10/boston-racist-reputation/; Akilah Johnson et al., "Boston. Racism. Image. Reality. The Spotlight Team Takes On Our Hardest Question," *Boston Globe*, December 10, 2017, https://apps.bostonglobe.com/spotlight/boston-racism-image-reality/series/image/.

4. Ilona Kickbusch, "The Political Determinants of Health—10 Years On," *BMJ* 350 (2015): h81, https://doi.org/10.1136/bmj.h81.

5. Martin Gilens and Benjamin I. Page, "Critics Argued with Our Analysis of U.S. Political Inequality: Here Are 5 Ways They're Wrong," *Washington Post*, May 23, 2016, https://www.washingtonpost.com/news/monkey-cage/wp/2016/05/23/critics-challenge-our-portrait-of-americas-political-inequality-heres-5-ways-they-are-wrong/.

6. Nicole F. Bernier and Carole Clavier, "Public Health Policy Research: Making the Case for a Political Science Approach," *Health Promotion International* 26, no. 1 (2011): 109, https://doi.org/10.1093/heapro/daq079.

7. Scott L. Greer et al., "Policy, Politics and Public Health," *European Journal of Public Health* 27, no. 4 (2017): 40, https://doi.org/10.1093/eurpub/ckx152.

8. "Derrick Harriell vs. the Clock," *VS* (podcast), Poetry Foundation, May 28, 2019, https://www.poetryfoundation.org/podcasts/150143/derrick-harriell-vs-the-clock.

9. Ibram X. Kendi, *How to Be an Antiracist* (New York: One World, 2019), 238.

Index

Note: Page numbers in *italics* refer to illustrative matter.

Aaron Henry Community Health Center, 196, 207
Abernathy, Ralph, 90
acceptability of health care, 210–15. *See also* health care
accommodation of health care, 207–10. *See also* health care
Act to Restore Hope, Opportunity and Prosperity for Everyone (HOPE Act), 42
affordability: of food, 33, 36–38; of health care, 197–204. *See also* food insecurity; poverty
Affordable Care Act (ACA), xv–xvi, 198, 202–4
Agriculture and Consumer Protection Act (1973), 29
Alabama, 94, 166
Allen, Sheena, 117
American Rescue Plan Act (2021), 38–39
amputations, 215–17
anti-Black violence, xix–xx, 73–74, 107, 190, 217. *See also* racism; violence
antiracism, xi, 7, 60, 89, 93, 232. *See also* racism
Arbery, Ahmaud, xx, 72
Arkansas, 100, 166
Assari, Shervin, 95
assimilationism, 7
auditing, 119–20
author's positionality, xi, xii, xv–xxii
availability of health care, 204–7. *See also* health care

Baby Cafés, 50–51
bank deserts, 116–18. *See also* economic and job opportunities
Barksdale, Jim, 145
Barksdale Reading Institute, 145
Barnes, Helen, 214
Barnett, Ross, 131
Bellmon, Eva, 85
Belue, Judy, 51
Betz, Ryan, 52
Bingham, Willie Lee, 72–73
birth statistics, 10, *11*, *12*, 168, 193, 211
Black Caucus, 24
Black East Side High School, 140
Black Lives Matter movement, xx
Black-owned businesses, 112–14, 189. *See also* economic and job opportunities
Black politicians: in nineteenth century, 21–22, 189; in twentieth century, 23–24
Black population statistics, 19
Blakney, E. B., 125–26
blues music and tourism, 107–10, *111*
Bolivar County, Mississippi, 19
Braveman, Paula, 4
Brooks, Anne, 220
Brown v. Board of Education, 137
Bruce, Blanche, 21
Bryant, Patrick, 72
Bryant, Phil, 42, 221
burial mounds, 18
Bush, Emma, 84
Bush, George W., 147
Bynum, Bill, 83–84

Calhoon, Solomon, 21
CapWay, 117
care coordination, 206–7. *See also* health care
Carmichael, Stokely, 132
Carr, Brendan, 222
casinos, 102–5
certification of teachers, 156. *See also* education system
CHART (Creating Healthy and Responsible Teens), 170
charter schools, 139–40. *See also* education system
Chetty, Raj, 92
Chickasaw, 18, 96
children with disabilities, 166
Chinese Exclusion Act (1882), 19
Chinese immigrants, 19
Choctaw, 18, 96
cholera, 2
chronically poor, as label, 13. *See also* poverty
Civil Rights Act (1964), 22
civil rights movement, xix–xx, 85, 107, 189–90
Clark, John, 96, 109
Clark, Joseph, 27, 87
Clark, Robert, 24
Clark House, 109
Clarksdale, Mississippi: economic and job opportunities in, 105, 108–10, 118, 120, 123–26; education in, 132, 137, 138, 143, 149–50, 157, 165, 172, 173, 175–81; exercise and accessibility in, 76, 79, 81, 82–83, 96; food insecurity in, 30, 32, 34, 36, 38, 46, 48, 49, 50–51, 56; health care in, 196, 208, 209–10; housing in, 65; neighborhood safety in, 61, 62, 68–74; teen pregnancy in, 168, 171
Clarksdale Baby Café, 50–51
Clarksdale Collegiate Public Charter School, 175–78. *See also* education system
Clarksdale Municipal School District, 137

Cleveland, Mississippi: economic and job opportunities in, 98, 100–102, 110, 114, 116, 118–19; education system in, 140–42; gentrification in, 112; GRAMMY Museum in, 107, 112, 120–21; Keep Cleveland Boring campaign in, 120–23; neighborhood safety in, 59, 64, 68, 70, 72–73, 76–77, 81–82; 2017 court ruling in, xxi; walking trail in, 85–87
Cleveland High School, 140–41
Cleveland trail, 85–87
Coahoma Early College High School, 137
Common Core education standards, 150–52
Congressional Peripheral Artery Disease Caucus, 217
Connor, Mike, 37
Constitution (1890), 21–22
Cooke, Sam, 108, 109
Cormack, Michael, 144–45
corn, 100
Coronavirus Aid, Relief, and Economic Security Act, 123, 163
corporal punishment, 165–68. *See also* education system
Cosby, Arthur, 13, 92
cotton, 96, 100
COVID-19 pandemic, xx, 1–2, 123, 155, 177, 194, 228
Curae Health, 195

Delta Bohemian Tours, 109
Delta Council, 97
Delta Edible Agriculture Teaching Students (EATS), 53
Delta Foundation, 126–28
Delta Fresh Foods Initiative (DFFI), 51
Delta Hands for Hope summer camp, 47
Delta Health Alliance, 53, 181–82
Delta Health Center, 190
Delta Meat Market, 123
Delta Regional Authority, 15
Delta Rides, 197

Delta State University (DSU), 120–22
Democratic Party, 21
demographics: of health care team, 214–15; shifts and political sentiments in, 19–21
desegregation of Cleveland schools, 140–42. *See also* education system
DeSoto County, Mississippi, 14, 15
diabetes, 215–17
Diabetes Telehealth Network, 221
discipline in schools, 165–68. *See also* education system
disenfranchisement, Black political, 21–22
displacement, 18, 95–97
domestic violence, 88, 105, 159. *See also* violence
Dorsey, L. C., 190
Dying of Whiteness (Metzl), 8

Early Learning Collaborative Act, 164
Earned Income Tax Credit (EITC), 119
economic and job opportunities, 90–92; auditing and, 119–20; bank deserts and, 116–18; Black-owned businesses, 112–14; Delta Foundation and, 126–28; gambling industry, 102–5; gaps and root causes of, 92–93; gentrification and unequal access to, 93, 110–12; historical roots of, 93, 95–99; job training and, 114–16; Keep Cleveland Boring campaign, 120–23; lottery industry, 105–7; major industries today, 93, 99–102; Meraki Roasting Company, 123–26; in Mississippi, 93–94; payday lending and, 118–19; policy reform for, 128–30; ripples of hope in, 120–28; tourism industry, 107–10
Edelman, Peter, 28
education system, 131–33; charter schools in, 139–40; Clarksdale Collegiate Public Charter School, 175–78; Common Core, 150–52; corporal punishment in, 165–68; economic and job opportunities and, 100; emotional support of students, 136, 159–62; funding of, 136, 142–44; gaps and root causes of, 134–36; health and, 133–34; higher education, 171–73; Indianola Promise Community, 181–85; MAEP program, 145–47; policy reform for, 185–88; Quitman County experiment of, 144–45; racism and, xx–xxi; ripples of hope in, 173–85; RISE program, 174–75; school-based health centers, 162–63; sex education in, 168–71; Spring Initiative, 178–81; teachers of, 153–59; testing in, 136, 147–50; third-grade gate, 152–53; universal preschool, 163–65; white flight and, 137–39
elections (1867), 21
elections (1869), 21
Elementary and Secondary Education Act (1965), 147
Ellington, Duke, 109
emergency-based culture of health, 208–9. *See also* health care
emotional support of students, 136, 159–62. *See also* education system
enslaved persons, 18–21
equity, defined, 7
Espy, Chuck, 74
Evers, Medgar, 85, 190
Every Student Succeeds Act, 147
exercise, 60, 74–83

Fakorede, Foluso, 215–16
farmers' markets, 44–45. *See also* food insecurity
farming, 96, 100
Federal Home Loan Bank of Dallas, 85
Ferguson, Billy Joe, 143
Fielding-Singh, Priya, 49
financial instability, 62–63. *See also* economic and job opportunities
flags, 24
Floyd, George, xx, 72
Fodor's Travel, 108

Index 299

food apartheid, 36
food deserts, 34
food equity policy, 33, 56–58
food insecurity: Baby Cafés for, 50–51; food affordability and, 33, 36–38; gaps and root causes of, 29–33; gardens and farmers' markets for, 44–45; Good Food Revolution for, 51–53; James C. Kennedy Wellness Center for, 53–56; Kennedy and Wright's Edelman Delta tour on, 27–29; policy reform for, 33, 56–58; ripples of hope in, 50–56; school lunches for, 45–47; SNAP for, 38–44; understanding meaning of food and, 33–34, 48–51. *See also* obesity; poverty
Food Stamp Act Amendment (1970), 29
food stamp program, 29, 38–44
food swamps, 34–36
forced displacement, 18
Fordice, Kirk, 146
Freedom Schools, 132
Freedom Summer, 22, 127
Freedom Village, 127
Freeman, Orville, 28
funding, educational, 136, 142–44. *See also* education system

gambling industry, 102–5. *See also* economic and job opportunities
gangs, 71–72
gardens, 44–45. *See also* food insecurity
Geiger, Jack, 190
generational wealth, 5
gentrification, 110–12
gerrymandering, 23–25
Gilens, Martin, 231
Good Food Revolution, 51–53
Gottlieb, Laura, 4
GRAMMY Museum, 107, 112, 120–21
Great Flood (1927), 87
Great Migration, 71, 87, 97–98
Green, Benjamin T., 189
Greenville, Mississippi: burial mounds in, 18; economic and job opportunities in, 63, 104, 112, 113, 117, 128; education in, 135, 138, 142, 150; exercise and accessibility in, 71, 78, 86–87; food insecurity in, 34, 35, 46, 50; health care in, 196–97, 203, 207–8, 210; population statistics in, 96; violence in, 62, 71
Greenville Baby Café, 50
Griot Arts, 123–24
Griot Grit (documentary), 125
Ground Zero, xvi, 108, 110

Hamer, Fannie Lou, 22, 190, 218
Hatch, John, 190
Head Start, 27, 90
health care, 189–91; acceptability of, 210–15; accommodation of, 207–10; affordability of, 197–204; availability of, 204–7; facility closures, 194–96; gaps and root causes in, 191; geographic accessibility of, 191–94; policy reform in, 3, 5–9, 25–26, 222–26; ripples of hope in, 215–22; telehealth, 221–22; transportation to, 196–97
health care sector, 101–2
health inequities: COVID-19 and, 1–2; in Mississippi Delta, 9–11; political determinants of, 16–25, 230–31; social determinants of, 2, 3, 6, 190
health insurance, xxii, 2, 133, 197–224. *See also* Medicaid
health policy reform, overview, 3, 5–9, 25–26. 222–232
Health Resources and Services Administration, 55
Healthy People 2020 program, 50
Henry, Aaron, 22. *See also* Aaron Henry Community Health Center
Hey Joe's restaurant, 122, 123
higher education, 171–73. *See also* education system
Hispanic/Latinx population, 19
home ownership, 64–67. *See also* housing inequities

hope, 1, 232. *See also* ripples of hope
HOPE Credit Union, 83–85, 117
Hopson Plantation, 96, 108, 111
House Committee on Agriculture, 43
housing inequities, 60–67. *See also* neighborhood safety
Howard, Theodore Roosevelt Mason, 190
Howell, "Chilly Billy," 109
Huerta, Justin, 121
Hughes, Langston, xx, 132
Human Genome Project, 5
Human Rights Watch, 166
Humes, H. H., 97
hunger. *See* food insecurity

"I, Too" (Hughes), xx
Indianola Baby Café, 50
Indianola Promise Community, 181–85. *See also* education system
Indian Removal Act, 18
Indigenous populations, 18–21
intimate partner violence, 68, 88, 105. *See also* violence
IRS (Internal Revenue Service) auditing, 119–20

Jackson, Andrew, 18
James C. Kennedy Wellness Center, 53–56
Jarrett, Zakia, xx
Jewish immigrants, 18–19
job centers, 115–16
jobs. *See* economic and job opportunities
job training, 114–16. *See also* economic and job opportunities
Johnson, Amanda, 175–78
Johnson, Chris, 53
Johnson, Kenneth, 11–12
Johnson, Lyndon B., 27, 190
Johnson, Robert, 107, 108

Keep Cleveland Boring campaign, 120–23
Kendi, Ibram X., 7, 147–48, 232

Kennedy, Edward, 132, 147
Kennedy, Jim and Sarah, 55
Kennedy, John F., 27, 91
Kennedy, Robert F.: assassination of, 91, 132; on education and health correlation, 131; education legislation by, 147; on individual acts and change, 1, 25; 1967 Mississippi Delta trip of, xvi, 59–61, 87
Kickbusch, Ilona, 230
King, B. B., 107, 182
King, Martin Luther, Jr., 29, 85, 90–91, 132, 144–45
King, Stephen A., 111
King v. Burwell, xv
KIPP Delta Elementary Literacy Academy, 176

Lampkin, Tim, 117
Langford, Clifford, 59
Leatherman, Shea, 104
Lee Academy, 138
Lewis, Ben, 124
LGBTQ+ community members, 122, 161, 170
life expectancy, 9
literacy tests, 21, 22, 23
location and health outcomes, 4
lottery industry, 105–7. *See also* economic and job opportunities
Louisiana, 10
Luckett, Bill, 108

Magnolia Health Plan, 207
malnutrition, 27–29. *See also* food insecurity
maps, 11, 12, 15, 17, 30, 31, 40, 195
March of Dimes, 10
Marlow, Billy, 219
Massachusetts, 228–29
Medicaid, xv, xvi, 162, 180, 198–99, 201, 202–4, 220–22, 224. *See also* health insurance
Meraki Roasting Company, 123–26
Meredith, James, 131

Metzl, Jonathan, xvii, 8
Mhoon Landing, 103
Mickey, Robert, 22, 23
migration, 97–99
Milton, Massachusetts, xxi
Milton Anti-Racist Coalition, xi
Mississippi Adequate Education Program (MAEP), 145–47. *See also* education system
Mississippi Band of Choctaw Indians, 18
Mississippi Constitution, 21
Mississippi Delta, overview, 9–11, 14–16
Mississippi Department of Agriculture and Commerce, 44
Mississippi Department of Human Services, 42
Mississippi Lottery, 105–7. *See also* economic and job opportunities
Mississippi Nurses Association, 218
Mississippi Optometric Association, 153
Mississippi Works Training Fund, 115
Mo' Money, 120
Montgomery, Isaiah T., 189
Moore, Amzie, 22
mortality penalty, 13
mortality rates, 13
mortgage loans, 5, 66, 67, 95, 227
Mosquito Burrito, 122, 123
Mound Bayou, 189–90
multimember districting, 23
Musgrove, Ronnie, 146

Nash, Spencer, 127–28
National School Lunch Act, 45
neighborhood safety: exercise and, 74–83; gang activity and, 71–72; gaps and root causes of, 60; police and law enforcement and, 72–74; policy reform for, 87–89; ripples of hope in, 83–87; stress and, 69–71; violence and, 67–69. *See also* housing inequities

No Child Left Behind, 147
Noland, Cali, 123
North Bolivar Good Food Revolution, 52
North Sunflower Medical Center, 218–20
Northwest Mississippi Regional Medical Center, 195
no-spray, as term, 48
"Now More Than Ever" (Parker), xviii–xix

Obama, Barack, 147
obesity, 29, *31*, 34–35, 39. *See also* food insecurity
O'Keefe, Bubba, 108, 110
organic, as term, 48
Otherfest, 121–22

paddling, 167–68. *See also* corporal punishment
Page, Benjamin, 231
Parker, Morgan, xviii–xix
patient experience, 209–10. *See also* health care
payday lending, 118–19
Perez, Thomas, 140
physical activity, 60, 74–83
physical punishment, 165–68
police and law enforcement, 72–74
policy reform agendas, 6–7; in economic and job opportunities, 128–30; in education system, 185–88; in food insecurity, 33, 56–58; in health care, 3, 5–9, 25–26, 222–26; in neighborhood safety, 87–89
political activism, 21–25
political determinants of health, 16–25, 230–31
poll taxes, 21, 22, 23
Poor People's Campaign, 90–91, 144–45
population statistics, 9–13, 18–21, 96
poverty, 4–5, 7–8; in Clarksdale, 168; eating habits and, 48–50; nineteenth-

302 Index

century politics and, 21–22; in rural America, 11–13. *See also* affordability; food insecurity
power, 7–8
presidential elections, xvi
Presley, Chelesa, 50–51
Presley, Elvis, 111
privilege, xvii, xxii, 7, 37, 120, 133, 138, 228
property requirements for voters, 21, 23
public health framework, 6

Quapaw, 18
Quitman County experiment, 144–45. *See also* education system

race, as construct, 5
racism: economic and job opportunities and, 110–12; educational system and, xx–xxi; of forced displacement, 18–19; in health care, 211–14; home ownership and, 64–65; in policies, 6–7; political power and, 21–22, 23–25; poverty and, 4–5, 7–8; school segregation, 136, 140–42; 2016 primary elections and, xvi. *See also* anti-Black violence; antiracism
racist policies, as term, 7
Ratliff, Zee, 109
recruitment of teachers, 136
redistricting, 23
Regional Initiatives for Sustainable Education (RISE), 174–75. *See also* education system
research methods, xix, xxii–xxv
retention of teachers, 136. *See also* education system
Revels, Hiram, 21
reverse migration, 98–99
ripples of hope: in economic and job opportunities, 120–28; in education system, 173–85; in food insecurity, 50–56; in health care, 215–22; in neighborhood safety, 83–87. *See also* hope
Riverside Hotel, 108–9
Robert Wood Johnson Foundation's Action Center, 26
Rogers, William "Weejy," 121
Ross, Rick, 108
Ruleville, Mississippi, 218–20
rural Americans, health of, 11–13
Rural Health Care Services Program (Health Resources and Services Administration), 55
Rural Physicians Scholarship Program (University of Mississippi), 192

safe places to live, 61–62
safety. *See* neighborhood safety
salaries of teachers, 157–58. *See also* education system
Sam's Town Casino and Gambling Hall, 104
Schanzenbach, Diane Whitmore, 41, 43
school-based health centers, 162–63. *See also* education system
school lunches, 45–47. *See also* food insecurity
segregationism, 7
sex education, 168–71. *See also* education system
Shack Up Inn, 111–12
Shafir, Eldar, 48–49
Simmons, Errick, 86–87
slavery, 18–19, 24. *See also* enslaved persons
Smith, Bessie, 109
Smither, Ricky, 141
Smith v. Allwright, 22
SNAP (Supplemental Nutrition Assistance Program), 29, 38–44, 245n76
Snow, John, 2
social determinants of health, 2, 3, 6, 190. *See also* individual choice

Southern Christian Leadership Conference, 90–91
soybeans, 100
Spire, C, 221
Splash casino, 103
Spring Initiative, 178–81. *See also* education system
standardized testing, educational, 136, 147–52. *See also* education system
state flag (Mississippi), 24
Stolle, Roger, 108
stress, 69–71
structural racism, as term, 7. *See also* racism
Student Nonviolent Coordinating Committee (SNCC), xx
student support, 136, 159–73. *See also* education system
Summer Food Service Program, 46
Sunflower County Freedom Project, 178
Sunflower Management Group, 219
Supplemental Nutrition Assistance Program (SNAP), 29, 38–44, 245n76
systemic racism. *See* racism

Taborian Hospital, 190
Tallahatchie County Courthouse, xix–xx
Tallahatchie Early Learning Alliance, 164
Taylor, Breonna, xx, 72
teachers, 153–59
Teach for America (TFA) program, 158–59. *See also* education system
telehealth, 221–22
Tennessee, 94
testing, educational, 136. *See also* education system
Texas, 166
Thiessen, Anja, 178–81
third-grade gate, 152–53
Thirteenth Amendment, US Constitution, 24

Thompson, Bennie, 214
Till, Emmett, xix–xx, 85, 87, 107, 190, 217
Till-Mobley, Mamie, 190, 217
timber industry, 96
tourism industry, 107–10. *See also* economic and job opportunities
transportation, 196–97
Travelers Hotel, 109
Treaty of Dancing Rabbit Creek (1830), 18
Tunica County, Mississippi, 14–15, 102–5
Turner, Ike, 108

universal preschool, 163–65. *See also* education system
University of Mississippi, 192
University of Mississippi Medical Center (UMMC), 221
US Constitution, 22, 24
US Senate Subcommittee Hearing on Employment, Manpower, and Poverty, 27

violence, 67–69, 70, 71–72, 132, 138, 160, 165–66. *See also* anti-Black violence; domestic violence; intimate partner violence; neighborhood safety
voting restrictions, 21
Voting Rights Act (1965), 22

walkability of communities, 75–77
walking trails, 85–87
War on Poverty, 190
Washington, Booker T., 189–90
Washington, Karen, 36
Waters, Muddy, 107, 109
wealth, 5, 22, 37, 48, 49, 65, 92, 113. *See also* economic and job opportunities; privilege
Wells, Peggy, 214
West Bolivar High School, 137

white flight, xxi, 137–39. *See also* education system
White House Council of Economic Advisors, 115
Whitney, Eli, 96
Wicker, Roger, 222
Williams, Mary, 214
Williams, Sandra, 74
Wilson, Catherine, 132

Workforce Development Center, 115
Workforce Investment Network (WIN) Job Centers, 115, 116
World Health Organization, 230
Wright, Jermall, 148
Wright Edelman, Marian, 27, 90

Zaharescu, Bianca, 178–81

www.ingramcontent.com/pod-product-compliance
Lightning Source LLC
Chambersburg PA
CBHW031615160426
43196CB00006B/133